BLACK '47

Black '47

Britain and the Famine Irish

Frank Neal
Professor of Economic and Social History
European Studies Research Institute
The University of Salford
Salford, England

First published in Great Britain 1998 by
MACMILLAN PRESS LTD
Houndmills, Basingstoke, Hampshire RG21 6XS and London
Companies and representatives throughout the world

A catalogue record for this book is available from the British Library.

ISBN 0–333–66595–3

First published in the United States of America 1998 by
ST. MARTIN'S PRESS, INC.,
Scholarly and Reference Division,
175 Fifth Avenue, New York, N.Y. 10010

ISBN 0–312–17662–7

Library of Congress Cataloging-in-Publication Data
Neal, Frank, 1932–
Black '47 : Britain and the famine Irish / Frank Neal.
p. cm.
Includes bibliographical references and index.
ISBN 0–312–17662–7
1. Irish—Great Britain—History—19th century. 2. Great Britain–
–Emigration and immigration—History—19th century. 3. Ireland–
–Emigration and immigration—History—19th century. 4. Great
Britain—History—Victoria, 1837–1901. 5. Famines—Ireland–
–History—19th century. 6. Ireland—History—1837–1901. I. Title.
DA125.I7N43 1997
941'.0049162—dc21 97–16913
CIP

This book is printed on paper suitable for recycling and made from fully managed and sustained forest sources.

10 9 8 7 6 5 4 3 2 1
07 06 05 04 03 02 01 00 99 98

Printed in Great Britain by
The Ipswich Book Company Ltd
Ipswich, Suffolk

In loving memory of Frank and Lizzie Neal
my parents

CONTENTS

Acknowledgements

Throughout the researching for, and preparation of this book, I have received help and assistance from a large number of people. The staff of various libraries and archives provided advice and cheerful effort to trace material. In particular I would like to thank the library staff at Cheltenham, Durham City Library, Gateshead, Liverpool City Library, in particular the microfilm unit, Manchester Central Library, Mitchell Library, Glasgow particularly the staff of the Strathclyde Archives, Newcastle, Newport, the staff of the Library of Propaganda Fide, Rome, the staff of the Local History section of Salford City Library. I am especially indebted to Gordon Read and his staff at the Merseyside Maritime Museum Archives. Mary McHugh, Archivist of the Glasgow Archdiocese kindly gave me the information on the deaths of Catholic priests in Glasgow.

Academic colleagues at Salford and elsewhere, many of them outside of the discipline of history, read various chapters and made helpful comments. These include Roger Mason, John Dobson, Carole Roberts, Mike Crosbie and Bill Lukin of Bolton Institute of Higher Education. Mervyn Busteed of the University of Manchester has provided many suggestions for improving the text.

I owe a huge debt to Josie McCann for her mammoth task of extracting over six thousand entries from the Liverpool Workhouse Admissions and Discharge Register for the year 1847. These have enabled me to provide new material on the Irish famine refugee experience in England. Similarly, I am indebted to Josie, Tom McIntyre and Keith Fox for also extracting over seven thousand Liverpool pauper burial records for the year 1847. I am indebted to Mary Carey who transcribed more than two thousand burial records for St Anthony's Catholic Church, Scotland Road. Thanks are especially due to my wife Evelyn and daughter Joanne for inputting these records on to a database. I would not have been able to cope without their assistance. This large body of archival data has yet to be fully exploited. My gratitude is also expressed to Gus Dobrynski of the Department of Geography who produced the maps inserted in the text.

I am very much indebted to Stuart McAllister and to the H.M.V. Music Group for financial assistance for a research project on Irish communities in the north east of England. I would also like to thank the committee of the Simon Fellowship at the University of Manchester for the award of a Simon Senior Research Fellowship during the academic year 1990-1. This gave me time to think. Conversations with Patrick O'Sullivan were invariably stimulating and thought provoking.

Finally, my greatest indebtedness is to Marnie Mason, whose skills in wordprocessing and her intelligence in understanding both the text and the best layouts for the material have enabled the project to be finished on time.

Frank Neal
University of Salford
January 1997

Figures

Tables

Appendices

Abbreviations

British Parliamentary Papers (BPP) House of Commons (HC) House of Lords (HL)

SC (Health) 1840. BPP (HC) 1840, Select Committee on the Health of Towns, Minutes of Evidence.

Chadwick Report (1842) BPP (HL) 1842, XXVI, Report from the Poor Law Commissioners of an Inquiry into the Sanitary Condition of the Labouring Population of Great Britain.

Chadwick Report (England) 1842. BPP (HL) XXVII Report on the Sanitary Conditions of the Labouring Population of England, Local Reports.

Chadwick Report (Scotland) 1842. Report on the Sanitary Conditions of the Labouring Population of Scotland, Local Reports.

First Report Large Towns. BPP (HC) Volume 1, 1844, First Report of the Commissioners for an Inquiry into the State of Large Towns and Populous Districts.

Second Report Large Towns. BPP (HC) 1845 (601) XVIII. Second Report of the Commissioners for an Inquiry into the State of Large Towns and Populous Districts.

Irish Poor (1836). BPP, 1836, (40) XXXIV Report on the State of the Irish Poor in Great Britain.

Irish Poor (1847). BPP (HC) Accounts and Papers 1847-48 (569) LIII Return of the Number of Irish Poor who, between the 31st day of December 1846 and the 31st day of December 1847, have received Relief out of the Poor Rates in the several Parishes comprised within the City of London, the Borough of Marylebone, the City of Westminster, the Borough of Lambeth, the Borough of Southwark, the Borough of Tower Hamlets, and the Borough of Finsbury respectively, and the Money Value of the Relief so afforded: And, the Number of Irish Poor relieved during the same Period out of the Poor Rates in the Parishes comprised of the Borough of Liverpool, the City of Glasgow and the City of Bristol, and the Money Value of the Relief so afforded.

Irish Poor (1848) BPP (HC) 1849, XLVII. Returns of the Irish Poor who, between the 31st day of December 1847 and the 31st Day of December 1848, have received Relief out of the Poor Rates in the several Parishes comprised within the City of London, the Borough of Marylebone, the City of Westminster, the Borough of Lambeth, the Borough of Southwark, the Borough of Tower Hamlets, and the Borough of Finsbury, respectively and the Money Value of the Relief so afforded.

SC (1847). BPP (HC) 1847, XI, Sixth Report of the Select Committee on Settlement and Poor Removal

SC (1854). BPP (HC) 1854-5, XIII, Report of the Select Committee on Settlement, Minutes of Evidence.

Emigrant Ships. 1854: BPP (HC) 1854 (349) XIII, Second Report of the Select Committee on Emigrant Ships.
Famine Papers. BPP (HC) Accounts and Papers, 1847 (764) L, Relief of Distress in Ireland.
Austin (1847). BPP (HC) 1847, (873) XXVII, Thirteenth Annual Report of the Poor Law Commissioners, Appendix No 8, Austin, Report on the Relief of the Irish Poor in Liverpool.
Vagrancy (1848). BPP (HC) 1848, Reports and Communications on Vagrancy, Report of W.D.Boase to the Poor Law Board, p. 17.
Sanitary Report, Scotland, No 9: BPP (HC) 1842. Reports of the Sanitary Conditions of the Labouring Population of Scotland. Local reports, No. 9, 'On the General and Sanitary Condition of Working Classes and the Poor in the City of Glasgow'.

Libraries and Archives

LIVRO	Liverpool City Record Office
MCL	Manchester Central Reference Library
MMM	Merseyside Maritime Museum
PRO	Public Record Office, Kew, London
Strathclyde	Strathclyde Archives, Mitchell Library, Glasgow
TWA	Tyne and Wear Archives, Blandford House, Newcastle

1 Introduction

I

This book is concerned with certain events which took place in Britain during one year, 1847. They were an integral part of the Irish Famine tragedy of the eighteen forties, a calamity that has scarred the Irish national psyche through to the present day. Tens of thousands of destitute Irish, men, women and children, poured into British cities and towns, hoping to escape the nightmare being lived by a significant proportion of the population of Ireland. This influx of refugees took place at a time when the urban squalor in Britain was assuming crisis proportions. Far from Britain proving a haven, for many Irish, the experience of the British slums was a continuation of the horrors being endured in Ireland. In the Registrar General's report for 1847, Liverpool was described as 'the cemetery of Ireland'. It is the story of these famine refugees which forms the substantive content of this study.

In writing this book I had two principal objectives in mind. One was to use all the available statistical evidence to establish the parameters of sensible discussion. Exaggerated claims regarding the scale of the suffering among the refugees which are subsequently found to be wrong, cast doubt on the reality of the horrors which occurred. However, statistics are a necessary but not sufficient condition for establishing the truth in this particular tragedy. This brings me to the second of my objectives. Also needed is an evaluation of the nature of the ordeal in terms of individual tragedies. I have tried to rescue from obscurity not only some of these famine victims who died lonely deaths, but also those who survived and who often had to watch their loved ones succumb to the ravages of cold, malnutrition, typhus and other famine related diseases. People don't have to die to suffer. During 1847, a majority of the famine refugees had to share grossly overcrowded cellars and rooms, with no water or sanitation. Many walked long distances after arrival in Britain, often lacking adequate clothing and sleeping rough in cold weather. By any objective appraisal of the evidence, the experience of a large proportion of the pauperised Irish refugees in 1847 was of a level of deprivation below that of the lowest sections of the English, Welsh and Scottish working classes. In claiming this, I am fully aware of the fact that 1847 was a year of economic depression in Britain and that many of the indigenous poor were living in extreme poverty.

I hope that professional academic historians and students of social history will find this account of the crisis both thought provoking and suggestive of new areas of inquiry. Much primary material concerning particular towns has yet to be utilized and there are plenty of doctoral theses and masters' dissertations to be written which could fill in the remaining gaps in our knowledge about the lesser known areas of Irish settlement. In particular, our understanding of the Irish experience in Britain needs to be extended beyond the analysis of census data, useful as that is.

When thinking about this introduction, I faced a dilemma. How much knowledge of Irish history does the reader need to have in order to fully understand the significance of the events which form the core of this book? Should I treat the refugee crisis in Britain during 1847 as a discrete piece of working class history? On reflection, I concluded that the famine refugee experience cannot be understood without some reference both to the Famine itself and its central place in Irish nationalist iconography. In fact, the poor law authorities and politicians in Britain were very much influenced in their policy making by events in Ireland over the period 1845-52. For anyone coming to Irish history for the first time, it is usually a matter of considerable surprise to find out that so little professional scholarship has been devoted to such a catastrophe, occurring as it did, in the heart of the British Empire. This gap in Irish historiography has been much commented on since 1995, the 150th commemoration of the onset of the potato blight. Paradoxically, this lacuna in scholarship exists side by side with a general awareness in Britain that there was an 'Irish potato famine' but this awareness of the fact is rarely accompanied by any knowledge or understanding of the event or its significance.

II

A great deal of writing on Irish history is about literature. When turning to political and social history, the reader should be aware of the fissiparous nature of much Irish historical writing. It is not surprising that in a nation so recently involved in a bloody struggle for independence from Britain, emotions run high when that history is reviewed. The uprising of 1916, the guerilla war against the British after 1918 and the civil war following the 1921 settlement, all are within living memory. Indeed, as events in Northern Ireland testify, for some Irishmen and women, this chapter in Irish history is not yet completed. All of this means that dispassionate academic historical reviews of Ireland's recent history do not meet the needs of many Irish nationalists.

The last thirty years has witnessed a rate of output in studies of Irish history which exceeds anything that has gone before. The most comprehensive detailed work on Irish history available in recent times is the series *A New History of Ireland*, ten volumes in all. Particularly relevant to the study of the Famine and emigration is W.E.Vaughan (ed) volume five, *Ireland under the Union (1) 1820-1870* (Oxford: 1989). Over the last ten years, the outpouring from the publishers has increased at an even faster rate. Interestingly, many of the new books and journal articles are the work of non-Irish scholars. Accompanying this latest stream of works on Irish history, has been the development of a world wide increased awareness of Ireland and things Irish. In the more cloistered world of academic historians, a major development has been the outbreak of intellectual warfare over the so-called 'revisionist' school of Irish history. Much nineteenth century history of Ireland was written, not by academics but by men involved in the political process. For many of those who were Irish nationalists, Irish history was viewed in terms of a struggle against a brutal colonial power. A central feature of such works has been an emphasis on political history and also the sufferings of the Irish people under British rule. Part of this viewpoint was the perception of an ancient Irish nation, Gaelic speaking, whose culture and identity had all but been destroyed by the Anglo-Saxons. From this perspective, the Union had done nothing for Ireland. For some writers, history was a tool or weapon to be used in both propagandising the Nationalist cause and engendering Nationalist solidarity. Such a use of history was not exclusive to Irish nationalists. All modern nation states use a combination of historical events, half truths, myths and sheer invention to engender a sense of national identity.[1]

In crude terms, critics of such nationalist writings accuse them of lacking rigour, not paying attention to evidence and, in the extreme, being simply story tellers with a political objective. In a reaction to such polemical history, there has emerged, relatively recently, a new genre of Irish history, characterised by an attempt to be 'value free' and paying scrupulous attention to sources and evidence. Some of these studies have utilized economic theory, statistics and demographic methods to rigorously investigate the economic and social structure of Ireland, the cause of economic change and its social consequences. Ostensibly, all of these studies have no political agenda of their own. The result has been to challenge some of the most deeply held beliefs of Irish nationalists. In turn, these works have provoked the counter claim that the 'revisionists' are ignoring the sufferings of the Irish people and the sacrifices made in the struggle for Irish independence. It is no part of this study to analyse the minutiae of the revisionist controversy, the contributions of the principal combatants or the range of issues it raises. It is worth noting, however, that the most discussed work is that of Roy Foster, *A Modern History of Ireland*, (Oxford: 1985). For some, Foster is the arch 'revisionist'. In fact, few historians fall entirely within one of these two viewpoints, they are not mutually exclusive standpoints. For the interested reader, an excellent introduction to the whole debate is D.G.Boyce and A.O'Day (eds) *The Making of Modern Irish History: Revisionism and the Revisionist Controversy'*, (London: 1996). This volume covers a wide range of topics and particularly germane to this book is the article by Mary Daly, 'Revisionism and Irish History: The Great Famine', chapter four. Also highly recommended is G.Davis, 'The Historiography of the Famine', in P.O'Sullivan (ed) *The Irish Worldwide*, volume six, *The Meaning of the Famine* (Leicester: 1996), chapter one. Davis makes the telling point that there is a yawning gap between the perceptions of many ordinary Irish people regarding events of Irish history, and those of many academics. Space does not permit this issue to be pursued. In any case, it is not central to the contents of this book. In conclusion, I suggest that in essence, the revisionist debate is not simply about Irish history, it is also concerned with the nature of historical research, its methods, objectives and uses.[2]

III

An ecological disaster struck Ireland in August 1845, in the form of *phythophtora infestans*, a fungus which attacked the potato crops, reducing them to a stinking, slimy inedible mess. As over 50 per cent of the population, small farmers, labourers and their families, depended on the potato for survival, the 1845 crop failure posed a serious threat to the health and lives of a significant proportion of the Irish population. The re-appearance of the fungus over the period 1846-9 was both incredible bad luck and the cause of a tragedy on such a scale that it can be objectively described as a watershed in the modern history of Ireland. The destruction of the potato crops was not evenly spread out, the worst hit counties being Clare, Cork, Galway, Kerry, Mayo and Roscommon. Correspondingly, the sufferings of the destitute were not evenly distributed. Even at this distance in time, the eyewitness accounts of the suffering endured and the horror of deaths on a large scale, still make chilling reading. This disaster struck a population in which large numbers normally subsisted at low standards of living.

Changes in the size of the population give some indication of the impact of the blight. The 1841 census, the first to approach modern standards of censuses, recorded a population of 8 175 000. Ten years later, a decade in which the Famine calamity occurred, the population of Ireland had dropped to 6 552 255. It is probable that at least one million died of starvation and/or famine related diseases. This means that in relative terms, the Irish Famine of 1845-51 was more devastating in its effects than more recent famines in India, China, Russia and Africa. The rest of the reduction in Ireland's population over the decade was accounted for by emigration to the

United States of America, British North America and mainland Britain. Of all British ports, Liverpool dominated the emigration traffic. A catastrophe on such a scale, in what was in effect a colony existing in close physical proximity to the richer colonial power, inevitably raises a host of questions which have, until fairly recently, received scant treatment. Given the nature of Ireland's economic structure, was the calamity inevitable? When did the Famine end? What was the British government's response to the crisis? Was it adequate? Was the British Treasury a malign influence, putting financial probity before compassion? If food supplies had not been allowed out of Ireland, would it have made much difference to the mortality and suffering? Did Catholic middlemen benefit from the food shortages? Were Irish landlords universally avaricious and/or stupid? What influence did economic theory have on British policy? How important was Providentialism, the view that the Famine was God's solution to the Irish problem? On the extreme of the spectrum of nationalist beliefs was the view that the British response to the Famine was an example of genocide.

The process of professional historians addressing the many issues raised by the Famine began in 1956 with the publication of the *Great Famine: Studies in Irish History*, R.D.Edwards and T.D.Williams, 2nd ed, (Dublin: 1994). This was a collection of essays dealing with various aspects of the Famine, medical, administrative and political. Though highly regarded by academics as a starting point in the process of understanding the Famine tragedy, it left many important questions unasked. In 1962, Cecil Woodham Smith's, *The Great Hunger: Ireland 1845-49*, was published. This became a bestseller and brought the horror of the Famine before a much wider readership. She identified Charles Trevelyn as the villain of the episode and laid blame on an inadequate British response. The book is well researched and written but was dismissed by many academics as being too emotive and lacking in objectivity. This writer does not share such opinions.

More recently, a number of important works on the Famine have appeared. In 1986, Mary Daly's book on the topic was published, *The Great Famine in Ireland* (Dublin: 1986). One of Daly's concerns was her perception of a 'victim mentality' establishing itself among sections of the Irish population. Cormac O'Grada's, *The Great Irish Famine* (Macmillan: 1989) provides the most concise, coherent and authoritative introduction to the Famine, its causes and consequences. After considering all the economic, political and social interstices of the Famine crisis, O'Grada concludes: 'In sum, the Great Famine of the 1840s, instead of being inevitable and inherent in the potato economy, was a tragic ecological accident. Ireland's experience during these years supports neither the complacency exemplified by the Whig view of political economy nor the genocide theories formerly espoused by a few Nationalist historians'.[3]

I have read nothing since that leads me to disagree with O'Grada's conclusion but, as he admitted in the introduction to the new edition of the Edwards' and Williams' book, there is much we don't know about the Famine. Many of the questions listed above await authoritative and convincing answers. O'Grada extended our knowledge further with his more detailed study, *Ireland before and after the Famine: Explorations in Economic History* (MUP: 1988). J.S.Donnelly, jr contributed several important essays on the Famine in volume five of *The History of Ireland* series. The gaps in famine history were further reduced with the appearance of Christine Kinealy's book, *This Great Calamity: The Irish Famine 1845-52* (Dublin: 1994). This has added a great deal to our understanding of the relief operations during the crisis. She concludes that the British relief operation was inadequate and that laissez faire economics triumphed over compassion. More particularly, she argues that British policy during the Famine was driven by a desire to bring about '...economic, social and agrarian reform'.

IV

The failure of the potato crops in 1846, the harsh winter and the policy decision in June 1847 to throw Irish famine relief back on to the Irish landlords, all combined to dramatically increase the exodus of refugees to Britain. Like much else in Irish history, emigration history has been neglected but in 1984, David Fitzpatrick's book appeared, *Irish Emigration 1801-1921* (Dublin: Economic and Social History Society of Ireland). This is both an excellent survey of the literature and analysis of the nature and scale of emigration. David Fitzpatrick also contributed an excellent essay on emigration in volume five of the *New History of Ireland*, pp. 562-616. An immensely important more recent contribution to the history of the Irish diaspora is the six volume series, *The Irish Worldwide: History, Heritage and Identity*. The editor is Patrick O'Sullivan (see bibliography). Volume one of this series, *Patterns of Migration*, throws further light on Irish emigration, while volume six, *The Meaning of the Famine* (1996) is particularly recommended for those interested in the subject. The Famine did not trigger Irish emigration, in pre-famine Ireland a rising level of emigration was already established, reflecting the harshness of life for many, particularly during the many partial failures of the potato crop. There is no doubt that the Famine increased the exodus massively, not only because of the flight of the absolutely destitute but also because it persuaded many less impoverished farmers and labourers that a better life was on offer out of Ireland. The clearly discernible flow of Irish labour to Britain before the Famine is hardly surprising. The island of Ireland was a part of the

British economic system and between all parts of the Union, there were no significant barriers to the movement of capital and labour. For labour markets to operate, two necessary conditions are information flows and mobility of labour. Information is necessary to inform workers in low paid employment of opportunities of higher pay and/or better conditions elsewhere. Mobility is needed for the labour force to respond to the stimuli of wage differentials. On the eve of the Famine, information flows were well established, both oral and written. Seasonal workers in British agriculture, priests, soldiers, hawkers and others all provided information to friends and relations in Ireland. The triumph of steamships on the routes between Ireland and Britain made travel much easier. In effect they were maritime 'motorways'. Competition brought the fares within the reach of all but the most destitute. Simultaneously, the demand for labour in Britain's industrial areas attracted Irish men and women long before the Famine crisis erupted. Unlike unemployed agricultural labourers in the south of England the geographical mobility of the Irish was not inhibited by the laws of settlement. The excitement of life in the big cities of Britain was in itself an attraction to young Irish men and women. The 1841 census registered 417000 Irish born persons in Britain. By 1851, this number had risen to 727000, of the 310 000 increase, a large but unknowable proportion would have been famine refugees.

Table 1.1: Irish-born population of England, Scotland and Wales 1841-1861

Area	*Numbers of Irish-born residents (nearest 1,000)*	*Percentage of the population Irish-born*
1841		
England & Wales	291 000	1.8
Scotland	126 000	4.8
1851		
England & Wales	520 000	2.9
Scotland	207 000	7.2
1861		
England & Wales	602 000	3.0
Scotland	204 000	6.6

Source: Census Reports: 1841, 1851, 1861, Birthplaces of the People

In the twenty-year period 1841-61 the number of Irish born rose by 311 000 in England and Wales or 107 per cent. From 1861 onwards the numbers of Irish born in Britain declined until an upsurge occurred in the 1930s. The aggregate figures in Table 1.1 must be broken down further to gain a full understanding of the impact of Irish immigration on England and Wales. For example, the figure of 520 000 Irish born citizens in 1851 does not seem unduly dramatic in a British population of over 18 million, but when we look at their geographical distribution, a pattern presents itself that has different implications. Of the 520 000 Irish born residents recorded in the 1851 census, over 20 per cent lived in London; of the rest, 299 640 lived in the nine northern counties, and, together, these represented 58 per cent of the total number of Irish immigrants. The county that exceeded all others in the number of Irish born residents was Lancashire. The distribution of the Irish in the North of England is shown in Table 1.2

Table 1.2: The Irish born population of the nine northern counties, 1841 and 1851

County	*Irish born residents 1841*		*Irish born residents 1851*	
	No	*% of Irish*	*No*	*% of Irish*
Lancashire	105 916	70	191 506	64
Cheshire	11 577	8	22 812	7½
West Riding	15 177	10	36 307	12
East Riding	1 945	1	6 052	2
North Riding	905	½	1 323	½
Durham	5 407	3½	18 501	6
Northumberland	5 218	3	12 666	4
Cumberland	4 881	3	9 866	3
Westmorland	242	-	607	-
Total	151 268	100	299 640	100

Source: Census reports, 1851, Birthplaces of the People.

Though there was hardly a town in Britain that did not experience an influx during the decade 1841-51, the major centres of immigration were clearly London, Liverpool, Glasgow, Manchester and Salford, and they remained so throughout the nineteenth century. Though London had the largest number of Irish born people within its boundaries in 1851, as Dr Lees has shown, their impact on the community at large was much less than in the case of the other towns because they were spread out over a much greater area.[4] Of the 36 registration districts in the metropolitan London area, those with the largest Irish born populations in 1851 were Whitechapel (8988), Marylebone (8456), St Giles (6030), Greenwich (6132), Pancras (5835) and Lambeth (4372), see Appendix No 4.4. Outside London, Liverpool had the greatest *number* of Irish born within its boundaries and the greatest *proportion* of its population who were Irish born. Four towns - Liverpool, Glasgow, Manchester and Salford - accounted for 27 per cent of all the Irish born in Britain in 1851. The concentration of the immigrants into these towns is emphasised dramatically when they are compared with 16 other large towns in which the Irish had established themselves.

Table 1.3: Irish born residents of Liverpool, Glasgow, Manchester, Salford and London, 1841-91.

Town	1841	1851	1861	1871	1891
Liverpool (borough)					
Population	286 656	375 955	443 938	493 405	517 980
Number of Irish born	49 639	83 813	83 949	76 761	66 071
Irish as % of population	17.3	22.3	18.9	15.5	12.6
Glasgow (burgh)					
Population	274 533	329 097	-	477 156	565 840
Number of Irish born	44 345	59 801	-	68 330	60 182
Irish as % of population	16.1	18.1	-	14.3	10.6
Manchester and Salford (borough and town)					
Population	306 991	401 321	460 428	379 374	703 507
Number of Irish born	33 490	52 504	52 076	34 066	32 270
Irish as % of population	11.06	13.1	11.3	9.0	4.6
London					
Population	1 873 676	2 362 236	2 803 989	3 254 260	4 211 743
Number of Irish born	73 133	108 548	106 879	91 171	66 465
Irish as % or population	3.9	4.6	3.8	2.8	1.6

Source: Census Reports, 1841, 1851, 1861, 1871, 1891.

Table 1.4: The size of the Irish born population in 16 towns of England, Scotland and Wales in 1851.

Place	*Total population*	*Number of Irish born*	*Irish as % of total*
Edinburgh (inc. Leith)	191 221	12 514	6.5
Birmingham (borough)	232 841	9 341	4.0
Bradford (borough)	103 778	9 279	9.0
Leeds (borough)	172 270	8 446	4.9
Newcastle (borough)	87 784	7 124	8.1
Bristol (city)	137 328	4 761	3.5
Sheffield (borough)	135 310	4 477	3.3
Sunderland	13 897	3 601	5.6
Merthyr Tydfil (town)	63 080	3 051	4.8
Kingston upon Hull	84 690	2 983	3.5
Gateshead	25 568	2 195	8.6
Newport (borough)	19 323	2 069	10.7
Nottingham (borough)	57 407	1 557	2.7
Swansea (borough)	31 061	1 333	4.3
Tynemouth	29 107	1 108	3.8
South Shields	28 974	922	3.2
Total	1 413 702	74 761	5.2

Source: Census reports, 1851, Birthplaces of the People.

The total number of Irish born in these 16 towns, taken together, was *still* fewer than the number in Liverpool. Indeed, the concentration in Liverpool was greater than the statistics reveal. For example, in 1851, parts of the union of West Derby (now part of Liverpool city) were outside the borough boundary but adjacent to it. The Irish born population of West Derby was 16 380, while in the next poor law union, Prescot, there were an additional 9341 Irish born. Across the river Mersey the township of Birkenhead was home to 3135 Irish.[5] Thus bordering the borough of Liverpool were at least another 28 856 Irish, giving a total of 112 669 for the whole district, an area still smaller than London. Many of the immigrants came from small towns and rural areas in the west of Ireland and on arrival in Liverpool they found more Irish gathered together than most of them had ever previously experienced. The Irish born population of Liverpool exceeded in numbers the population of the majority of Irish towns.

Reference has been made above to the dramatic increase in the output of works in Irish history. This last 12 years has seen an equally dramatic increase in books on the Irish in Britain. Some of these are collections of essays, while others concentrate on Irish settlements and their experiences in particular towns. Anyone wishing to make a quick entry into the literature could usefully start with the two volumes edited by Swift and Gilley. First is R.Swift and S.Gilley (eds), *The Irish in the Victorian City* (Croomhelm: 1985). Particularly recommended in this volume is D.Fitzpatrick, 'A Curious Middle Place'. Their second volume is *The Irish in Britain* (Pinter: 1989). Specific towns covered by these essays are Bristol, Edinburgh, Glasgow, Liverpool, Stafford, Stockport, York and Wolverhampton. More focused books on the Irish in Britain include Lyn Hollen Lees, *Exiles of Erin, Irish Migrants in Mid-Victorian London* (MUP: 1979). This is a study of Irish settlements in London using 1851 census data. The city of York is the subject of a study by Frances Finnegan, *Poverty and Prejudice: Irish Immigrants in York, 1840-75* (Cork University Press: 1982). This was followed by T.Gallagher, *Glasgow, The Uneasy Peace: Religious Tensions in Modern Scotland: 1819-1914* (MUP: 1988), F.Neal *Sectarian Violence: The Liverpool Experience, 1819-1914* (MUP: 1988). W.J.Lowe, *The Irish in Mid-Victorian Lancashire* (Peter Lang: 1989). Alan O'Day, *A Survey of the Irish in England, 1872* (Reprint: Hambledon Press: 1990). G.Davis, *The Irish in Britain 1815-1914* (Gill and Macmillan: 1991). This work is an exhaustive survey of the themes and literature concerning the history of the Irish in Britain. Elaine McFarland, *Protestants First: Orangeism in Nineteenth Century Scotland* (Edinburgh University Press: 1990) T.M.Devine (ed) *The Irish Immigrants and Scottish Society in the Nineteenth and Twentieth Centuries* (Donald: 1991). S.Fielding, *Class and Ethnicity: Irish Catholics in England and Wales, 1880-1903* (Open University Press:

1993). Last in this list is M.J.Hickman, *Religion, Class and Ethnicity: The State, The Catholic Church and the Education of the Irish in Britain* (Avebury Press: 1995). What is remarkable is the short period over which these works appeared. Collectively, the themes covered include the spatial distribution of the Irish communities, occupational profiles, the Catholic church and the immigrants, religious tensions, crime and so on. Many studies use census data, usually 1851 and less frequently 1861. A brilliant survey article is strongly recommended, David Fitzpatrick, 'A Peculiar Tramping People: the Irish in Britain, 1810-70', in W.E.Vaughan, *A New History of Ireland* volume five, *Ireland under the Union,* (Oxford: 1989) chapter 29, pp. 623-660. However, it is now discernible that much of the work on the Irish in Britain is going over old ground. There is a need to move beyond census data and to use as yet unexploited primary archive material in the Public Record Office, County and Church archives.

In all the studies of the Irish in mid-Victorian Britain there is a curious absence of attention paid to one of the most dramatic periods of the Famine crisis, the eruption of starving and diseased refugees into our towns and cities. The exceptions, as far as I can ascertain, are two pieces I wrote in the 1990s. In 1986 I completed a study of the conditions under which the Famine refugees were carried to Liverpool over the period 1847-51. This appeared under the title 'Liverpool, the Irish Steamship Companies and the Famine Irish', in *Immigrants and Minorities*, volume 5, March 1986, pp. 28-61. In 1988 my book on the Catholic/Orange conflict in Liverpool came out, entitled *Sectarian Violence: The Liverpool Experience, 1819-1914* (Manchester University Press: 1988). Chapter four of this is devoted to the impact of the Famine Irish influx on Liverpool. Since then, I have exploited much unused archival material of the period, including Workhouse, Custom Bills of Entry and burial records. These records, as yet not fully analysed, provide some of the material in this book. Similarly, I have used archival material for other towns covered by this study. In concluding this brief listing of the literature, it needs to be noted that comprehensive histories of the Irish in Liverpool, London, Glasgow and Manchester have still to be written.

I hope this work proves interesting and illuminating, and that it will stimulate others to fill the gaps in what is not only the history of the Irish but also part of the history of the working classes in general.

Notes and References

1 An excellent treatise on the issue of national identity is A.D.Smith, *National Identity* (Penguin: 1991). See also B.Jenkins and S.A.Sofos, *National Identity in Contemporary Europe* (Routledge: 1996)

2 A useful introduction to the debate about the nature of historical investigations, see E.H.Carr, *What is History?* (Penguin: 1961, 2nd ed 1987). D.Thomson, *The Aims of History*, (Thames and Hudson:1970). M.Stanford, *The Nature of Historical Knowledge*, (Blackwell: 1986).

3 C.O'Grada, *The Great Irish Famine* (Macmillan: 1989), p. 76.

4 L.H.Lees, *Exiles of Erin* (MUP: 1979), see chapter three, 'The Social Geography of Irish London'.

5 I am grateful to Chris Boyle for the data on the township of Birkenhead, based on the 1851 census enumerators' sheets.

2 The Urban Environment and Pre-famine Irish Settlements

I

From 1815 onwards, the Irish presence in Britain was increasingly the subject of comment. Throughout the nineteenth century, the Irish in Britain had a bad press. The epithets heaped on their heads usually included 'dirty', 'filthy', 'violent', 'disgusting' and 'ungrateful'. Just as frequently, the character of the Irish, their moral fibre and lifestyle, was subject to critical analysis in column inches of the London and provincial press. The contrast with the comment, or lack of comment, on the Welsh and Scots living in English towns is startling. The modern reader could be forgiven for concluding that between all the Irish poor and the English poor generally there existed a yawning gap in both living conditions and moral fibre. Such a conclusion would be false and the validity or otherwise of the attacks on the Irish character and lifestyle must be judged, in part, on the basis of the urban environment in which a large proportion of the Irish immigrants were forced to live.[1] Any immigrants arriving in a new country, devoid of economic resources, are forced into those sectors of the labour market in which there are no barriers to entry and, by definition, these are the lowest paid jobs. However, low pay was not the only factor bearing down on the poor in Victorian Britain; the casual nature of much employment meant that earnings per week were such that millions of people were always on the margin of destitution over the whole of the period under review, and beyond.[2] From the fact of low income and intermittent employment followed a number of consequences guaranteed to produce a wretched lifestyle; the necessity to enter the bottom end of the housing market, overcrowding, lack of water and sanitation, poor diet, minimal furniture, endemic typhus and epidemic cholera.

T.J.Dykes, a doctor working for the Poor Law Guardians in Merthyr Tydfil, wrote to the Poor Law Commissioners in London on 14 May 1847. At this time Merthyr was beginning to experience the arrival of famine Irish, entering through Cardiff and Newport.

> Permit me to call your attention to the following cases of extreme distress. I know your humanity will find some means of alleviating their misery. Josiah Robins, a ragman, lives in two cellars under the row of

> houses between Bethesda chapel and Mr D.W.James. These cellars are about ten feet square, all lighted by a small window in each, the floor is partly pitch and partly earth. There are two fireplaces, one only is used. In the first cellar, there is one straw bed, in the other two strawbeds and a heap of straw in one corner. The place is damp, the little clothing they have is filthy. In these two cellars *thirteen persons* are now living. Robins took in a woman to lodge about a month back, she died of fever. J. Robins, his wife and child, Thomas Robins and his wife, a young man of seventeen and a young woman of the same age, an old woman, a man, his wife and two children, also a woman who came there to nurse them, all these persons are labouring under fever in different shapes. These persons have been diligently attended to by the medical attendants of the parish but what can medical skill do in such cases as these. It is food, light and air they require. They are in receipt of relief from the Board, but until they are removed from the noisome den in which they breathe the impure air, which has caused them to be affected with disease, there is no hope for their permanent recovery.[3]

In fact the Board did nothing. Official publications of the period contain thousands of such descriptions.[4] The Irish did not create these conditions and they were shared with sections of the English, Welsh and Scots poor. The famine crisis however exacerbated the wretchedness of many Irish in British cities and towns.

By the time large scale Irish immigration into Britain commenced, coinciding with the appearance of cross channel steamers, the Industrial Revolution was well underway. Much of the pre-famine emigration from Ireland was a response to changing economic opportunities.[5] The main features of Britain's industrial takeoff need to be appreciated in order to understand some of the economic forces affecting Irish society. In Britain, the application of waterpower to the driving of machines was accompanied by the construction of a widespread canal system which by the end of the eighteenth century played a central role in reducing transport costs. As a consequence of the development of steam engines, the need for riverside locations was removed, new factories were constructed in urban areas, benefiting from inward migration as a solution to labour shortages.[6] These developments were followed by the utilisation of steam to provide motive power, first for marine engines and then locomotives. In 1814 the first steam driven vessels appeared on the Mersey and the Clyde and by 1820 Liverpool, Glasgow and other ports were connected with all the major Irish ports by paddle steamer (see chapter three).[7] Plentiful supplies of coal and iron ore, the development of sophisticated financial markets, an explosion of inventive genius and an aggressive entrepreneurial class all coalesced to propel Britain into the position of being *the* world's dominant economic power by the time of the Irish famine. This pre-eminent economic power was not seriously challenged until about 1880 onwards.[8] Despite cyclical setbacks, the secular trend of Britain's aggregate gross national product was firmly upwards, as was Gross National Product per head. There is no doubt that this led to higher living standards in the long run for the majority but, as Lord Keynes pointed out, 'in the long run we are all dead'. It is undeniable that economic growth, dictated by the impersonal workings of market forces, necessarily leaves casualties in the short run and the short run may last for most of the life of many individuals. Technological developments, or more precisely, their innovation, mean that existing technologies become obsolete and the people they employ face falling real incomes and then unemployment. Whether or not they work again depends on the occupational and geographical mobility of the unemployed.

The Irish textile industry was badly hit by the mechanisation of weaving and from 1820 onwards, thousands of Irish and English handloom weavers faced low incomes, desperate poverty and ultimately the elimination of their occupation. Many Irish handloom weavers moved to British textile towns, particularly Glasgow and Manchester, but they could not escape the consequences of the new technology. A similar fate, for example, befell the woolcombers of West Yorkshire, machinery displaced people.[9] However, though invention and innovation destroy jobs, they also create new opportunities. For instance, the rapid growth of the railway system after the Rainhill trials in 1829, killed off hundreds of jobs in the stage coach industry but created a demand for thousands of people to work in railway construction, manufacturing rolling stock and railway operations. In addition the new form of transport created non-railway jobs as distribution costs were lowered, markets opened up and business communications became much faster. Given the unequal economic development of both countries, it was inevitable that such growth would draw people from Ireland to Britain.

Despite the fact of secular growth in output, for large numbers of people in nineteenth century Britain, low incomes and poverty were present throughout their lives, the 'short run' of economic analysis. By 1830, the fact of widespread poverty was giving rise to concern among sections of the middle classes, who because of the social apartheid in British towns, had their perceptions of the poor shaped by the reports of middle class investigators of life among the working classes.[10] From the point of view of this study, the social costs of economic growth need to be noted, in particular those arising directly from the dramatic increase in Britain's population throughout the nineteenth century. Again, this is not the place to analyse the factors which removed the Malthusian constraints on population growth in Britain but the social consequences of that growth need to be recognized in any assessment of the experience of the Irish in Britain. More specifically, the growth of urban areas consequent on the mechanisation of production requires comment, as most Irish immigrants moved into British towns rather than rural areas.

By 1841 England's population was eighty per cent bigger than it had been in 1801, an annual *average* growth rate of 1.5 per cent.[11] One consequence of this demographic pattern of development was an extremely rapid increase in the size of towns, especially in the areas experiencing accelerated economic growth. At the time of the Irish Famine, one could, with respect to England, meaningfully refer to the 'booming' north and the 'depressed' south. For example, the population of Lancashire exhibited an annual average growth in its population of 2.2 per cent between 1831 and 1841 and this was maintained over the next decade. Similarly, over the decade 1841-51, the population of the borough of Liverpool had an average annual growth rate of 2.7 per cent, as did the township of Manchester. In both cases, inward migration accounted for most of the increases. In the case of Liverpool in 1851, only 42.4 per cent of the population was born within the borough, the rest were migrants.[12] In the case of *short distance* migrants, 42 470 came from Lancashire and Cheshire, some 11.3 per cent. However, in the case of long distance migrants, 83 813 were born in Ireland, 22 per cent of the total population and 39 per cent of *all* inward migrants. In addition to the Irish, there were 20 285 Welsh and 14 039 Scots born persons recorded in the 1851 census. This gives a total of 118 137 from the Celtic areas, or 55 per cent of all inward migrants. The Celtic influence on Liverpool was even greater when one considers that about 10 per cent of those persons recorded as Liverpool born would be the children of Celtic parents.[13]

If we examine the case of Manchester borough and Salford township together, the 1851 census revealed that 45 per cent of the population were born within the two towns and 195 748 were short distance immigrants from Lancashire and Cheshire. Of the *total* number of inward migrants (219 126), 52 304 were Irish born, some 13 per cent of the gross population and 24 per cent of all inward migrants. To these can be added 6850 Welsh born and 6351 Scots, making a total of 65 905 Celts or 30 per cent of all inward migration.[14] The mass internal migration which took place in nineteenth century Britain simply reflects the response of individuals then, as now, to the stimuli of labour markets.[15] Given information flows, transport facilities, and no barriers to entry, people move from low wage areas to higher wage areas. How quickly or easily labour responds to market forces depends to a large extent on rigidities in the markets but inexorably, large numbers of people in Victorian Britain responded to regional wage differentials. The principal example of rigidities in labour markets however, were the laws of settlement and removal. By giving people security in terms of the right to poor relief in their parish, many English poor in the South were deterred from migrating north.

The rapid growth of Britain's industrial towns was not accompanied by a corresponding growth in the social infrastructure. The process took urban élites by surprise. As early as 1832, it was clear to the more thoughtful politicians, local and national, that major crises were imminent with respect to housing, water and sanitation. This awareness coincided with the coming to power in 1830 of a crusading Whig administration which, among a plethora of policies reformed the poor law and, in 1835, the administration of local government. The latter in particular, gave rise to new urban élites, with their power base in manufacturing industry and trade.[16] A manifestation of the growing crisis were the periodic outbreaks of typhus and cholera. Even the aristocracy, living on their estates and so removed from the scenes of urban squalor, could not avoid cholera. The urban middle classes also could ignore the unpleasant facts of working class life by the simple expedient of never visiting the slums but they could not escape disease. Typhus and cholera affected all classes, though not evenly. The cholera outbreaks in 1832 and 1837-8 triggered off a number of detailed investigations into the social condition of the population in Britain's towns. These were carried out just before the Irish famine, the most notable investigator being Edwin Chadwick, the Secretary to the Poor Law Commissioners. The subsequent reports contain much data, statistical and anecdotal, on social conditions in general and on the Irish in particular.[17] In addition to state sponsored inquiries, a large number of private surveys were carried out in particular towns and all confirmed the findings of the official investigations.[18] In their essential details, the various reports were consistent in both their description and their conclusions. Horrific overcrowding, lack of clean water and totally inadequate sanitation were conditions which large numbers of people endured in addition to low income levels. Though in some sense related, the issues of poverty and lack of social infrastructure were essentially separate matters. The rapid population growth and, simultaneously, mass immigration into the towns, during the first half of the nineteenth century was unprecedented and the resultant urban squalor, initially unavoidable. The local élites had no previous experience to guide them but from 1832 onwards, the growing fear of death from disease produced a heightened interest in problems of sanitation, water supplies, burying the dead and housing improvements.

However, when the middle class investigators turned their attention to the phenomenon of widespread poverty, two separate strands of analysis entered into their comments on the working class. There was a recognition that low income and casual employment contributed to poverty stricken lifestyles. In addition they incorporated into their texts, moral judgements on the poor, attributing much poverty to fecklessness and a lack of moral fibre. To support such a view, cases were often cited in which families on the same income level displayed, on the one hand, cleanliness and decency while on the other hand, families in similar economic circumstances, lived in dirt, squalor and dissoluteness. The investigators, in many cases, had entered a world previously unknown to them and the poverty and degradation that they witnessed was almost beyond their comprehension. Their reports formed a bridge between the alien world of the poor and that of the middle classes, the latter simultaneously fascinated and repelled. The 'bridge' was language and the language used, in a sense, 'constructed' the poor in terms of middle class values. The standards against which the poor were judged were the middle class virtues of neatness, cleanliness, respectability, sobriety and so on. Departure from these criteria marked degradation, irrespective of economic circumstances. The use of metonymy was part of this process. The populations of slums,'teemed' and 'swarmed'; the homes of the poor were 'lairs' or 'dens'. The necessity of many poor of both sexes to share rooms or even beds was dubbed promiscuity. The downturn in the economy in 1841-2, and 1847, exacerbated the problem of poverty and it was into this environment that the famine Irish arrived.

II

Moving from macro analysis to micro, detailed attention must now be turned to the particular conditions in three towns which were targets of Irish immigration; Liverpool, Manchester and Glasgow. The first major source of evidence concerning the social conditions of the Irish in Britain before the famine influx is the report of George Cornwallis on the state of the Irish poor in Britain. This was undertaken at the behest of the Home Secretary and the evidence was gathered during 1834 and published in December of the same year.[19] A feature of the document is a number of reports dealing with the Irish in specific towns. The reports on Liverpool, Manchester and Glasgow are particularly detailed.[20]

The Irish Catholic population of Liverpool in 1833 was estimated to be 24 156.[21] This is almost certainly an underestimate in view of the 1841 census revelation that the pre-famine Irish born population of Liverpool was nearly 50 000. George Forwood was an assistant overseer of the poor in Liverpool. He told the investigators that many Irish rented houses at £10 p.a. or more (These were houses bigger than most working class people rented). The objective was then to rent out the rooms to lodgers, the tenants living in the cellar. To the extent that this practice occurred it was probably one of the factors that led to the overcrowding of Irish houses noticed by many observers of the social scene.[22] An alternative available to immigrants was the lodging house. These were, in general, pestiferous places but cheap, twopence or threepence per night. A third option was the Night Asylum. This was run by private charitable individuals, providing spartan overnight accommodation under a very strict regime. In July 1833, 40 per cent of all persons admitted to the Liverpool Night Asylum were Irish.[23]

In 1834, Father Vincent Glover was the English born parish priest of St Peter's in Seel Street, Liverpool and an Englishman. He claimed his parish was split fifty: fifty in terms of respectable, hardworking Irish, on the one hand, and the drunken and idle on the other. He sided with those who believed that much working class poverty was self imposed due to fecklessness and not low wages.

> The Irish are not good managers, they do not live equally well with the English on equal wages. Of those who earn from 14s to 16s a week, the better class maintain their families in tolerable comfort; the worse do not. Many who live in squalid filth in cellars are earning good wages.

There is no way of establishing retrospectively the accuracy of Glover's observation but as a Catholic priest, he was intimately involved with the Irish in his parish. In his own words, 50 per cent of his Irish parishioners were respectable and hardworking so his claim that the Irish were not good managers clearly is ambiguous. Glover also argued that there was little upward occupational mobility among the Irish in Liverpool but did not believe this was due to discrimination. He identified lack of education and training as the main reasons.[24]

The problem of evaluating this anecdotal evidence is illustrated by the evidence of Thomas Robinson, an English Catholic priest in the same parish as Glover. Robinson admitted that there were 'great numbers of Irish in extreme poverty' but, 'I do not perceive much difference between English and Irish labourers in the same circumstances'.[25] Father Thomas Fisher was the parish priest of St Mary's, Edmund Street. He also was English, his church had 3,000 communicants during the year and he estimated about 67 per cent were Irish:

> A large proportion of the Irish in my flock are in a very low state, living in cellars and garrets, their furniture is very poor, a pallet of straw, a stool, sometimes a table, an iron pot and a frying pan, a jug for water, a few plates and a leaden or pewter pan. Persons in this class live on potatoes and stirabout, now and then perhaps, they may get a herring or a little bacon.

He went on to contradict Father Robinson by expressing the view that an Irishman on the same wages as an Englishman did not live as well.[26] This opinion was also supported by Father Francis Murphy, of St Patrick's, Toxteth. By contrast, he was an Irishman who had lived in Liverpool for six years. 'They do not live equally well with the English on equal money, because they squander their money'.[27]

Samuel Holmes was the largest builder in Liverpool and had employed Irishmen over a long period. He commented on the 'wretched way of living' and put it down to their improvidence. He also believed that earning the same as English labourers, the Irish lived less well. However, he did not attribute this to drunkenness but to their hospitality to other Irish people. 'They are very kind to each other'.[28]

In 1834, William Henry Duncan was an honorary physician at the North Dispensary in Liverpool. He was later to emerge as a major figure in the handling of the famine immigration crisis in Liverpool. In 1833, 45 per cent of all the patients passing through the North Dispensary were Irish and Duncan had an extensive experience of visiting the Irish in their 'dwellings'. As a result of this, Duncan formed firm opinions about the conditions experienced by the Liverpool Irish.

> The Irish poor are about one third of the poor population of this town. I attribute the greater proportion of disease among the Irish to their living in crowded, ill-ventilated, dirty habitations. The Irish live chiefly in lodging houses and cellars, four or five families - frequently more than that - inhabiting the same house; sometimes two or more families in the same cellar. They are frequently liable to rheumatism, fever and chronic diseases of the lung. These are the prevailing diseases of all the poor in Liverpool; but as these arise from the badness of the dwellings, and as the Irish live in the worst dwellings, they are more liable to them than others... The Irish seem to be contented amidst dirt and filth, and close confined air, as in clean and airy situations... Frequently there are four or five beds in a room, just large enough to hold them and four or five persons sleep in each bed.[29]

What the Cornwallis report revealed about Liverpool was that for a variety of reasons, low wages, intermittent periods of employment, and in some cases, fecklessness, large numbers of pre-famine Irish inhabited the bottom end of the generally poor housing stock of the borough of Liverpool. How bad was this housing situation?

By the commencement of 1836, a large proportion of all of Liverpool's working class were living in cellars and courts. A court was entered off the street, through a narrow entrance, often arched. The courts were up to fifteen feet wide, with three storey houses, up to nine on each side which blocked out most sunlight. At the end of the court were usually two privies, ashpits, used by all the people in the court and also by many from the street houses, which frequently had no privies. The privies were rarely emptied and so excrement and urine often overflowed into the courts, creating a stench which in summer was almost unbearable. Often the ends of the courts were blocked off by the rear wall of the houses in the next street (closed courts). The street houses had cellars, generally consisting of one room, about ten feet by twelve feet, below street level and frequently less that six feet in height. As early as 1789/90, it was estimated that Liverpool had 1728 cellars, homes to 6780 persons.[30] Relatively few cellars were in court houses. In the 1832 cholera outbreak, the Irish in Liverpool figured disproportionately in the death toll. J.R.Wood of the Manchester Statistical Society carried out a detailed survey of the educational system in Liverpool over the last few months of 1835 and the beginning of 1836, soon after the Cornwallis investigation.[31] In the course of this he examined closely the living conditions in the slums. He estimated that there were 2271 courts, 7493 occupied cellars and 369 unoccupied.[32] This figure of 369 unoccupied cellars is of interest in that in indicates that in 1836, ten years before the famine crisis, there was little spare accommodation available at the *bottom end* of the housing market. Wood put the cellar population between 31 000 and 32 000 persons and reported that most of the cellars were damp, all were below street level, most had only one window, no privy and no water. Water was obtained from stand pipes in the courts and these were usually on three times a day. His description of Liverpool's working class streets is reminiscent of present day descriptions of third world countries.

> I think there is one circumstance which very much effects the atmosphere in those districts in which the cellars are particularly; there is a great deal of broken ground in which there are pits, the water accumulates in those pits, and of course at the fall of the year, there is a good deal of water in them, in which have been thrown dead dogs and cats, and a great many offensive articles. The water is nonetheless used for culinary purposes. I thought it was only used for washing, but I found it was used by the poorest inhabitants for culinary purposes.[33]

In his report, Wood pointed out that the population living between Scotland Road and the river was 'wretched'. This was the principal area of Irish settlement in Liverpool.

Four years later Duncan gave evidence to the Select Committee on the Health of Towns. He estimated the number of people living in court houses to be 86 000 and about 38 000 were living in cellars.[34] He highlighted the problems of sanitation, water supplies and poor housing. Economic forces reinforced unhealthy activities. Duncan was told by a town missioner of a case in which a family living in a cellar had collected three cartloads of manure out of the streets and courts and *stored it in their cellar*. This would be sold later to market gardeners on the outskirts of the borough. At the time, there was no nuisance legislation to stop such activities.[35] In many courts, the landlords paid the water companies for a supply and in turn the courtdwellers paid about 3d a week in advance, for the standpipes to be turned on. Often the landlords got in arrears with their water payments and the whole supply to the court would be cut off.[36] Duncan described one visit he made to Union Court, off Banastre Street in the Vauxhall Ward.

> In one court I visited the other day I found the whole place was inundated with filth, having a most intolerable stench, and I found that it proceeded from two ash pits in the adjoining courts having oozed through the wall; the liquid portion of it had oozed through, in consequence of the imperfection of the wall, and the nuisance was so great that one of the houses had been uninhabited for three years until just before, when the landlord flagged the floor to prevent its oozing through, but is still oozed through. In that court there were 63 cases of fever in 12 months; there was no drain whatsoever to the court. Part of the court belonged to one landlord and part to another; one of the landlords had offered to be at half the expense of making a drain, if the other would subscribe; but he would not and in consequence, nothing was done.[37]

This case illustrates the problems of the poor. An individual tenant in a court could do little to improve conditions. To persuade others to keep the communal privy clean was a difficult if not impossible task, given the transitory nature of much occupation of the houses. Even if neighbours co-operated, the privies were not emptied on a regular basis. Insistence on neighbours observing certain standards could result in a physical assault. Duncan described a cellar in Preston Street where 30 persons slept every night. In the centre of the cellar, they had dug a hole to collect the liquids that drained to the cellar floor. When fever broke out, eight of the 30 died.[38]

The sheer difficulties associated with the ordinary mechanics of living provoked people into drastic and seemingly foolish action. For example, persons living in street cellars would have to carry their rubbish and contents of chamber pots upstairs, along the street and into the nearest court in order to put it in an ashpit or dunghill. The Superintendent of the Unitarian Town Mission told Duncan that he had visited a cellar in which the floor was constantly covered in water and the inhabitants had taken the door off its hinges and laid it on bricks so that they had a dry surface. In addition, they had knocked a hole in the back wall of the cellar, creating an opening onto an ashpit. This enabled them to throw refuse into the ashpit without going upstairs and round to the court.[39] Before the 1841 census revealed the size of Liverpool's Irish born population to be 50 000, Duncan had identified the areas of dense Irish settlement. In the North-End, Lace Street, in the Vauxhall Ward, was estimated to be 87 per cent Irish. Also in the North End, North Street was 83 per cent Irish while Crosbie Street in the South End, was 87 per cent Irish born. All of these streets were characterized by the most desperate social conditions within a generally prevailing environment of extreme poverty.[40]

In 1844, it was estimated that there were about 45 000 persons living in cellars.[41] Under an act of 1842 it was laid down that from 1 July 1844, cellars could not be used as dwelling places unless they conformed to certain standards.[42] As it was impossible for most of the cellars to be improved, it meant that on 1 July 1844, at least 23 000 of the poorest people would be forced to leave them, with nowhere to go. James Aspinal, chairman of the Health of Town Committee confessed that he had no idea what would happen if the law was enforced and expressed the opinion that many would finish up on the parish or move into the already overcrowded courts.[43] By the end of 1846, some 3000 cellars had been cleared under the 1842 Act but by this time, Irish paupers were arriving in large numbers and so the famine crisis put an end to the plans for an early clearance of the cellar population. During 1847, a policy of ejecting cellar dwellers was implemented but abandoned when the numbers of destitute Irish arriving in the port precipitated an even worse accommodation crisis.[44] Samuel Holmes, a prominent builder and a leading member of Liverpool's Conservative party, described the conditions in the streets occupied by the poor in 1845:

> In numberless instances courts and alleys have been formed without any declination for the discharge of surface water. Many are laid without channels: and while the solid refuse thrown upon them rots upon the surface, the liquid matter is absorbed, and much finds its way into the inhabited cellars of the courts. The north end of the town is full of pits of stagnant water, which forms so many receptacles for the putrid matter that is constantly thrown into them, such as dead animals, the drainage from starch and other manufacturies, and in hot weather, the stench from these places is intolerable... There are thousands of houses and hundreds of courts in this town without a simple drain of any description; and I never hail anything with greater delight than I do a violent tempest or terrific thunderstorm, accompanied by heavy rain; For these are the only scavengers that thousands have had to cleanse away the impurities and the filth in which they live, or rather exist.[45]

Holmes had consistently criticized the poor housing stock in Liverpool and spoken out for tighter building regulations. Another problem for Liverpool's poor in 1844 was the fact that the water companies only provided water every other day in many areas of the borough. If families did not have sufficient receptacles for holding water, they had to go without. If they were out when the stand pipes were working, they also missed out the chance of obtaining water.[46]

William Duncan was appointed Liverpool's Medical Officer of Health in 1847 as a result of the 1842 Act, the first Medical Officer of Health in the country. Following on from his earlier investigations he produced a number of valuable reports, all of which confirm the evidence of both his earlier work and that of other investigators. In 1844, Duncan had produced a detailed investigation of the causes of death in Liverpool.[47] With a death ratio of one in 29.75 of the population, Liverpool was worse than London, Manchester, Birmingham, Leeds and Bristol. He found that of 6294 cellars, 44 per cent were damp or wet and 84 per cent had no window at the front. As in all Victorian towns, sanitation was a major problem. Duncan estimated that the population of Liverpool excreted 6000 tons of solid matter a year and that the whole of the cellar population 'are absolutely without any place of deposit for their refuse matter'.[48] Like other commentators, Duncan identified the area between Scotland Road and Vauxhall Road as being particularly deprived, at least 67 per cent of the front (street) houses having no privy, ashpit or yard. The inhabitants had to use the privies in the courts. Another feature contributing significantly to its general unhealthy state, was the density of population. One district in the north-end had a population of 12 000 living in a space of 49 000 square yards, giving a ratio of 657 963 to the square mile, two and three quarters times greater than the density of London.[49] Duncan quoted a case of four families sharing a room no more than ten feet square.[50] Collectively the investigations of Cornwallis, Wood, Holmes and Duncan all demonstrate that the urban environment of Liverpool was normally unhealthy; that the housing stock was of poor quality, even by the standards of Victorian England and that, on the eve of the Irish famine, the town was the most densely populated in Britain. Both Irish and non Irish working classes lived in such conditions.

The main area of Irish settlement in Liverpool, was the north-end. Six months before the 1841 census enumeration, a survey was taken of the population living in courts and cellars in the parish of Liverpool.

Table No 2.1 below shows the increase in the Irish born population in the various wards over the period of the famine crisis. The striking feature is the high proportion of court and cellar dwellers in the wards containing large numbers of Irish. In Vauxhall, 57 per cent of the population were living in cellars and courts while in St Pauls, Exchange and Scotland, the percentages were also high, 40, 36 and 39 respectively. The correlation between cellar and court dwellings on the one hand and Irish settlement on the other is confirmed by the census data.

Table 2.1 The population inhabiting the twelve wards in the parish of Liverpool in 1842 distinguishing between courts and cellars

Wards	*Pop. in 1841*	*Pop. of courts in 1840*	*Pop. of cellars in 1840*	*Total pop. in courts and cellars*	*Per cent of ward's total*	*Number of fever deaths 1835-9*
Vauxhall	26 146	11 585	3 253	14 838	57	4 346
St Pauls	18 002	5 209	1 981	7 190	40	1 615
Exchange	17 769	3 975	2 491	6 466	36	2 955
Castle St	9 691	1 829	570	2 399	25	955
St Annes	18 882	5 588	1 983	7 571	40	1 078
Lime St	18 848	4 079	900	4 979	26	480
Scotland	35 613	10 628	3 166	13 794	39	1 867
St Peters	9 533	1 589	499	2 088	22	673
Pitt Street	15 263	1 742	2 103	3 845	25	1 108
Gt George	19 645	4 590	1 337	5 927	30	1 863
Rodney St	15 202	2 567	903	3 470	23	265
Abercromby	15 899	2 153	982	3 135	20	264
Total	220 493	55 534	20 168	75 702	34	17 469

Source: First Report, Large Towns, Appendix Liverpool, Table 10, p. 24.

During the years following the 1841 census the Vauxhall, Exchange and Scotland wards experienced nearly 18 000 Irish move into the area. The fall in the population of St Pauls, also in the north-end, was caused by the demolition of housing to make way for a railway, so increasing the pressure of demand for low cost housing in the other wards. In the south-end, Great George and north and south Toxteth witnessed an increase of 5850 in the numbers of Irish born. The wards with the high percentages of Irish were also the wards with the largest numbers of court and cellar dwellings. It is interesting to observe, for example, that the numbers of Irish born persons in the Vauxhall, Scotland and Exchange wards alone, exceeded the total number of Irish born in the whole of Co. Durham and Northumberland.

In all the reports on Victorian social conditions, investigators picked out sections of the Irish communities as examples of absolute destitution, the ubiquitous 'low Irish'. William Duncan was no exception but his investigations do reveal the misery of much of the Irish experience in Britain and he did show some understanding that the root problem was poverty. To finish this survey of the urban environment in Liverpool on the eve of the famine, we give Duncan the last word. Writing in 1840 of the filthy nature of working class areas in Liverpool, he stated:

> ...but when it is considered that there are not less than 50 000 of the lower Irish resident in Liverpool, it will be understood that some portion of it, at least, must be the result of their own indifference. Even when a plentiful supply of water is at hand, the inhabitants of the filthy courts inhabited by the Irish too often neglect to avail themselves of its services, and when the removal of a nuisance is in their power, they seem to think it hardly worth the trouble which it would occasion them... But it must be remembered that many of the evils which I have pointed out are, perhaps, the inevitable result of poverty and I believe the fever, to a certain extent, is an inseparable accompaniment of extreme poverty affecting large masses of the population. Among the causes of fever in Liverpool I might have enumerated the large proportion of poor Irish among the working population. It is they who inhabit the filthiest and worst ventilated courts and cellars, who congregate the most numerously in dirty lodging houses, who are least clean in their habits and the most apathetic about everything that befalls them. It is among the Irish that fever especially commits its ravages and it is they who object most strongly to be removed to the hospital from their miserable abodes... No one interested in the welfare of his poorer brethren can contemplate the prospect without a feeling of melancholy foreboding; and I am persuaded that so long as the native inhabitants are exposed to the invasion of numerous hordes of uneducated Irish, spreading physical and moral contamination around them, it will be in vain to expect any sanitary code can cause fever to disappear from Liverpool.[51]

With regard to fever, Black '47 was to confirm Duncan's worst fears.

III

Manchester exhibited similar problems of poor social infra-structure as Liverpool at this time, Unfortunately, at present (1997) no large scale, detailed analysis of the census enumerators' returns on the scale of Dr Papworth's work on Liverpool exists for Manchester, although that task has now been initiated by Mervyn Busteed.[52] However, a number of detailed private investigations of Manchester's working classes were undertaken in the period immediately preceding the famine and these provide reasonable evidence, statistical and anecdotal, concerning the pre-famine Irish settlements in Manchester township.

The most referred to study is that carried out by James Phillips Kay, published in 1832, under the title of *The Moral and Physical Conditions of the Working Classes Employed in Cotton Manufacture in Manchester*.[53] In this, the Irish claim a disproportionate amount of attention and because

Kay's report was influential in helping to frame middle-class perceptions of the Irish in Manchester, his ideological stance needs to be understood. Kay was a medical doctor and, like Duncan in Liverpool, was trained in Edinburgh. In 1828 he became senior Physician at the Ancoats and Ardwick Dispensary in Manchester. Kay was a committed Christian, a laissez faire economist and an empiricist. He held an unequivocal view that capitalism was the form of economic organization which promoted the maximum amount of happiness for the greatest number of people:

> Believing that the natural tendency of unrestricted commerce (unchecked by the prevailing want of education, and the incentives afforded by imperfect laws to improvidence and vice) is to develop the energies of society, to increase the comforts and luxuries of life, and to *elevate the physical conditions* of every member of the social body, we have exposed, with a faithful, though a friendly hand, the condition of the lower orders connected with the manufactures of this town, because we conceive that the evils affecting them result from foreign and accidental causes. A system, which promotes the advance of civilization and diffuses it over the world - which promises to maintain the peace of nations, by establishing permanent international law, founded on the benefits of commercial association, cannot be inconsistent with the happiness of the *great mass of the people*... The evils affecting the working classes, *so far from being the necessary results of the commercial system, furnish evidence of a disease which impairs its energies, if it does not threaten its vitality.*[54]

This is the core of Kay's economic philosophy. Unrestricted trade raises material living standards for the majority of people. International trade promotes international accord. Crucially, Kay believed that the wretchedness of many of the working classes was not the necessary consequence of the capitalist system of production but was due entirely to exogenous factors which could, by diligent analysis and private action, be removed. The factors which, in Kay's view, inhibited the improvement of the poorest section of society were both economic and moral. The 'disease' that Kay refers to was what he felt was the irreligion, ignorance, dissoluteness and lack of forethought of a significant proportion of the working class. The 'imperfect laws' he referred to were those governing the sale of alcohol and the licensing of dance halls and such things as the corn laws. He clearly understood that the rate of urban growth had outstripped the growth of social institutions, infra-structure and organisational structures necessary to ameliorate the animal existence of many people. But improvements could be achieved, it was within the power of the middle-classes to provide.

Capitalism was inherently beneficial to the majority of persons and, in the long run, the evils existing could be removed by the enlightened self-interest of the middle classes. Kay understood that both changing patterns of demand and technological innovation could create unemployment. However, he shows little understanding of what that did to the human spirit despite his familiarity with life in the slums. He appreciated that the handloom weavers in Manchester had suffered from the mechanisation of weaving and that wages were very low even when work could be obtained. The majority of this group of workers were Irish. Speaking of the short period in economic analysis, Kay described their conditions:

> The handloom weavers, existing in *this state of transition* (my italics) still continue a numerous class, and though they labour fourteen hours and upwards daily, earn only from five to eight shillings a week. They consist chiefly of Irish and are affected by all the causes of moral and physical depression which we have enumerated. Ill-fed, ill-clothed, half-sheltered and ignorant; weaving in close damp cellars or crowded workshops, it only remains that they should become as too frequently the case, demoralized and reckless, to render perfect, the portraiture of savage life.[55]

Kay went on to argue that the Irish had had a deleterious effect on the morals of the English working-classes with whom they were in contact. Kay's view that the state of the handloom weavers was 'transitory' was undoubtedly true but it took nearly a generation of hardship for the handloom weavers to adjust to the new market situation. Occupational mobility was hindered by unlimited competition in all the alternative unskilled jobs open to the weavers.

He was against any inhibitions on free trade, such as, for example, the corn laws, the navigation laws and trade unions. Tariffs on foreign imports invited retaliation, thus reducing the volume of world trade. In turn, this reduced the demand for labour, brought about falling wages and increased poverty. Capitalists faced with falling demand, can only employ labour at lower wages. In Kay's view (and that of Karl Marx) the Irish met the demand for labour at rock bottom wages:

> Those districts where the poor dwell are of recent origin. The rapid growth of the cotton manufacture has attracted hither operatives from every part of the kingdom, and Ireland has poured forth the most destitute of her hordes, to supply the constantly increasing demand for labour. This immigration has been in one important respect, a serious evil. The Irish have taught the labouring classes of this country a pernicious

> lesson.... Debased alike by ignorance and pauperism, they have discovered with the savage, what is the minimum means of life upon which existence may be prolonged. The paucity of the amount of means and comforts *necessary for the mere support of life* is not known by a more civilized population, and this secret has been taught the labourers of this country, by the Irish. As competition and the restrictions and burdens of trade diminished the profits of capital, and consequently reduced the price of labour, the contagious example of ignorance and a barbarous disregard of forethought and economy exhibited by the Irish, spread.[56]

The Irish immigrants, used to a much lower level of physical, well-being had, in Kay's view, taught the English lower orders how to survive on the minimum income necessary for bare survival. The intellectual inconsistency of Kay's position is made clear in the above passage. The existence of a group of workers willing to accept the lowest wage produced by market forces, consistent with subsistence, is something that a committed adherent of laissez-faire economics should have welcomed. It was the ability of the Irish, often transient workers, to exist at such low wage levels, that benefitted employers. The price to be paid however was the sight of a lifestyle that Kay found repellent. Despite this, he would not have supported minimum wage legislation! Teaching English people to survive on minimum income during a trade depression is not what worries Kay about the Irish. He accuses the Irish of importing a permanent life style of dissoluteness and improvidence likely to contaminate the English lower orders, Duncan's 'moral contamination'. His other target was the poor law, which at this time, was under investigation with a view to reform. He believed that the system of outdoor relief encouraged significant numbers of the working-classes to rely on poor relief, removing the incentive to provide for the future. Thus the poor law had to be reformed, reintroducing the distinction between deserving and undeserving poor. For Kay, the Irish encouraged the English to use poor relief as a fall back position to be used when current income was spent, thus becoming welfare dependent. Kay was fully aware of the detrimental effects of long hours spent in factory employment. He also understood that, faced with unremitting toil followed by returning home to poverty stricken, unhealthy and uncongenial dwellings, men would go to the tavern and drink excessively. The solution was education, religious instruction and a reform of the poor law in such a way as to reserve relief for the deserving poor. Kay's report was aimed at persuading the middle-classes of Manchester and other towns, that, in cost/benefit terms, it was in their interests to promote such policies, in effect to inculcate middle class values.

Manchester had 14 police districts at the time of Kay's investigation. For purposes of collecting information the districts were divided into four groups, Ancoats (district number 1); Deansgate (districts nos. 10, 11, 13 & 14); London Road (district nos. 4 & 7) Market Street (district nos. 3,5,6,8,9 & 12) and St George's (district no. 2). Kay's study revealed that the poorest elements in Manchester's population lived mainly in Police Districts 1,2,3,4 & 10. Of a total of 6951 homes inspected, 2221 or 32 per cent did not have privies. Of these, 959 or 43 per cent were in the poorest districts. In the case of homes needing their drains repairing, 56 per cent were in the same districts.

Some of the worst disease ridden dwellings were the lodging houses and in 1832 there were 267 of these in Manchester township. Of this number, 64 per cent were in the poorest districts. Kay pointed out that these bare statistics did not convey the full reality of the awful living conditions endured by large numbers of people, including the lack of bedding, food, fuel and clothing. Referring specifically to the Irish, he wrote:

> In these respects, the habitations of the Irish are most destitute. They can scarcely be said to be furnished. They contain one or two chairs, a mean table, the most scant culinary apparatus and one or two beds, loathsome with filth. A whole family is often accommodated on a single bed, and sometimes a heap of filthy straw and a covering of old sacking to hide them in one undistinguished heap, debased alike by penury, want of economy and dissolute habits... and often more than one family lived in a damp cellar, containing only one room in whose pestilential atmosphere from twelve to sixteen persons were crowded. To these fertile sources of disease were sometimes added the keeping of pigs and other animals in the house, with other nuisances of the most revolting character.[57]

In this passage, he was referring to the Irish dwellings in general, but a particular area was picked out for special comment. This was a collection of houses, about two hundred in number, situated on low lying ground on a bend in the River Medlock below Oxford Road. This was known locally as 'Little Ireland' although in fact it was a relatively small Irish settlement. A report by a sub-committee reported on the condition of Little Ireland and described damp cellars, overcrowding, lack of ventilation, lack of clothing and dampness. The area was particularly awful because it was low lying and liable to floods.[58] In 1841 the total Irish born population of these streets was 963 with another 187 British born children of two Irish parents. This made a total of 1150 living in 239 houses. This district entered into the iconography of Irish destitution in Britain but there were much larger Irish settlements in Manchester, in Ancoats and Newtown districts, the latter sometimes referred to as 'Irish Town'. Angel Meadow was situated between Rochdale Road and the River Irk. A recent study of this area using the 1851 census reveals a total population of 10 995 of which number 4735 were born in Ireland and 807 were British born children of two Irish parents, making a total Irish settlement of 5542 or 50.4 per cent.[59] Kay believed that the house building speculators had identified the needs of the impoverished Irish immigrants as a niche in the housing market. He expressed the opinion that the speculators provided houses for the Irish by buying the cheapest sites, which usually meant the unhealthiest. These builders, he claimed, were 'adventurers' who seem to speculate on the existence of a race of inhabitants who are satisfied with the 'minimum' comforts of life. Two years after Kay's pamphlet was published, the Cornwallis investigation into the Irish poor in Britain provides more information on the pre-famine Irish settlements in Manchester. Some of the evidence given to the Commissioners acts as a counter balance to Kay's opinions and conclusions. Kay gave evidence: '... the tendency to speculate on the barbarous habits of the people in selecting inconvenient houses, etc, is much greater in those towns which are colonized by the Irish'.[60]

His critical views of the undesirable activities of building speculators in providing for a particular need at the bottom end of the housing market does not fit easily into a belief in the efficacy of the market system as a means of maximising society's welfare. Kay also seems to have had problems in distinguishing between profit maximisation and welfare maximisation. Despite his generally adverse views on the Irish in Manchester, Kay did not think the Irish were inherently inferior to the English. He believed they were intellectual equals and their conditions were the result of the lifestyle in Ireland.[61]

Turning first to the estimates of the size of the Irish settlements in Manchester in 1834, these vary between 30 000 and 40 000. Given the 1841 census figure of 30 304 in the borough of Manchester, the estimate in 1834 of 30 000 seems the most realistic figure. Salford had an Irish born population of 3996 in 1841.[62] A very large proportion of Irish at this time had been attracted by the possibility of finding work, including handloom weavers. The perception of endemic Irish poverty was established from the onset of large scale pre-famine Irish immigration into Manchester township. For example, for the financial year ending 25 March 1824, expenditure on the Irish poor in Manchester was £818. For the financial year ending 25 March 1833, the amount so spent was £3327, almost a quadrupling. Over the same period, expenditure on the English poor increased less than two times.[63] Despite a widespread pre-occupation with Irish poverty and alleged dissolute lifestyle, many knowledgeable individuals in Manchester testified to the crucial role of the Irish in the region's industrial development. Few seemed to share Kay's view of the demoralising effect of the Irish in Manchester. Giving evidence to the Cornwallis enquiry Mr Gardiner, Directing Overseer of the township of Manchester, stated:

> I do not consider, with respect to the relief of the Irish poor, that there is any difference between Manchester and other manufacturing places. I think that Lancashire has so increased by her manufacturies, that in all probability we might have been deficient in labourers if it had not been for the immigration of the Irish. From that I conclude that it is not unfair in principle that where they have given their best services for a number of years, for the best period of their life, they should receive assistance on emergencies when they fall into distress, sickness, old age or any other casualty. As there are no poor laws in Ireland, there can be no means by which they can prolong life if they are passed back.

Gardiner was intimately concerned with the operation of poor relief in Manchester and while this did not make him an expert on labour markets, his opinion is noteworthy.[64] His views on the importance of the Irish to the regional economy were shared by other influential persons giving evidence to the same investigators. For example, John Frederick Foster, the stipendiary magistrate of Manchester and Salford, declared:

> The practice of not passing the Irish [sic. back to Ireland] after a long residence originated from the feeling that the manufacturers of Manchester could not have increased as they did, had it not been for the labours of Irish workmen and that it was therefore unjust when they were past labour to send them back to Ireland.[65]

Many of those giving evidence to the Cornwallis enquiry regarding Manchester, were in manufacturing, particularly textiles, and can reasonably be regarded as authoritative regarding labour issues. The body of anecdotal evidence, on balance, supports the argument that Irish labour was crucial to the industry of both Manchester and its surrounding districts. In effect, this meant that employers had access to a reserved army of unemployed unskilled workers *and* handloom weavers.

The opinion that Irish immigration had held down wages was not unanimous but it *was* a majority opinion amongst those giving evidence. James Guest, a Manchester cotton manufacturer expressed the opinion that many of the Irish immigrants (pre-famine) were weavers: '...an English agricultural labourer would find no employment in our mills, if he were to come. I never heard of a case of an instance of an English agricultural family bringing their children to Manchester to work in the factories'.[66]

Another cotton manufacturer, James Aspinall Turner, told the enquiry: 'I consider that the Irish have been a great advantage to the manufacturers of this town... On the whole I do not think that the English agricultural labourer would be so well able, as the Irish, to undertake the employments afforded them in Manchester'.[67]

James Taylor owed a silk mill in Newton Heath which employed five hundred as winders of silk. Of this number 190 were Irish. He reiterated the view that rigidities in internal English labour markets meant that Irish labour was of central importance to industry. He had commissioned the building of a mill and *all* the bricklayers were Irish. He tried, but failed, to recruit English bricklayers: 'I never heard of any men coming from Kent, Surrey or any of the Southern counties and asking for work in Lancashire or Cheshire. I never received any application of that kind'.[68]

One of the reasons for this immobility of labour referred to by these witnesses, was the effect of the laws of settlement. If an English worker left his parish of birth at this time (1834) he lost the right to poor relief should he need it. The widespread support for the view that Irish immigration into Manchester had held down the wages of the unskilled was undoubtedly part of the explanation proffered by many, of why Manchester had benefitted from the presence of the Irish. However, with regard to the English handloom weavers, mechanisation not immigration was responsible for the reduced level of demand for their services. The Cornwallis enquiry produced evidence to back up Kay's findings regarding the poorest areas of Manchester. John Redman, visiting overseer to Manchester township, had been responsible for the Newtown district and he confirmed the generally held view that large numbers of Irish lived there. 'I have heard it called 'Irish town' from this circumstance'. John Butcher, also a visiting overseer, told the enquiry 'I once had the district of Oldham Rd, in which there is a very large Irish population'.[69] Turning to the issue of housing, John Robertson, a surgeon at Manchester's lying-in hospital, claimed: 'Although I have entered the abodes, perhaps of many thousand Irish, I do not remember to have seen any furniture in them except a small deal table, a chair or two and only occasionally a bed. In very many instances, no furniture whatsoever, was to be seen'.

He estimated that (in 1834) there were not less than 6000 cellars in Manchester and that most of them were inhabited by the Irish.[70] Kay gave evidence to the enquiry when it visited Manchester in January and February 1834, and he returned to his theme of the deleterious influence of the Irish on the English: 'In some cellars in Little Ireland, I have known eighteen people, adults and children, sleep in one room about four yards square, without window or any other means of ventilation except through a door which opened into an adjoining apartment... In general I should say that the house of an Irishman is that of a person in a lower state of civilisation than that of the population of this country'.[71]

Yet another contradiction in his value system included the opinion that, despite his adherence to laissez faire economic policy, the state should interfere in the 'amusements' of the poor, 'to be within the range of its fostering care... a more enlightened and paternal care might have restrained them from evil'. Here he was referring to the drink trade, music halls and so on.[72] A particularly densely populated area of Manchester was around the Collegiate Church (now Manchester Cathedral), bounded by Shude Hill, Hanover Street, Long Millgate, Todd Street and Withy Grove. Within this area, Garden Street, Back Garden Street, Back Hanover Street, Wells Street and Huntsman Street, were all notorious for their poverty. Another area of acute destitution was Angel Meadow, in particular Crown Lane, Nelson Street, Back Ashley Lane, Charlotte Street, Park Street, Irish Row and Water Street. Richard Baron Howard was a Manchester doctor, who gave detailed evidence to the Sanitary Inquiry of 1842. Writing of the areas in Manchester where most of the poor lived, Howard described the normal state of affairs as they then existed:

> ...whole streets in these quarters are unpaved and without drains or main sewers, all worn into deep ruts and holes, in which water constantly stagnates, and are so covered with refuse and excrementitous matter as to be almost impassable from the depth of mud, and intolerable from stench.... In many of these places are to be seen privies in the most disgusting state of filth, open cesspools, obstructed drains, ditches full of stagnant water, dunghills, pigsties, etc.[73]

After more description of the external environment in which thousands of Manchester's poor were living, Howard then described the inside of their houses:

> They are dirty in an extreme degree, damp, shamefully out of repair and barely furnished. Many indeed, can scarcely be said to be furnished at all - a table, a chair or a stool, a few, and very few articles of culinary apparatus, some shavings or a little straw in one corner, with a scanty piece or two of filthy bed covering, constitute the whole furniture of numerous habitations in this town... The wretched conditions of many of the cellars will scarcely be credited by those who have not visited them - dark, damp and filthy, incapable of ventilation and constantly liable to be flooded, they present a most dismal appearance and are quite unfit to be inhabited by civilized human beings. The walls are scarcely ever white washed, the windows neither keep out the wind or rain, and the floors are

> sometimes not half covered with bricks or flags. I have occasionally visited patients where the bedding or straw on which they lay, was placed without any protection, on a floor not only damp but literally wet.[74]

Howard's view on the condition of Manchester's poor received support from a report on a survey of 12 000 poor families in Manchester, undertaken at the behest of a number of socially concerned members of the middle class. This was published in 1842, before the results of the Sanitary Enquiry. The objective was to establish the scale of the poverty problem before giving private relief.

The author of the report was Joseph Adshead.[75] The investigators visited 1551 handloom weavers' households in 1840, consisting of a total of 6978 individual weavers and members of their families. The concentration of the handloom weavers in Ancoats and New Town is obvious (Police districts one and two) as is the number of Irish handloom weavers, 60 per cent of the families and, coincidentally, 60 per cent of the individuals. Both of these districts were consistently identified both as areas of extreme deprivation and of relatively dense Irish settlement. Though the cellar population of Manchester and Salford was much less than that of Liverpool, it was still considerable. The Relief Committee found that 2040 families out of the total 10 132 families visited, lived in cellars, the majority being in the Ancoats, Deansgate and New Town districts.[76]

Table 2.2 The geographical distribution within Manchester of 1551 families of handloom weavers identified by the Relief Committee in 1840.

District	*English*		*Irish*	
	Families	*Individuals*	*Families*	*Individuals*
Ancoats	332	1494	328	1476
New Town	191	859	509	2290
Deansgate	42	189	44	198
Portland	62	279	43	193
Total	627	2821	924	4157

Source: Adshead, 1842.

IV

Turning to Glasgow, the available evidence paints a similar picture to that of Liverpool and Manchester. When examining the statistics of population in the case of Glasgow it is important to keep in mind that frequently the term 'Glasgow' refers to the city of Glasgow and its suburbs of Barony parish and part of the Gorbals district. In 1841, the city of Glasgow had a population of 120 183; Barony parish 106 075 and Gorbals district (part), 48 066, making a total of 274 324 for the city of Glasgow and its suburbs. The 1841 census counted 44 346 Irish born for this administrative area, smaller than the numbers in Liverpool but larger than in Manchester and Salford. The earliest estimate of the size of the Irish born population for this same area is that of Dr Cleland, who claimed that in 1819, the Irish born population was 35 554. This does not seem unreasonable given the 1841 census count of 44 346. Interestingly, he claims that 46 per cent of these were Protestants. Bishop Scott, the Catholic bishop in Glasgow stated in 1834 that the majority of Catholics in Glasgow were Irish from the north of Ireland.[77]

The Cornwallis Report is the best source of evidence concerning the Irish in Glasgow before the famine crisis. Again the anecdotal evidence in the report is often contradictory but, despite this, a fairly detailed picture emerges of the pre-famine Irish settlements. In the case of Glasgow, 29 persons gave evidence, including clergymen, textile manufacturers, coal mine proprietors, poor law officials, policemen and doctors. The anecdotal evidence is overwhelmingly of the view that the economic opportunities in the west of Scotland were the magnet for the majority of Irish immigrants into the area. In contrast to Liverpool, Glasgow had a manufacturing base of textiles, together with coalmining and ironworks. Like Liverpool, it had a shipbuilding and ship repair industry. The attraction for job seekers of the textile industry, and the opportunities it gave the women and children, made the comparison with Manchester and the surrounding Lancashire mill towns more apposite. Few spinners in the Glasgow area were Irish, unlike weavers among whom the Irish were heavily represented. James Thompson was a cotton manufacturer employing three to four hundred looms in Glasgow, Girvan and Lanark: 'Probably two thirds of these weavers are Irish. Nearly all those at Girvan are Irish or the descendants of Irish'.[78]

James Hutchinson employed from 1500 to 2000 handloom weavers producing muslin in Glasgow, 'a good many of these are Irish'.[79] A Mr Scott managed a cotton mill at Blantyre and told the Cornwallis enquiry that 'the Irish at Blantyre are almost all Protestants'.[80] The predominance of the Irish in the textile industry seems to have reflected an aversion to working in mills on the part of the Scots. Originally, this reluctance seems to have been due to the fact that in the early stages of the mechanisation of the Scottish textile industry, handloom weaving paid more and so the Scots were reluctant to give it up, hence Irish workers were recruited to make up the labour shortfall in the mills. William Dixon owned a number of coal mines, an ironworks and ironstone mine. His main colliery was at Govan. On 22 February 1834, he employed 580 people at Govan. Of this total 320 or 55 per cent were Irish. At the Calderstone Ironstone mine, also owned by Dixon, 585 men were employed, of which number 22 per cent were Irish.[81]

The 1841 census confirmed the importance of the textile industry in providing job opportunities in the Glasgow area. Males dominated the handloom weaving sector and many of these were Irish. By way of contrast, power loom weaving was principally undertaken by women and in the cotton mills generally, women predominated. Overall, the textile industry provided equal employment for males and females. Compared with textiles, coalmining offered few job opportunities in that the total number employed in coalmining in 1841 in the Glasgow and its suburbs, was only 1576. One area which should have offered Irish women employment opportunities was the market for domestic servants. The 1841 census recorded 11 921 women describing themselves as servants in the Glasgow area.

Table 2.3: The numbers in each occupational group within the textile industry as recorded in the 1841 census for the city of Glasgow and its suburbs.

Occupation	*Male*	*Female*	*Total*
Powerloom weavers	384	2 666	3 050
Handloom weavers	1 967	354	2 321
Weavers (not specified)	584	108	692
Cotton manufacture	9 437	11 349	20 786
Dyeing	729	112	841
Cotton calico printing	886	204	1 090
Woollen manufacture	1 040	224	1 264
Total	15 027	15 017	30 044

Source: 1841 Census: Abstract and Answers (Occupations) County of Lanark, pp. 47-57.

There is some anecdotal evidence that Irish women were not in demand as domestic servants. George Williamson, Procurator Fiscal of Greenock expressed the view that: 'The Irish females, from their not being much liked as servants in families, are forced to remain in their parents' homes and become dissolute and untidy, and merry persons just like their parents'.[82]

Alexander Carlile, a cotton thread manufacturer of Paisley claimed 'the domestic servants of Paisley are almost all Scotch girls'.[83] The balance of the Glasgow evidence given to the Cornwallis inquiry in 1834 was of the opinion that the Irish had been indispensable in meeting the labour requirements of the regional economy. This was not because they had held back the rate of increase of wages across a number of segments of the labour market but because the labour supply would have been insufficient without the Irish, even given higher wages. In addition to the view of their indispensable contribution, it was also believed that the Irish were hardworking, intelligent and desirable labour force. William Wilson, a brick and tilemaker preferred Irish workers to Highlanders. 'In general, the Highland labourers are not such hardworking men as the Irish'.[84] James Hutchinson, an employer of large numbers of Irish handloom weavers, declared. 'The Irish are as good workmen as the Scotch'.[85] Joseph Browne, the owner of a dye factory at Glasgow, expressed the positive opinion: 'I am inclined to think that if the Irish had the same facilities as our countrymen, they would surpass them and the English in intelligence and usefulness. I have found in them an acuteness and cleverness which I do not think my own countrymen possess'.[86]

These views are important in counterbalancing the well established stereotype of the Irishmen in the press, literature and drama. There is plentiful evidence that among those who dealt with working class Irishmen and women, there was a widespread opinion that the Irish were intelligent, quick and resourceful, as well as being of economic benefit to Britain. Despite these accolades, there were, paradoxically, widespread reservations over the lifestyle of many Irish and the influence which many assumed the Irish to exercise over the lower orders of British. Simultaneously, there were contradictions in such views. James Neilson, manager of the Glasgow Gas Works told the Cornwallis inquiry that 'the Irish are excellent workmen, the best labour we get. If possible, when I put them together, I get threequarters Irish and one fourth Highlanders'. Yet in the same evidence, he blames the Irish for the deterioration which he perceived to have occurred among the Scots working class, echoing the views of Kay in Manchester and Rushton in Liverpool.[87]

The population of Glasgow and its suburbs increased from 202 426 in 1831 to 274 324 in 1841. This represented a very high, average annual rate of growth, 3.1 per cent. The census of 1841 gave the figure of Irish born in Glasgow 44 350, Over the famine decade 1841-51, the population of Glasgow city and its suburbs increased from 274 324 to 322 986, an average annual growth rate of 2.3 per cent and both famine Irish immigrants and Highlanders, were a significant element in this growth. In 1851, the population of the four parishes of Glasgow totalled 358 951, with a total number of Irish born of 62 925. As was the case in respect of all other large towns, we find the familiar story of urban development outstripping the growth of social and organisational infrastructure in the spheres of housing, water and sanitation.

At the present time (1997) no detailed analysis of the 1841 census enumerators' sheets has been done for Glasgow and so the precise geographical location of the pre-famine Irish in Glasgow is not known with certainty. Richard Curtis was a pawnbroker with a shop in Trongate and he did a lot of business with the Irish:

> The Irish are scattered all over the town, but mostly they live in the suburbs (sic Barony and Gorbals). The wynds and closes leading from Trongate to Bridgegate, in the centre of the town, are also chiefly occupied by Irish and the poorest order of Scotch.[88]

Moses Steven Buchanan, was senior surgeon at the Glasgow Royal Infirmary and he told the Cornwallis inquiry:

> In consequence of the crowded state of the Irish lodging houses, typhus has prevailed in Glasgow among the Irish more extensively than among the Scotch.. In the lodging houses I have often seen from eight to twelve in one apartment, lying on straw with little or no bedding and almost no blankets. The worst are towards the south part of the old and new wynds; they are dark, damp, crowded and ill-ventilated hovels; there are few cellar residences in Glasgow.. generally speaking, the dwellings of the Irish are a grade inferior in regard to furniture; the lowest part of the populations being Irish, we find that in comfort, education and moral feeling, they are inferior to the Scotch... There are no streets or districts in Glasgow exclusively inhabited by Irish.. they appear to be quite amalgamated and mixed up with the poor population of the town.[89]

John Stirling, surgeon, claimed:

> The dwellings of the Irish are poorer than those of the Scotch in the same class of life; more of them are huddled together, the homes are ill-furnished, ill-aired and dirty in the extreme. The poor Irish frequently live on the floor, on straw or shavings; frequently however, they have beds. It is the practice for as many to sleep on the same bed as can be crowded into it - it is not uncommon for three or four to lie in the same bed - frequently three or four beds and in the same apartment, in which males and females sleep next to one another.[90]

Jelinge Symons was an Assistant Handloom Weaver Commissioner, who had written various reports on social conditions. On 3 March 1840, he told the Select Committee on the Health of Towns that 'I am not aware that I have ever seen a town in which the state of the working classes was worse, as regards the points of cleanliness and health'.[91] He identified what was, in his opinion, the most wretched part of Glasgow:

> I allude to the dense and motley community who inhabit the low districts of Glasgow, consisting chiefly of the alleys leading out of the High Street, the lanes in Calton, but particularly the closes and wynds which

> lie between the Tron-gate and the Bridge Street, the Salt Market and Maxwell Street. These districts contain a motley population, consisting almost all the lower branches of occupation, but chiefly of a community whose sole means of subsistence consists of plunder and prostitution.[92]

Symons estimated that 20 000 to 30 000 lived in this district and that the living conditions were such that 'no person of common humanity to animals would stable his horse in'.[93] He described the pieces of dung lying around the courts and claimed that in the lodging houses up to twenty persons, male and female and all ages 'sleep promiscuously on the floor in different degrees of nakedness'. He went on to express the opinion that the worst of the houses were in a dangerous state and that conditions in Glasgow were worse than in Liverpool and Manchester.[94] In some instances he quoted, people had no privy and nowhere to dump excrement other than the courtyard. The provision of water was a single pump in each district and people had to take receptacles to be filled.[95] The problem of evaluating this kind of anecdotal evidence is demonstrated by contrasting the statements of various investigators of the same phenomena. Symonds, describing the population in the 'low districts' of Glasgow referred to above, stated: 'I have seen human degradation in some of its worst phases, both in England and abroad, but I can advisedly say that I did not believe, until I visited the wynds of Glasgow, that so large an amount of filth, crime, misery and disease existed in one spot in any civilized country'.[96]

Dr Baird carried out a survey of conditions in Glasgow for the Chadwick Sanitary Enquiry.[97] Writing in 1841, he expressed the contrary view to that of Symonds that at least 80 per cent of Glasgow's population belonged to the working classes and that they 'are in general civil and industrious and in point of moral and mental worth, at least equal to the same classes in any other city or town I have visited'. He also confirmed the existence of cellars occupied by the poorest elements in Glasgow's society. He made the point that though many of Glasgow's operatives lived comfortably, that they lived on the margin; bad weather, trade fluctuations or rising food prices could easily impel them into pauperism.[98] As in all similar towns, fever was constantly present and Baird pointed to the bad housing conditions as a major contributor to the high death rate. The economic pressures channelling Glasgow's poor into the worst housing were identified in a report submitted to the same inquiry:

> That regular manufactories of pauperism exist in the damp and unventilated cellars and the ground floors in the lanes and closes of the city is a fact of easy demonstration. In almost every helpless and hopeless case of rheumatism (and they are not a few) I could trace its origin to the

> person having lived on some damp ground floor, in a close or lane, or in the sunk flat of some house in a more reputable locality, and it has often happened that no sooner has one diseased tenant been driven out than another healthy person succeeds to undergo the same disqualifying process, *merely tempted by a few shillings of lower rent or that he may be able to sell coals, or some commodity in the densely populated vicinity* (my italics)... I was induced to inquire and notice where the disease [fever] had been most deadly, and again and again have I observed that it was in closes and homes where no thorough ventilation existed, or could be made to operate, that this had happened; where a close was shut on *three* sides, perhaps on four, with the exception of the passage or entry, which acted as a mere conducting force to carry the malaria or contagion to the inhabitants of the upper floors or houses. And I observed that particular houses, where the disease had been destructive, were situated close by the receptacles of impurity, common to the neighbourhood, where fluid abominations were continually exhaling their noxious vapours.[99]

The lodging houses of Glasgow were similar to those elsewhere with regard to the miserable conditions that characterized them.

In 1841, the City missionaries and church elders answered a survey carried out by Baird. Fifteen out of the 16 districts sending in answers stated that the last winter had seen a great deal of destitution among the population. The district of Calton (part of Barony parish) had a population of 28 000. The Commissioners of police, church elders and parish surgeons inspected the district and found five hundred families without bedding or fire and all poorly clothed.[100] Captain Miller, Superintendent of the Glasgow Police identified the centre of Glasgow as possessing 'an accumulated mass of squalid wretchedness which is probably unequalled in any other town in the British dominions'. He picked out the interior of a square bounded on the east by Salt Market, on the west by Stockwell Street, on the north by Trongate and in the south by the river. (Six years later, the *Glasgow Courier* identified the worst areas of Glasgow as the closes and wynds on the south side of Trongate and Argyll Street including the Salt Market and Bridgegate, the east side of High Street and a large part of Gallowgate).[101] In concluding his report, Baird accused the 'higher classes' of being indifferent to the condition of the poor and expressed the view that given their terrible conditions it was surprising they were not more discontented. Commenting on the evidence given him by police, missionaries, poor law officials and others, Baird stated:

> It will be noticed that several of my informants specify the "great influx of the lower orders of Irish" into Glasgow as another cause of the destitution here. Doubtless the vast number of Irish immigrants must have affected the price of labour and rendered employment more scarce and so had increased the amount of destitution in Glasgow, but not, I think, to so great an extent as is generally supposed; and it should be borne in mind that Glasgow otherwise has reaped immense advantage from the exercise of their lusty thighs and sinews. When, on this point, I may be allowed to remark that the poor Irish in Glasgow have completely verified the common adage, 'Give a dog a bad name', etc. The bad name was many years ago fixed upon them, and it has adhered too closely. It is more refreshing, therefore, to meet testimony in their favour.[102]

V

The picture painted of urban conditions in Britain on the eve of the Famine is unequivocal. Rapid urban growth, unmatched by a simultaneous investment in infrastructure such as water supplies, sanitation and adequate housing, produced horrific conditions which large numbers of people had to endure. Equally unequivocal, was the view of practically all observers of the social scene, that a large section of the immigrant Irish occupied the worst of these conditions, together with some of the least able elements of the English, Welsh and Scots. The Irish did not create these conditions and given their place in the unskilled labour markets, they had little choice. The middle class seemed oblivious to the sheer difficulties of life in the slums. The critics were not only English, Frederick Engels, the German, was as savage in his condemnation of the Irish lifestyle as anyone else. 'The worst quarters of all towns are inhabited by Irishmen'.[103] However, there is ample anecdotal evidence in these reports that the Irish were highly regarded as workers and that their contribution to economic growth was important. Part of the reason for their usefulness was their mobility, a factor which does not contribute to stable lifestyles.

Notes and References

1 For a detailed treatment of English attitudes towards the Irish, see L.P.Curtis, *Apes and Angels: The Irishman in Victorian Caricature,* David Charles, (Newton Abbot: 1971). S.Gilley, 'English Attitudes towards the Irish in England, 1798-1900' in C.Holmes (ed) *Immigrants and Minorities in Britain Society*, (London: 1978) pp. 81-110.

2 J.H.Treble, *Urban Poverty in Britain, 1830-1914*, paperback, (Methuen, London: 1983) (referred to hereafter as Treble), chapters, 1 and 2.

3 PRO/MH12/16328/Merthyr/11043B. T.J.Dyke to Poor Law Board, 14 May 1847.

4 Examples are (1) BPP (HC), *Accounts and Papers,* 1841, 2 (58), Correspondence between the Home Office and the Poor Law Commissioners on 'Distress in Bolton: Report of Assistant Commissioner'. (2) BPP (HC) *Accounts and Papers,* 1842 (77) XXXV, 'Distress in Stockport'. (3) BPP (HC) *Accounts and Papers,* 1837 (376), LI, Report of Dr Kay to Poor Law Commissioners on 'Distress in Spitalfield's.

5 D.Fitzpatrick, *Irish Emigration, 1801-1921,* (Dundalgan Press: 1984), part 4. Also C.O'Grada, *Ireland: A New Economic History,* (Oxford: 1994) ch. 9, section 9.3.

6 A.Redford, *Labour Migration in England, 1800-1850,* (Manchester: 1926). Also A.K.Cairncross, 'Trends in Internal Migration', *Transactions of the Manchester Statistical Society,* 1938-9, group meetings. pp. 21-5.

7 F.Neal, 'Liverpool, The Irish Steamship companies and the famine Irish', *Immigrants and Minorities,* volume 5, March 1986, No.1, pp. 28-61. J.Kennedy, *The History of Steam Navigation,* (Liverpool: 1903).

8 For coverage of this phase in British economic history, see F.Crouzet, *The Victorian Economy,* (Metheun, London: 1982), ch. 2. D.N.McCloskey,'The Industrial Revolution 1780-1860: a survey', in R.Floud and D.McCloskey (eds.), *The Economic History of Britain since 1700,* volume 1, 1700-1860, (Cambridge University Press: 1981) pp. 103-127. P.K.O'Brien, 'Modern Conceptions of the Industrial Revolution', in P.K.O'Brien and R.Quinault (eds.) *The Industrial Revolution and British Society,* (Cambridge University Press: 1993), pp. 1-30. For a succinct survey of Britain's shipping industry, see 'The Shipping Industry' (ch. 7) in G.Jackson, M.J.Freeman & D.K.Aldcroft, *Transport in Victorian Britain,* (Manchester University Press: 1988).

9 R.Reid, *The Land of Lost Content: The Luddite Revolt of 1812,* (Penguin: 1986). An account of the impact of new technology on textile workers and their reaction to it.

10 For the modern scholar, the reading of these reports present problems because of the conventions of representation adopted by middle class people describing a world utterly beyond their previous experience. For a full discussion of the issues involved, see J.W.Childers, 'Observation and Representation: Mr Chadwick writes the Poor', *Albion,* Spring, 1994, pp. 405-432.

11 I have calculated this and the following growth rates by using the census reports for 1841 and 1851 to obtain populations at each year and used the basic compound interest formula, $a = p\,(1+r)^n$ where a equals amount, p = principal, r = rate of interest and n = number of years. We obtain $\sqrt[n]{a/p}$ where a = population in 1851, p = population in 1841, n = 10, and r = average annual growth rate.

12 1851 Census, *Birthplaces of the People*: 'Birthplaces of the Inhabitants of Principal Towns', Div. XVIII, Liverpool Borough, p. 664.

13 I have multiplied the actual Irish-born population by a factor of 1.1. My own, as yet unpublished, study of the whole Irish-born population of Newcastle, Gateshead, Warrington, Leigh and Prescot, together with large samples of the same from County Durham's small towns, yields a figure varying between 10% and 15% in terms of the ratio of English-born children of two Irish parents, to the whole Irish population. This is crude but not unrealistic as an estimator of the total 'Irish' in a town, including their English-born children. I have used the conservative estimate of 10%.

14 1851 Census, *Birthplaces of the People:* 'Birthplaces of the Inhabitants of Principal Towns', Div. VIII, Manchester (City) and Salford (Borough), p. 664.

15 J.G.Williamson, 'The Impact of the Irish on British Labour: Markets during the Industrial Revolution', *Journal of Economic History,* XIVI, No. 3, September 1986, pp. 639-721.

16 J.Garrard, *Leadership and Power in Victorian Industrial Towns 1830-80,* (Manchester University Press: 1983). This is a study of the exercise of power in three industrial towns, Salford, Bolton and Rochdale. See also D.Frazer, *Power and Authority in the Victorian City*, (Blackwell, Oxford: 1979).

17 The growing awareness of an urban crisis was noticeable by 1830 and the next two decades witnessed the production of a number of reports by government agencies. These provide a wealth of detailed information, statistical and descriptive, of the social conditions in Britain's towns, with many references to the Irish. For anyone coming to the subject for the first time, they provide the natural inroad into the topic. See i. SC (Health) 1840; ii, First Report, Large Towns; iii, Second Report, Large Towns. All these reports contain material dealing with conditions in specific towns in Britain. In addition to these there are a large number of reports from various bodies and committees dealing with every aspect of urban squalor and problems generally, both local and national. Especially recommended, in addition to Treble referred to above are A.S.Wohl, *Endangered Lives: Public Health and Victorian Britain*, paperback, (Methuen, London: 1983). J.Burnett, *A Social History of Housing,* paperback, (Methuen, London: 1980). Gareth Stedman Jones, *Outcast London: A Study of the Relationship between Classes in Victorian Society*, (Oxford University Press: 1971); F.B.Smith, *The People's Health,* paperback, (Weidenfeld & Nicolson, London: 1990). *The Unknown Mayhew: Selections from the Morning Chronicle 1849-50*, (Penguin: 1984). *Labour and Poor in England and Wales 1849-51*: *Letters to the Morning Chronicle,* volume 1, (Frank Cass, London: 1983).

18 For Liverpool, see John Finch, *Statistics of the Vauxhall Ward of Liverpool*, (Liverpool: 1842). A.Hume, *Missions at Home or a Clergyman's Account of a Portion of the Town of Liverpool,* (Liverpool: 1850). Manchester is particularly well served. See, James Phillips Kay, *The Moral and Physical Condition of the Working Classes Employed in the Cotton Manufacture in Manchester*, (London: 1832), referred to hereafter as Kay, 1832. Joseph Adshead, *Distress in Manchester: Evidence of the State of the Labouring Classes in 1840-42*, (London: 1842), referred to hereafter as Adshead, 1842. Richard Parkinson, *On the Present Conditions of the Labouring Poor in Manchester, with Hints for Improving it*, (London: 1841), referred to hereafter as Parkinson, 1841. Leon Faucher, *Manchester in 1844: Its Present Condition and Future Prospects*, (London: 1844), reprinted F. Cass, 1969, referred to hereafter as Faucher, 1844.

19 Irish Poor (1836)

20 Irish Poor (1836). Liverpool, pp. 8-41, Manchester, pp. 42-84, Glasgow, pp. 101-41.

21 Irish Poor (1836) p. 9.

22 Irish Poor (1836) p. 10.

23 Irish Poor (1836) p. 18.

24 Irish Poor (1836) p. 22.

25 Irish Poor (1836) p. 23.

26 Irish Poor (1836) p. 23.

27 Irish Poor (1836) p. 24.

28 Irish Poor (1836) p. 28.

29 Irish Poor (1836) p. 18.

30 I.C.Taylor, 'The Court and Cellar Dwellings: The Eighteenth Century Origins of the Liverpool Slum', *Transactions of the Historical Society of Lancashire and Cheshire*, volume 122 (1970) pp. 67-90.

31 SC (Health) 1840, Minutes of Evidence, J.R.Wood, pp. 128-173.

32 SC (Health) 1840, Wood, q. 2136-7, p.128.

33 SC (Health) 1840, Wood. q. 2205, p. 132.
34 SC (Health) 1840, Duncan, q. 2374, p. 141.
35 SC (Health) 1840, Duncan, q. 2416, p. 144.
36 SC (Health) 1840, Duncan, p. 2442-43, p. 145.
37 SC (Health) 1840, Duncan, q. 2511, p. 149.
38 SC (Health) 1840, Duncan, q. 2513, p. 149.
39 SC (Health) 1840, Duncan, q. 2516, p. 149.
40 First Report (Large Towns), W.H.Duncan 'On the Physical Causes of the High Rate of Mortality in Liverpool', p. 29.
41 Second Report (Large Towns), Minutes of Evidence, 'Causes of Disease Among the Inhabitants', J.Aspinall, q. 23, p. 78.
42 Second Report (Large Towns), Minutes of Evidence, 'Causes of Disease Among the Inhabitants', J.Aspinall, qq. 26-8, p.78.
43 Second Report (Large Towns), Minutes of Evidence, 'Causes of Disease Among the Inhabitants', J.Aspinall, qq. 34-6, pp. 78-9.
44 See *Manchester Guardian* 7 July 1847. The stipendiary magistrate, Rushton, refused to sign any ejection orders until he was assured that alternative arrangements had been made for sick cellar dwellers. The fit persons were to be sent back to Ireland. A week later, receiving such assurances, Rushton ordered the cellars to be cleared but the policy was not fully implemented.
45 Second Report (Large Towns), Evidence of S. Holmes, p. 187.
46 SC (Health) 1840, Appendix, J.R.Wood, q. 2206.
47 First Report (Large Towns), Appendix, W.H.Duncan, 'On the Physical Causes of the High Rates of Mortality in Liverpool', pp. 12-33.
48 ibid, p. 15.
49 ibid, p. 28.
50 SC (Health) 1840, Minutes of Evidence, W.H.Duncan, q. 2403, p. 143.
51 Chadwick Report (England), Liverpool, pp. 293-94.
52 M.A.Busteed and R.I.Hodgson, 'Irish Migration and Settlement in Nineteenth Century Manchester, with special reference to Angel Meadow', *Irish Geography*, 27 (1), 1994, pp. 1-13. M.A.Busteed, R.I.Hodgson and T.F. Kennedy, 'Myth and Reality of Irish Migrants in Mid-Nineteenth Century Manchester: a preliminary study', in P.O'Sullivan (ed.), *The Irish World Wide, History, Heritage, Identity, volume 2, The Irish in New Communities,* (Leicester: 1992), pp. 26-51. M.A.Busteed and R.I.Hodgson, 'Coping with Urbanisation: The Irish in Early Manchester', in S.J.Neary, M.S.Symes and F.E.Brown (eds.) *Proceedings of the 13th Conference of the International Association for People - Environment Studies*, (Chapman: 1994).
53 Kay, 1832.
54 Kay, 1832, pp. 77-8.
55 Kay, 1832, p. 44.
56 Kay, 1832, pp. 20-1.
57 Kay, 1832, p. 32.
58 Kay, 1832, p. 34-6. Another description of Little Ireland in Manchester, see Sanitary Inquiry, Local Report, No. 20, pp. 307-8. M.A.Busteed, 'The Most Horrible Spot? The Legend of Manchester's Little Ireland', *Irish Studies Review*, 13, 1995-6, pp.12-20.
59 M.A.Busteed and R.I.Hodgson, 'Angel Meadow: a study of the geography of Irish settlements in mid-nineteenth century Manchester', *Manchester Geography*, 14, pp. 3-26. See also Busteed and Hodgson, 'Irish Migration and Settlement in Early Nineteenth Century Manchester with special reference to the Angel Meadow District in 1851', *Irish Geographer*, 27, pp. 1-13.

60 Irish Poor (1836) p. 61.
61 Irish Poor (1836) p. 59.
62 Irish Poor (1836) pp. 42-3. Estimate of Manchester's Irish-born population made by Fr T.Parker and Fr D.Hearne. The Salford figure is from the 1841 Census Report.
63 Irish Poor (1836) pp. p.44.
64 Irish Poor (1836) p. 47.
65 Irish Poor (1836) p. 51.
66 Irish Poor (1836) p. 66.
67 Irish Poor (1836) p. 65.
68 Irish Poor (1836) p. 69.
69 Irish Poor (1836) p. 48-9.
70 Irish Poor (1836) p. 56.
71 Irish Poor (1836) p. 57.
72 Irish Poor (1836) p. 58.
73 Chadwick Report (England) R.B.Howard. 'On the Prevalence of Diseases Arising from Contagion, Malaria and Certain Other Physical Causes Amongst the Working Classes in Manchester', p. 305.
74 ibid, p. 306.
75 Adshead, 1842, p.v. These people had contributed £4000 for the relief of Manchester's indigent workers.
76 Adshead, 1842, p.14. Table 'Families living in cellars'.
77 Irish Poor (1836) p. 101.
78 Irish Poor (1836) p. 110.
79 Irish Poor (1836) Glasgow, p. 111.
80 Irish Poor (1836) p. 108.
81 Irish Poor (1836) pp.113-4.
82 Irish Poor (1836) p 141.
83 Irish Poor (1836) p. 133.
84 Irish Poor (1836) p. 116.
85 Irish Poor (1836) p. 111.
86 Irish Poor (1836) p. 112.
87 Irish Poor (1836) p. 116.
88 Irish Poor (1836) p. 117.
89 Irish Poor (1836) p. 118.
90 Irish Poor (1836) p. 119.
91 SC (Health) 1840, J.C.Symons, q. 1068, p. 60.
92 SC (Health) 1840, J.C.Symons, q. 1072, p. 61.
93 SC (Health) 1840, J.C.Symons, q. 1078, p. 61.
94 SC (Health) 1840, J.C.Symons, qq. 1144-5, p. 65.
95 SC (Health) 1840, J.C.Symons, qq. 1150-1, p. 65.
96 SC (Health) 1840, J.C.Symons, q. 1074, p. 61.
97 Chadwick Report (Scotland) 'Sanitary Condition of the Working Classes and the Poor in the City of Glasgow', pp. 159-195.
98 Chadwick Report (Scotland) p. 166.
99 Chadwick Report (Scotland) p. 181-2.
100 Chadwick Report (Scotland) p. 196.
101 *Glasgow Courier*, 24 April 1847.
102 Chadwick Report (Scotland) p. 185.
103 F.Engels, *Condition of the Working Class* (Manchester: 1844) p.91.

3 Escape

I

John Fitzpatrick, a Roman Catholic priest, wrote a letter to the Catholic journal *The Tablet*, dated 4 January 1847. He was writing from Skibbereen to thank the readers of *The Tablet* for monetary gifts sent to help his parishioners:

> Most of the labouring and trade population are literally naked, having pawned for their support, day and night clothes. I have often seen, in visiting the houses, entire families labouring under fever and lying together on a sop of dirty straw without any covering than the rags which they wear by day. I have found the living and dead lying together on the same floor. I have known some bodies to be buried without coffins, in consequence of the poverty of the people; and in some cases, from the inability of surviving friends to purchase a coffin and their repugnance to bury the deceased without one, the body has been kept for five days until it was in a state of putrefaction and I have known the children in fever lying with the corpse during this time.

Increasingly during the winter of 1846, the English papers published harrowing accounts of the desperate condition of a significant proportion of the Irish population. However, given the scale of the tragedy, the coverage is less than modern newspaper readers would expect. *The Tablet* published Fitzpatrick's letter in an edition of 9 January 1847 and this was one of a growing number of reports of the horrors occurring in Ireland. Again, the later coverage is less than one would expect, but enough evidence was produced to indicate to the newspaper reading public the indisputable horror of the famine. At the time Fitzpatrick's letter was written, Hugh McNeile, an Irish Anglican priest in Liverpool and a leader of the 'No Popery' campaigners in England, preached a sermon pleading for help for the starving Irish. In the course of a powerful address, he read extracts from letters written by the Dean of Cork and another Anglican priest in the south of Ireland. The priest, an old friend of McNeile, told him that on the morning of writing the letter, he had ridden round his parish. Fifty persons had died of 'absolute starvation' and he had been told by the local doctor that 'hundreds, if not thousands, are so reduced that neither medicine or food can restore them'. This letter, and McNeile's sermon, was published in the Liverpool press during the first two weeks of January 1847.[1] Further evidence of the absolute level of destitution is contained in a letter written by Commander Caffin, R.N., who commanded the navy steam ship *Scourge*, to the Secretary of the Admiralty. The letter is dated 15 February 1847 and was given a wide circulation in the press.[2] Caffin had been in charge of unloading foodstuffs, principally meal, at Schull. Dr Traill, the rector of Schull, took him on a tour of the parish. Every house they entered had someone in it who was either dead or dying. In one cabin, three miles from the rectory, Dr Traill asked a woman 'Well Phyllis, how is your mother today'. Traill had visited the cabin the day before:

> ...and there, fearful reality, was the daughter, a skeleton herself, crouched and crying over the lifeless body of her mother, which was on the floor, cramped up as she had died, with her rags and cloak about her, by the side of few embers of peat. In the next cabin were three young children belonging to the daughter, whose husband had run away from her, all pictures of death. The poor creature said she did not know what to do with the corpse. She had no means of getting it removed and she was too exhausted to remove it herself.

Caffin was clearly shocked both by what he himself saw and what he was told by indisputably reputable persons and finished his letter by asking 'what is government doing?' [3]

Given the large body of evidence available concerning the nightmarish nature of the calamity, it seems somewhat superfluous to ask 'why were unprecedentedly large numbers of Irish fleeing to Britain?' In addition to those escaping probable death or unacceptable levels of destitution, others were seeking better long term economic opportunities. There is no reason to believe that the ordinary workings of labour markets stopped operating during the years 1845-1851. Despite the economic downturns of 1841-2 and 1847, the demand for labour in Britain's industrial areas presented potential employment to many Irish and the information networks existed for such opportunities to be known throughout Ireland. The consequences of the potato blight, particularly in the winter of 1846, must have convinced many not on the verge of starvation, that Britain presented better opportunities for acquiring an improved standard of living.

II

A major factor influencing the size of the famine inflow into Britain was the easy availability of cross channel steamers. The first half of the nineteenth century witnessed rapid changes in the technology of shipping.[4] In broad terms, the principal developments were the move from timber to iron as a construction material and the substitution of steampower for sail. Such issues are of more than passing interest in the context of the flight of famine victims from Ireland to Britain. Steampower brought a regularity of channel crossings that sail could never match because of the reliance on weather conditions. Additionally, the new steamers were relatively fast and competition between the steamship companies forced down passenger fares to a level within the reach of all but the most destitute. Had these technological changes not occurred, or if the famine had happened before 1820, then it is probable that the scale of the movement of people to Britain would have been significantly less.

With regard to the changing technology of propulsion, the first vessels were paddle steamers, clumsy to manoeuvre and relatively inefficient in fuel terms. By 1845, screw driven vessels were beginning to replace paddle steamers on the Irish routes and, in the context of the famine exodus, it is important to remember that none of these ships were built primarily as passenger vessels. All had a limited amount of cabin accommodation but the overwhelming majority of passengers were carried on deck. The principal cargoes carried were agricultural products and animals.[5] It is also important to keep in mind with regard to passenger traffic between Irish ports and Britain, steamers dominated over sail in terms of the tonnage involved. By contrast the traffic in emigrants from Britain and Ireland to the USA, Canada and Australia was overwhelmingly in sailing ships. It was only in the eighteen sixties that the economics of marine steam propulsion proved more successful than the clipper ships. In 1847, Liverpool dominated this emigrant trade, more Irish left through Liverpool than all the traffic from Irish ports.

Paddle steamers were popular with Irish deck passengers because the wooden housing covering the paddles gave some shelter from the seas. By contrast, the propeller driven vessels gave no such protection, deck passengers were more exposed to the elements and the vessels rolled a great deal, inducing sea sickness. On 22 July 1819, the *Waterloo*, a paddle steamer, owned by Messrs. Langton of Belfast, became the first steamer to enter the Mersey from Ireland and after this events moved rapidly.[6] In 1822, the St George Steamship Company was founded and in April the company inaugurated a service between Liverpool and Dublin. In October, one of its vessels made the Liverpool to Dublin crossing in 11½ hours.[7] Competition soon followed in the form of the City of Dublin Steampacket Company and in February 1823, this company ordered two steamships to be built at Liverpool for the Liverpool-Dublin route. One of these was called the *City of Dublin*. The driving force behind this company was Charles Wye Williams. In September 1824, another company, The Dublin and Liverpool Steam Navigation Company entered the battle for cross channel business and by 1825, competition was so severe that a vessel sailed from Dublin carrying 700 passengers at sixpence per head.[8] With this degree of competition, amalgamation was inevitable but cut throat pricing continued throughout the famine years. This price war was a factor in facilitating the movement of the destitute Irish to Britain.

Before 1846, emigration and an increasing volume of trade with Britain, principally in agricultural products and animals, produced a rising demand for steamers. Liverpool shipbuilders benefitted from this. For example, in September 1843, the *Nimrod* was launched at the Liverpool yard of Thomas Vernon. She was built for the City of Cork Steam Packet Company and was to become very familiar to those Irish travelling between Cork and Liverpool.[9] In October 1845, Peter Cato's yard in Liverpool had three steamers in the course of construction for the City of Dublin Steamship Company. Two were for the Liverpool-Dublin route and the third, for the Liverpool-Cork crossing.[10] In January 1846, Vernon's launched the *Windsor,* built for the City of Dublin Steamship Company and the *Ajax*, built for the City of Cork Steamship Company.[11] By 1847, the port had steamer connections with Cork, Waterford, Wexford, Port Rush, Londonderry, Sligo, Belfast, Dublin, Drogheda, Dundalk and Newry. At the same time, ports on the south coast of England and South Wales also had steamer connections with the principal Irish ports. London, Bristol, Cardiff and Swansea had strong ties with Cork, Waterford and the south-east of Ireland generally, the London bound vessels often calling at Portsmouth en route. The coal trade of Cardiff employed a fleet of ships carrying coal to Cork and Waterford while Newport in Monmouthshire was also a major port for the coal trade with Ireland. The outward trip to Ireland involved the carrying of coal but return cargoes were often difficult to find and the colliers frequently carried passengers in the holds on the journey back to Wales. In Scotland, all the ports on the Clyde had steamer connections with Ireland, principally the north of Ireland.

For deck passengers, the journey from Ireland to Britain was usually uncomfortable, both because of the lack of protection against the rain and the seas running over the decks. However, quite apart from such physical discomfort, the Irish channel was intrinsically a dangerous passage and the loss of steamers was not uncommon. For example, 18 April 1837, the steamer *Albion* outward bound from Dublin for Bristol, was wrecked after striking a rock.[12] In January 1838, the steamer *Killarney*, outward from Cork to Bristol, sank and 25 people drowned.[13] Three years later, the steamer *Thames*, out from Dublin to London, sank with the loss of 20 dead.[14] This tragedy was followed almost immediately by another. The steamer *Nottingham* out from Dublin to Liverpool, in February 1841, collided with an American sailing ship but in this instance, the sailing ship sank with the loss of 122 persons.[15] The paddle steamer *Victory* outward from Liverpool to Waterford, struck the Barrels, a rock formation off the coast of Waterford, and became a total loss. In 1847, the *Grana Uaile* a new vessel on the Liverpool-Dublin route, caught fire outward bound from Liverpool to Dublin, with a loss of life, including Captain Bowden.[16] These events reflected a permanent risk on the Irish routes. Bad weather, strong tides, collisions, fires and dangerous coasts all increased the danger facing the famine refugee. Keeping such factors in mind, it is first necessary to identify the main shipping routes to Britain available in 1847 to the tens of thousands leaving Ireland and second, to examine the conditions under which the famine refugees crossed to Britain.

III

The decision to emigrate was usually undertaken after careful consideration of the options available. Individuals or families often had information regarding job prospects in America, Canada and Australia, sent to them by friends and families already abroad. Equally, many persons had their fare paid for them by their contacts in America and elsewhere. Many of those who emigrated were poor but not destitute.[17] A different category of persons were those whose lives were completely devastated by the potato failures, disease and in some cases forcible eviction. For this category, the term 'refugee' seems more appropriate; they left Ireland bereft of economic resources, often ill, with no possessions and no plan other than to cross to Britain. A significant proportion would never have seen the sea and could have had only the vaguest idea of how to get to the towns of Wales, Scotland and England. The forces pushing them out of Ireland were the high probability of premature death or long term destitution whilst the 'pull' factors were the hope of a job in Britain and the knowledge that the system of outdoor relief across the water was better than what was on offer in Ireland.

The following individual instances illustrate the experience of many. John Waters, his wife and seven children, walked from Mayo to Dublin in order to take a steamer to Liverpool, a much cheaper crossing than Sligo-Liverpool.[18] Jeremiah Sullivan, his wife and five children were evicted from their farm, near Schull. Sullivan sold his cow for three pounds and when the money had been spent, the family walked to Cork and took a vessel for Newport, the total fare being eight shillings.[19] Such experiences were repeated throughout the famine crisis. Julia Leonard, a widow with three children, walked the 164 miles from Cork to Dublin to take advantage of the cheap steamer crossing.[20] Winefred Kelly, with six children, had sold all her furniture to obtain the fare from Dublin to Liverpool. She landed in England with threepence in her pocket.[21]

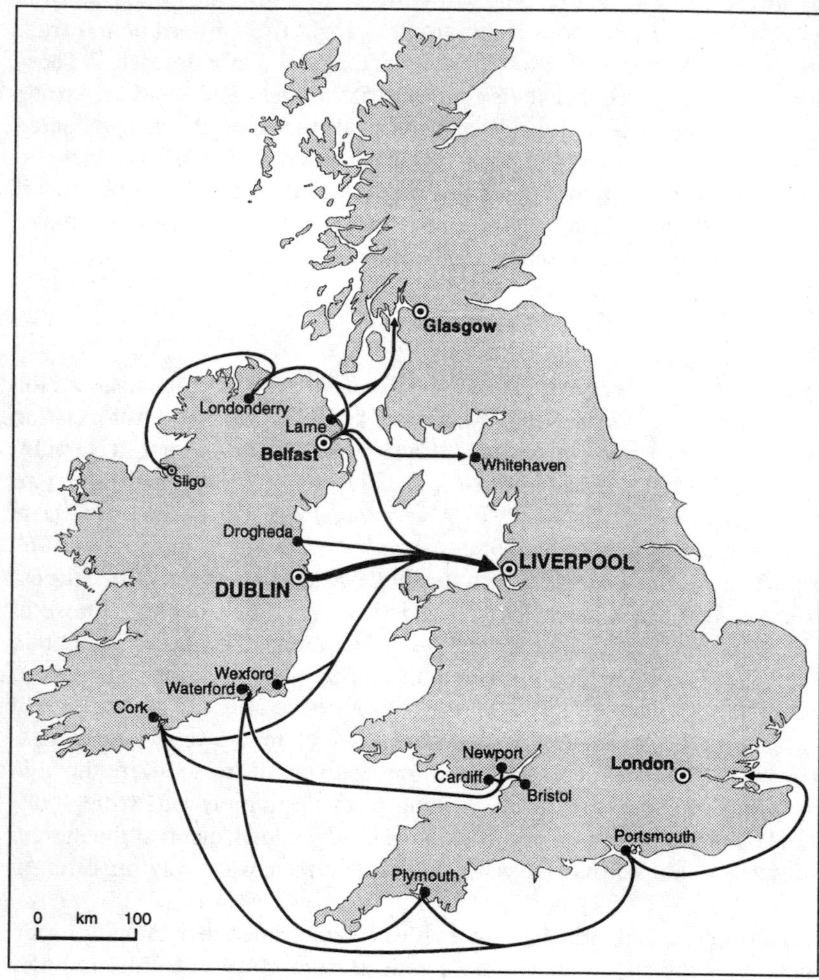

Figure 3.1 Principal shipping routes between Ireland and Britain in 1847

IV

Given the scale of the movement of people from Ireland to Britain during 1847, the obvious question is 'how was it accomplished?' The equally obvious answer is that they used the existing trade routes and shipping capacity. The volume of commercial traffic between Britain and Ireland was such that the large numbers of refugees and emigrants were easily transported to Britain. It is instructive to examine the Irish traffic into the principal ports of entry, for example, Liverpool, Glasgow, Bristol, Newport and London. Of lesser significance were such places as Fleetwood, Whitehaven and Portsmouth. Using the Customs Bills of Entry, it is possible to obtain aggregates of the volume of traffic arriving at British ports from Ireland during 1847, the Irish ports of departure and the relative importance of sailing ships and steamers.[22] The picture which emerges is the absolute primacy of Liverpool as *the* port of entry for vessels from Ireland.

Table 3.1: The tonnage of vessels arriving at Liverpool, Glasgow, London, Bristol and Newport from Ireland during 1847.

Port of arrival	*Tonnage*		*Total*
	Sail	*Steam*	
Liverpool	73 827	484 143	557 970
Glasgow	55 064	190 268	245 332
London	21 612	82 559	104 171
Bristol	10 285	71 633	81 918
Newport	nd	nd	19 409

Sources: MMM, *Customs Bills of Entry, 1847, for Liverpool, Glasgow, Bristol and London.* PRO/Cust/130, 'An Account of Coasting Vessels entering Inward and Outward at the Port of Newport, 1842-51'.

The pre-eminence of Liverpool as *the* Irish port is immediately obvious, handling more than twice the tonnage of Glasgow and five times the London traffic. The size of sailing vessels was, in the case of all ports, small, For example, on the Liverpool crossing, the average was only seventy tons, (median = 64 tons). In the case of Glasgow, the average was only sixty four register tons.[23] In the absence of steamers, the movement of people would have been severely curtailed, not simply because their capacity was less but also because small sailing vessels were slow, depending on the vagaries of the wind. For this reason, and the fact that they were cheap, the majority of those travelling to Britain chose to use steamers. The volume of shipping entered in at each port in Table 3.1 was also an index of job opportunities. The volume of traffic was big because each had industrial hinterlands, presenting the best chances of obtaining work and finding established Irish settlements. Another factor to be kept in mind when examining the refugee experience is that the routes to Liverpool were longer than those to Glasgow, with the result that crossing times to Liverpool were longer, thus prolonging the harrowing experience of being a deck passenger. It is true that journeys from Cork, Waterford, Dublin and Wexford to London and South Wales were long but the numbers travelling to those ports were much smaller than in the case of Liverpool.

Even in the case of steamers, bad weather could increase significantly the time taken to reach British ports, resulting in atrocious conditions for deck passengers. In 1847, there were twelve companies operating steamers between Ireland and Liverpool, the most important being the City of Dublin Steam Packet Company. The average time of voyages to Liverpool are given below in Table 3.2.

Table 3.2: The average time taken by steamships on routes from the principal Irish ports to Liverpool, distinguishing between screw driven vessels and paddle steamers, in 1847.

Port of departure	*Name of vessel*	*Method of propulsion*	*Average time taken*	*Company*
Belfast	Blenheim	Paddle	13½ hrs	Belfast Steam Packet
Cork	Minerva	Paddle	22 hrs	Cork Steam Packet
Drogheda	various	Paddle	11 hrs	Drogheda Steam Packet
Dublin	various (22)	" (19) screw (3)	12-14 hrs	City of Dublin Steamship
Dublin	Liverpool	Screw	13½ hrs	Dublin & Liverpool Steam Packet
Dublin	Dublin	Screw	14 hrs	Dublin & Liverpool Steam Packet
Dublin	Waterwitch	Screw	16 hrs	Dublin & Liverpool Steam Packet
Londonderry	Maiden City	Paddle	23 hrs	NW of Ireland Steam Packet
Newry	Sea Nymph	Paddle	11 hrs	Newry Steam Packet
Port Rush	various	Paddle	22 hrs	Port Rush Steam Packet
Waterford	William Penn	Paddle	27 hrs	Waterford Steam Packet
Wexford	Town of Wexford	Paddle	24 hrs	Wexford Steam Packet

Source: BPP (HC) 1849 (339), L1, 'Captain Denham's report on passenger accommodation in steamers, between Liverpool and Ireland' Appendix 13, pp. 26, 29, 30, 32-5.

The City of Dublin Steam Packet Company operated 22 steamers on the Dublin-Liverpool route at the time of the famine crisis and the average time taken was between 12-14 hours. In bad weather conditions a steamer could take *twice* as long to reach Liverpool, the screw driven vessels generally taking longer than the paddle steamers.[24] The next question is that of the principal Irish ports of departure. The table below shows the tonnage entered in at Liverpool from Irish ports during 1847.

Table 3.3: The number and tonnage of vessels arriving at Liverpool from Irish ports during the year 1847, distinguishing between sailing vessels and steamers.

Port of departure	*Number*			*Tonnage*		
	Sail	*Steam*	*Total*	*Sail*	*Steam*	*Total*
Belfast	45	150	195	3 453	62 631	66 084
Cork	55	50	105	6 623	23 541	30 164
Drogheda	21	336	357	2 110	84 806	86 916
Dublin	108	718	826	10 254	192 597	202 851
Dundalk	15	118	133	596	47 790	48 386
Limerick	55	-	55	5 285	-	5 285
Londonderry	18	57	75	1 114	18 052	19 166
Newry	47	54	101	2 994	17 442	20 436
Port Rush	7	23	30	547	5 711	6 258
Sligo	21	17	38	1 443	3 400	4 843
Waterford	24	63	87	2 016	17 320	19 336
Wexford	24	22	46	1 860	10 488	12 348
Rest	320	24	344	35 532	365	35 897
Total	760	1632	2392	73 827	484 143	557 970

Source: MMM, *Customs Bills of Entry for Liverpool, 1847.*

Of the total tonnage entering in at Liverpool from Ireland, 484 143 tons, or 87 per cent, was steam tonnage. Dublin stands out as by far the most important port of departure. With regard to steamers, 40 per cent of all the tonnage arriving at Liverpool was from Dublin. If the Drogheda tonnage is added to this, then 57 per cent of all tonnage entered was from the Dublin region. By contrast, Waterford, Wexford and Cork traffic made up only 51 349 tons, or 11 per cent, of Liverpool's Irish traffic, while Dundalk, Belfast, Port Rush, Newry and Londonderry accounted for 27 per cent of the total. It cannot be presumed that the primacy of Dublin as a port of embarkation meant that refugees came principally from the Dublin area. As we have noted, people walked long distances to take advantage of the cheaper fares. The majority of famine refugees entering Britain through Liverpool came from the famine stricken counties of the west coast of Ireland. In contrast to Liverpool, the main Irish ports in the Glasgow-Irish trade were those in the north, in particular, Belfast, Londonderry and Larne, accounting for 62 per cent of tonnage entering in from Ireland during 1847, while Dublin traffic was 24 per cent (see Table 3.4 below). The pre-eminence of steam again is clear, 78 per cent of total tonnage. In absolute tonnage, Glasgow's Dublin traffic was less than a third of Liverpool's. Given the geography of the British Isles, this is what one would expect. Similar geographical considerations are reflected in the cases of London and Bristol.

Table 3.4: The number and tonnage of vessels arriving at Glasgow from Irish ports during 1847, distinguishing between sailing ships and steamers.

Port of departure	Number			Tonnage		
	Sail	*Steam*	*Total*	*Sail*	*Steam*	*Total*
Ballina	13	-	13	1 024	-	1 024
Belfast	78	221	299	4 992	86 824	91 816
Cork	8	17	25	512	6 202	6 714
Drogheda	22	-	22	1 408	-	1 408
Dublin	23	91	114	1 472	57 072	58 544
Dundalk	18	-	18	1 152	-	1 152
Glenarm	13	-	13	832	-	832
Kilrush	6	-	6	384	-	384
Larne	352	-	352	22 528	-	22 528
Limerick	134	-	134	8 576	-	8 576
Londonderry	29	177	206	1 856	35 384	37 240
Newry	22	-	22	1 408	-	1 408
Port Rush	6	2	8	384	278	662
Sligo	34	11	45	2 176	3 726	5 902
Tralee	20	-	20	1 280	-	1 280
Waterford	9	-	9	216	-	216
Westport	7	-	7	448	-	448
Wexford	32	-	32	2 048	-	2 048
Rest	37	2	39	2 368	800	3 168
Total	863	521	1384	55 064	190 286	245 350

Source: MMM, *Customs Bills of Entry, Glasgow, 1847.*

Turning next to London, the ports of Belfast, Londonderry and Dundalk were relatively insignificant elements in London's Irish trade. By contrast, Cork, Limerick, Waterford and Tralee made up 53 per cent of London's traffic while Dublin accounted for 32 per cent (see Table 3.5 below). Bristol exhibited the same trade pattern as London with Cork, Limerick and Waterford accounting for 75 per cent of the port's Irish traffic. Dublin represented 20 per cent. Notably, 87 per cent of all tonnage entering Bristol was steamer traffic (Table 3.6 below).

The situation at the Irish ports of embarkation during 1847 was chaotic. There were a number of reasons for this and in taking these into account, it is important to keep in mind the fact that the steamers on the Irish routes were not built as passenger vessels. The steamer companies were not organized to carry large numbers of passengers, that aspect of their business developed almost by accident. Their main and most profitable business was carrying agricultural products and animals for Britain's ever growing urban populations. In the words of Charles Wye Williams, the managing director of the City of Dublin Steam Packet Company: 'The company's system is to load with goods and cattle, and then receive such deck passengers as may come at the starting hour; certainly without limit, and must settle down as best they can'.[25]

Table 3.5: The number and tonnage of vessels arriving at London from Irish ports during 1847, distinguishing between sailing ships and steamers.

	Numbers			*Tonnage*		
Port of departure	*Sail*	*Steam*	*Total*	*Sail*	*Steam*	*Total*
Ballina	1	-	1	91	4 265	91
Belfast	1	22	23	74	4 195	4 339
Clare	2	1	3	133	112	245
Cork	17	69	86	1 405	31 307	32 712
Dublin	3	134	137	216	35 100	35 316
Dundalk	2	-	2	272	-	272
Dungarvan	2	-	2	158	-	158
Galway	18	1	19	2 055	369	2 424
Kilrush	9	-	9	753	-	753
Kinsale	1	-	1	97	-	97
Limerick	78	10	88	10 024	1 716	11 740
Londonderry	4	6	10	254	1082	1 336
Ross	1	-	1	72	-	72
Sligo	20	7	27	1 802	1 176	2 978
Tralee	14	-	14	989	-	989
Valencia	1	-	1	83	-	83
Waterford	62	11	73	1748	7 432	9 180
Westport	3	-	3	307	-	307
Youghall	11	-	11	1 079	-	1 079
Total	250	261	511	21 612	82 559	104 171

Source: MMM, *Customs Bills of Entry, 1847,* London.

Williams' statement is remarkable for lacking any expression of concern over the atrocious conditions on his company's vessels. A major cause of chaos was the system of issuing tickets. Agents of the shipping companies sold tickets inland, without any concern about which vessel was involved, what day or time of sailing. The result was that large numbers of people turned up on the quayside, far in excess of the room available. A government inquiry was informed:

> The class of passenger called 'deckers' go to the offices where tickets are issued without limit, or even distinguishing one vessel from another; the consequence is, they accumulate on the quay, ready for a rush, to any one vessel they take a fancy to, so that she belongs to the company the tickets hails from. It is in vain to call out to them to divide themselves

> with other vessels also ready to start; we have no control, nor right to appeal to the police as the matter stands; we are obliged to draw the planks away at all risks, to stop the rush on board.[26]

For example, 9 April 1847, the *Nimrod* was loading at St. Patrick's quay, Cork, for Liverpool. She had *800 adult passengers*, in addition to some children, when another 100 rushed aboard just as she was ready to cast off. In this instance the fare was 10 shillings per head, this was all profit as the pay load was the animals and the produce carried as cargo.[27] The inability of the steamer companies (or rather, their unwillingness) to take action to control numbers boarding produced bizarre situations. For example, on 3 April 1849, three steamers arrived in Liverpool, one had two deck passengers, one 418 passengers and the third, 123 passengers. On the 14 April, three more vessels arrived, one carried 18 passengers, a second had 574 passengers and a third, 78.[28] The principal reason for the frequent maldistributionof passengers among vessels was that people wanted to travel with friends and family. They were often frightened of the sea voyage and needed the confidence of travelling with people they knew. This example of wide variations in the number of passengers carried highlights the nature of the economics of steamship operations at the time. Throughout 1847, all of the Irish vessels entering inwards at British ports carried food and livestock. The probable exceptions to this claim were the colliers returning to South Wales and the ships carrying iron ore and sulphur from Arklow. By 1845, the trade in animals and foodstuffs was steady and the volumes predictable. For example, 186 483 oxen, bulls and cows, 6363 calves, 259 257 sheep and lambs and 480 827 pigs, were imported into Britain from Ireland in the year ending 5 January 1847.[29] By contrast, passenger traffic was unpredictable and the seasonal increase due to harvesters crossing to Britain did not justify special provision of passenger vessels. For a company at this time to commission vessels with sheltered accommodation below deck was simply unprofitable, given the constant demand for space for animals and foodstuffs. So, as Charles Wye Williams stated, deck passengers had to fend for themselves, but their fares represented pure profit. They imposed no marginal cost on a passage. Why then, if passengers were a bonus, was there extreme competition for the deck passengers during 1847? One answer is that they *were* pure profit. Another probable explanation is that the volume of food exported from Ireland dropped significantly in 1847, thus reducing revenues. Falling food exports to Britain illustrate the effect of the worsening of the famine in the autumn of 1846. The drop in the exporting of wheat and wheatflour, of 17 521 tons in 1846 was a 78 per cent decline on the previous year.

Figure 3.2 The *Nimrod* and the *Patrick* loading at Cork bound for Liverpool

Such a falling off in exports to Britain must have affected the revenues of steamship companies when, fortunately for them, the same causes of the decline in food exports were forcing large numbers to leave Ireland (see Appendices Nos. 3.3 and 3.4)

How many paupers crossed to Britain during 1847? Unfortunately, with the exception of Liverpool and Glasgow, no data exists. The scale of the Irish pauper problem facing the Liverpool authorities became clear by the end of December 1846.

Table 3.6: The number and tonnage of vessels arriving at Bristol from Irish ports during 1847, distinguishing between sailing vessels and steamers.

Port of departure	*Numbers*			*Tonnage*		
	Sail	*Steam*	*Total*	*Sail*	*Steam*	*Total*
Arklow	17	-	17	1 445	-	1 445
Belfast	5	-	5	425	-	425
Cork	35	101	136	2 975	33 166	36 141
Dublin	21	49	70	1 785	14 749	16 534
Dungarvan	5	-	5	425	-	425
Galway	2	1	2	170	-	170
Kinsale	4	-	4	340	-	340
Limerick	8	-	8	680	-	680
Newry	3	-	3	255	-	255
Ross	1	-	1	85	-	85
Sligo	2	-	2	170	-	170
Tralee	1	-	1	85	-	85
Waterford	8	94	102	680	23 718	24 398
Wicklow	5	-	5	425	-	425
Youghal	4	-	4	340	-	340
Total	121	244	365	10 285	71 633	81 918

Note: As the Bills did not record the tonnage of sailing ships, a sample of 1391 sailing ships from Irish ports to Liverpool, Glasgow and Newport, for which data was available, was used to calculate an average of 71 tons per vessel. This was then used to estimate the sailing ship tonnage for Bristol.
Source: MMM, *Customs Bills of Entry, 1847, Bristol.*

Edward Rushton, the stipendiary magistrate claimed that 15 000 Irish paupers landed at Liverpool during December 1846 and the parish authorities were so worried that they called an emergency meeting of the Select Vestry in order to draw up a petition to the Home Secretary.[30] During the whole of the famine crisis, Edward Rushton was the stipendiary magistrate at Liverpool. In assessing the size of the immigration it is fortunate that, on 13 January 1847, Rushton ordered the Liverpool police to count the number of 'poor persons' arriving from Ireland at the Liverpool docks, and for the next seven years, this enumeration took place.[31] Initially this was in response to a request from the Home Office. It was left to the police to distinguish between 'poor' and 'pauper' and this was done on the basis of appearance, so there is an arbitrary element in the classification. For example, many of the Irish travelling to Liverpool in order to emigrate to America were themselves very poor and could only emigrate because their fares had been sent from America by relatives. Thus, many of these could easily have been classified as poor. However, such emigrants would have some luggage whereas the absolutely destitute Irish had none, in most cases literally possessing nothing but the rags they wore. The distinction between 'poor' and 'pauper' was important because the political campaign to stop Irish immigration, led by the authorities in Liverpool, was aimed at those immigrants looking for poor relief and not those who were coming to England looking for work. In practice, the distinction was almost impossible to make. However, despite these complications, the figures provide the best available estimate of the traffic in paupers from Ireland to Liverpool during the famine crisis.[32]

Table 3.7 The number of Irish poor arriving at the port of Liverpool 1847-54 (inclusive) distinguishing as far as possible those who remained in England from those who had emigrated overseas.

Year	*Deck passengers emigrants jobbers*	*Deck passengers apparently paupers*	*Total*	*Paupers as a percentage of total*
1847	180 213	116 000	296 213	39
1848	158 582	94 190	252 772	37
1849	160 457	80 468	240 925	33
1850	173 236	77 765	251 001	31
1851	215 369	68 134	283 503	24
1852	153 909	78 422	232 331	34
1853	162 299	71 353	233 652	29
1854	147 810	6 679	154 489	4

Source: The data for the year 1847 were given by Edward Rushton in a letter to the Home Secretary, SC (1854), Minutes of Evidence, A.Campbell, q. 4954. The data for 1848 are based on newspaper reports of arrivals at Liverpool. With regard to arrivals over the period 1849-53, the source is Emigrants Ships, p. 107, 'Return of the Number of Irish Poor Brought Over Monthly to the Port of Liverpool From Ireland over the Last Five Years', and SC on Poor Removal (1854-55) 308, XIII, Table D, showing the number of ship passengers who arrived at Liverpool from Ireland during the years 1853-54 and 1854-55, pp. 330-1.

Unfortunately, the information gathered by the police was not put together systematically for the years 1847 and 1848 and it has had to be gleaned from a variety of sources, such as evidence given to Select Committees, newspaper reports, Head Constables' reports and other official sources. With regard to 1847, the most authoritative statement is contained in a letter written by Rushton to the Home Secretary, in which he stated that between 13 January 1847 and 13 December 1847 inclusive, 296 213 persons landed at Liverpool from Ireland. Of these, he claimed 116 000 were 'half naked and starving' some 39 per cent of the total.[33] The Head Constable's report for 1848 also quoted the same aggregate figure for 1847 and both were presumably based on police estimates. A corresponding figure for 1848 is more elusive but contemporary newspapers give some idea of the rate of arrivals.[34]

Allowing for the arbitrary classification of paupers, the picture presented by the statistics is clear enough. From the peak of 296 231 arrivals in 1847, the inflow of people from Ireland to Liverpool remained at a high level until 1854. The severity of the famine in 1847 is reflected in the extremely large, and unprecedented numbers of people arriving from Ireland during that year and the fact that 39 per cent were described as paupers. The continuing distress in Ireland is logged by the large numbers of arrivals in each year upto 1854. Remarkably, there was a spectacular fall in the number of paupers recorded as coming ashore at Liverpool in 1854. There are a number of possible explanations. There is a clerical error. If so it went uncommented upon. There was an improvement in poor relief payments in Ireland. Not so, there were no legislative or policy changes at this time. A more plausible explanation is that the huge outflow over the period 1847-53 had removed the most destitute elements in Irish society *and* the economy was picking up. In other words, the immediate famine crisis was over. It needs to be noted that over the period 1847 to 1850, inclusive, these data record an estimated 368 423 paupers landed at Liverpool. Taken against the fact that over the ten year intercensus period 1841-51, the *total* increase in the number of Irish-born persons in Britain was only 229 000, we must conclude that either many of those landing at Liverpool returned home at some stage or that many described as paupers were in fact emigrants. However, none of these considerations alter the fact that during 1847, the flow of destitute persons into Liverpool was overwhelming for the local poor law officials. The authorities in Glasgow, faced with similar problems to those existing in Liverpool, appear to have kept statistics regarding the number of Irish coming ashore in 1847. However, no full data sets have survived. During the week ending 10 August 1847, there were ten arrivals of Irish vessels at Glasgow, Broomielaw. Nine were steamers, two were sailing vessels. The two sailing smacks carried 106 passengers between them, the nine steamers carried 4928, and 98 per cent of the total were officially described as 'poor class'.[35] Over the period 15 June to 12 September, 33 267 persons arrived from Ireland. Of these, 30 189 or 91 per cent were described as being '... men, women and children in the last stages of wretchedness'.[36] Between January and 30 November 1847, 49 993 'destitute' Irish landed at the Broomielaw. This was a monthly rate of arrivals of 4545, which over the year would have yielded 54 538, half of the estimated number of paupers which arrived in Liverpool.[37] We simply do not know how many landed at Greenock and other ports on the Clyde. No data exists for South Wales, nor Newport before 1849.

V

Reasons have already been suggested as to why the Irish should have wanted to cross to British ports and the major obstacle to be overcome was the steamer fare. How did the destitute find the fare? There were good reasons why landlords and other ratepayers in Ireland should want to assist paupers in obtaining a passage to England. Many Irish poor law unions were financially impoverished because often ratepayers could not find the funds to pay the rates because the potato blight had destroyed their incomes. By facilitating the movement of the destitute to Britain, Irish ratepayers reduced the demand on their own resources and it was the belief that this was happening on a large scale which caused much bitter comment in England. There were well-documented cases of Irish landlords sending their tenants to America and Australia but, with regard to the claim that landlords were sending paupers to England, hard evidence is not easy to come by and much of the available evidence is anecdotal.[38] *The Times*, implacably opposed to the Irish landlords, carried a leader of 6 January 1847 in which it stated:

> Shiploads of the most miserable destitution daily arrive at these devoted shores... the influx has been going on for more than two months and it is said to be chiefly from Mayo and the other western counties, where they are fairly starved out and compelled, as well as privately helped, to emigrate by persons whose place it is to help them.

On 19 February 1847, *The Times* made the further accusation that agents in Ireland were providing passages to Newport where the Irish were told 'they can find employment on the South Wales railway at 4 shillings per day'. Edward Rushton was very experienced in the administration of the poor law system in Liverpool and must be regarded as authoritative. Writing to the Home Secretary on 21 April 1849, he said:

> Beyond all doubt, the towns on the seacoast in Ireland and many of the landed proprietors in Ireland furnish the wretched Irish with the means of coming to Liverpool. I have often discovered this from the

> examination of the poor and only the other day an Irish offender, when asked where he came from, said he was sent with one shilling from the Irish workhouse to Liverpool.[39]

John Evans, Assistant Overseer for Liverpool's Select Vestry, gave evidence to the Select Committee on Poor Removal in 1854. When asked if many paupers were carried free of charge by steamship companies, he replied:

> I think there is little of it at present but in 1847, 1848 and 1849, unquestionably great numbers came to Liverpool from different ports in Ireland, especially from Dublin, and on questioning these poor persons, I was told over and over again by some, that they came over free; by others that they did not know who paid their fares; and by very many that some strange gentleman on the quay in Dublin gave them their tickets to come over.[40]

Other officials in Liverpool shared the same belief. For example, George Carr, the Master of Liverpool Workhouse, giving evidence to the same committee as Evans, quoted at great length the case of James Gormally, a 13-year-old orphan who had been in the Ballinrobe union in Mayo. The boy alleged that three gentleman visited the workhouse and he had been given seven shillings to go to England, but Carr admitted he knew of no organized efforts to finance the passage of paupers from Ireland to England. He did say that when he worked at the Cork workhouse, some merchants in the coal trade gave paupers free passages to England on their colliers.[41] No-one subsequently produced any evidence of the large scale, organized subsidizing of voyages to Britain but the belief that such actions took place persisted throughout the period under review. The ratepayers in Liverpool became even more convinced following an incident in April 1847. Early in that month, an American ship, the *Rochester*, left Liverpool with 250 Irish emigrants. She ran aground on the Arklow Bank off the coast of Wexford but fortunately everyone was rescued, although the emigrants lost all their possessions. They were taken to Wexford town where the Mayor raised private subscriptions to cover their fares back to Liverpool to obtain 'justice and charity in Liverpool'. On 19 April 1847, Edward Rushton was called to Liverpool Town Hall, to be faced with 250 destitute Irish. The Select Vestry had to provide them with relief and Rushton organized the re-financing of their passage to America at something like six pounds per head.[42] There can be little doubt that some subsidizing of paupers' fares did take place and, while there were economic incentives for landlords and others to do so, it is probable it was also undertaken from humanitarian motives, a concern to help people escape the appalling misery in Ireland.

A more important factor in encouraging the movement of famine Irish to Britain was the level of fares charged by the steamship companies. Concern over steamer fares in Liverpool was based on the view that the majority of the Irish immigrants were so poor that it was only the low fares on the cross-channel steamers that made it possible for paupers to travel to Liverpool. Passengers to British ports on the cross-channel ferries travelled in cabins, steerage, or on deck. Cabin fares were such that only a minority could afford them and so little cabin accommodation was provided *because* of the low demand. Steerage accommodation, where available, was in a space below decks and was provided with bunks, which appealed to passengers who could not afford cabins but who did not want the hazards of a passage on deck. Travelling on deck was cold, miserable and dangerous and in the winter months particularly, was undertaken only by those who could not afford anything else. However, many vessels sailing from Liverpool had no steerage. The Cork, Dublin and Wexford steamers had none, while one of the two vessels on the Drogheda run also had none, and so travelling on deck was the only option open to the majority of immigrants.

The view that competition between steamship companies forced down deck fares to very low levels was widespread among officials during the famine crisis. The managing director of the City of Dublin Steam Packet Company openly admitted in 1849 that the firm's screw vessels were not designed to carry passengers. However when competitors, the Dublin and Liverpool Screw Schooner Company started to carry passengers, his company had dropped the fare to Liverpool to one shilling per head.[43] When Mr Hart, Clerk to the Select Vestry, was questioned concerning the probable effects on Irish immigration into Liverpool if the law allowing the removal of Irish paupers without settlement rights was changed, he stated that: 'Immigration of vast numbers would set in, encouraged as it would be again, by low fares which have sometimes been from sixpence to one shilling per head, owing to competition between the rival steamship companies'.[44] Hart was referring to the famine years. It was on the Dublin-Liverpool crossing that competition was fiercest, frequently reducing the fares for deck passengers from the usual price of two shillings and sixpence to one shilling or sixpence per head. The occurrence of price-cutting on the part of one company depended on whether or not a rival company had a vessel loading at the same time. If it had, prices fell as low as was necessary to obtain passengers. If there was no opposition, the fare was varied to whatever level the traffic would bear, which in the case of most deck passengers would not be very much. Rarely did non-price competition take place in the form of offering better conditions for the passengers, principally because the steamship companies were not in the passenger business. One instance of this occurred when the Belfast Steamship Company put its vessel the *Telegraph* on the Cork-Liverpool run, to compete with the Cork Steamship Company The *Telegraph* had a space forward fitted out with seats and a stove and another small room was made available with a table and stove, to enable passengers to prepare and eat food. The fare charged was the same as that for a deck passage on the vessels of the Cork Steamship Company. This episode was short-lived, the two companies came to an agreement; the *Telegraph* being withdrawn after just two voyages. In 1853, the fare for deck passengers on screw steamers from Dublin to Liverpool was again one shilling per head. In December 1852, the agent of the City of Dublin Steamship Company had been asked by the parish officials not to carry passengers at that price as the conditions on deck were very bad. The agent replied that the company would rather not have such business but they had little choice as a rival company had lowered its prices to a shilling per head.[45] At a meeting of the Glasgow Parochial Board in January 1847, Archibald McClellan reported that he had visited the agents of the steamship companies in Glasgow and asked them to explain the low level of steamer fare from Ireland to Glasgow. The Board was incensed because the companies charged the Board much more (regular fare) when Irish paupers were sent back to Ireland. Unfortunately, the reply has not been preserved.[46] In Liverpool, the same question was met with the answer that they, the steamer companies, did not bring paupers over cheaply. This was clearly untrue.

A situation in which the prices of deck passengers fell to very low levels suggests that there was excess carrying capacity at the time this occurred; elementary economic theory predicts that price in a competitive market will fall when supply exceeds demand at the prevailing market price. Yet the numbers wanting to cross the sea to England during the famine years were very large. However, economic theory also suggests another explanation of the periods of low prices. If space on deck was not used for anything else, then allowing several hundred people to travel on deck would involve very little addition to the cost of the voyage, simply the cost of the extra fuel. Anything above zero revenue received from such passengers was a contribution towards overheads. On the other hand, deck passengers were extremely poor so that the companies could not have charged very much, otherwise they would have cut off the demand. Thus they charged what the traffic would bear and these factors, rather than excess capacity, explain the prices of sixpence and one shilling that prevailed for certain periods. Whatever the reasons, there is no doubt that the Irish poor were sensitive to price differentials between the various crossings to British ports. Consistent with this view that low fares encouraged paupers to travel to Liverpool (or encouraged others to pay their fares) was the argument that higher fares would discourage this traffic. In 1854, the deck fare from Cork-Liverpool was ten shillings and Augustus Campbell expressed the view that a fare of 12 shillings a head would deter immigration from the port of Cork.[47] However, it is extremely unlikely that fare increases would have significantly discouraged the outflow from Ireland during 1847 as the Irish were very determined to leave and would go to great lengths to obtain the fare.

VI

Quite apart from concern over the possible influence of the low fares on the volume of immigration of Irish poor, there was, over the period 1846 to 1853, a growing alarm in Liverpool and elsewhere over the conditions under which people were carried on the steamers. Part of this anxiety on the part of the citizens of Liverpool and Glasgow was concern over their own well-being. The outbreak of typhus in Liverpool in February 1847 was the beginning of a nightmare in which thousands died and, in the view of many, a major factor in the spread of the infectious diseases was the presence of the Irish immigrants. (see chapters five and six). Typhus was commonly referred to as 'Irish Fever', and there was the belief that many of the immigrants already had typhus on arrival in Liverpool. Local opinion was incensed because the steamship companies operated no system of checking the condition of the immigrants as they embarked at the Irish ports.

In Liverpool, the epidemic was so bad by May 1847 that the Home Secretary announced that two vessels normally used for quarantine purposes would be made available as floating hospitals. These were the *Akbar* and the *Newcastle*. These lazarettos, as they were referred to, were later joined by the *Druid* and the *Lancaster*, all to be fitted out at the expense of the ratepayers. The *Akbar* was to receive any typhus cases from the Irish steamers. It was also announced that the steamship companies were to be warned about carrying passengers who were suffering from the fever.[48]

Taking his lead from the Home Secretary, the Mayor of Liverpool sent for the representatives of the companies to request their co-operation in implementing a new system of checks. They were asked to inspect passengers embarking in Ireland and to refuse to carry anyone who appeared to be ill from the fever. On arrival at Liverpool, their vessels were to stand in the river where they would be boarded by medical officers and inspected for typhus victims and, until the vessels were given clearance, they were to fly a yellow flag. Any vessel that arrived for a second time with infected passengers would be put into quarantine for a period. Such a system would obviously hinder the operations of the steamship companies, but they reluctantly agreed. On 10 May 1847 the City of Dublin, the Drogheda, the

Dundalk, and the Newry Steamship Companies issued orders that their vessels would allow no deck passengers on board unless they were first examined by a doctor and declared free of fever. The pressure on the companies to co-operate with the authorities in Liverpool must have been great because the companies also announced that no destitute person would be allowed on board a steamer who could not support himself or herself in Britain. It was not said how the status of such persons would be established and was almost certainly a public relations operation as it had no discernible effect on the volume of traffic in Irish poor. It was simply impossible for a ship's master to check potential passengers. The companies also announced that in future the return fare to Liverpool would be five shillings each way.[49] Again this appears to have been a reaction to criticism of fare policies and seems to have lasted but without stemming the inflow in immigrants. However, the medical provisions proved effective and on 19 May 1847, the *Manchester Guardian* announced that since the regulations had come into force, only four fever victims had been found on Irish steamers arriving at Liverpool. However, it did admit that people suffering from typhus were hiding themselves when the doctors went aboard. On 16 June 1847, the same paper reported on the current situation: 'The effects of the regulations as to the Irish vessels is obvious from the fact that not a single individual suffering from the fever has been found upon any of the steamers'.[50] However, during the same week, the crew of the *Akbar* were given a 50 per cent wage increase to induce them to stay on board.[51]

The same preoccupation with fear of the Irish steamers importing typhus surfaced at the meeting of the Glasgow Parochial Board held 17 May 1847. The chairman, Archibald McClellan, told the meeting that they needed to adopt the same procedures as the Liverpool authorities. The Board decided to approach the steamship companies and ask them not to allow sick people on board in Ireland. Again, this was a futile request.[52] In June, the Glasgow authorities received authorization from Whitehall to inspect steamers arriving from Ireland. It was decided that vessels must stop and be inspected at Greenock. The first steamer to arrive under this system was the *Thetis*, from Belfast. In ignorance, she did not stop at Greenock, going straight to the Broomielaw in Glasgow. Fortunately, there were no fever victims.[53] However, the Glasgow Parochial Board then memorialized the Home Office that the system should be applied to Ardrossan, Troon, Ayr, Greenock, Port Glasgow, Dumbarton and Bowling. This approach was unsuccessful.[54]

The quays used by the Irish vessels arriving in London were Alderman's Stairs, Scovells Wharf, Dublin Wharf and Carpenter Smith's Wharf. On 19 April, the *Prussian Eagle*, from Cork, and the *Limerick* from Dublin, landed 1200 Irish at Alderman's Stairs, in Lower East Smithfield, in 'a most wretched state of distress'.[55] A particular problem for the London unions was that the refugees simply disappeared into London's vastness. On 18 May, the Guardians of the Stepney Union wrote to the Poor Law Commissioners, complaining that many of the newly arrived Irish had typhus. The Commissioners suggested a quarantine in the Thames.[56] The Marylebone Union, also in London, met 6 November and sent a memorial to the Home Office regarding the need for quarantining of arrivals from Irish steamers. The meeting of Guardians discussed petitioning Parliament over the issue but a resolution to that effect failed to attract sufficient votes.

VII

Although the populations at the ports of entry were concerned about the dangers to their health arising from sick immigrants coming ashore there was also some sympathy for the Irish over the conditions endured on the sea voyage to Britain. Even in the summer, night crossings were cold and, for people in a debilitated state and without adequate clothing, the voyage was still an unpleasant experience. In the winter and in bad weather, it was a terrible ordeal. The main causes of the distress were exposure to the elements, with no protection whatsoever, and overcrowding, all the more frightening to the passengers because the majority had no idea of what was in store for them, arriving at the Irish ports as they did, from rural areas inland.

At the port of Cork, as we have seen, the majority of persons took vessels to South Wales and the south coast of England, including London. The need of the coal vessels for ballast on their return trip to Cardiff meant that the shipmasters could afford to offer passages at low prices. In some cases, ships carried up to two hundred in the holds, such passengers providing the weight otherwise provided by shingles and lime.[57] In many cases, the price of a passage fell to two shillings and sixpence, or lower. The Medical Officer of Health for Cardiff, writing in 1854, with reference to the famine, stated: '...these poor wretches are brought over as ballast, without any payment for their passage. The Captains, it appears, find it cheaper to ship and unship this living ballast than one of lime or shingle'.[58]

Initially during the famine crisis, the colliers landed Irish immigrants at Cardiff but the Cardiff Poor Law Guardians established that the vessels were not licensed to carry any passengers and prosecuted. The Masters then adopted the policy of landing the refugees at Newport.[59] From November 1846 onwards an increasing proportion of Irish arriving at British ports were in a bad physical condition, exacerbated by the voyage to Britain. Worse, many were already in the grip of typhus, requiring hospital treatment immediately on arrival. The *Cardiff and Merthyr Guardian* of 12 February 1847 carried a report from its correspondent at Newport, dated 8 February:

> '...a vessel named the *Wanderer* has just arrived here with nearly two hundred of the wretched famished creatures, chiefly from Skibbereen, huddled together in a mass of wretchedness unparalleled. On examining the crowded vessel, it was found that between twenty and thirty starving men, women and children were lying on the ballast in the hold in dying condition. Their state was most deplorable and had it not been that surgical and charitable aid was rendered the moment the vessel came alongside the wharf, it is said that many would have been brought ashore dead'.

Following the removal of the people from the hold, five died. Given the fact that in 1847, there was no direct steamer service between Ireland and Cardiff, any Irish entering Cardiff by sea must have travelled in a sailing ship. As already noted, these were much smaller than steamers and slower. The case of the *Industry* of Cork illustrates the nature of the refugee experience at this time. The *Industry* was a small sailing vessel of 86 tons. She left Cork on Monday, 29 March, bound for Cardiff to pick up a cargo of iron railway lines. Her master was John Hart and there were four other crew members. She carried 150 sheep and ballast and it is not clear whether or not she was licensed to carry passengers. The vessel had no food for passengers and no medical equipment. Before sailing she took on board about 35 Irish men, women and children. The adults paid two shillings and sixpence each for the voyage. They clearly had no idea of what the voyage entailed. They had provisions for the journey but several asked the mate how long the trip would take. The *Industry* left Cork bound first for the New Passage, then Penarth and finally Cardiff. Soon after leaving Ireland, the passengers started with sea sickness. On Wednesday, 31 March some of the passengers asked the master for food and water. He gave them some biscuits and a water allowance of four pints a day. The mate complained that the Irish were roasting salt fish and this was making them particularly thirsty. On Thursday, 1 April, an Irishman, who had boarded alone, complained of feeling ill and vomiting. On 2 April he asked the master for some bread as he had none. This prompted the master to reprimand him, telling him he should have come prepared. On 1 April the *Industry* reached the New Passage and the sheep were put ashore. Several Irish went with them to help drive them to Bristol. When the sheep vacated the hold some of the remaining passengers then left the deck and stayed in the hold. The same night, the unknown Irishman died on the deck of the *Industry*. The inquest was held at Cardiff on 4 April and the verdict was 'died by the visitation of God'. The unknown Irishman joined other dead Irish in the pauper graveyard.[60] This example, small vessel, probably unlicensed, refugees unprepared for a journey, is almost certainly typical of the South

Wales immigrant traffic during 1847. Similarly, the inquest verdict made no reference to malnutrition though this was probably the single, most contributory factor in the man's death. With regard to the question of unlicensed vessels carrying passengers, there is some evidence that the authorities did occasionally implement the law throughout the famine crisis. The *Lady Ann*, of Kinsale arrived at Cardiff in April 1847. The master had been observed landing 40 Irish paupers on the coast and he was arrested, appeared before the magistrates and fined ten pounds. The Customs impounded the vessel until the fine was paid.[61] On 22 May 1849, the vessel, *James* also of Kinsale, arrived at Newport. She was 78 tons and licensed to carry only 98 persons. In fact she carried 119 adults and 78 children, three children counting as one adult for the purpose of fares. In addition she carried 16 horses and 30 sheep. Captain James Savers was charged with carrying excess passengers and fined £200 or two months in prison.[62] The severity of this sentence suggests the authorities were becoming more determined to stamp out the trade in paupers.

The ships' masters incurred a great deal of hostility in the South Wales ports and Newport. Essentially, during 1847, the resentments were twofold. First, the rising level of concern over the amount of relief spent on the Irish immigrants and second, fear that the Irish were bringing typhus with them. This anger reached such levels that some masters began to put the refugees ashore before reaching Newport. However, this practice was not only to avoid incurring the anger of the townspeople of Newport but also to avoid being charged with carrying too many passengers. The favourite place for putting the Irish ashore was called the *Lighthouse*, about three miles out from Newport harbour. It was claimed that the immigrants were usually told that there was not enough water on board to last until they reached Newport. Also, they were advised that by going ashore there they would reach Newport much more easily and obtain poor relief much earlier. In practice, being disorientated, many finished up in Cardiff or did not reach Newport until three days later.[63] Many of those put ashore in this manner were in a weak physical condition and not surprisingly, some died. This was not a short term phenomenon. An example is the case of an Irishman called Donovan. In May 1849, a vessel called the *Three Brothers* was observed making its way along the Welsh coast, landing parties of people at various points. It was claimed the vessel carried three hundred Irish, all in a bad physical condition. Donovan died after being put ashore and his wife, assisted by other Irish, buried his body in the mud. The corpse was washed ashore at Peterstone. At the subsequent coroner's court, another inquest was also held on the body of an Irishman who had been put ashore and who had died of starvation soon after.[64] In July 1849, the Secretary of State wrote to the Mayor of Cardiff, saying that the Coast Guard Officers of the Swansea district had been instructed to keep a lookout for vessels landing Irish passengers and to check if they had infringed any laws.[65]

Speaking of emigrants arriving at Cork to take the Liverpool steamer, John Besnard, the general weighmaster at Cork said: 'Because the order comes from America to the parties to proceed from Liverpool to ship, and these parties coming from the interior of the country, have no idea of what a deck passage is or what they have to suffer, I am quite sure that nine out of ten have never seen a steamer and have not the most remote idea of what a deck passage means'.[66] Besnard seems to have been a humane man who was very concerned over what he saw every day on the quayside at Cork and in his evidence to the Select Committee on Emigrant Ships he further stated:

> I have gone to Liverpool expressly to await the arrival of Irish steamers and no language at my command can describe the scenes I witnessed there: the people were positively prostrated, and scarcely able to walk after they got out of the steamers, and then they were seized hold of by those unprincipled runners so well known in Liverpool. In fact, I consider the manner in which these passengers are carried from Irish to English ports is disgraceful, dangerous and inhuman.

Bernard described how the sea washed over the decks, drenching the passengers and sweeping luggage overboard. On occasions, a tarpaulin was rigged up to provide some shelter but this was only small and offered no protection against the sea.[67] Sylvester Redmond was a journalist and author who lived in Liverpool and who travelled frequently to Dublin. Redmond became concerned over the conditions on the Irish steamers and, giving evidence to the same Select Committee as Besnard, he described a voyage from Dublin to Liverpool which he had recently undertaken. Referring to deck passengers, he stated:

> ...they were generally crowded around the funnel of the steamer or huddled together in a most disgraceful manner; and as they have not been used to sea voyages, they get sick, and perfectly helpless, and covered with the dirt and filth of each other. I have seen the sea washing over the deck of a steamer that I came over in one night, completely drenching the unfortunate people, so much so that several of them got perfectly senseless. There were 250 deck passengers on board; and they were in a most dreadful state; it was an extremely stormy night and the vessel heaved about in a very awful manner; the sea washed over her tremendously, and it was only by great exertions that some of these people were not carried overboard. I could not get further than the head

of the stairs, but early in the morning, when it became light, I saw 50 or 60 of these people, including four or five children, perfectly stiff and cold. The Captain was a very humane man and although it was blowing a stiff gale of wind, I suggested to him to have those people taken into cabins, and he did so, bringing the worst in first. They were perfectly wet, and whatever clothes they had on, they were obliged to be taken off. There was a fine boy, apparently dead, but by a great deal of exertion and rubbing him in hot water and laying him before a fire, he revived.[68]

He went on to quote the case of a 20-year-old girl on the same voyage, who had apparently died of cold. On arrival at Liverpool a doctor was sent for and fortunately she recovered. In reference to the problem of overcrowding, Besnard stated that the fare from Cork to Liverpool was ten shillings, and he had witnessed a steamer sail carrying 1100 deck passengers and 300 pigs below deck. The fare for the pigs was half that for a passenger but the pigs, were better looked after because they were of value to someone.[69]

The Liverpool press carried many reports of the desperate plight of the famine immigrants. For example, the Dowling family, father, mother and five young children, arrived at night at Liverpool in February 1847, on the steamer *St Patrick*. Immediately on coming ashore the youngest child died.[70] In another case, a woman who had asked the parochial authorities to be sent back to Ireland went on her knees and begged the official not to send her back on a screw-driven vessel. On her journey to Liverpool as a deck passenger on such a vessel, she and her child had nothing to eat and were wet-through for the whole journey, having spent a night on deck completely exposed to the weather.[71] Though the volume of passenger traffic from Ireland to Britain peaked in 1847, the atrocious conditions on board steamers continued to exist over the whole famine crisis.

The conditions on the Irish steamers were brought before the British public in December 1848 in a particularly horrific way. At 4.00pm on 1 December 1848 the steamer *Londonderry* left Sligo, bound for Liverpool with a crew of twenty two and carrying 206 passengers who, according to the *Liverpool Mercury* '... appear to have chiefly consisted of the wretched and destitute class who are pouring into England and in such multitudes and who are landed daily in our streets without a penny of money, and with scarcely rags enough to cover them'.[72] Of the 206 passengers, three people occupied the cabin accommodation and the rest were deck passengers. The weather quickly deteriorated and the vessel was pitching in high seas, the danger to the passengers increased by the presence of cattle on deck. Captain Johnson ordered 170 deck passengers below into a space that was 18 feet long, ten or 12 feet wide and seven feet high. The master then had the entrance covered with a tarpaulin and fastened by ropes. The consequences of forcing that many people into such a confined space were horrific. The available oxygen was insufficient and people began to die of suffocation; in the panic, people fought to get out but the entrance was secured. (Appendix No 3.2) Eventually a man escaped and raised the alarm. The sight that greeted the master and crew was such that the vessel stood-to in Lough Foyle for 12 hours before Captain Johnson had the courage to pull alongside the quay at Derry. The scene that faced the Mayor and magistrates of Derry when they went aboard was described by *The Times*:

> The scene on entering the steerage of the steamer was as awful a spectacle as could be witnessed. Seventy-two dead bodies of men, women and children, lay piled indiscriminately over each other, four deep, all presenting the ghastly appearance of persons who had died in the agonies of suffocation; very many of them covered with blood which had gushed from the mouth or nose, or had flowed from the wounds inflicted by the trampling of nail-studded brogues, and by the frantic violence of those who struggled to escape. For it was but too evident that, in the struggle, the poor creatures had torn the clothes from each others backs and even the flesh from each others limbs.

The violence of the storm is indicated by the fact that twenty cattle died, principally as a result of being trampled to death on deck. Captain Johnson and the first and second mates were arrested and charged with manslaughter. The affair set off an outcry against conditions on the steamers. The jury found the men guilty and also recommended the proprietors of 'steamboats' to treat as an urgent necessity, the provision of better accommodation for the 'poorer class of passengers'. A correspondent of the *Northern Whig* repeated the view of *The Times* that the captain and crew of the *Londonderry* had no murderous intent when they forced the passengers into the steerage but they were guilty of the 'most gross inconsideration, however... We do not blame them very much. The system requires alteration. We are bound to say that a vast change is demanded in favour of deck passengers carried by our steamers and it will be surprising if this terrible slaughter fails to induce legislative interference'.

The casual and chaotic nature of the business of transporting passengers on what were essentially cargo vessels is revealed by the confession of the first mate that he had no idea how many passengers were aboard when they left Sligo. *The Times* felt the case of the *Londonderry* was even more horrible than that of the fire on board the *Ocean Monarch* and, as a preface to its reporting of the details of the event, stated: 'If we here repeat the details of what occurred, it is with no wish to harrow up the public feeling nor even of signalling to public indignation the persons by whose gross indiscretion and most criminal carelessness the tragedy was brought about. It is rather with a view that government may at last be *compelled* by public opinion to look more closely into the condition not only of emigrant ships but of all throughout the United Kingdom'.

Michael McNulty had left Sligo in November 1848 and went to Liverpool to try and earn the passage fare to America.

> When famine commenced in Connaught, I had been in good opulence, and though I was encumbered with a large, helpless family I stemmed it up manfully, until poor rates and exorbitant taxes became so enormous in the aggregate, that I started for Liverpool about a month ago to improve my condition and in summer to proceed to America, when I might get employment for the greater part of my family. During this time I was communicating with my family and in compliance to my call, they embarked on that unfortunate steamer, in Sligo on the 1st December 1848.

McNulty's family on board the *Londonderry* were his wife Ellen, sons Michael and Jerry and daughters Anne, Nancy, Catherine, Biddy, Mary. All died except Mary and Jerry McNulty. In addition a cousin also died and all the family's money, being carried by Ellen McNulty had not been found by December 16.

The tragedy on board the steamship *Londonderry* attracted a lot of attention but elicited no immediate response from the government and it needed more deaths to provoke some action. On the night of Thursday, 19 April 1849, the steamship *Britannia* left Dublin for Liverpool carrying 414 deck passengers who, as usual, had no protection of any kind against the weather. Conditions worsened rapidly and snow and hail added to the desperate situation facing the passengers. At about 6 o'clock on the Friday morning, Elizabeth Noon and her six-year old son were observed to be in a bad way and the woman was taken into the cabin quarters where she died. Her son was taken into the engine room to benefit from the warmth but he also died. At about 9 o'clock on Friday morning, an unknown man was found dead on deck. On arrival in Liverpool, Dr Laycock was sent for and declared all three to be dead from exposure, a verdict repeated next day by the borough coroner. Laycock was so upset by what he saw on the *Britannia* that he wrote immediately to the *Liverpool Mercury*, asking the paper to publicize the case in an effort to mobilize opinion in favour of controls over the companies. The paper published his letter of 21 April and introduced it with a statement of its own: 'The facts elicited at the inquest elsewhere reported speak trumpet edged in support in an argument as to the inhumanity of the human cattle trade, for we can call it nothing less, now carried on for the mutual benefit of the steamboat owners and of persons on the other side of the water, who find it convenient to ship their paupers here than to maintain them at home'.[73]

The case was raised in the House of Commons on 26 April when J O'Connell asked the President of the Board of Trade whether or not the government intended to bring in measures to regulate the carriage of passengers between the various parts of the United Kingdom. O'Connell referred specifically to the cases of the *Londonderry* and the *Britannia*. Mr Labouchere, President of the Board of Trade, replied that the government's attention had been brought to the cases referred to and he went on to say that:

> The subject was one which was not unattended with difficulty; and it would be most inadvisable to throw any obstruction in the way of the cheap means of conveyance at present enjoyed by the humbler classes in Ireland, who came over to the harvest, or for other purposes. On the other hand, the overcrowding had been affected with such serious results, that it would be necessary to interpose.[74]

Whether the 'humbler classes' actually enjoyed the voyage to England is debatable but Labouchere's reluctance to interfere in the Irish Sea traffic was consistent with a laissez-faire mood in economic policy. However, as an indication of the government's concern, Labouchere asked Captain Denham, a Board of Trade official, to go to Liverpool and prepare a report on the conditions experienced by deck passengers on the Irish steamers, particularly on the Liverpool-Dublin crossing. He also promised that no time would be lost in taking action if Denham's report indicated the need.[75]

Meanwhile tragedies of all kinds continued to occur on steamers. For example, in December 1849, Catherine Neary embarked on the steamer *Nimrod* from Cork to Liverpool. On the voyage she killed her baby and on arrival at Liverpool was arrested and subsequently charged with murder.[76]

VIII

At the time of Denham's dispatch to Liverpool, the law regarding the carrying of passengers on steamships was slowly responding to changing conditions. In 1846, a statute had been enacted for '*The Regulation of Steam Navigation and for Requiring Sea Going Vessels to Carry Boats*' (9 and 10 Vic. Cap. 100). This Act required the owners of steamships to make certain declarations to the Board of Trade each year concerning the condition of the hull and machinery, these to be provided by a surveyor and engineer respectively. On receipt of these, the Board of Trade would grant a sea-going certificate. With respect to passengers, the Act laid down specific regulations concerning the number of lifeboats to be carried. This Act came into force on 1 January 1847 and stated that no vessel could go to sea carrying passengers unless it had a valid certificate. At this time, the problem of overcrowding had not become scandalous. As noted earlier with respect to the *Lady Ann* and the *James* even when possessing a certificate masters ignored the limit on numbers which could be carried.

By 1848, the problem of overcrowding was sufficiently recognized at government level to bring about further legislation in the form of '*An Act for the Further Regulation of Steam Navigation and for Limiting in Certain Cases, the Number of Passengers to be Conveyed in Steam Vessels*' (11 and 12 Vic. Cap. 81).

This Act gave the Board of Trade the power to limit *where it thought fit*, the number of passengers a steam vessel could carry and to insert this limit into the sea-going certificate. A fine not exceeding five shillings could be imposed for every passenger carried over the maximum permitted number. However, this Act was permissive and there is no evidence that it was widely used. On the contrary, the evidence points in the other direction. On 25 April 1849, Labouchere told the House of Commons that the provisions of the Act regarding the limitations on the number of passengers carried on steam vessels had been restricted to vessels travelling on rivers, but this cannot be construed from reading the Act. This, then, was the situation at the time of the deaths aboard the *Britannia*. Denham reported to the Board of Trade on the 21 May 1849 and its contents were made known to the House of Commons on 21 June. His investigations revealed, unequivocally, that the journey to Liverpool from Irish ports was normally one of extreme hardship for deck passengers. Priority was given to the cargo and animals. The animals were carried both below and on deck. In heavy weather they would panic, causing chaos. The animals' dung and urine covered the decks yet people sometimes went among them to keep warm. The medical officers employed by Liverpool parish inspected vessels on arrival and their evidence confirms the barbaric nature of the trade. They claimed that sometimes a vessel would carry over one thousand passengers:

> As to the area space available for each deck passenger, it may be observed that no portions of the vessels were set apart for such accommodation. The decks and holds were generally filled with cattle, so that even in an uncrowded state there was great difficulty in moving; but when passengers were in such numbers [sic 1000], they were so jammed together in the erect posture that motion was impossible. One woman stated that she had been obliged to sit during the whole of the passage, from the want of room to save herself, while her children were placed

> under her legs for safety. The common offices of nature, including vomiting from sea sickness, were consequently done on the spot... The passengers and cattle were therefore indiscriminately mixed together; the sea and urine pouring on their clothes from the animals, and they stood in the midst of filth and mire... The smell from the filth, mire, effects of sea-sickness and the engine, were most intolerable.[77]

These descriptions, given by doctors in Liverpool, were applicable to a large proportion of the arrivals in Liverpool during 1847. In case there is a suspicion that the medical men were exaggerating, the police also gave evidence to Denham's inquiry:

> During the years 1847 and 1848, there were frequently from 600 to 800 deck passengers on board of one steamer at a time, arriving from the ports of Dublin, Drogheda, Dundalk and Sligo, crowded together on deck, mixed among the cattle and besmeared with their dung, clothed in rags and saturated with wet (the spray of the sea having washed over them during the voyage), so that on their arrival, from the fatigue of the passage, the want of proper food and clothing, many of them have been unable to go ashore without assistance, and to all appearances were not likely to survive many days; and the hardships of such unfortunate deck passengers are frequently augmented by a contrary wind, as the paddle steamers are not able to make the passage (with a strong east wind) in less than 18 to 20 hours, and the screw steamers (under similar circumstances) have often been 30 hours coming from Dublin, with a number of passengers on deck, most of whom had no food or other refreshment to get during that time so that on their arrival they are greatly exhausted and in a most deplorable state.[78]

The number of deaths on the passages was small. During 1847 it was less than ten, but as Denham pointed out, human beings can endure a lot of suffering without actually dying. It is clear that the representatives of the steamship companies showed little concern for the suffering of the passengers. Commenting on his meetings with them and their views of the problem, Denham reported:

> In these sentiments no acquiescence in regulations for humanity's sake is traceable or to be expected. Impunity is attached to the complained of system, because few deaths are recorded in its exercise, forgetting that human endurance can reach a fearful height without actually dying. Unlimited and promiscuous crowding of men, women and children, are held as desirable for the crowded. And of animal creation, the human

being is of the class not to be provided for; or, if included in any regulations, a scale is proposed that would authorize a greater number than has hitherto been carried... Such inconsistencies and inconsiderate propositions serve to show what little amelioration of the present system is to be expected from the trading party.[79]

Thus Denham believed that the steamer companies would volunteer no action which would reduce profits. The report, which covered the famine years 1847 to 1848, established beyond any doubt that the conditions of deck passengers on the Irish steamers *were ordinarily those of extreme hardship and frequent degradation.* The ships' masters interviewed by Denham blamed the ticket agents in Irish ports who, they alleged, sold as many tickets as possible without any thought of the consequences in terms of overcrowding. There were allegations from passengers that, when on board, they were exploited by the sailors. The crews often charged them a one penny a quart for water and the privilege of being admitted to the forecastle cost two shillings in some cases. In other cases, sailors charged freezing immigrants sixpence for three hours' stay in the engine-room. Denham listed seven suggestions to improve the situation and argued that the existing Act (11 and 12 Vic. Cap. 81) would be sufficient to achieve the desired improvements except that the penalties were too small.

It is not surprising that Denham's report upset the proprietors of the steamship companies whose basic defence was that they were not in the passenger business and that they had simply carried people who were desperate to escape from Ireland. Charles Wye Williams, Managing Director of the City of Dublin Steam Packet Company wrote to the *Morning Chronicle* (letter appeared 26 July 1849) calling the report 'unfair'. He attacked the authorities in Liverpool for their campaign to stop the steamers carrying paupers to Britain. 'What the parish of Liverpool seeks is to prevent immigration, in other words, the free intercourse between England and Ireland. Will the Board of Trade undertake the responsibility for such a measure?'[80] Clearly the answer was always, no. There is no doubt that the conditions under which the Irish travelled to Britain, in particular Liverpool, during the famine exodus were horrific. These were tolerated for a number of reasons. First and foremost, the eruption of refugees in 1847 took everyone by surprise. The steamship companies were not primarily in the passenger business and it would have been impossible for them, overnight, to have invested in passenger steamers. Also long term investment in steamers to meet a short term crisis would, from their point of view, have been economic madness. Where they are open to criticism is allowing overcrowding. It is true it was chaotic on the Irish quays as the refugees sought passages. At little extra cost, the companies could have controlled the numbers carried on individual vessels, Even this, however, would not have removed entirely the awfulness of those journeys for people ill-clad, hungry and often already suffering from famine related illnesses. The terrible conditions were tolerated because Irish paupers and immigrants had no friends in high places. Also, apart from those concerned with the steamer trade and the docks, few would witness the heart rending scenes on the docksides, certainly not middle-class decision makers. During 1847, local authorities in Britain were struggling with their own problems of sanitation, poor housing, inadequate water supplies and an increase in indigenous poverty. The central government was pre-occupied with the famine relief problems in Ireland. The whole episode must be viewed as an integral part of the famine tragedy in which the suffering of the Irish people at home continued on their journey to Britain or their voyage to North America, or was endured in the slums of British towns.[81] Robert Scally has drawn attention to the passivity of the refugees and emigrants, the acceptance of the overcrowding, the often brutal treatment from officials and seamen. There is no doubt that many of the people fleeing Ireland during 1847 were disorientated, often from rural communities with little travel experience, unused to negotiating with officials for tickets and accommodation, even unused to dealing with cash. The result in many cases was an acceptance of their fate which Scally has likened to that of negro slaves on the voyage to America and the Jews of the Holocaust. Whether or not one accepts the analogy, it is undisputable that many of the most destitute people leaving Ireland at the height of the crisis were disorientated, passive and fatalistic. In such a condition they were easier to pack onto the decks of cross-channel steamers or into the holds of emigration ships.[82] The controversy surrounding the steamer traffic did eventually produce more legislation aimed at improving conditions but too late to ameliorate the passage for those fleeing Ireland. The prize for those reaching the 'promised land' was life in Victorian Britain's overcrowded and disease ridden slums.

Appendices

Appendix 3.1 The tonnage of wheat, wheat flour, oats and oatmeal, imported into Great Britain from Ireland over the year 1845-1851, inclusive.

Product	1845	1846	1847	1848	1849	1850	1851
Wheat & wheatflour	22 439	4 918	2 300	3 811	2 933	2 207	1 189
Oats & oatmeal	34 329	16 395	8 793	19 332	14 043	13 442	14 275
Barley & barley meal	nd	1 161	595	999	580	510	556

Note: Where the original data is recorded in quarters, these have been converted into tons, using the conversion rate of 28 lbs = one quarter. *Sources:* For the year 1845, BPP (HC) *Accounts and Papers,* 1846 XLIV, 'An Account of the Quantities of Wheat, Barley, Oats, Wheatflour and Oatmeal Imported into Great Britain from Ireland in the year 1842, 1843, 1844 and 1845.' For the year 1846, BPP (HC) Accounts and Papers... For the years 1847-51 BPP (HC) *Accounts and Papers*, 1852 (538) LI, 487. Quantities of Corn, Grain, Meal and Flour, stated in Quarters, Imported into Great Britain from Ireland in Each Year from 1847-1851.'

Appendix 3.2 The names of 50 persons who died on board the SS *Londonderry*, on 1 December 1848. In total, 72 people died.

Thady Armstrong
son of Thady Armstrong
Bridget Bailly
Bridget Bourke
Hannah Browne
Dominic Carty
son of Dominic Carty
Mary Cain
Pat Clancy
Pat Clark
James Cathey
John Connaughton
Margaret Connaughton
Anne Cullan
Ann Cullan
Michael Egan
Brian Flynn
Catherine Gilgan
Pat Glin
Owen Haughrey
Mary Kane
Anthony Martin
Pat Milmo
Brian Melvin
James M'Griskin
Ellen M'Anulty
Anne M'Anulty
Michael M'Anulty
Nancy M'Anulty
Catherine M'Anulty
Biddy M'Anulty
Mary M'Donagh
John M'Gowan
Catherine M'Gowan
Michael M'Gowan
John M'Loughlin
Mary M'Loughlin
James M'Cormick
Pat Nealon
Catherine Reilly
Mary Rowen
Mary Rowen
Owen Scanlon
Owen Scanlon
George Stephenson
Mary Talland
Biddy Terney
John Ternan
Thady Tierney
Thomas Tonner

Source: Mayo and Sligo Intelligencer, 14 December 1848. Note: at the time of this report, 22 bodies were unidentified.

Appendix: 3.3 Ships carrying food arriving at Liverpool from Ireland on Monday 11 October 1847

Name of vessel	*Tonnage*	*Irish port of departure*	*Dock*	*Cargo*
Blair	88	Limerick	Colourg	560 bags oats, 640 barrels wheat
Dublin	154	Dublin	Clarence	60 sacks oats, 111 sacks wheat, 88 bags oatmeal, 29 sacks oatmeal, 170 firkins butter, 148 bags beans, 12 barrels tapioca.
Duchess of Kent	268	Dublin	Clarence	132 sacks wheat, 64 sacks oatmeal, 7 packets eggs, 1 puncheon whiskey, 1 cask wine, 2 barrels Porter, 10 sacks malt, 116 cows, 200 sheep
Emerald	81	Wexford	Georges	250 quarters oats, 220 quarters beans
Emerald	179	Dublin	Clarence	8 barrels butter, 100 firkins butter, 117 hogshead porter, 10 puncheons treacle
Ida	70	Newry	Kings	54 tons oats, 220 tons oatmeal, 20 tons wheat
Irishman	232	Drogheda	Clarence	202 lds oatmeal, 79 cows, 580 sheep
Geraldine	83	Limerick	Georges	232 barrels oats, 644 barrels wheat, 40 barrels pork, 8 barrels porter
Lord Byron	116	Dublin	Georges	500 quarters Indian corn
Leeds	242	Dublin	Clarence	58 sacks oats, 8 bags malt, 3 boxes eggs, 117 cows, 300 sheep
Nimrod	497	Cork	Clarence	733 sacks oats, 20 sacks oatmeal, 438 sacks wheat, 584 firkins butter, 10 cattle, 50 pigs
Pride of Erin	478	Dundalk	Clarence	16 bags oats, 186 bags meal, 198 bags barley, 27 firkins butter, 119 cows, 212 sheep, 84 pigs
St Patrick	378	Drogheda	Clarence	239 lds oatmeal, 100 barrels wheat, 2 boxes eggs, 103 cows, 560 sheep, 10 horses
Tynwald	374	Belfast	Clarence	300 firkins butter, 42 boxes butter, 20 barrels bacon, 10 puncheons whiskey, 22 hogshead ham, 48 cows, 157 sheep
Victoria	62	Limerick	Kings	16 tons oats, 80 tons wheat

Source: MMM Customs Bills of Entry

Appendix 3.4 The number of private ships and emigrants carried, departing from ports under the superintendence of Government emigration officers.

Port of departure	*1847*		*1848*		*1849*		*1850*		*1851*	
	ships	*passengers*	*ships*	*passengers*	*ships*	*passengers*	*ships*	*passengers*	*ships*	*passengers*
London	71	10 576	109	13 372	162	22 778	136	14 137	124	22 095
Liverpool	514	129 663	519	125 504	562	147 685	568	166 090	606	196 217
Plymouth	19	2 689	74	4 996	109	7 976	82	6 697	72	7 778
Glasgow (etc)	42	4 593	79	7 496	102	13 789	80	12 900	86	13 745
Belfast	53	10 999	49	8 730	57	9 650	35	5 870	21	3 752
Dublin	44	9 169	46	7 680	47	9 861	32	7 368	41	9 079
Londonderry	66	12 385	42	7 076	47	7 808	27	4 142	33	6 310
Sligo (etc)	64	13 050	24	3 078	38	3 978	19	2 404	17	2 047
Limerick	81	11 624	76	9 401	76	11 554	80	10 667	79	11 773
Cork	114	18 601	91	11 627	84	9 721	64	8 099	79	12 462
Waterford	39	4 748	20	1 607	33	4 173	29	3 039	28	2 689
New Ross	24	5 062	12	1 866	15	2 963	13	2 858	19	5 241
Totals	1131	233 159	1141	202 433	1332	251 936	1165	244 271	1205	293 188

Sources: BPP (HC) 1853, Emigration Ships. 'A Return showing the Number of Passenger Ships which had sailed from Ports in the United Kingdom with emigrants on board, 1847-51 inclusive'.

Appendix 3.5 The number of people landing at Glasgow from Ireland during the week ending 10 August 1847.

Name of vessel	*Port of departure*	*Respectable class*		*Poor class*		*Children*		*Grand total*
		Males	*Females*	*Males*	*Females*	*Under 10yrs*	*10yrs+*	
Londonderry (S)	Derry	6	7	929	71	54	11	1078
Vanguard (S)	Dublin	30	5	-	-	7	-	42
Tartan (S)	Belfast	4	6	151	30	13	4	208
Shamrock (S)	-	14	8	1173	31	7	-	1233
Aurora (S)	Belfast	2	2	569	74	50	10	707
Neptune (Smack)	Port Rush	-	-	18	5	3	-	26
Albion (Smack)	Port Rush	-	-	39	6	8	-	53
Ocrean (S)	Dublin	30	3	10	2	10	-	55
Tartar (S)	Belfast	-	-	145	25	5	3	178
Londonderry (S)	Derry	4	1	361	44	34	10	454
-	-	64	-	827	69	23	17	1000
Railway	-	-	-	-	-	-	-	741
Total	-	154	32	4222	357	214	55	5775

nb: 170 of the total number landing were too old to walk.

Source: Mitchell Library, Glasgow. Minutes of the Meeting of the Glasgow Parochial Board held 24 August 1847, pp. 162-164.

Notes and References

1 *Liverpool Courier*, 6 January 1847.
2 *Liverpool Journal*, 20 February 1847. This edition carried the full text of Commander Caffin's report.
3 ibid.
4 For a treatment of some of these technological changes see, J.Kennedy, *The History of Steam Navigation*, (Liverpool: 1903). F.Neal, 'Shipbuilding in the North-West of England', in S.Ville (ed) *Shipbuilding in the United Kingdom in the Nineteenth Century: a regional approach*; E.Corlett, *The Iron Ship*, 2nd ed. (Moonraker Press: 1990).
5 The nature and scale of the Irish cross channel trade has received relatively little attention from maritime historians. See F.Harcourt, 'Charles Wye Williams and Irish Steam Shipping', *The Journal of Transport History*, 3rd series, volume 13, no. 2, September, 1992, pp. 141-62. H.S.Irvine, 'Some Aspects of Passengers Traffic Between Britain and Ireland, 1820-50', *The Journal of Transport History*. F.Neal, 'Liverpool, The Irish Steamship Companies and the Famine Irish', *Immigrants and Minorities*, volume 5, no. 1, (March, 1986), pp. 28-61, referred to hereafter as Neal (Steamships). An important source of information on the Irish steamer trade during the famine period is the report by Captain Denham on his investigations carried out in 1849. PRO/BPP/HC (1849) 'Captain Denham's Report on Passenger Accommodation in Steamers Between Ireland and Liverpool', referred to hereafter as Denham, 1849. For an idiosyncratic, but insightful look at the Irish emigration trade over the period under review see, R.Scally, 'Liverpool Ships and Irish Emigrants in the Age of Sail', *Journal of Social History*', volume 17, no. 1, (Fall: 1983) pp. 5-30.
6 Kennedy, op.cit, p. 33.
7 Kennedy, op.cit, p. 37.
8 Kennedy, op.cit, p. 37. Harcourt, op.cit, p. 142.
9 *Gore's General Advertiser*, 28 September 1843.
10 *Liverpool Mercury*, 3 October 1845. This edition carries a report on the orders for Irish steamers placed with Peter Cato's. The *Emerald* was launched by Cato, 15 January 1846. She was an iron steamship, 130 feet long, 21 feet wide and was screw driven, 60 h.p. engines, see *Liverpool Mercury*, 16 January 1846 and *Liverpool Times*, 20 January 1846.
11 *Liverpool Mercury*, 23 and 30 January 1846. The *Ajax* was intended for the London-Cork route. See also *Liverpool Mercury*, 27 March and 3 April 1846 for reports on the launching of the *Black Diamond*, an iron steamship for the City of Dublin Steam Packet Company. She was 330 tons burden, 60 h.p. engines and was to be used on the Liverpool-Dublin crossing.
12 *Manchester Guardian*, 29 April 1837.
13 *Manchester Guardian*, 27 January 1838.
14 *Gore's General Advertiser*, 14 January 1841.
15 *Gore's General Advertiser*, 25 February and 18 March 1841.
16 *Liverpool Mercury*, 16 April 1847.
17 There is a large, and growing literature on Irish emigration. The most authoritative works are D.Fitzpatrick, *Irish Emigration, 1801-1921* (Dublin: 1984). D.Fitzpatrick, *Oceans of Consolation: personal accounts of Irish migration to Australia*, (Cork: 1994). P.O'Farrell, *The Irish in Australia* (N.S.W. University Press: 1986), chapter three is particularly useful. O.MacDonagh, 'Irish Emigration to the United States of America and British Colonies during the Famine' in R.Dudley Edwards, T.D.Williams (eds),

The Great Famine: studies in Irish history, 1845-52, (Dublin: 1956), chapter vi. B.Collins, 'The Origins of Irish Immigration to Scotland in the Nineteenth and Twentieth Centuries', in T.M.Devine (ed), *Irish Immigrants in Scottish Society in the Nineteenth and Twentieth Centuries*, (Edinburgh: 1991), pp. 1-18. A detailed treatment of the emigration of Irish women is P.O'Sullivan (ed), *The Irish World Wide History, Heritage, Identity*, volume 4, 'Irish Women and Irish Migration', (Leicester U.P: 1995). W.D.McKay, *Flight from Famine: the coming of the Irish to Canada*, (Toronto: 1990), The author of this work is a journalist and is not authoritative but is frequently quoted. C.Kinealy, *This Great Calamity: the Irish famine 1848-52*, (Dublin: 1994), in particular chapter eight. C.O'Grada, *Ireland: a new economic history, 1780-1939*, part II, chapter four and part IV, chapter nine, (Oxford: 1994).

18 *Manchester Guardian*, 2 January 1847, *Stockport Advertiser*, 8 January 1847. Waters died of malnutrition in Stockport. (see p. 183), *Sunderland Herald*, 16 April 1847.

19 *Bristol Gazette*, 27 April 1847, *Cheltenham Examiner*, 28 April 1847. Three Sullivan children died of malnutrition in *Cheltenham*, see pp. 178-9.

20 SC (1854) J.Evans, q. 5333.

21 SC (1854) J.Evans, q. 5339.

22 The Customs' Bills of Entry record each vessel arriving at a port, including the name of the vessel, its port of departure, a detailed list of its cargo, date of arrival, tonnage of the vessel, master's name and number of crew. Unfortunately, the amount of detail recorded varies between ports. Thus, for example, in the case of the Glasgow bills, the tonnage of a ship is not always recorded. The bills have not survived for all ports. From the point of view of this study, it is disappointing that the bills for Cardiff, Swansea and Newport, cannot be traced.

23 When the tonnage of a vessel is not recorded it can be obtained elsewhere. In the case of steamers, the companies advertised their sailings and often gave the tonnage of the vessel. Sailing vessels were very small and it was rarely that their trips were advertised. In the case of the Glasgow Bills, however, for the year 1847, 413 sailing ships had their tonnage recorded, providing a large sample from which to estimate the overall average tonnage of sailing vessels arriving at Glasgow (64 tons)

24 Captain Denham inspected the *Emerald* on her arrival at Liverpool 6 May 1849. She had taken nearly 31 hours on the trip from Dublin to Liverpool. She carried 306 deck passengers and a woman gave birth in the ship's engine room. Denham, 1849, pp. 10-11.

25 Denham, 1849, p. 3.

26 Denham, 1849, p. 4.

27 *The Tablet*, 17 April 1847. (This report was taken from the *Cork Register*).

28 Denham, 1849, p. 9.

29 BPP (HC) Accounts and Papers, 1847. The Number of Cattle, Sheep and Pigs Imported into Great Britain during the year ending 5 January 1847.

30 *Liverpool Mail*, 26 December 1846. Report on the meeting of the Select Vestry.

31 SC, 1847, Minutes of Evidence, E.Rushton, qq. 4370-1. See also SC (1854) Minutes of Evidence, A.Campbell, qq. 4969-4971. Campbell explains the source of some data on emigration arrivals from Ireland.

32 No data of arrivals at Liverpool from Ireland appears to have been kept for any year after 1855.

33 SC (1854) Minutes of Evidence, qq. 4952-54. This is a complete copy of Rushton's letter to the Home Secretary.

34 The statistics for 1848 and 1849 were estimated using the data of weekly arrivals at Liverpool recorded in the press. The *Manchester Guardian* carried such reports.

35 Strathclyde, Glasgow Parochial Board meeting held 24 August 1847, p. 162.
36 *Glasgow Herald*, 27 September 1847, report on the meeting of the Glasgow Parochial Board at which a memorial was prepared for the Privy Council, complaining of Irish pauper immigration.
37 Strathclyde, Glasgow Parochial Board meeting, 30 November 1847.
38 SC (1854) Minutes of Evidence contain lots of anecdotal evidence, claiming that various agencies and individuals in Ireland were financing the trip to England of many destitute Irish.
39 SC (1850) Minutes of Evidence, A. Campbell, q. 4954, p. 359, copy of Rushton's letter.
40 SC (1854) Minutes of Evidence, J.Evans, qq. 5340-1.
41 SC (1854) Minutes of Evidence, G.Carr, qq. 5546-5576.
42 SC, 1847, Minutes of Evidence, E.Rushton, qq. 4397-99. Also *Liverpool Courier*, 28 April 1847. Report on the meeting of the Select Vestry 27 April at which details of the *Rochester* incident were discussed.
43 Denham, 1849, p. 3.
44 SC (1854) Minutes of Evidence, A.Campbell, q. 5025. Campbell quoted Hart.
45 For a detailed analysis of competition on the Irish-Liverpool crossing see Neal (Steamships).
46 Strathclyde,, Minutes of Glasgow Parochial Board held 26 January 1847. Also reported in the *Glasgow Herald*, 29 January 1847.
47 SC (1854) Minutes of Evidence, A.Campbell, qq. 5076-5082.
48 *The Times*, 8 May 1847. Report on questions in the House of Commons on 7 May regarding the situation in Liverpool. Sir George Grey, Home Secretary, said that the steamship companies had been warned about carrying fever victims.
49 *Manchester Guardian*, 12 May 1847.
50 *Liverpool Standard*, 15 June 1847, report on the meeting of the Select Vestry held on 8 June 1847. Charles Wye Williams, Managing Director of the City of Dublin Steamship Company tried to persuade the Vestry to agree that on arrival in Liverpool, steamers flying a quarantine flag should dock first and sick persons then be removed to the lazarettos. Clearly, this proposal was beneficial to the companies but it was rejected.
51 *Manchester Guardian*, 9 June 1847.
52 *Glasgow Herald*, 21 May 1847. Report on the meeting of the Glasgow Parochial Board held 17 May 1847.
53 *Glasgow Herald*, 14 June 1847. When the *Thetis* arrived at the Broomielaw, a detachment of police was on hand in case there was resistance to a medical inspection. In the event there was no reaction among the passengers.
54 Strathclyde, Minutes of the meeting of the Glasgow Parochial Board held on 25 June 1847, p. 121.
55 *The Cambrian*, 30 April 1847.
56 PRO/MH12/7802/Stepney Union/8696A. Stepney Guardians to E.Chadwick, Secretary to the Poor Law Commissioners, dated 18 May 1847. Mr Hall of the Poor Law Commissioners commented on the back of the letter that there was nothing they could do to stem the inflow of Irish immigration.
57 SC (1854) Minutes of Evidence, E.David, q. 6471.
58 SC (1854) Minutes of Evidence, E.David, q. 6452.
59 SC (1854) Minutes of Evidence, E.David, q. 6473.

60 *Cardiff and Merthyr Guardian*, 10 April 1847. This carried a detailed report of the inquest. PRO/Customs/71/49. Letter to the Customs House, London from Newport, dated 21 July 1847. The captain of the *Industry* had arrived without completing the necessary paperwork.
61 *Cardiff and Merthyr Guardian*, 17 April 1847.
62 The zeal with which harbourmasters and custom officers enforced passenger legislation varied considerably. Also long after Denham's report, masters continued to flout the law. See *Liverpool Mail*, 15 January 1853.
63 SC (1854) Minutes of Evidence, J.Salter, Newport Relieving Officer, q. 6740-5
64 *Manchester Guardian*, 19 May 1849.
65 *The Times*, 2 July 1849.
66 Emigrant Ships (1854) Minutes of Evidence, J. Besnard, qq. 4896-7.
67 Emigrant Ships (1854) Minutes of Evidence, J.Besnard, q. 4700.
68 Emigrant Ships (1854) Minutes of Evidence, S.Redmond, q. 1527. Redmond claimed he had never seen tarpaulins provided.
69 Emigrant Ships (1854) Minutes of Evidence, J.Besnard, qq. 4896-7.
70 *Liverpool Journal*, 27 February 1847.
71 SC (1854) Minutes of Evidence, J.Evans, q. 5305.
72 The account given here of the *Londonderry* tragedy is based on contemporary press reports. See *Londonderry Journal*, 6 December 1848, *Mayo and Sligo Intelligencer*, 7 and 14 December 1847, *Liverpool Mercury*, 8 December 1848, *Times*, 8 and 13 December 1848, *Manchester Guardian*, 9 December 1848, *Sunderland Herald*, 15 December 1848 and *Newcastle Journal*, 9 December 1848.
73 *Liverpool Mercury*, 21 April 1849. See also *Liverpool Albion*, 23 April 1849.
74 *Hansard* (Commons) volume 106, 1849, p. 670.
75 ibid.
76 *Liverpool Chronicle*, 8 December 1849.
77 Denham, 1849, p. 17. Evidence of the Medical Officers' in charge of quarantine at Liverpool.
78 Denham, 1849, p. 18. Evidence of Inspector Johnson.
79 Denham, 1849, p. 10.
80 *Liverpool Mail*, 28 July 1849. This edition of the paper carries a full copy of Charles Wye William's letter to the *Morning Chronicle*.
81 For a detailed account of the battle for a tightening up of legislation regarding Irish steamers see Neal (Steamships).
82 R.Scally, op.cit, pp. 7-9.

4 Arrival

I

Given the scale of immigration during 1847 and the poor physical condition of many of those landing at British ports, it is not surprising that the poor law system immediately came under severe strain. In England and Wales, under the terms of the 1834 Poor Law Amendment Act, parishes had been organized into larger administrative units known as poor law unions. The individual parishes within a union were responsible for the provision of poor relief and all contributed towards its overheads, usually such things as the provision of a workhouse, hospital wards and industrial schools. The paid employees of a union were the staff of the workhouse, the relieving officers, nurses, doctors and teachers. The relieving officiers were the men in direct contact with the poor, assessing claims for relief and also carrying the responsibility of ensuring the provision of medical treatment for those who needed it. The management of the union was in the hands of a Board of Guardians who were elected annually by the ratepayers. The financing of poor relief was through the simple expedient of taxing the local ratepayers, be they tenants or houseowners. The unit of assessment was the annual rental value of the property. This meant that, unlike today's system, in which central financing of social security payments is the norm, at the time of the famine, the amount spent on poor relief in a parish was raised from local people who, in turn could decide not to re-elect guardians whose policies they disapproved of. Though there were slight variations in the collecting of poor rate income throughout England and Wales, in its basic features, the system was as described above.

The guardians of the poor were normally businessmen, farmers and merchants, the kind of people whom ratepayers felt would pursue sound financial policies consistent with fulfilling their responsibilities to the poor. Poor relief was given in two forms. Indoor relief involved a person entering the workhouse while outdoor relief, in the form of food, clothing and money, was given to paupers without any necessity to enter the workhouse. In general, workhouse populations were the very old, the very young, the sick and widows with children. To establish the right to poor relief in a parish, a person had to have the legal status of 'settlement', achieved by being born in the parish or by one of a number of arcane criteria. Alternatively, after August 1846, a person who had lived for five years *continuously in a particular parish,* acquired the status of 'irremovable poor'. Outside of these categories, persons claiming poor relief of more than a temporary nature, could be physically removed to the parish in which they had settlement. From the point of view of this study, the important fact to note is that under this system the famine Irish landing at British ports had no legal claim to long term poor relief and were subject to the laws of removal. However, the poor law unions, as described above, had a legal obligation to ensure that nobody died of starvation, malnutrition or 'the want of the necessaries of life'.[1] In Liverpool, the parish of Liverpool *was* the union and the board of guardians was known as the Select Vestry.

In the case of Scotland, different legislation applied in the form of the Poor Law Amendment (Scotland) Act, 1845, but the organisational structure and financial principles were similar. The overall control body was called the Board of Supervision and the unions were known as the parochial boards. In the case of the City of Glasgow there were, at the time of the Irish famine, four unions; these were Glasgow parish, Barony parish, Gorbals parish and Govan parish. Each of these had a parochial board, with functions and responsibilities similar to the boards of guardians in England and Wales. Also, the laws of Settlement and Removal applied in Scotland. However, there were differences, in particular the methods of raising revenue, the role of private charity and the degree of control over the parishes exercised by the Board of Supervision. In particular, the churches in Scotland, in providing funds for the poor, played a central role in the poor relief system.[2] The Irish poor relief system dates from 1838 and at the time of the onset of the famine, outdoor relief was not given to able bodied persons and the provision of workhouse places was inadequate relative to the numbers seeking indoor relief.[3] The British system of poor relief came under severe stress in the mid eighteen forties, both as a result of a major downturn in the British economy, and the mass immigration of destitute Irish into Britain's towns and cities.

II

When did the authorities in British ports and towns become aware that they had a major problem on their doorstep in terms of Irish pauper immigration? Again the experience of Liverpool deserves our attention first, for two reasons. As has already been noted, the numbers of Irish entering the port exceeded those going to Glasgow or any other port. Also, more data exists in the case of Liverpool than anywhere else. Despite the re-appearance of the potato blight in Ireland in 1846, there was, initially, no sense of impending catastrophe. An example of this is the leader article which appeared in the *Liverpool Journal* of the 19 September 1846. By this date, it was clear to those in Ireland that a serious crop failure had occurred. The leader was headed 'Is there any cause for alarm?' Even allowing for the fallibility of leader writers, the piece is remarkable for its complacency:

> The Irish people are alarmed lest they should be starved; the Irish landlords are alarmed lest they should be pauperized, and the good and humane men in this country, are alarmed lest the scarcity of food should raise prices to a famine rate and disorganize the monetary system of the country... One of the marked blessings of a civilisation is the security it affords against famine. In barbarous and semi-civilized states, populations often perish... but the operations of a civilized society forbid the possibility of famine... On the whole, there is a great cause for caution but there is no danger of famine.

This article may have reflected the ignorance of an individual leader writer or, more likely, it revealed the widespread ignorance among the British public of the full significance of what was happening in Ireland. Nine weeks later, the same paper reported 'immense numbers of Irish paupers were landing in Liverpool, escaping from the threat of death by starvation in Ireland'. The paper went on to air what, immediately, became a central public concern, namely the probable consequences of the immigration of refugees on local rates.[4] Such worries found official expression when, on Tuesday 22 December, the Select Vestry held a special meeting to discuss the full implications of the large numbers of destitute Irish coming ashore at the port. The chairman of the Select Vestry, and chairman of the meeting, was Augustus Campbell, rector of Liverpool parish church. Campbell was a patrician figure who knew little of life in the teeming slums near his church. The main objective of the meeting was to draw up a memorial to the Home Secretary, Sir George Grey, asking for help, both financial and political. It was pointed out to the Secretary of State, that during the week ending 19 December 1845, 888 individual Irish had received relief from the parish. For the week ending 20 December 1846, the number was 13 471. The memorial, in its final draft, asked Sir George to take steps to ensure that persons boarding steamers in Irish ports should not be allowed to do so unless they could prove they had work awaiting them in England or could show that they had means to support themselves on arrival. The memorial claimed, not unreasonably, that Liverpool was in a special position vis-a-vis Ireland and should therefore receive special assistance at a time of crisis. Specifically, the Vestry requested that Liverpool's expenditure on the famine Irish should be re-imbursed from the Consolidated Fund. While there is no doubt that Liverpool was shouldering a financial burden as a direct consequence of the 1846 potato blight, the requests were forlorn, based on desperation or a total misunderstanding of both the problems on the ground in Ireland and the constitutional and economic implications of the Act of Union. As noted in chapter three, at the ports of embarkation in Ireland, the quaysides were crowded with desperate people, often rushing on board steamers, with the crews helpless to stop them. Even if the authorities had imposed a queuing system, how could the claims of work or a supportive family waiting in England be verified? Under the Act of Union, capital and labour were free to move anywhere within the Union. What the memorial reveals is that by December 1846, the authorities in Liverpool were beginning to panic. The memorial also makes it clear that the influx of famine Irish into Liverpool had started in November 1846.[5] On December 28, the Home Office wrote to the Liverpool authorities in reply:

> Sir George Grey regrets to learn that, from the cause stated in the memorial, so large an increase has taken place in the numbers of casual poor relieved by the parish of Liverpool, but he is unaware of any means by which Her Majesty's Government could prevent the departure from Ireland of such of the Irish as may be desirous of leaving their country, and who are able to obtain a passage to England. Neither are there any funds at the disposal of Her Majesty's Government, applicable to the repayment of the parish of Liverpool of the amount of extraordinary expenses to which, from the causes stated, they have this year become liable.[6]

This firm refusal to help was predictable yet as the crisis worsened, the Liverpool authorities appealed once more for help and again the government held to its position. It was reluctant to interfere with the steamship companies over the issue of overcrowding and was even more reluctant to interfere with the freedom of movement.

Though Campbell and the members of the Select Vestry met weekly to exercise overall management of poor relief, they were not in the front line of the operation. The buffer between the middle classes in general and the horrors of the slums were the people who actually witnessed the destitution and dealt with poverty at first hand, the doctors, relieving officers, workhouse staff, police and town missionaries. One figure central to the crisis management at street level was Edward Rushton, the stipendiary magistrate of Liverpool and also legal advisor to the Select Vestry. He sat daily in court, dealing with vagrants and others running foul of the law as a result of their desperation. A close friend of Rushton's was John Loch, agent to the Duke of Bridgewater. On 23 December 1846 Loch went to Liverpool from Worsley Old Hall near Manchester, and dined with Rushton, who told him of the situation in the port regarding Irish immigration. The next day Loch wrote to Sir George Grey and told him of 'the numbers of starving Irish' arriving in Liverpool. Grey received this letter soon after the memorial from the Select Vestry. Referring to his conversation with Rushton, Loch told Sir George that:

> ... within the last month, he says that 15 000 have arrived, *all* of whom are now being maintained in Liverpool at the expense of the community. He anticipated that within the next month, the number will be doubled, and there can be no reason why it should be stopped there; indeed, on the contrary, there is every reason for the numbers going vastly beyond it, so long as there is starvation in Ireland, and charitable aid here. This is very dreadful; there is already enough of distress, want of employment, and of suffering in store for Lancashire, without the addition of this ocean of starving immigration. It is not only due to, but it is indispensable for the preservation of the moral, the physical and the social condition of the people in this part of the country, that it should be stopped. Rushton acknowledged the necessity of this, while he deplored the absence of any means by which it might be affected, he seemed to think that nothing was left but to deal with the evil in the best possible manner on its arrival here. If this really be so, it must be submitted to, but if it should seem right to the Government to try and check this flood at its source, I can't help thinking the means to doing so might be had... I am informed the steamers are bringing the poor people over gratis; where they derive their remuneration I don't know.[7]

It is significant that Loch expresses that all pervading concern felt among the higher echelons of society, of the threat posed by the Irish to the moral condition of the English poor. As a law officer, Rushton knew, unlike Loch and Augustus Campbell, that there was no law preventing the movement of people from Ireland to Britain. He also recognized that given starvation in Ireland, a harsh Irish poor law and the perception of a better poor law system in Britain, particularly with respect to the provision of outdoor relief, people were behaving rationally, and legally, in moving to Britain. Rushton's view that the situation would worsen was absolutely correct and the sense of crisis heightened. On 15 January 1847, the *Liverpool Mercury* carried a leader headed 'Frightful Distress in Liverpool'. In this the *Mercury* argued that the burden of Irish relief in Liverpool was a national problem. *The Mercury* restated the objections of the Select Vestry, that Liverpool should not bear the financial consequences of famine in Ireland. However, the evidence is clear, that from November 1846, Liverpool was feeling the fallout from the return of the potato blight in Ireland.

Following the Select Vestry's memorial to the Home Secretary, the situation worsened. Between 13 January and 30 April 1847, inclusive, 76 959 adult males, 49 613 adult females, and 25 540 children, a total of 144 112 landed in Liverpool from the Irish ports.[8] During 1847 a total of 296 231 disembarked from the Irish steamers and over 116 000 were designated paupers.[9] Few, if any, of these destitute people would have had any legal right to poor relief but the Select Vestry, like all poor law guardians, had a statutory obligation to see that no one died for want of 'the necessaries of life'. What were the immediate options open to the Irish landing in Liverpool, lacking the financial resources which would have enabled them to rent a room and support themselves over a period of unemployment? Basically there were four choices; private charity, begging, the help of friends already established in Liverpool or parochial relief. The principal private charity in Liverpool at the time was the Liverpool District Provident Society. During 1845, 3488 English and 4446 Irish families received handouts. For 1846, the figures were 9447 and 18 987 respectively. These increased numbers reflect both the severity of the economic downturn and, in the case of the Irish, the increased level of immigration. In 1847, the numbers receiving help from the Provident Society were 3633 non-Irish and 5465 Irish families.[10] These decreases were the result of legal changes in 1846 which gave people with five years' continual residence in a parish the right to poor relief, without the threat of removal. This resulted in more people claiming parochial relief. Also more charities were set up to help with the crisis, handing out soup and bread and so diverting some requests from the Provident Society.

Begging became a widely practised tactic in the survival strategy of many immigrants. In Ireland the lack of a poor law before 1838 meant that in Ireland, begging was widespread. Even if a family obtained only a few pence a day, it meant that in Liverpool a bed could be bought for a night either in the Night Asylum or in a lodging house. As obnoxious as the lodging houses were, they were preferable to spending a night in the open during the cold weather and the use of children as beggars increased the family income, ensuring that some food could be purchased. Though begging was a crime under the Vagrancy Acts, the sheer numbers of Irish beggars meant that for various practical reasons, the law could not be implemented. For example, if all the beggars or the street hawkers had been arrested, sentenced and taken to prison, the local prison at Kirkdale could not have accommodated them. Additionally, the threat of prison did not deter begging, because prison meant warmth and food, much more preferable to living on the streets or in the lodging houses. The dilemma was illustrated by a case that came before Edward Rushton in November 1846. An Irish woman, with six children, was brought before Rushton, charged with begging. Rushton concluded it was a bad case and said he would send her to prison. Immediately the poor law official in court objected on the grounds that if the woman went to prison, the parish would have to take the children and hire a nurse to look after them, causing the ratepayers to foot a large bill. As a result of this intervention, Rushton did not sentence her to prison, she went to the workhouse with the children, a cheaper solution than hiring a nurse. This incident caused Rushton to exclaim 'If this be the process, there is an end to the Vagrant Act in Liverpool.. the case illustrates practically the working which has attended the influx and its effect upon our parochial funds'.[11]

The brunt of the provision of emergency relief for the famine Irish was borne by the ratepayers. Under normal circumstances, applicants for relief would go to the parish offices in Fenwick Street in the centre of the town. The four relieving officers of the poor who staffed the office would then investigate the legitimacy of the applicants' claims. By December 1846, the system was breaking down. On coming ashore at the Clarence dock, a majority of the immigrants would make their way to Fenwick Street to seek assistance in the form of tickets for soup and bread and/or money. By January 1847, Fenwick Street was daily crowded with such large numbers of destitute Irish that the officials could not cope. They were already under pressure because of the increased claims of the indigenous population and resident 'irremovable' Irish. The swarms of famine Irish broke the system and the relieving officers gave up any pretence of assessing the validity of claims for relief.

During January they simply handed out tickets in an effort to get rid of people. The result was an astonishing rise in numbers receiving outdoor relief. Any attempt at establishing the number of individual Irish receiving relief during 1847, using the published data regarding weekly claims, runs into the problem that units of counting used are not clearly defined. For example, a 'case' of Irish relief may refer to an individual or a head of a family, claiming on behalf of say, five or six others. Also, an individual may have been claiming for days or months.

The statistics in Table 4.1 below refer to 'instances' of relief, not individuals.

Table 4.1 The number of instances of Irish poor relieved outdoors with bread and soup at Liverpool during January 1847.

Week ending	*Males*	*Females*	*Children*	*Total*
9 January	5 313	6 932	21 269	33 514
16 January	11 616	12 354	46 634	70 604
23 January	22 719	22 928	80 272	125 919
30 January	24 588	24 991	93 565	143 144
Total	64 236	67 205	241 740	373 181

Source: Austin (1847), Appendix A, Relief of the Irish in Liverpool, pp.115-116.

If the weekly total is divided by six (relief not given on Sundays) then we obtain a rough estimate of the number of *individuals* receiving relief aid.

For example, for the week ended 9 January, 33 514 instances were approximately equal to 5587 individuals; for the week ending 30 January 143 144 instances were approximately equivalent to 23 857 individuals. These averages are the *minimum* numbers of individuals, as many would not seek relief every day. Either way, the month of January saw a dramatic increase in the number of Irish recipients of relief. This fact attracted the attention of Albert Austin, Assistant Poor Law Commissioner for the North West, who went to Liverpool to investigate the reason for the escalation in claimants.

Austin was immediately struck not only by the numbers claiming poor relief but also the ratio of children to females among the claimants. In table no 4.1 above, the overall ratio is 3.59:1. This ratio was totally at odds with the official statistics of arrivals. For example, in the period 13 January to 30 April 1847, 41 613 female immigrants entered Liverpool from Ireland, accompanied by 25 540 children. This gives a ratio of children to women of 0.61:1. Based on the January figures Austin quickly concluded that massive fraud was occurring; in fact people were borrowing children in order to make enhanced claims. Given the chaos in Fenwick Street, it's not surprising that fraud took place, including English pretending to be Irish. Many Irish waiting to emigrate to North America and Australia also took the opportunity of using the parish to subsidize their transhipment.

Under the urging of Austin, the Select Vestry moved quickly to tighten up the system, conscious of a rising level of ratepayers' discontent. An Irish famine sub-committee was set up to supervise the giving of relief to the casual Irish applicants for relief. The areas of Liverpool in which most Irish lived were divided up into thirteen districts. In each district a relief office was opened to deal specifically with Irish applicants. In eleven of these districts, two assistant relieving officers were appointed to oversee the giving of relief, in the other two, each had one overseer. The size of each district was based on the estimated numbers of Irish living in them. Many of the extra relieving officers were policeman, seconded from the borough police force specially for the period of the crisis. Supervising the thirteen district offices and the new twenty four relieving officers, were two inspectors, one each for the north and south end of the town. Their principal responsibility was to co-ordinate the flow of information from the relief officers to the Select Vestry, the body with final responsibility for the administration of poor relief. Within each of the eleven most populated relief districts, there was a further sub-division into two halves, each supervised by an overseer. Under the new system, each assistant relieving officer had a book in which the name of every applicant for relief was to be entered, the amount of relief given, together with the number, age and sex of any children. Those seeking help had to apply every morning at the relief office of the district in which he or she resided. All applicants had to be visited in the place at which they resided and, in general, the relief tickets for bread, soup, clothes, medicine, or alternatively, money, were distributed at the district office. The relieving officers were instructed to acquaint themselves with the places in which the Irish lived, including lodging houses and cellars. In particular they were told to visit every case of sickness they heard of, without waiting for a formal application for relief. The objective of the new system was twofold. First to cut down on fraudulent claims and second, to minimize the chances of paupers dying because the parochial officers, in the confused, chaotic condition of the slums, did not know they were ill. The members of the Select Vestry were particularly sensitive to accusations of neglect and indifference to suffering. The new system, a total overhauling of the previous system, was a direct response to the famine crisis, and its thoroughness was indicative of the alarm felt by the authorities concerning the scale of the problem.

The reorganisation was justified immediately on its implementation. On 1 February 1847, relief in the form of soup and bread was given to 3496 Irish males, 3592 Irish females and 15 260 Irish children, a total of 22 348 individuals. The new scheme was introduced on 2 February with startling results. The numbers of Irish receiving bread and soup was 895 males, 1283 females and 2818 children, a total of 4996. This was a fall of 82 per cent in the numbers of children previously claimed for and 78 per cent overall. It is particularly important to note that because of the rigorous inspection of claims introduced on 2 February, many Irish were scared off applying because they thought they ran the risk of being sent back to Ireland under the laws of settlement and removal. Though Austin's reforms succeeded in almost eliminating fraudulent claims, the number of genuine claims continued to rise, but a slower rate. During the first four months of 1847, the *daily* number of Irish receiving relief peaked at 10895 on 10 April. It needs to be kept in mind that the scale of outdoor relief available to an individual was minimal, enough to stave off death from starvation and, it was hoped, not appealing enough to attract new paupers from Ireland nor encourage malingering in Liverpool. The parish cuisine, even for the hungry, was not appetizing. The soup distributed by the Select Vestry was made of fish, mixed with pimento and treacle. A ticket gave a person the right to quart of this concoction, as well as a portion of bread. The best available evidence of the numbers of Irish-born individuals receiving relief in Liverpool during 1847 is 47 194. However it is certain that this number was a minimum. The chaos of the early months meant that many cases were not recorded and the true figure is likely to have been 50 000 or more.[12] The statistics of Irish poor relief given above are necessary in order to establish the parameters of sensible discussion. During the whole of 1847, the parish of Liverpool provided outdoor relief for (at a minimum) 47 194 individuals born in Ireland, at a cost, excluding medical services and overhead charges, of £20 750.[13] There is no evidence that the Irish paupers received significantly less aid than the non-Irish but the fact remains that the level of relief was minimal. For example, for the week ending 21 March 1847, the expenditure on 9503 individuals was one shilling, twopence and one farthing per head.[14] However, necessary though the statistics are, they have a certain one dimensional character: references to 'numbers of Irish relieved' impart little flavour of the reality of life for the individuals who made up the numbers. The reasons why we know so little of the majority of actors in the drama are fairly obvious but it is possible to get some idea of the qualitative nature of the Irish immigrant experience in Britain at this particular time.

III

We have already noted the wretched conditions on the cross channel steamers, the desperate nature of the pre-famine Irish settlements, and the options open to the destitute immigrant with regard to a survival strategy on landing at Liverpool. The pressing need, particularly during the winter months, was overnight shelter and for those at the bottom of the economic pile, the lodging house or the night asylum were often the first choices available, at about 1d per person per night. Thus, sevenpence from the parish would secure a bed for seven nights, usually shared with a least one other person. The lodging houses were desperate places *before* the famine crisis and Dr Duncan was familiar with them in his official capacity. In the course of a survey of Liverpool's community health in 1844, he described them:

> ... with regard to individual dwellings, it is in the 'lodging houses' - usually situated in the front street, but sometimes in the courts - that the overcrowding of inmates is carried to the highest pitch. The worst description of houses of this type are kept by Irishmen, and they are resorted to by the migratory Irish, among others, who may, perhaps, not remain more than a night or two in the town, as well as by vagrants and vagabonds of all descriptions. In every room of such houses, with the exception of the kitchen or cooking room, the floor is usually covered with bedsteads, each of which receives at night, as many human beings as can be crowded into it; and this too, without any distinction of sex or regard to decency. But there are cellars, usually the double cellars I have described, which are used for the same purpose... At night the floor of these cellars - often bare earth - is covered with straw and there the

lodgers - all who can afford to pay a penny for the accommodation - arrange themselves as best they may, until scarcely a single available inch of space is left unoccupied. In this way as many as 30 human beings or more are sometimes packed together underground, each inhaling the poison which his neighbour generates, and presenting a picture in miniature of the Black Hole of Calcutta.[15]

The extraordinary numbers coming ashore in 1847 greatly exacerbated an already bad situation. The press provided plenty of examples of the problem facing the Select Vestry, both before and after its tightly organized relief operation was functioning. On 20 November 1846, a group of Irish, mainly women and children, appeared in court before Rushton, charged with begging in the street. Their clothing was described as rags. One old woman, with five children, claimed they literally had had nothing to eat and were subsisting on water. In its report of this case, the *Liverpool Journal* wrote:

> Mayo and Roscommon seem to be the principal counties in Ireland which at present are sending us their pauper population in droves and the cost per head of sending these unfortunate people back again to the harbour of Westport, which lies on the west coast of Ireland, is becoming enormous. Its seems the creatures do not come here from Westport but they walk to Dublin on foot and they come here from Dublin. How they manage to pay their passage is a mystery to Mr Rushton and the Parish Office, for when landed on our quays, they are in a most destitute condition, seldom or never having even so much as sixpence in their possession.[16]

However, the physically debilitating effort of walking from Mayo or Cork to Dublin, followed by the gruelling conditions on board the steamers, guaranteed that Liverpool would have a major humanitarian relief problem on its doorstep. The evidence is overwhelming in support of the proposition that the situation in Liverpool was unprecedented. The examples that follow should not obscure the fact that people endured much suffering without actually dying. Mary Maganey of Vauxhall Road, was found dead in bed. It was claimed that all she had consumed over a three or four day period, was a cup of tea.[17] Soon after, an unknown man was found on the pavement in Marybone, the heart of Irish Liverpool. He was dead on arrival at hospital and the inquest verdict, delivered 26 January, was death from starvation. At the inquest the coroner absolved the relieving officers from any blame. He acknowledged that they were struggling with the hordes of immigrants asking for relief. Currie, the coroner, claimed it was the seventh case within the last few weeks and he expressed the view that many people in Liverpool were on the point of starvation.[18] At about the same time, an Irish woman collapsed outside the Waterloo Hotel, her baby and a four year old standing over her. A crowd gathered and a passerby gave her the money to go to the night asylum.[19] Dennis Curran, his wife and six children had arrived in Liverpool on Christmas Eve, 1846, with eight shillings to support the family. They took a cellar in Ashby Street, having by now only three shillings left. Curran made this money last as long as possible and did not apply for parish outdoor relief, probably out of fear of being sent back to Ireland. On 7 January, his son Patrick died. Richard Hobson, surgeon, declared it to be death by starvation, 'one of the worst cases I have ever seen'. On the day of Patrick's death, all the family had were three pounds of bread to support eight people.[20] On the same day, another inquest in Liverpool was held on the death of nine month old Mary Brady. Her father, mother and four children occupied a cellar in Lace Street, notoriously the most unhealthy street in Liverpool. The verdict was death from starvation, and it was claimed that if the parish overseers had not intervened, they would all have died.[21]

Anthony Cawley arrived in Liverpool from Ireland sometime in December 1846, with a pound in his pocket. He managed to survive on this for a while, without asking for parochial relief. On Sunday 1 February 1847 his wife arrived from Ireland and 'joined him in a cellar in Dolling Street' on 3 February. Cawley applied for parochial relief to Mr Tompkins, a Toxteth Park relieving officer. Tompkins went to the cellar to investigate the family's circumstances, in accordance with the new procedures just implemented. He found Mrs Cawley on a bed with a child. On starting to leave he noticed a bundle of rags which aroused his curiosity and on examining it, found it was the corpse of a child. Cawley had not mentioned the child's death to Tompkins and it was not clear what he planned to do. The subsequent inquest verdict was 'death from starvation'. At the inquest, the coroner asked Gilmour, one of the parochial surgeons, what he intended to do about the parents, who were both in a bad way. Gilmour replied that as they were not on his list, he would not do anything. The coroner threatened him with legal action if he did nothing and this threat moved Gilmour to action.[22] Later the same month, an Irishman named Dowling, his wife and five children walked into one of the district relieving offices, the wife carrying a dead child. They had travelled to Liverpool on the steamer *St Patrick* and the child died immediately on the family coming ashore. The parish provided a pauper funeral.[23] The Judge family left Sligo on 23 March 1847, travelling on the steamer *Rover* for Liverpool. Two year old Michael Judge took ill and asked for water. His mother asked members of the crew for water but, it was alleged, they refused unless the Judge family paid for it. (This was a common complaint against the crews of steamers.) They no money and it was only the intervention of a fellow passenger that resulted in the mother obtaining water for the child. Despite this the child died before reaching Liverpool and the parish had another pauper funeral.[24]

The inquest verdicts at this period seem strange, reflecting the fact that deaths were rarely recorded as from starvation but more usually as from famine related conditions. The death of two year old Michael Judge was recorded as ' death from disease of the bowels'. Soon after the death of Michael Judge, a policeman was patrolling his beat in London Road, a main road leading out of Liverpool. He noticed a woman sitting on a step, holding a baby. He ordered her to move on but on returning he noticed she was still there. The baby was dead. It transpired she was an Irishwoman and at the inquest, the verdict was that the cause of death was by diarrhoea. The mother did not turn up for the inquest.[25] Less than a month later, another inquest was held, this time on the death of Mary Hasien. Mary had arrived in Liverpool from Ireland sometime in March. On 12 April she went to lodge in a house in Roe Street but became ill soon after. The landlord turned her out, probably because he suspected typhus, a common fear. She could not walk and died in the street. The inquest verdict was 'death from natural causes - inflammation of the lungs'. There was no reference to the conduct of the landlord.[26] Eleven year Deborah Cummins came ashore in Liverpool from the steamer *Limerick.* She immediately went to lodgings in Barter Street and died the following morning, verdict 'died from disease of the bowels'[27]

Despite a number of such inquests it was the death of eight year old Luke Brothers which awakened middle-class Liverpool to the desperate social conditions existing in the town. The Brothers family, father, mother and several children, arrived in Liverpool from Ireland, already ill. They acquired a cellar in Banastre Street, in the Vauxhall district of Liverpool. The father applied to the district relieving officer for parochial aid and was given three shillings. All the family went down with typhus and could rarely leave the cellar, which had a mud floor. Occasionally, during this period, the children would go out begging even though ill. Luke Brothers, died on 1 May. The surgeon attending the family said the corpse was surrounded by five other typhus victims and that the room was unfit for human habitation. Under questioning by the coroner, Joseph Bleven, the relieving officer pointed out that he was working seven days a week and simply could not visit all those at risk, as laid down under the new scheme of administering poor relief. The borough coroner was so appalled by the case that he urged all the members of the press to give maximum publicity to the case, 'in the hope that some speedy measures would be taken by the authorities to arrest the progress of the dreadful state of things by which we are surrounded'. Mr Christmas Humphries the surgeon carried out a post mortem and declared that the boy's stomach was 'totally devoid of food' and the inquest verdict was 'death of starvation'. The coroner ordered the jury to accompany him to the cellar in Banastre Street. His verdict after the visit was that it' was not fit for pigs' and that the Brothers' family would have been better off if they had slept on the quayside, under a piece of sailcloth. Not content with forcing the members of the jury to visit the cellar, the coroner also went to see the Mayor and described the conditions in which people were living in Banastre Street. While there he met a member of the Select Vestry who was 'astonished' to hear that such an environment existed in Liverpool. The *Liverpool Albion* in its reporting of the case commented that there were not many on the Select Vestry who visited the miserable hovels in which so many of the recipients of relief existed.[28] The incredulity expressed by the Select Vestry member illustrates the fact that despite the contiguity of the social classes, there existed a deep social apartheid, bridged only by the reports of the various social investigators, parish employees or the press. On 5 June Nancy Doherty and her daughter went to the Night Asylum in the hope of getting a bed for the night. It was full up and so they slept in the street with other destitute people. In the morning Nancy was dead; inquest verdict 'natural causes'. In fact her lungs were diseased, a famine related condition.[29] The famine also claimed victims among those passing through Liverpool. David McCarthy was a twenty-two year old Irishman who boarded the emigrant ship *James Moran*, in the Waterloo dock. He died on board before she sailed and the inquest verdict was 'death from the want of food and disease of the lungs.[30] The examples given above are intended to give some feeling for the reality behind the statistics of relief. These people fell through the poor relief net but even for those who were in receipt of relief, life was extremely wretched, hard and precarious. For the timid and respectable fallen on hard times, existence in Liverpool's cellars, courts and lodging houses was brutalising and fearful. Though, by 2 February, the Select Vestry had implemented an efficient system of giving outdoor relief, the volume of applications remained at well above pre-famine levels. In the case of the Irish, many of these were long term residents who had gained the status of 'irremovability' (see chapter eight) However, in the heated debate over the rates burden, the distinction between irremovable and casual Irish relief was lost. Despite the rebuttal of their previous memorial to the Home Secretary, the Select Vestry, on 26 January, drew up another memorial, this time to the House of Commons, asking for legislation, arguing that because of the accident of geography, Liverpool should not have to bear, unassisted, the consequence of unrestricted Irish immigration. At the meeting held to draw up the memorial, it was suggested that, as legislation was being sought, a meeting of all ratepayers ought to be involved in signing the memorial. This was unanimously agreed.[31] In the meantime Augustus Campbell wrote again to the Home Secretary. In the course of repeating the mantra concerning Liverpool's rates burden, he asked for restrictions to be placed on the policy of the steamship companies carrying paupers to Liverpool at low prices. He explained that fraud was widespread and there was a need to be discerning in giving relief:

> The position of the Select Vestry is, therefore, very painful to them; they know it is their duty as guardians of the poor, and it must be their desire as Christian men, to relieve real destitution and prevent the probability of starvation; but while they owe this duty to the casual Irish poor, they feel that they owe a higher duty to their own settled poor, and that they are under very serious moral and legal obligations to their own ratepayers, as trustees of the parochial funds.

He informed Sir George Grey that there was a real fear in the town of typhus and, by implication, the Irish immigrants posed the biggest threat; he told of forty-one people being found in one house and the average degree of overcrowding was twenty-five: '...the working classes are becoming exasperated at the supposed preference of Irish to English poor. The ratepayers are becoming clamorous under a sense of injustice by which they think that they are made to pay such an undue proportion of what they consider at least to be a national burden'.[32]

Though this letter had no more effect than the memorial sent in December 1846, it was a clear statement of the ratepayers' views of the problem. On a priori grounds, one would have expected such a reaction on the part of ratepayers yet other views were also expressed. Three months later in contrast to Campbell's views, Edward Rushton told a select committee that the working classes had responded with 'the greatest possible kindness' to the Irish, with no hard feelings. Subsequent events in Liverpool showed that the patrician Campbell, remote from contact with the masses, was nearer the truth with regard to the reactions of the working classes to mass immigration.[33]

Events in Liverpool were being watched closely throughout the country and the *London Times* of 1 February praised Liverpool citizens for their generosity towards the Irish and said it was an example the whole empire 'must take and endure in this unparalleled act of relief'. The same day, Lord Brougham presented a petition from the Select Vestry to the House of Lords but in his speech, he appeared to defend the Irish landlords. This elicited a ferocious attack on him in *The Times* the next day.

> There's comfort for Liverpool. Did the Mayor, magistrates and respectable inhabitants of that city expect their advocate would wind up

> their case with the grand principle of leaving the poor to shift for themselves... Liverpool happens just now to have the full benefit of the two systems... It feeds its own poor by the protective laws of this country and receives a free trade importation of Irish misery. Giving the poor no inducement to stay at home and every faculty for going abroad is not the way to help that port just at this moment.

What was clear by February 1847 was that Liverpool was to get no special treatment from central government. However, political pressure on Westminster was to pay off, in that by June, changes in the law regarding the Irish poor law and also removal, brought about nationally, a reduction in claims for poor relief on the part of Irish famine refugees.

IV

The parochial authorities in Glasgow faced the same kind of difficulties that the Select Vestry in Liverpool was struggling with but with two additional problems. First, simultaneously with the famine Irish immigration, large numbers of Highlanders were flooding into the city and its suburbs. Many of them spoke only Gaelic, adding to the difficulties of providing poor relief. Second, the 1845 reforms of the poor law system in Scotland had produced administrative repercussions which had not been fully absorbed by the time the Irish famine refugee problem erupted. A significant difference in the Scots system of relief was that voluntary contributions by ratepayers were still a feature of the system in 1847, a totally inadequate source of crisis funding.[34] Despite these drawbacks the poor law authorities in Glasgow city, Barony and Govan parishes had the same legal obligation as the English authorities to provide relief irrespective of the settlement status of those seeking help.

The organisation of relief in Glasgow in 1847 involved two lists of paupers, regular and casual poor. In January the applications for relief were heard only once a week. In the crisis such an interval of time between hearing applications was unacceptable. Huge crowds of Irish and Highlanders blocked the street outside the office of the Glasgow Parochial Board, estimated at up to one thousand at a time. Under such pressure the granting of relief orders was changed to three times a week. The Night Refuge was besieged by so many Irish poor that the police were necessary to maintain order.[35] On 21 January 75 cases of destitute persons were up before the Lieutenant at the Glasgow Police Office charged with begging. On 22 January, two hundred, men, women and children were brought before the magistrates, all on begging charges and all in a very poor physical condition.[36] The seriousness of the situation was quickly recognized, composed as it was not only of Irish and Highland refugees, but a significant amount of indigenous poverty. At the beginning of January, a soup kitchen had been opened at the Night Asylum in St Enoch's Square. One penny bought a bowl of soup and a piece of bread and over the six days ending 23 January, 2371 tickets were sold. During the next two weeks, the numbers of tickets sold were 4513 and 5740 respectively. Reporting on these statistics, the *Glasgow Chronicle* observed that the majority buying tickets were Irish, 'emaciated by disease and want'.[37] There is no doubt that this soup kitchen kept many alive who would otherwise have perished.

During a three week period ending 13 February, 786 individuals were arrested for begging and of this number, 76 per cent were Irish. It was at this early stage in the crisis that adverse press comments began to appear, containing a combination of sympathy, exasperation with behaviour of Irish landlords and alarm over the probable financial consequences of the famine immigration. *The Glasgow Herald*, commenting on the 786 arrests for begging, opined:

> ...these investigations are most irksome and thankless, which the magistrates engage in; but unless the city is to be over run with stranger vagrants, as Liverpool has been, this course of procedure must be followed, and rigidly too. No doubt there is much actual suffering among this new class of pauper, and a pity it is so but the Glasgow public cannot be expected to carry its charity so far as to exempt the pockets of Irish landlords at the expense of increased privation and bitterness on the part of those who have long resided among us.[38]

This comment is interesting on a number of counts. Explicitly, it recognizes the Irish famine refugees as 'a new class of paupers'. Implicit, is the idea that there is a fixed sum available for poor relief and that the more is spent on relieving the Irish poor, the less there is for the Scots poor. The Glaswegian poor were going to bear the burden resulting from the incompetence and recklessness of Irish landlords. Of course, there was an alternative to such an outcome, the burden be shifted on to the ratepayers of Glasgow city, Govan and Barony. In the event, this is what actually happened. Also the press report did not seem to recognize that the magistrates could not solve the problem. The beggars could not pay fines and there was not the space available in local gaols to make imprisonment a feasible option. Even if prison had been an option, it would not have discouraged begging, being a preferable alternative to life on the streets. Liverpool had learned that particular lesson. Not even removal of beggars to Ireland was a viable alternative (see chapter eight). Baillie Liddell told the Glasgow Parochial Board on 15 February that the police could not accommodate those families arrested for begging, sometimes numbering two hundred in a day.[39] In the six week period ending 27 February, 1245 individuals had been arrested for begging. Of this total, 938 were Irish, described as 'ill and desperate'.[40] The authorities sent 163 back to Ireland.[41] A woman arrested at this time said that she, her husband and children had come from Derry only four days before. They had two pounds in money when they left Ireland and had paid six shillings for the steamer fare. After three days in Glasgow that money had gone and so they had been forced to beg.[42]

The accelerating magnitude of the relief problem facing Glasgow city parish was revealed at a meeting of the Parochial Board held 5 March. The members present were told that the total number of those classified as 'casual poor' and receiving relief during January had been 4541. During February, the number had risen to 6000. The financial cost of the January relief had been £700 while an additional £133 was spent on removing some of the Irish back to Ireland. What proportion of the relief expenditure was spent on Irish refugees was not stated but all the available evidence suggests that it was a very significant amount. At the same meeting, a report was tabled by members of a Board sub-committee charged with levying the poor rate. This report, while acknowledging the sufferings of our 'fellow subjects', went on to claim that the Irish were importing disease and were absorbing a large proportion of the funds available for relieving the indigenous poor. Most worrying of all, in the view of the authors of the report, the Irish 'were setting a most pernicious example to the lower orders of Glasgow'.[43] In effect, the charge levied against the Irish famine refugees was that they were showing the Scots poor how to become welfare dependent, echoes of James Phillips Kay in Manchester. As in other places, exasperation with the Irish in Glasgow was fuelled by press stories of Irish persons claiming poor relief when in fact they had money. For example, *The Glasgow Herald* 15 February reported the case of a 'wretched' looking Irishman who had asked for relief. He told the Relieving Officer that he and his family had not eaten for two days and that he and his children were suffering from the famine. When searched by the Relieving Officer, he was found to have five shillings and tenpence. He was sent back to Ireland and his money was confiscated as a contribution to the parish's expense in paying for the steamer fare. *The Glasgow Chronicle* 10 March carried the story of an Irishman who travelled from Ardrossan to Glasgow by train. He avoided paying for the rail fare but was arrested at Glasgow station. The point of the story was that he was 'emaciated' but was found to have twenty pounds in his pockets. The report of the sub-committee referred to above concluded that while the famine Irish continued to arrive on the Clyde in such large numbers, it was impossible to 'raise the temporal and spiritual condition of the lower orders of this city'. On the 5 March 1847, the town council discussed the problems posed by the influx of Irish paupers.

Table 4.2 The number of Irish paupers receiving relief in Glasgow and the surrounding parishes over the period 1-29 January in each of the years 1846 and 1847.

Parish	*Nos. receiving relief*		*1847 as %*
	1846	*1847*	*of 1846*
Glasgow	765	4541	594
Barony	395	1966	498
Govan	111	581	523
Total	1271	7088	558

Source: *Glasgow Herald* 5 March 1847, Report on the meeting of the town council held 4 March, 1847.

The parish of Glasgow experienced both the largest, absolute increase in numbers and also the greatest percentage increase. In each of the three parishes, the large increases in the number of paupers receiving relief reflected *both* the increase in Irish famine immigrants *and* the arrival of people from the Scottish highlands escaping from the consequences of failed crops. The evidence suggests that the Irish accounted for the larger part of the increase. Over the period referred to in Table 4.2, the number of Scots receiving relief increased by only 168 per cent. At the same time as the town council of Glasgow was given this report, the Parochial Board of Glasgow was told that an additional rate would have to be levied because the increased level of claims for relief was expected to continue.

The estimated shortfall in revenue was given as £8 500 and it was anticipated that a penny rate would have brought in £10 867.[44] The various local authorities on Clydeside were aware of Liverpool's attempts to obtain central government financing of its expenditure on the famine refugees. Equally, they were also aware that such attempts had failed and this discouraged them from trying the same tactic. Instead, attention was concentrated on a policy of pressuring central government to change the Irish poor law. On 27 March, Glasgow Parochial Board drew up a petition to Parliament on this issue. In the preamble, they laid out their view of the cause of Glasgow's social and financial problems:

> That your petitioners, as the representatives of the ratepayers of this populous city parish, in the discharge of their arduous and responsible duties imposed on them as managers' of the poor's fund, experience much difficulty and annoyance, as well as an unprecedented increase of expenditure, arising almost entirely from the extraordinary influx of impotent, infantile and diseased Irish paupers into this passage.[45]

Here we have again the view that the majority of the paupers claiming casual relief were Irish and that they brought disease with them. Despite the increased amount of indigenous poverty *and* the invasion of distressed Highlanders, the Irish famine refugees are picked out as *the problem* facing Glasgow. Like similar petitions elsewhere, it was aimed at changes in the Irish poor law which would transfer the burden of Irish poverty in Glasgow back on to the Irish landlords. To this end, it was good tactics in blaming the Irish for the difficulties that Glasgow was experiencing. The resentments against the Irish landlords were further fuelled by the continued circulation of rumours that the landlords were financing the paupers' steamer fares to Glasgow. This belief was shared by the ratepayers of Liverpool, Cardiff and Newport. For example, four 'stout' Irishmen arrived in Glasgow, hungry. They went into an eating house, consumed a meal and refused to pay. On being arrested they claimed that their steamer fares to Glasgow had been paid by 'gentlemen' in Ireland.[46] As in many similar instances, they could not, or would not, remember the name of the person who paid their fares.

In chapter two, the physical environment of Glasgow was examined and the picture which emerged was one of unremitting poverty-stricken housing and the lack of sanitation and water characteristic of mid-nineteenth century towns. The Irish famine immigration caused ever greater overcrowding. The number of cellars in Glasgow was less than in Liverpool and so lodging houses became even more overcrowded.

At the beginning of April 1847, there were in Glasgow, 915 lodging houses in the area of High Street, the Wynds, Bridgegate, Gallowgate and the Salt Market. These had 2848 beds which, because of multiple occupancy, provided a total of 3136 lodgings. Together with the lodging houses, the Night Asylum took the brunt of the famine immigration but severe overcrowding took place everywhere in the accommodation market. In one instance, 17 persons were reported as living in a garret.[47] We have already noted that in 1847, 50 000 Irish paupers landed at Glasgow. The only available official statistics reveal that in 1847, the city of Glasgow parish gave relief to 17 864 Irish. The cost to Glasgow parish arising from the relief operation was £20 031.13s.9d. In neighbouring Barony parish, 13 952 received relief at a cost of £9092 4s. The average cost for Glasgow parish was £1. 3s. 4d. compared with 13s.3d. in Barony. However, too much cannot be made of these statistics in the absence of other statistical data.[48] As in all the other crisis centres, the level of relief per head was small though not significantly different to the payments to the non-Irish paupers. It is certain that the relief payments and soup and bread, though keeping people alive, could do little to ameliorate the awfulness of the physical environment.

V

With regard to the ports of Cardiff, Swansea and Newport, there is a relative paucity of data and anecdotal evidence relating to the events of 1847. The regional economy had received a boost with the completion of the Bute dock at Cardiff in 1839 and the Taff Vale railway in 1841. In 1841, the population of the borough of Cardiff (St John's and St Mary's parish) was 10 077 and the Irish-born population was recorded in the 1841 census as numbering 965. The population of the borough of Swansea was 16 787 of which number 428 were born in Ireland. The town of Newport's population in 1841 was 8225. The increase in population in the region between 1831 and 1841 reflected the railway and dock construction works and the growth in the iron and coal industries.[49]

Table 4.3 The number of passengers landed at Newport from Irish ports during the years 1849-53 inclusive.

Month	*1849*	*1850*	*1851*	*1852*	*1853*
January	21	43	-	52	85
February	344	195	33	135	165
March	169	705	178	43	150
April	259	438	342	602	1558
May	534	421	744	1183	1344
June	345	157	978	564	1005
July	-	34	909	342	377
August	-	34	297	40	52
September	-	40	80	12	58
October	-	21	106	47	18
November	-	32	59	32	-
December	30	20	13	-	-
Total	1702	2140	3739	3052	4812

Source: BPP (HC) 1854 (300) LV, 'Report of the Number of Poor Brought Over to the Ports of Liverpool, Glasgow, Swansea, Neath and Newport over the last Five Years'.

Newport seems to have been the major port of entry for the Irish during the famine years. No official data exists with respect to arrivals from Ireland before 1849. Using the number of vessels entering in at Newport in 1847 as a base, then an *upper limit* in terms of estimated arrivals is 19 275.[50] None of these ports were significantly involved in the emigration business and so most people coming ashore from Irish vessels would have been refugees from the famine. The exception would have been harvesters, but in 1847 the people who normally came as harvesters would also have been feeling the effects of the famine. Table 4.3 above gives the arrivals at

Newport from Ireland over the period 1849-53. Given the fact that five months data is missing from 1849 figures, it is certain that the total was greater than 1702. A figure of 2000 does not seem unreasonable. Whatever the correct figure it is certain it was much less than the unknown total of arrivals at Newport during 1847. Speaking in 1854, John Salter, relieving officer at Newport, stated nothing that had occurred since 1847 had been so bad.[51] The estimated 19 275 arrivals given above does not look unreasonable when placed against the number of applications for relief, there being some correlation between the number of arrivals in 1847 and Irish claims for outdoor relief.

Table 4.4: The number of Irish poor relieved at Newport over the period 1848-53 inclusive.

Year	*Number of applications*
1848	12 661
1849	11 007
1850	7 713
1851	4 992
1852	6 698
1853	3 299

Source: SC (1854) Minutes of Evidence, J. Salter, q. 6778, p.496. Salter provided the statistics for 1849-53. For the year 1848 the source is Irish Poor (1848).

In 1847, the total number of persons relieved at the Newport House of Refuge was 25 319. If we assume that 75 per cent of these were Irish, then we obtain an estimate of 18 989 Irish applications for relief. This does not seem unreasonable and is probably on the low side. We know that during the first 21 weeks of 1847, W. Harries, the relieving officer at Newport Union, handled 11 000 Irish applications for relief. Over a year, this would total 27 238.[52] As late as 1852, the 6698 Irish applications for relief represented 60 per cent of all applications.[53] For these reasons the estimate of 19 275 arrivals based on ships docking from Ireland in 1847, does not seem unduly exaggerated. The fall off in applications for relief in 1848 is what one would expect given the change in the law regarding removals. As we observed in the case of Liverpool, Irish applications for relief fell significantly in 1848. The argument that Newport was the most important regional port for the famine Irish during the famine is supported when the data concerning relief in Cardiff is examined.

The 18 month period month ending 25 March 1848 covered the 1847 crisis and the total number of Irish relieved in Cardiff township was 4775. This was obviously far fewer than is the case of Newport. This was no short term phenomenon. The number of applications for the year ending 25 March 1850 was 3152 compared with 11 007 in Newport during 1849.

Table 4.5 The number of Irish relieved in the township of Cardiff, 30 September 1846 to 30 September 1851.

Period	*Numbers relieved*
Half year ending 25 March 1847	1804
Year ending 25 March 1848	2971
Year ending 25 March 1849	2219
Year ending 25 March 1850	3152
Half year ending 30 September 1850	1308

Source: SC (1854) Appendix 14, p.612.

In chapter three, evidence from newspapers was provided concerning the wretched state of many of the refugees travelling to South Wales and Newport. This receives support from official quarters. W.Boase was a poor law official who was given the job of examining the vagrancy problem in England and Wales during 1847 and the early months of 1848. Famine Irish immigrants were included in the investigation. Boase was unequivocal in his opinion that no one knew how many Irish came ashore in South Wales during 1847. He had himself witnessed arrivals at the docks in the region and he reported that '...a great many harvesters land at South Wales ports, but by far the greater proportion of the Irish I saw in Wales were women with small children, old men, apparently feeble; pregnant women, and girls and boys about ten years old'.[54]

Boase's views on the make up of the immigrants was shared by Mr John, relieving officer at Cardiff in 1847.[55] In his final report to the Poor Law Board in London, Boase went on to draw contrasts between the Irish landing in South Wales and those coming ashore at Liverpool:

> Indeed the contrasts between the Irish immigrants at Liverpool and in Wales is most striking, the former, by their own account, come from the distant part of Ireland, walking from Mayo to Drogheda, and from Roscommon and Sligo, to take ship which none but the able bodied could do. And they really are, judging from what I have seen, chiefly lusty young men, willing to work and unencumbered by women and children. But on the contrary, those landing in Wales are nearly all helpless and burdensome to the community. The incredible number of widows, with three or four small children who came over to 'get a bit for the children', others professing to be married women whose husbands are supposed to be in London, young girls and boys looking for parents, brothers and uncles who may or may not be found.[56]

Boase's views on the condition of the Irish coming ashore in Wales is similar to other opinions but his statement that the Irish arriving in

Liverpool were bursting with health is ludicrous. It can be only explained in terms of his observing some arrivals of harvesters and even such people suffered from the famine. Also Liverpool was the main port for Irish emigrating to North America and Australia and these were probably in a better state of health than the paupers. Few emigrants went via South Wales. John Salter, recalling 1847 in Newport, remembered the relieving officer's house being under seige '... with these poor creatures in the street, who were evidently in the greatest want and the greatest state of sickness with fever raging'.[57] Jeremiah Box Stockdale was the superintendent of police in Cardiff in 1847 and describing the Irish coming ashore, recalled '...many of them apparently starving and in an advanced state of disease'.[58]

The principal source of temporary accommodation for the newly arrived Irish in Newport was the House of Refuge. This was managed by a policeman, Sergeant Huxtable and his wife Harriet acted as matron. An applicant for relief went to the house of W.W.Harries, relieving officer, and obtained a ticket, enabling him or her to sleep at the House of Refuge. On 27 May, Harries complained to the Poor Law Board in London, '... the immigration of Irish has caused me an immense increase of labour to me, having relieved 11 000 since the first of January'.[59] After receiving a ticket from Harries, paupers went to the House of Refuge for food and from there to a converted former police station which would accommodate 200. Those who did not then move on were sent to work at the workhouse.[60] Persons staying at the House of Refuge slept on the floor. An indication of the severity of Newport's problem is the fact that during 1846, the House of Refuge provided relief for 3953 persons. The corresponding figure for 1847 was 25 319, a 651 per cent increase.[61] The view that the majority of Irish were transients, using Newport as a brief stopover, is reinforced by the level of relief provided. For example, during 1848, 12 661 Irish received relief at Newport at a cost of threepence halfpenny per head.[62] This meant that the applicants were given soup and bread and a floor to sleep on before they moved inland.

The Irish refugees arriving in Cardiff made for those streets which already had an Irish presence, reinforced by labourers working on the construction of the Taff Vale railway. The burgeoning Irish settlement was centred on Stanley Street, David Street, Love Lane, Landore Court, Little Frederick Street, Whitmore Lane and Newtown.[63] The condition of these streets replicated the conditions of the slums in other towns of the time. In Stanley Street it was claimed that it was the custom for four or five families to sleep in one room. In number 17, Stanley Street, Michael Harrington ran a lodging house, 54 people were observed to lived in one room measuring 15'10" by 17'2" by 8'6".[64] The Catholic chapel of St David's was sited at the corner of Stanley Street and David Street, in the centre of the growing

Irish Catholic settlement.[65] It too, like the relieving officer's home, would be a destination of those newly arrived Irish needing help and advice.

As in other regions of Britain, there was in Wales an initial upsurge in sympathy for the Irish in Ireland and the Highlanders in Scotland. This sympathy was reinforced by the distressing scenes witnessed at the ports of arrival. Illustrative of the Welsh response was the meeting held 18 January 1847. James Lewis, the Mayor of Cardiff, chaired a meeting to raise money for the Irish and Scots.[66] A similar meeting was held at Merthyr Tydfil on 21 January while at Dowlais the Reverend Daniel Roberts addressed a similar meeting in Welsh.[67] Soon after, a Welsh Calvinist chapel raised two guineas while a meeting at Aberdare on 9 February raised 20 pounds (this was equal to a week's wages for each of twenty labourers).[68] Any antagonism to Roman Catholicism was swept aside by a wave of horror and compassion. Equally, the reaction of the local press reflected the nationwide, ambiguous attitudes of the indigenous population towards the Irish generally and the refugees in particular. The belief that the Irish were welfare dependent, irrespective of the famine, was widespread and the press continually highlighted what they believed to be examples of an Irish propensity to abuse British hospitality'. There was also the inevitable resentment felt by some of the indigenous poor at what was perceived to be the draining of the available poor relief to support strangers. On 25 February 1847, the *Bristol Gazette* carried a networked report from the *Monmouthshire Merlin* describing the situation in Newport with respect to Irish refugees ... cast as most of them have been, brutally on our shores, emaciated and in many instances diseased, they find the hope of employment an empty vision'. The paper went on to describe the 'indefatigable efforts of Sergeant Huxtable and his wife' in managing the House of Refuge and commenting on the cost to Newport ratepayers.

> ...this is a matter of lasting credit to our town and we praise God, that we may be enabled to keep life in these miserable strangers until better times arrive, but it cannot be disguised that the poor of the place complain bitterly of the increased privations brought upon them; and that many persons who have thus been subscribers to the very munificent relief fund of above £1000 - a larger sum, by the way, than the Irish landlords of half a dozen counties have contributed - consider that Newport has been very ungratefully treated by those communities in the sister isle.

Three weeks later, the *Gazette* returned to the Irish problem in a leader: '...this is no question of party, sect or class. All feel the pressure...all are interested. Through every pore is felt the exhausting drain of Irish distress and except the property of Ireland is made to bear its share of Irish burden, England will be dragged down to the level of Irish pauperism'.[69]

The Cambrian newspaper complained of the Irish who 'infested' the Greenhill district of Swansea and it took up the increasingly repeated theme that many Irish were claiming relief when in fact they had money.[70] In a later leader article it claimed that the Irish were 'ungrateful'. Paradoxically, such reports of events were side by side with sympathetic reports of the terrible condition of many of the Irish coming ashore. Compassion and exasperation intermingle in the accounts. On 22 February, a young Irishwoman 'whose appearance betokened the utmost wretchedness and physical degradation', gave birth on the mail road near Cardiff bridge. She was removed to the workhouse. The *Cardiff and Merthyr Guardian* claimed that she tried to get out of the workhouse: 'It is surmised by those who profess to know the character of these Irish immigrants that her object in endeavouring to leave her present abode, where she receives proper attention and comfort, was to obtain liberal contributions by retailing her story and sufferings around the town'.

The article contained no factual material whatsoever other than that she gave birth and went into Cardiff workhouse. The rest is, as the article admits, surmise.[71] However, the steady flow of such comments was part of a process which 'constructed' the Irish immigrants for middle class society, a society equally lacking in first hand experience of the indigenous poor. Underlying much of the adverse comment was a deep felt anti-Catholicism. Patrick Keating was searched on applying for relief and found to possess two pounds. *The Cardiff and Merthyr Guardian* described him as '...a newly imported Irishman under the new system adopted by landlords and Catholic priests for transporting paupers to England'.[72] In a case at Cardiff magistrates court in July 1847, a number of Irishmen and women appeared on a charge of fighting in the street. Superintendent Stockdale told the court, 'Oh yes your worship, they always fight after attending Mass'. This was clearly untrue but it was part of the process of constructing the stereotype of Paddy, the fighting Irishman.[73]

The situation in Cardiff, Swansea and Newport in 1847 reflected many of the features of the famine influx crisis in Liverpool and Glasgow. Equally, the evidence is clear that the famine refugee crisis was not over by the end of 1847. Early in May 1849, the dead body of an Irishman was found in an outhouse near Rhumney and it was concluded that he had died of cold and extreme hunger.[74] Soon after an Irish family landed at Cardiff, husband, wife and four children. The husband went immediately to seek work while the woman and children obtained lodgings. Soon after, they were turned out when they could not pay for the night's lodging and they wandered the streets. While trying to find new shelter the youngest child died in the mother's arms. The inquest verdict was 'death by visitation of God'.[75] Evan David, chairman of the Cardiff Board of Guardians, told of a case in the winter of 1853/4 in which a large Irish family landed at Cardiff's dock. They were all in a bad physical condition and were taken in a cart to the relieving officer's house. At this stage, the woman was holding a child that was observed to be in a dying state; hours after being taken into the workhouse, the child died.[76] James Salter, relieving officer at Newport recalled a case he came across in June 1854. The Keene family arrived at Newport from Bantry, man, wife and five children. In Salter's words they were emaciated and Keene himself said they were literally starving. Salter sent the family to the union Hospital, 150 yards from his office but before the family reached the hospital, one of the children died.[77]

In conclusion, the question remains, where in Ireland did the refugees come from? The lack of Bills of Entry for Swansea, Cardiff and Newport makes in impossible to identify the tonnage of shipping arriving at these ports from specific Irish ports of departure. However, the overwhelming body of anecdotal evidence is that the refugees came from Cork and the south eastern counties. Writing in April 1848, W. Boase, told the Poor Law Board that:

> ...a remarkable fact is that all the Irish I met on my route between Wales and London said they came from Cork county. This is also confirmed by the officers who relieve them at Chepstow, Newport and Cardiff. Mr John, relieving officer at the latter place told me, in his examination, that not one out of every hundred of the Irish came from any other county than Cork. There are few Tipperary men but these do not trouble us; they are more industrious in their habits than Cork people.[78]

Finally, the importance of Newport as the port of entry in the South Wales region is emphasized by the official statistics of the number of Irish who received relief at the expense of ratepayers. In 1848, Merthyr Tydfil relieved 1346 Irish paupers, Cardiff 2063, Bristol, 4403, while Newport relieved 12 661.[79]

Appendices

Appendix 4.1 The increase in the numbers of Irish-born persons in the main English counties of Irish settlement: 1841-1851.

County	*1841*	*1851*	*Increase*	%
Durham	5 407	18 501	13 094	242
Staffordshire	4 803	15 858	11 055	230
Northumberland	5 218	12 636	7 418	142
West Riding (Yorks)	15 127	36 307	21 180	140
Derbyshire	1 849	3 979	2 130	115
Cumberland	4 881	9 866	4 985	102
Monmouth	2 925	5 888	2 963	101
Cheshire	11 577	22 812	11 235	97
Lancashire	105 916	191 506	85 590	81
Warwickshire	6 333	11 294	4 961	78
London	82 291	108 548	26 257	32
Gloucestershire	5 778	6 563	785	14
Devonshire	4 084	4 940	856	21
Kent *extra metropolitan*	10 401	8 275	-2126	-20

Source: 1841 Census, Enumeration Abstracts, M.DCCC.XLI. Summary of England, p.399. 1851 Census, Birthplaces of the People, England.

Appendix 4.2: The Irish-born populations of Welsh counties 1841 and 1851, indicating increases over the decade.

County	*1841*	*1851*	*Increase*	%
Anglesey	137	340	203	148
Brecon	282	674	392	139
Cardigan	70	272	202	289
Carmarthen	163	514	351	218
Carnarvon	292	583	291	100
Denbigh	316	1 030	714	226
Flint	370	612	242	65
Glamorgan	3174	9 737	6563	207
Merioneth	52	77	25	48
Montgomery	95	190	95	100
Pembroke	292	703	411	141
Radnor	33	90	57	173
Total	5276	14 822	9546	181

Source: 1841 Census, Enumeration Abstracts, M.DCCC.MLI. Summary of Wales, p.458. 1851 Census, Div.XI, Monmouthshire and Wales, Birthplaces of the People, pp. 887-91.

Appendix 4.3 The numbers of Irish-born in the registration districts of Wales and Monmouthshire: 1851

District no	*District*	*Total pop.*	*Irish-born*	*Irish as %*
576	Chepstow	19 057	248	1.3
577	Monmouth	27 379	152	0.1
578	Abergavenny	59 229	1 733	2.9
579	Pontypool	27 993	1 018	3.6
580	Newport	43 472	2 737	6.3
581	Cardiff	46 491	3 317	7.1
582	Merthyr Tydfil	76 804	3 646	4.7
583	Bridgend	23 422	412	1.8
584	Neath	46 471	993	2.1
585	Swansea	46 907	1 389	3.0
586	Llanelly	23 507	187	0.8
587	Llandovery	15 055	33	0.2
588	Llandilofawr	17 968	43	0.2
589	Curmarthen	38 142	251	0.7
590	Narberth	22 130	40	0.2
591	Pembroke	22 960	322	1.4
592	Haverfordwest	39 382	341	0.9
593	Cardigan	20 186	90	0.4
594	Newcastle-in-Emlyn	20 173	39	0.2
595	Lampeter	9 875	3	-
596	Aberavon	13 224	18	-
597	Aberystwyth	23 753	116	0.5
598	Tregaron	10 404	5	-
599	Builth	8 345	23	0.3
600	Brecknock	18 174	426	2.3
601	Crick-Howell	21 697	213	1.0
602	Hay	10 962	12	-
603	Presteigne	15 149	51	0.3
604	Knighton	9 480	28	0.3
605	Rhagades	6 796	11	0.2
606	Machynelleth	12 116	6	-
607	Newton	25 107	72	0.3
608	Montgomery	20 381	112	0.5
609	Llanfyllin	19 538	15	0.1
610	Holywell	41 047	615	1.5
611	Wrexham	42 295	711	1.7
612	Ruthin	16 853	71	0.4
613	St Asaph	25 288	225	0.9
614	Llanewst	12 479	23	0.2
615	Corwen	15 418	18	-
616	Bala	6 736	13	-
617	Dolgelly	12 971	19	-
618	Festiniog	16 182	23	0.2
619	Pwllheli	21 788	16	-
620	Carnarvon	30 446	141	0.5
621	Bangor	30 810	390	1.3
622	Conway	11 630	36	0.3
623	Anglesey	43 243	340	0.8
Total		1 188 914	20 738	1.74

Source: 1851 Census Reports, Birthplaces of the People.

Appendix 4.4 Irish-born population of the London registration districts 1851 census.

District name and number	*Total population*	*Irish-born population*	*Irish as % of total*
1. Kensington	120 004	4370	3.6
2. Chelsea	56 538	2450	4.3
3. St George, Hanover Sq	73 230	2682	3.7
4. Westminster	65 609	3864	5.9
5. St Martins in the Field	24 640	1250	5.1
6. St James, Westminster	36 406	2185	6.0
7. Marylebone	157 696	8456	5.4
8. Hampstead	11 986	138	1.2
9 Pancras	106 526	5835	5.5
10. Islington	95 329	2420	2.5
11. Hackney	58 429	683	1.2
12. St Giles	54 214	6030	11.1
13. Strand	44 460	2431	5.5
14. Holborn	46 621	4224	9.1
15. Clerkenwell	64 778	1676	2.6
16. St Luke	54 055	2192	4.1
17. East London	44 406	3626	8.2
18. West London	28 790	1921	6.7
19. London City	55 932	1647	2.9
20. Shoreditch	109 257	2293	2.1
21. Bethnal Green	90 193	813	0.9
22. Whitechapel	79 759	8998	11.3
23. St George in the East	48 376	3576	7.4
24. Stepney	110 775	6099	5.5
25. Poplar	47 162	2494	5.3
26. St Saviour, Southwark	35 731	1979	5.5
27. St Olave	19 375	2932	15.1
28. Bermondsey	48 128	2532	5.3
29. St George, Southwark	51 824	2467	4.8
30. Newington	64 816	1316	1.0
31. Lambeth	139 325	4372	3.1
32. Wandsworth	50 764	848	1.7
33. Camberwell	54 667	1604	2.9
34. Rotherhithe	17 805	920	5.2
35. Greenwich	99 365	6132	6.2
36. Lewisham	34 835	973	2.8

Source: 1851 Census, Birthplaces of the People, Division 1, London, pp. 31-35.

Appendix 4.5 The number of Irish-born persons in each of the counties of Scotland, 1851.

County	*Total population*	*Irish-born population*	*Irish as % of total*
Dumfries	78 213	2 166	2.8
Kirkcudbright	43 121	2 561	5.9
Wigtown	43 389	7 042	16.2
Ayr	189 858	20 967	11.0
Bute	16 608	585	3.5
Renfrew	161 091	25 678	15.9
Dumbarton	45 103	5 356	11.8
Lanark	530 169	89 330	16.8
Stirling	86 237	5 472	6.3
Linlithgow	30 135	2 843	9.4
Edinburgh	259 435	15 317	5.9
Peebles	10 738	323	3.0
Selkirk	9 809	286	2.9
Roxburgh	51 642	1 234	2.4
Berwick	36 297	252	0.7
Haddington	36 386	1 337	3.7
Fife	153 546	2 654	1.7
Kinross	8 894	30	0.3
Clackmannan	22 951	722	3.1
Perth	138 660	2 445	1.8
Forfar	191 264	16 219	8.5
Kincardine	34 598	327	0.9
Aberdeen	212 032	1 727	0.8
Banff	54 171	127	0.2
Elgin	38 959	44	0.1
Nairn	9 956	34	0.4
Inverness	9 650	38	0.4
Argyll	89 328	1 476	1.6
Ross & Cromary	82 707	167	0.2
Sutherland	25 793	37	0.1
Caithness	38 709	57	0.1
Orkney/Shetland	62 533	34	0.05
Scotland	2 888 742	207 367	7.2

Source: 1851 Census, Birthplaces of the People, Scotland, pp.1039-1040.

Appendix 4.6 The number of persons born in Ireland and receiving poor relief in Scotland in each of the years 1846-1853 inclusive.

Year	*Number relieved including dependents*
1846	18 841
1847	40 692
1848	47 170
1849	38 932
1850	30 519
1851	26 586
1852	23 167
1853	21 345
Total	247 252

Source: SC (1854) Appendix 6, p. 578.

Notes and References

1 There are a large number of texts describing the poor law system. See M.E.Rose (ed) *The Poor and the City: the English Poor Law in its Urban Context, 1834-1914*, (Leicester University Press: 1985). D.Fraser (ed) *The New Poor Law in the Nineteenth Century*, (Macmillan: 1976). P.Wood, *Poverty and the Workhouse in Victorian Britain*, (Allan Sutton: 1991).

2 A.Patterson, 'The Poor Law in Nineteenth Century Scotland', in D.Fraser (ed) *The New Poor Law in the Nineteenth Century*, (Methuen: 1976) pp. 171-193.

3 For a detailed treatment of the Irish poor law system during the famine, see C.Kinealy, *This Great Calamity: The Irish Famine 1845-52*, (Gill and Macmillan: 1994).

4 *Liverpool Journal*, 21 November 1846.

5 Famine Papers, Memorial of the Select Vestry of the Parish of Liverpool to Sir George Grey, Secretary of State of the Home Department', p. 435-6.

6 Famine Papers, Mr Phillips, Home Office, to Mr Hart, Clerk to the Select Vestry, letter dated 28 December 1846, p. 436.

7 Famine Papers, Mr Loch to Sir George Grey, dated 24 December 1846, pp. 436-7.

8 Austin (1847), Appendix no. 8, p.115.

9 SC (1854) A. Campbell, Chairman of the Liverpool Select Vestry, q.4954, p.358. Campbell is quoting from a letter written by E.Rushton, Stipendiary Magistrate, to Sir George Grey, dated 21 April 1849.

10 SC (1854) Appendix No. 8, Returns of the Mendicity Department of the Liverpool District Provident Society, p.593.

11 SC (1847) E.Rushton, q.4370, p.56. The Crown's Law Officers tried to pressurize Rushton into applying the Vagrancy Act by issuing a writ of Mandamus, but to no effect.

12 Austin (1847). This report gives details of the reorganization of the system of distributing poor relief to the Irish and the numbers relieved. The figure of 47 194 individual Irish cases is given by Campbell, SC (1854) Minutes of Evidence, q. 4951, p.358.

13 SC (1854) Minutes of Evidence, A.Campbell, q. 4951, p. 358.

14 *Liverpool Chronicle*, 27 March 1847, Report of the fortnightly meeting of the Select Vestry held on 23 March 1847.
15 First Report (Large Towns) Appendix, W.H.Duncan, 'On the Physical Causes of the High Rates of Mortality in Liverpool', pp. 16-17.
16 *Liverpool Journal*, 21 November 1846.
17 *Liverpool Courier*, 27 January 1847.
18 *Manchester Guardian*, 27 January 1847.
19 *Halifax Guardian*, 9 January 1847. *Gore's General Advertiser*, 7 January 1847.
20 *Halifax Guardian*, 9 January 1847, *Gore's General Advertiser*, 21 January 1847.
21 *Halifax Guardian*, 9 January 1847.
22 *Liverpool Chronicle*, 6 February 1847.
23 *Liverpool Journal*, 27 February 1847. See also *Liverpool Mercury*, 16 April 1847, 'Death of seven month old Maria Brannan on board the Drogheda steamer, inward bound for Liverpool'.
24 *Liverpool Chronicle*, 27 March 1847.
25 *Liverpool Chronicle*, 17 April 1847.
26 *Liverpool Courier*, 21 April 1847.
27 *Liverpool Courier*, 12 May 1847.
28 *Liverpool Albion*, 10 May 1847. *Liverpool Mercury*, 11 May 1847.
29 *Liverpool Chronicle*, 12 June 1847.
30 *Liverpool Chronicle*, 22 May 1847.
31 *Liverpool Courier*, 27 January 1847, Meeting of Select Vestry held on 26 January.
32 *Liverpool Mercury*, 29 January 1847. This edition carries a full copy of the letter from A.Campbell to Sir George Grey, dated 28 January 1847.
33 SC (1847) Minutes of Evidence, E.Rushton, q. 4418, p. 61.
34 A.Paterson, op.cit, p. 172.
35 *The Times*, 13 January 1847.
36 *Glasgow Courier*, 26 January 1847. *Glasgow Chronicle*, 27 January 1847.
37 *Glasgow Herald*, 29 January 1847. *Glasgow Chronicle*, 3 & 10 February 1847.
38 *Glasgow Herald*, 15 February 1847.
39 *Glasgow Courier*, 16 February 1849. Report of the meeting of the Glasgow Municipal Police Board held on 15 February 1847.
40 *Glasgow Herald*, 5 March 1847. Report of the meeting of the Glasgow Municipal Police Board held on 1 March 1847.
41 *Glasgow Chronicle*, 3 March 1847. Report of the Meeting of the Glasgow Municipal Police Board held 3 March 1847, Of the 163 Irish removals back to Ireland, 232 had been in Glasgow for less than eight days.
42 *Glasgow Courier*, 25 February 1847. At the same court appearance, a 14 year old Irish girl had stolen a loaf because she was hungry while another Irishman broke a window at the police station in order to obtain a warm cell.
43 Strathclyde, Minutes of the Glasgow Parochial Board Meeting held on 5 March 1847, Report of the Assessment Committee, pp. 74-5.
44 ibid.
45 Strathclyde, Minutes of the Glasgow Parochial Board Meeting. Also *The Times*, 7 April 1847. This edition carries a copy of the petition in its entirety.
46 *Glasgow Herald*, 19 April 1847.
47 *Glasgow Courier*, 20 April 1847. Report of the Meeting of the Glasgow Parochial Board, held on 19 April 1847.
48 Irish Poor (1847)

49 For a description of the regional economy, see G.E.Jones, *Modern Wales: A concise history, c.1485-1979*, (Cambridge: 1984), chapter 7. P.Jenkins, *A History of Modern Wales, 1536-1990*, (Longman: 1992), chapter 11.
50 PRO/Customs/71/130, An Account of Coasting Vessels entering in at Newport. In 1847, 257 vessels entered in at Newport from Ireland. If we assume on an average of 75 passengers per vessel, this gives a total of 19 275 arrivals.
51 SC (1854) Minutes of Evidence, J.Salter, q. 6745, p.493.
52 SC (1854) Minutes of Evidence, J.Salter, q. 6892, p.503.
53 PRO/MH12/8089/1847/Newport. Letter from W.W.Harries to Newport Guardians, dated 27 May 1847.
54 Vagrancy, 1848, p.17.
55 ibid, p. 36.
56 ibid, p.18.
57 SC (1854) Minutes of Evidence, J.Salter, p. 6744, p.493.
58 Vagrancy (1848) p. 31.
59 PRO/MH12/8089/1847/Newport, Letter from W.W.Harries to Newport Guardians, dated 27 May 1847.
60 PRO/MH12/8089/Newport, Report of John Lewis, assistant Poor Law Commissioner, to the Poor Law Commissioners on his visit to the Newport Union on 5 June 1847.
61 Vagrancy (1848) Number of Persons relieved at the House of Refuge, Newport, Monmouthshire during the year 1847, p.29.
62 Irish Poor, 1848.
63 The most detailed treatment of the Irish in Cardiff is the thirty year old work, J.Hickey, *Urban Catholics: Urban Catholicism in England and Wales from 1829 to the present day*, (London: 1967). For an examination of the development of an Irish Catholic community see chapters 3,4, and 5. For a treatment of spatial distribution of Catholics in Cardiff and some references to social conditions see C.Roy Lewis, 'The Irish in Cardiff in the Mid-Nineteenth Century', *Cambria*, volume 7, No.1, (1980) pp. 13-41.
64 op.cit, Hickey, p.75.
65 op.cit, Lewis, p.38.
66 *Cardiff and Merthyr Guardian*, 23 January 1847.
67 *Cardiff and Merthyr Guardian*, 30 January 1847.
68 *Cardiff and Merthyr Guardian*, 6 March 1847.
69 *Bristol Gazette*, 18 March 1847.
70 *Cambrian*, 23 April 1847.
71 *Cardiff and Merthyr Guardian*, 26 February 1847.
72 *Cardiff and Merthyr Guardian*, 17 April 1847. See also the same paper, 24 July 1847, 'Irish Woman fined for fighting produced one and half sovereigns from her pocket'.
73 *Cardiff and Merthyr Guardian*, 21 July 1847.
74 *Manchester Guardian*, 19 May 1849.
75 *Cardiff and Merthyr Guardian*, 15 May 1847.
76 SC (1854) Minutes of Evidence, E.David, q.6341, p. 479.
77 SC (1854) Minutes of Evidence, J.Salter, q.6715, p. 491.
78 Vagrancy (1848) p. 18. See also SC (1854) Minutes of Evidence, E.David, q. 6471, p. 474, q.6482, p. 475.
79 Irish Poor (1848)

5 Liverpool and the Irish Fever

I

As tragic as the deaths from starvation were, they were eclipsed, both in numbers and scale of suffering, by the consequences of the typhus epidemic of 1847. The problems that typhus posed for the authorities in Britain, particularly in the ports of arrival, far exceeded those arising from the economics and mechanics of paying outdoor poor relief. Whatever fears the ratepayers had concerning the financial consequences of the famine immigration, they soon took second place to the fear of death from what became universally known during 1847 as 'Irish fever'. Throughout urban Britain, poor law guardians struggled with the problems of finding extra hospital beds, doctors, nurses, coffins and graves.

The response of local authorities throughout the country to the typhus epidemic involved two separate groups of decision-makers. In England and Wales Boards of Guardians had the responsibility of providing medical treatment to the poor. Under normal circumstances this was not problematical. All workhouses had a general medical ward, nursing and medical staff. Often the poor law guardians in a union would also subscribe to a dispensary run by private donations. At times of crisis, these facilities would have to be expanded and the 1847 crisis appears to have posed greater problems than the previous typhus and cholera outbreaks.[1] The poor law guardians therefore had the additional responsibility of providing more hospital beds, nurses, doctors and medicine in a very short time. In turn, the medical doctors had to decide on the kinds of treatment to be offered to the sick and what preventative methods should be adopted to limit the spread of the epidemic.

In judging the efficacy of the medical community in dealing with the 1847 typhus crisis, it needs to be understood that the state of medical knowledge at the time rarely permitted a straightforward answer to the question 'what caused this disease?' Contemporary medical practice reflected an underlying tradition based on the doctrine of bodily humours, or fluids of the body. Health was conceived of as vitality, a sense of physical and mental wellbeing, maintained by the body. Similarly, disease was the upsetting of this equilibrium and lurking behind much treatment was the ancient conviction that all diseases were the results of disorders of the humours.[2] At a simplistic level, it can be argued that there were two basic etiological schools of thought in medicine at the time of Chadwick's investigation into public health. For probably the majority of doctors, the cause of disease was a large variety of 'predisposing' factors such as cold, dampness, lack of adequate food, overcrowding, poor air supplies, bad water and so on. These factors would affect different people in different ways but all of them predisposing individuals to illness. Adherents of this viewpoint would not subscribe to the theory that there was a single 'exciting' cause of a disease. For such people the important etiological questions concerned such matters as 'why did this particular person contract the disease and that person did not?' Why did this person die of the disease and that person did not?' Those who practised medicine in this tradition paid great emphasis on the individual patient's description of his or her own conditions.[3]

Essentially, physiology prevailed over aetiology. To the extent that causation was discussed, a distinction was often made between 'remote' causes and 'proximate' causes. By definition, remote causes could have been many things which upset the bodily equilibrium and in the extreme, the economic system which gave rise to poverty and its consequent life style. Proximate causes were considered the essence of a disease and such causes were ascribed on the basis of the pathological process that characterized a disease, such as, temperature, skin rashes, debility, diarrhoea and so on. For example, certain symptoms would lead to a diagnosis of typhus or 'fever'. The term 'contagionist' has been applied to that body of medical opinion which refused to accept the idea of a single cause of a disease. The adherents of this philosophy have been criticized as providing no basis for improvements in public health. Critics argued that they simply treated people after quarantining them in order to contain contagion, and when cured returned them to their former disease ridden habitats. They provided no public health prescription.

Counter-posed to the 'contagionists' are the 'anti-contagionists'. These were those doctors and scientists who believed there *was* a single cause to a disease, a single 'exciting' factor. This etiological view point gained ground in the second quarter of the nineteenth century. Its triumph was due in no small part to Edwin Chadwick, for whom it provided the raison d'être for his policy prescriptions. For Chadwick and his supporters, this belief in a single cause manifested itself in the assertion of a miasmatic theory of disease. Miasma was caused by the putrefaction of organic matter, which in turn gave rise to noxious substances which were agents in carrying disease. In the slum conditions described in chapter two, the way to improve health was to remove rotting organic matter. Good *sanitation* was the answer to the problem of disease. For Chadwick and his allies, quarantining victims of disease, without tackling the cause of disease was a waste of time. In fact, the contagionists, with their view on predisposing causes of disease, *did* provide a basis for policy prescription. Better diet, clothing, water and housing would have improved health. The crucial issue was that tackling the problem of poverty would have involved an unacceptable political agenda. Chadwick's sanitation policies of better drainage, sewers and building regulations were cheaper and also had the great attraction of immediately benefitting the middle classes.

By 1847, as far as public health was concerned, the Chadwickian anti-contagionists had triumphed. This was despite the fact that the detailed investigations into the causes of the typhus epidemic in Ireland in 1818 had almost unanimously produced evidence that poverty, poor diet, damp conditions, lack of clothing and low income were factors present in the majority of fever victims.[4] Admittedly, the precise cause of transmitting typhus was not understood but what was clear was the correlation between a particular lifestyle and the incidence of typhus. However, attempting to change these conditions would have been a highly politically charged matter. Whatever the public health policy implications of believing that disease had many pre-disposing causes or, by contrast, one 'exciting' cause, *once an epidemic broke out* all protagonists believed in the efficacy of taking the poor victims out of public circulation.

Before 1847, typhus was frequently confused with typhoid fever. William Jenner then demonstrated a diagnostic distinction between the two but it was only in 1908 that scientists at the Pasteur Institute in Paris showed that typhus infection occurs through body lice ingesting the blood of the typhus victims. The organisms which spread typhus are minute bodies known as *Rickettsia Prowazeki*.[5] The louse ingests the organisms from a victim's blood and once inside they spread rapidly in its intestines which swell and burst. The *rickettsiae* then pass out of the louse in its faeces. If the louse is on another host, infection usually takes place through the person scratching and breaking the surface of the skin and crushing the louse. Thus typhus was spread in conditions of dirt and overcrowding. However, typhus also was spread by means other than direct contact with someone lice-ridden. If a louse was crushed, the *rickettsiae* would survive in the remains which, when they dried, became dust. This meant the organism could be inhaled so that people without body lice could contact typhus. For a person infected, the onset of typhus was rapid. The symptoms included shivering, head and body aches, the face becomes bloated, the skin turns dark, severe toxaemia, muscular twitching was experienced and the victim's 'mental state' becomes confused. After about five days, body rashes appeared. In general the attack lasted about 14 days and the death rate varied between 20 per cent and 45 per cent. When the dead body of a victim cooled, the lice looked for warmer hosts, something easy to do in the overcrowded slums.

Until 1880, typhus was endemic in British and Irish towns and had been known by a variety of names such as gaol fever, spotted fever, camp fever, putrid fever and, in the nineteenth century, Irish fever.

The state of medical knowledge at the beginning of the famine was such that 'fever' was a generic term covering a number of conditions which were in some cases symptoms of quite different diseases. In particular, *relapsing fever* was often described as typhus, though in fact it was a distinct illness due to *Spirochaetae,* a thread like organism, larger than the *Rickettsia Prowazeki*. When it enters a louse, it multiplies, not in the intestines, but in the body. This meant it did not pass out of the louse through the agency of its faeces. When a louse was crushed, by scratching or anything else, the *spirochaetae* remained in the corpse of the insect which when dried, became dust. So the organism could be inhaled. Of course, if the corpse of the louse was on an open wound or scratch, the host was infected. The start of relapsing fever was much more rapid than was the case with typhus and the symptoms included stiffening of the body, stomach upsets, sick feeling and vomiting. A crisis was reached within about five days, accompanied by heavy sweating and exhaustion. However, one or more relapses occurred before the patient died or recovered. In the mid-nineteenth century lack of knowledge meant that the two diseases were often confused and so as a consequence, statistics regarding 'fever' victims are often not clear about which disease they refer to.[6] Given the living conditions of a significant proportion of the working classes in British towns, it is not surprising that the arrival of large numbers of destitute Irish exacerbated the endemic presence of typhus in the already overcrowded slums. In the popular mind, both diseases were associated with famine but the causal chain was not malnutrition leading to typhus and relapsing fever. Famine was accompanied by poverty, dirt and overcrowding among the famine victims, the ideal conditions for lice to flourish. Epidemic fever had appeared in some places in Ireland in 1845, for example, Kilkenny. In 1846 it appeared in Cork, Roscommon and Sligo at the back end of 1846 and early 1847. Dublin, Wicklow, Longford and Louth experienced the onset of fever early in 1847 and Derry in the spring of 1847.[7] Accompanying the scourge of fever was dysentery. This was caused by bacilli transmitted by flies, the eating of contaminated food, or the use of fingers which were not clean. When inside a person, the bacilli rapidly multiplied, attacking the intestinal walls, in some cases causing gangrene. The excreta of infected persons swarm with the bacilli and are highly infectious. The victim experiences bowel colic and violent diarrhoea, typically passing blood. Scurvy also accompanied famine, causing painful swelling of the joints, blood collecting under the skin surface resulting in great pain; the gums rot.

II

Any examination of Irish Fever in Britain during 1847 must start with the case of Liverpool. There are two reasons for proposing this. First, the sheer numbers of Irish passing through Liverpool exceeded those in any other British town so facilitating the spread of the disease. Second, more data exists for Liverpool than elsewhere in Britain. Liverpool was particularly vulnerable to typhus both because of its poor housing stock and also the constant movement of large numbers of Irish through the port. The 1841 census revealed that the town had an Irish-born population of nearly 50 000 but at any one time there were large numbers of transitory Irish as well as, or included, in the 50 000 . Many were emigrants waiting for ships to North America, others were Irish immigrants resting before moving inland to other British towns. The numbers of famine Irish arriving during 1847 were, as we have noted, extremely large and significant numbers spent time in Liverpool recovering from their journey to Britain. Another element in Liverpool's floating Irish population was the large numbers of Irish who made their way to Liverpool from towns inland in order to be passed back to Ireland by the Liverpool parish authorities. All of these temporary residents increased the desperate overcrowding in cellars, courts and lodging houses. When the fever epidemic erupted in March 1847, its affects were correspondingly devastating and Liverpool's fever victims were continually re-enforced by new arrivals from Ireland.

The Select Vestry, as the poor law guardians, had an unequivocal responsibility to provide medical aid to the poor. The Borough Council carried some statutory obligations in the field of public health and at times there was some confusion between the borough and the parish over respective responsibilities. In 1846, the Liverpool Sanitary Act went through Parliament and its provisions came into affect on 1 January 1847. The scope of the Act was to deal with private rights in such a manner as to make them subordinate to the public welfare and it was a sign of Chadwick's success in pushing his views on the cause of low standards of public health. Importantly, Dr William Duncan was appointed the first ever British Medical Officer of Health and an appropriately named Mr Fresh was appointed Inspector of Nuisances. Both these men had central roles to play in the battle against Irish Fever. William Henry Duncan was born in Seel Street, Liverpool in 1805. Like J.P. Kay in Manchester, he graduated in medicine from Edinburgh University and then he returned to Liverpool to practice medicine at a time when the great debates over public health were emerging.[8] As a result of the Sanitary Act, the Borough Council set up a Health Committee, a development that was the cause of further confusion regarding the matter of who Duncan was responsible to, the Health

Committee or the Select Vestry. Neither Duncan nor members of the Health Committee could have foreseen the calamity that was to face them in the first year of the Sanitary Act's existence. The issues to be addressed here are, what was the scale, chronology and geography of the Irish fever epidemic in Liverpool; which groups were most affected and what was the nature of the response of the authorities to the crisis?

III

Dealing first with the scale of the fever, two indices are the numbers dying of the disease and the numbers treated in hospitals and at home. During the summer of 1846, the town had experienced a particularly nasty and fatal outbreak of diarrhoea and dysentery but fever was not particularly present. As late as January 1847, out of a total of 855 deaths of all kinds during the month, only 44 were attributed to fever.[9] However, February saw a 70 per cent increase in fever deaths while in April there was an increase of 127 per cent over March. Table 5.1 below illustrates both the scale and chronology of fever deaths in the *parish* of Liverpool during 1847.

Table 5.1 Deaths from fever and diarrhoea in the parish of Liverpool during 1847.

Month	*Deaths from all causes*	*Deaths from fever*	*Deaths from diarrhoea*
January	855	44	69
February	947	75	109
March	1 273	123	173
April	1 420	279	200
May	1 652	551	245
June	1 768	813	188
July	2 054	828	346
August	2 097	817	488
September	1 489	582	231
October	1 196	498	90
November	998	333	55
December	1 531	296	42
Total	17 280	5239	2236

Source: LIVRO. MOH. 1847-50, p.10.

Over the year, 31 per cent of all deaths were attributable to fever. It is clear that the month of March witnessed the beginning of the crisis. The absolute number of deaths from fever peaked in July, at 828 and thereafter the decline continued throughout the rest of the year. Despite this, the 296 fever deaths in December were nearly seven times greater that the 44 deaths in

January. This reflects the continued immigration of famine Irish rather than the spreading of the disease among the resident population. The number of deaths from diarrhoea and dysentery followed closely the deaths from fever. (the coefficient of correlation = 0.71) but peaked in August and then fell continuously. By contrast with the fever deaths, the number of diarrhoea deaths in December was twenty seven *less* than those in January. The increased total of all deaths in December was due to an outbreak of influenza. On the basis of this evidence, 5239 persons died of typhus in 1847 and 2236 died of diarrhoea and dysentery. In fact the situation was worse than these figures suggest because they refer only to the parish. In the borough of Liverpool (the parish plus north and south Toxteth and Everton) the total number who died of fever, diarrhoea and dysentery was 8434.

The next issue is that of identifying the areas in which the epidemic struck. This is particularly important in testing the hypothesis that the majority of the victims were Irish. Thanks to the professionalism of Dr Duncan, there are reasonable data concerning the geographical incidence of the fatalities in the borough. Table 5.2 below gives a breakdown of the deaths on a ward basis, distinguishing as before, between deaths from fever and deaths from diarrhoea and dysentery.

Table 5.2 The distributions of deaths from fever, diarrhoea and dysentery in the borough of Liverpool during 1847, on a ward basis.

Ward	*Fever*	*Diarrhoea & dysentery*	*Totals*
Scotland	663	472	1135
Vauxhall	924	382	1306
St Paul's	145	84	229
Exchange	491	224	715
St Anne's	196	102	298
Lime Street	90	65	155
Castle Street	49	40	89
St Peter's	52	55	107
Pitt Street	81	73	154
Great George	446	213	659
Rodney Street	50	55	105
Abercromby	90	47	137
Workhouse	1011	395	1406
Hospitals	944	26	970
Borough Gaol	7	3	10
Total for parish	5239	2236	7475
Ex-parochial wards	606	353	959
Overall total	5845	2589	8434

Source: LIVRO. MOH. p.113, Table III.

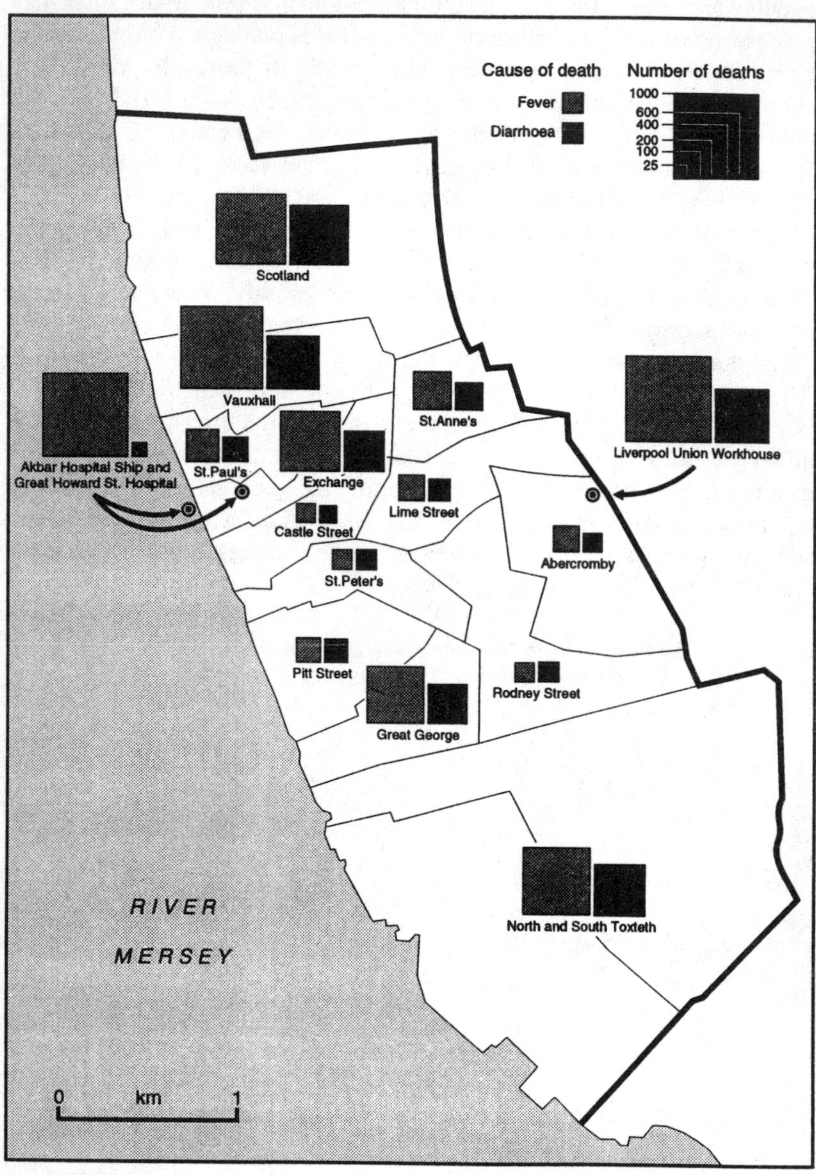

Figure 5.1 Distribution of deaths from fever and diarrhoea in Liverpool during 1847

A number of features of these data warrant comment. Measured in terms of the absolute numbers of deaths from fever, the greatest incidence occurred in Scotland, Vauxhall and Exchange in the North End and Great George in the South End. Each of these wards had large Irish-born populations. It is also the case that the numbers of deaths from fever are even more highly correlated with the deaths from diarrhoea and dysentery on the basis of *ward* distribution (r = 0.945). This is not surprising, the most overcrowded districts had the conditions that generated all the diseases associated with poverty. Using absolute numbers of deaths could be misleading without reference to the size of total population in each ward. If we use the basis of *relative* numbers of deaths, the conclusion that the Irish wards suffered most is unchanged.

Table 5.3 Death rates from fever, diarrhoea and dysentery in the various political wards of the borough of Liverpool during 1848.

Ward	*Death Rates from Fever*	*Death Rates from diarrhoea & dysentery*
Vauxhall*	one in 17	one in 55
Exchange*	one in 21	one in 61
Great George*	one in 22	one in 75
Scotland*	one in 48	one in 87
St Anne's	one in 69	one in 168
St Paul's	one in 71	one in 160
Castle Street	one in 114	one in 182
Pitt Street	one in 116	one in 169
St Peter's	one in 118	one in 143
Lime Street	one in 129	one in 234
Abercromby	one in 130	one in 318
Rodney Street	one in 228	one in 269
Parish	one in 46	one in 108
Extra Parochial Wards	one in 156	one in 269
Borough	one in 58	one in 130

Note: *These wards were districts in which there were large numbers of Irish.
Source LIVRO. MOH. 1847-50, p.14.

Not only did Vauxhall ward experience the greatest number of deaths from fever, it also had the highest mortality rate, one in seventeen of the population. Exchange was next with one in twenty one, followed by Great George and Scotland. By contrast the middle class areas of Abercromby and Rodney wards had rates of one in 130 and 228 respectively. The evidence provided by Duncan's reports is unequivocal, the areas with the highest densities of Irish immigrants suffered most in the 1847 calamity. Following the increase in the number of fever cases in March, Duncan wrote to Sir

George Grey, the Home Secretary, informing him that the fever was progressing in 'the North End Irish districts' and also that it had also spread to the 'Irish districts in the South End'.[10] Writing in his report for 1847, he recorded that:

> In the beginning of May the epidemic burst through the barriers which had hitherto seemed to confine it to the poorer classes of the inhabitants; it invaded the better conditioned districts of the town, establishing itself among the English population, who had previously escaped its ravages, and gradually creeping up among the wealthier class. In June it appeared for the first time in Toxteth Park and West Derby.[11]

The inference to be drawn from Duncan's report is that as late as May, the majority of victims were Irish. His choice of language is also of interest. For example, the use of the term 'English population' provides confirmation of the view that in Liverpool, we can refer to 'Irish districts'. There is also the implication that the *seriousness* of the crisis had deepened *because* the epidemic was putting the English *and* wealthier classes at risk.

Looking back on 1847, Duncan deplored the loss of many 'respectable and useful citizens'.[12] However, as we have noted, the citizens of Abercromby and Rodney wards were considerably safer than the inhabitants of Vauxhall, Exchange, Scotland and St George.

IV

The authorities in Liverpool, poor law guardians, police, town councillors and doctors, were facing an unprecedented experience. From the outset of the crisis in March 1847, Duncan, the Health Committee and the Select Vestry had three principal issues to address. First there was a desperate need for extra space in order to provide more hospital beds. There was also a need for extra doctors and nurses so that fever victims could be removed to hospital, nursed and, hopefully, so stopping the spread of typhus among the population. It was recognized however, that this second objective could not be achieved so long as large numbers of famine Irish were continually arriving in the port. However, there was an acceptance of the futility of trying to obtain governmental action to stop immigration and so attention was turned to the installation of efficient quarantine procedures in the river.[13]

The hospital facilities for treating fever victims, before the start of the typhus crisis, consisted of eighty iron beds in the fever ward in the grounds of the workhouse, in Mount Pleasant.[14] The workhouse was in the Abercromby ward on the site of what is now (1997) the site of the Roman

Catholic Cathedral. Under normal circumstances, this provision had proved adequate but as the number of fever victims increased in the first two months of 1847, it became clear more hospital beds were needed. Space in the town was at a premium because of dock construction, house building, and commercial developments and so the Select Vestry faced difficult problems in acquiring the required space.[15] Initially, the workhouse chapel and committee rooms were commandeered for use as hospital wards and were used as such from the first week in March.[16] That month witnessed a dramatic increase in deaths from typhus and so as a consequence, on 31 March, the Irish Relief Committee, a sub-committee of the Select Vestry, ordered the preparation of plans for the erection of temporary fever sheds within the grounds of the workhouse. On 5 April they contracted with builders to construct three sheds, each able to accommodate 100 patients, at a cost of £2100.[17] What followed was to become a familiar response to similar decisions about fever sheds throughout the country. As soon as the residents of properties near to the workhouse heard of the plans to build fever sheds, they organized a protest through their ward councillor. Their concerns were threefold. They feared that the presence of fever victims in the sheds would increase their risk of catching typhus. Duncan assured them there was absolutely no risk and pointed out there had always been a fever ward at the workhouse.

A second complaint was that crowds gathered each day in Mount Pleasant to watch the bodies of dead fever victims being removed to the pauper cemetery which was near the workhouse, in Cambridge Street. The new sheds would increase the number of burials in Cambridge Street and so in response to the protests the Select Vestry agreed to change the procedure for burying the dead in a manner that would be less offensive to local residents. Lastly, the owners of lodging houses in Mount Pleasant claimed their lodgers were leaving because of the increased fear of typhus resulting from the plans to build fever sheds, so imposing an economic burden on them. They were told little could be done about that particular problem.[18]

Simultaneously with the expansion of the number of beds at the workhouse, the Select Vestry continued to search for additional property. The objective was to find buildings easily converted into fever wards as the majority of fever victims were still at home. For example, on 13 March, Duncan told the Health Committee that a total of 530 patients were being treated for typhus and of this total, 300 were being treated at home.[19] On 3 April he recorded that there were 500 fever patients in four Irish streets alone.[20] On 19 April he told the Health Committee that the workhouse wards had been constantly full during the previous four weeks and cases of fever were being refused admission. The increasing number of typhus cases was, in his opinion, due to the spread of fever within the population *and* the continued influx of fever victims from Ireland.[21] By this time, the Select Vestry had acquired some empty buildings in Great Howard Street in Vauxhall, on the corner with Chadwick Street. These extra wards were opened 25 April.

The nature of the crisis at this time is illustrated by the discussion at the meeting of the Select Vestry 27 April. Despite the extra capacity, the demand for admission to fever wards continued to exceed supply. A letter was read out, from Mr George Evans, the workhouse governor. He said the dilemma he faced was that each day he had applications for admissions to the fever wards, which he had to turn down. He felt that by doing so he was 'perhaps to send them to their deaths in the streets'. To admit them put the existing patients at greater risk. He asked the Select Vestry what he should do? The response to this letter clearly reveals that the guardians were at their wits end. Mr Riding admitted they 'scarcely knew what to do'. He complained that the moment they provided extra accommodation, they were faced with protests. Another member called on the Vestry to take land on the north shore of the Mersey. This suggestion was met with the answer that the whole of Bootle would be up in arms. Someone else suggested that the Select Vestry ask the government for hospital ships. After more such inconsequential discussions, the unfortunate Governor was instructed to 'provide all the accommodation in his power' and when full, to admit no more! A committee was then formed to examine if more room could be found in the newly built addition to the workhouse.[22] One index of the problem facing the authorities is given by the number of pauper deaths. Over the period 1835-46, the average number of paupers buried *each year* in the pauper cemetery was 1367. During April 1847 alone, 654 paupers were buried in the same cemetery and over the year 7350 were buried in the two parochial cemeteries.[23] The number of coffins supplied by the Select Vestry to *outdoor* paupers also indicates the progress of the disease during the first four months of 1847. As Table 5.4 below illustrates, the rapid increase in the number of coffins provided from mid March onwards matches the increased virulence of the fever (these were in addition to those provided for the workhouse dead).

By 17 May the new sheds in Great Howard Street were full, accommodating between 300 and 400 patients, while there were 800 cases in the workhouse hospital and sheds.[24] As happened at Mount Pleasant, the residents in streets surrounding the Great Howard Street sheds protested at the presence of fever victims. Not only residents were frightened, it was reported that passengers riding in coaches from Bootle to Liverpool insisted that the vehicles bypass the fever sheds.

Again, Duncan assured all those concerned that they would not contract fever simply by passing the sheds.[25]

Table 5.4 The number of coffins provided for outdoor paupers by the parochial authorities in Liverpool: 1 January to 30 April (inc) 1846 and 1847.

Week-ending	*Number of coffins*		*Increase*	
	1846	*1847*	*absolute*	*%*
7 January	20	55	35	75
14 January	27	55	28	4
21 January	25	63	38	52
28 January	12	70	58	483
4 February	23	71	48	209
11 February	22	110	88	400
18 February	21	102	81	386
25 February	22	83	61	277
4 March	27	97	70	259
11 March	14	99	85	607
18 March	13	129	116	892
25 March	17	128	111	652
1 April	19	118	99	521
8 April	10	128	118	1180
15 April	25	138	113	452
22 April	17	126	109	641
29 April	24	138	114	475
30 April	1	21	20	2000
Total	339	1731	1392	411

Source: Austin (1847) Appendix A, No 8, p.117.

Despite this extra space, the demand for beds continued to rise. On 22 May, Duncan told the Health Committee that more beds were needed. As the sense of crisis heightened, more desperate measures were advocated. Some of the doctors involved suggested the building of fever sheds outside of the town, capable of holding 5000. They also asked for salary increases in recognition of the danger they ran in tending fever patients. In addition they asked that the Select Vestry should finance insurance on their lives.[26] Alfred Austin, the Assistant Poor Law Commissioner for the North West, suggested that the industrial school at Kirkdale be converted into a hospital because the Manchester poor law guardians had offered to take Liverpool children into their schools at Swinton. This also was rejected.[27] By the third week in June there were an estimated 1400 fever patients in the workhouse and other fever sheds, hospital and lazarettos. In addition there were 'nearly 4000' patients being treated at home.[28] On the 26 June, the *Liverpool Albion*, in a leader on the epidemic, suggested, unsuccessfully, using Hilbre Island in the Dee as a quarantine station. By this time it was claimed that 8000 people were being treated for fever.[29] More sensibly the Select Vestry had, by early May, obtained government permission to use two vessels on the Mersey, one, the *Newcastle* to act as a quarantine station for infected Irish arriving on steamers from Irish ports. The second vessel, the *Akbar,* a brig of 1200 tons, was to be used as a hospital ship for Liverpool patients. Each vessel could hold 300 patients. Twice a day, a steamer attended at the Albert Dock in order to convey fever patients into the river where the *Newcastle* was moored. Later another vessel, the *Druid* was used as a hospital ship.[30] Despite all efforts, none of these devices for providing extra beds kept up with demand and the majority of patients continued to be treated in their own homes, which were frequently overcrowded, dirty and certain to increase the spread of the disease.

The statistics of hospital provision and deaths cannot recreate the reality of the tragedies which occurred at this time, they can only be guessed at. The lonely deaths, often in stinking cellars, a long way from home, the bewilderment and fear, the wretchedness of losing one's family and friends in an alien environment, this was the nightmare relived in 1847 by thousands. Some vicarious sense of these terrible experiences can be gleaned from the workhouse register. On 13 May 1847, while the Luke Brothers case was being discussed in the local press, Roger Flynn (37), his wife Catherine (38) and their six children, all entered the workhouse fever ward. The family was Irish. On 15 May, Bridget (16) died. She was followed by her father, on 26 May, sister Catherine (14), on 11 June, brother Thomas (2) on 24 June, her mother on 12 July and brother John (4) on 28 July. Another sister Mary (9) died but no date was given. The sole survivor was seven year old Michael Flynn, who was sent to the orphanage on the 8 August. On 20 May, Bridget McIntyre aged 19 years and her sisters Mary (12) and Margaret (10), together with their brother John (7) all entered the workhouse fever ward. The fact that there were no parents recorded as entering the workhouse suggests that they were already dead. Margaret McIntyre died 4 June, John 14 June, Bridget on the 17th and Mary on 6 June.[31] The Liverpool coroner conducted an inquest into the death of a woman who had fallen down some cellar steps. It came out during the inquest that 17 people had died of typhus in that one house over the preceding two weeks. Also there were ten typhus victims still in the house.[32]

The policy of transferring fever victims from their homes to fever sheds was based on the anti-contagionist view that disease was spread by 'miasmas' arising from putrefying matter. Moving patients from their cellars and overcrowded rooms into a hospital where they were washed, placed in separate beds in well ventilated rooms appears to have had some success in reducing contagion. Deaths peaked in July although the immigration of destitute Irish continued unabated. This policy of hospitalisation was accompanied, from 1 July onwards, by a policy of clearing the cellars. On

12 May, Edward Rushton had told a meeting of ratepayers that 'no less that 27 000 people had taken up their quarters in cellars, which from the fact of their being deficient in dimensions, had been condemned by Act of Parliament'.[33] Rushton was referring to the 1846 Sanitary Act, which laid down clear regulations concerning the required dimensions of cellars used as living quarters. Had the famine crisis not erupted, the town council would have implemented its provisions and closed many of them. The arrival of the famine Irish put an end to such a policy. However, the changes in the law of Settlement and Removal in June 1847 and the amendment of the Irish Poor Law at the same time, encouraged the council to resurrect the policy of emptying the cellars. It was now easier to remove the famine Irish back to Ireland and this could be justified on the grounds that such persons had a legal right to outdoor relief in Ireland. (see chapter eight)

Immediately, after the legal changes, the Town Clerk announced that the 1846 Act, with regard to cellars, would be implemented. In addition, the same Act's provision regarding lodging houses would also be enforced.[34] The policy decisions were greeted with delight by the local press. In its edition of 5 July, the *Liverpool Albion* told its readers, under a leader of 'Cheering Prospect' that:

> Two items of intelligence we are rejoiced to be in a position to communicate to them today: the first, that all the abominable holes called cellars, which have been generating fever among the lower and middle classes of society to an alarming extent are in process of being cleared and rendered uninhabitable for the future: and second that the Irish paupers are being conveyed to their own country in hundreds, and will be debarked in the thousands, in the course of the present week upon the shores of their native land. On Friday and again on Saturday there were no fewer than eighty persons summoned before Mr Rushton for having let their cellars to Irish immigrants, the said cellars being only about six feet in height from floor to ceiling, and the ceiling being only about a foot to a foot and a half above the level of the street. Most of these cellars are situated in Lace Street, Midgehall Street, and in the vicinity of that low and densely populated part of the town; and it appeared that fever had been, and still is, raging in nearly the whole of them, and that not confining itself to the wretched occupants of the ground floor, it had spread its ravages to those occupying the room above, and was rapidly consigning its victims to premature graves.

Albion's euphoria was a little premature. During 1847, 15 000 Irish were removed from Liverpool to Ireland, but many of these would return.[35] The failure of the policy of pushing poor relief finance on to Irish ratepayers in

Ireland meant that many Irish preferred life in Britain. Also, many of the Irish removed from Liverpool were from other areas of Britain. The *Albion* itself admitted many Irish were refusing point blank to go.[36] More tellingly, the numbers that would be forced on the streets by the policy of closing cellars made it impracticable. During the first week in July, fifty six cellars were cleared. However, some of the people evicted were left in the street, suffering from fever. Rushton refused to sign any more eviction orders until the Select Vestry guaranteed that all sick persons evicted from the cellars would be given hospital treatment.[37] This guarantee was given and the cellar clearance proceeded. This eviction policy was combined with a tougher policy on removing those Irish back to Ireland who did not have settlement. Though there is no clear evidence of how successful this policy was in terms of controlling the spread of fever, there is reason to believe it was counter productive. Some Irish who became ill with fever, refused to apply for admission to the fever sheds *because* they knew that on recovery, they would be removed to Ireland. However by staying at home, they increased the risk of contagion.[38] By the end of September, the view of the authorities in Liverpool was that the height of the typhus crisis was passed. It was announced that the *Newcastle* was to be cleared of fever victims, they were to be dispersed among the fever sheds in Great Howard Street. At the same time it was reported that there were no fever victims aboard the *Akbar*.[39] Commenting on the decline in the number of fever cases, the *Albion* declared that though this was bad news for the parish coffin makers, for the driver of the parish hearse, it was good news 'for the unfortunate man has had a weary life over the last few weeks. He had had to convey five or six dead bodies in his hearse at one time'.[40] In November, the Registrar General's report on the deaths in Liverpool for the third quarter of 1847 provided some interesting statistics of death in the six sub-registration districts. With respect to the Dale Street sub-district, the *Liverpool Mercury* commented on the 747 deaths, which were 57 less than the previous quarter:

> This may be accounted for in a great measure by the removal of the lower Irish from the cellars, besides many being sent back to Ireland by the authorities; otherwise the mortality would have been greater than in the preceding quarter.[41]

In all British towns receiving famine refugees, the increased financial cost of relieving Irish paupers was in itself a source of growing resentment among sections of the host communities. The typhus epidemic fuelled such resentments. This was a particularly combustible ingredient in Liverpool where conflict between Irish and English was a well established feature of working class life before the famine crisis.

V

Overwhelming opinion among the English, lay, medical, local and national, was that fever was an *Irish* import. Certainly, the evidence is that the majority of victims were Irish. The report of the Registrar for St Thomas's sub-district in Liverpool, for the quarter ending 31 December 1846, recorded a large increase in the number of deaths compared with the same quarter in 1845.

> A considerable proportion of the increase arizes from the great influx of poor people from Ireland, most of whom are destitute when they arrive. Some have only a few days in the town previous to their death'.[42]

In February 1847, Duncan informed the Home Secretary, that fever affected 'almost exclusively the Irish and that 88 per cent of all the patients in the fever hospitals were Irish'. Of this number, 71 per cent came from the Vauxhall area between Vauxhall Road and Scotland Road, a district characterized by the worst housing in the town. He told Sir George Grey: 'Should the destitute Irish continue to flock into Liverpool as they are now doing, there can be no doubt that what we now see is only the commencement of the most severe and desolating epidemic what has visited Liverpool for the last ten years'.[43]

Few people have offered a more prophetically accurate opinion. Of all deaths from fever occurring in patients' homes over the first three quarters of 1847, 18 per cent occurred in only *four,* predominantly Irish streets, Lace Street, Crosbie Street, New Bird Street and Birch Street. Lace Street became a nightmare, 472 people from that one street died, or one third of all inhabitants.

On 13 March, Duncan again reported that the Irish districts were suffering most from fever and that 50 per cent of all patients under treatment at home were in the Vauxhall and Exchange wards in the North End and St George's in the South End. Further evidence of the predominance of the Irish among the typhus victims was Duncan's particular concern over the habit of holding back from burying the dead in order to have a wake. This was not a widespread custom among the English and Welsh working classes:

> I beg to direct the attention of the Health Committee to the objectionable custom of retaining the bodies of the dead, especially those who have died of infectious fevers, in the sleeping rooms of the living. On Sunday last a man died of typhus fever in a small room in Thomas Street, in which seven or eight other inmates slept, two of whom were also ill with

> fever. Their friends objected to the burial taking place before Sunday (tomorrow) and in the meantime, the other occupants continue to sleep in the same room with the dead body. Other cases have been reported to me over the last week. I myself have seen the body of a child who had died of smallpox lying in a cellar where fifteen individuals slept.

Duncan then urged the Health Committee to use their powers of enforcing compulsory burials. He went on to refer to the general sanitary conditions in the town but quickly returned to the theme of Irish immigration:

> But I cannot too emphatically report the opinion I formerly gave, that so long as the influx of destitute Irish is allowed to continue unchecked, no measure which is in the power of the Health Committee or Council to adopt, can materially diminish the amount of sickness and mortality in Liverpool.[44]

Laying the blame for the typhus epidemic on the Irish was not restricted to Duncan. It was an almost unanimously held opinion. Mr Fresh, the Inspector of Nuisances, had the responsibility for the removal of all the rubbish and ordure in the town and was very experienced in visiting the cellars and courts. He also told the Health Committee:

> I respectfully think that the overcrowding of the cellars and small houses in the Irish districts with the migratory and filthy Irish poor is the greatest cause of the spread of contagion and that notwithstanding every precaution which can be taken, much more than ordinary sickness and disease will continue to prevail until the immense inflow of Irish paupers shall cease.[45]

Fresh was not a doctor and he may have been simply repeating the views of Duncan. However, he had an expert knowledge of conditions in the working class areas of Liverpool. By the end of May, he and his men had visited 4348 cellars; of these only 174 were unoccupied. He reported that in the Irish districts *all* the cellars were being lived in but, despite these illegal occupations, he recognized that it was impossible to implement the law, '...yet a benevolent humanity will almost shudder at the idea of expelling the inmates of these places when they have nowhere else to lay their heads'.[46] This was a view shared by the police.[47]

Despite his experience of slum conditions Duncan still displayed a lack of understanding of the sheer difficulty which people who were destitute and living in awful circumstances, had in organizing their lives. For someone who had been nursing one or more sick persons, possibly sleeping on straw, short of food, living in permanent, cold, semi-darkness, lacking washing facilities, the simplest tasks presented huge challenges. When a person died in a cellar those wanting help *immediately* would have to have gone to the parish office. There they would have had to persuade a parish officer to visit their dwelling.[48] If a person went directly to the workhouse, there was no guarantee they would be dealt with. In his report to the Health Committee on 22 March, Duncan said he himself had witnessed a woman carry the body of her dead child into the workhouse and ask for it to be put in the charnel house. Her request was refused. Duncan asked the Health Committee to offer facilities to those relatives who were willing to deposit corpses in the workhouse deadhouse. Again, no policy decision was taken.[49]

As early as March the parochial medical officers were overstretched with the consequence that many persons were going unattended. Catherine O'Leary lived at 17 Westmorland Street where her child became seriously ill. She carried the baby to the house of Mr Cripps, a doctor, and asked for help. A servant turned her away. No doctor visited her and the child died.[50] On 5 April, *The London Times* ran a piece headed 'Irish invasion'. This described the crisis in Liverpool and the building of extra fever sheds. Readers were told that corpses were taken by relatives to the pauper churchyard (in the Abercromby ward) at all hours of the day and night. The reporter claimed that often the coffin lids were not nailed down and that if the gates were closed at night time, the coffins were shoved over the wall. In other cases, they were left outside the wall. The report was dated 1 April but there is no reason to believe it was incredible. Some people could not afford coffins and of these, some were so disorientated that they did not use the poor law facilities available. A policeman was called to Gloucester Street by frightened residents. An Irish woman was carrying a dead baby and knocking on doors, asking for money in order to bury the child. The policeman removed her from the street.[51] Though the district relieving officers tried to visit the poor regularly, when illness struck help was needed immediately. If all the family were ill, then the effort needed to contact the relieving officers or doctors was often beyond their capability. This was particularly the case if the sick were newly arrived immigrants, not conversant with the geography of the town or the system. There are numerous examples of breakdowns in the system. A man and his four children living in Scotland Road were turned out of their home because one child had the fever. They could not get to the hospital, no one else would take the child, which was left all night in the street.[52] In yet another case, an Irish family of four were found lying in a field in the Potteries in Toxteth on Tuesday, 7 June. They had been lying their since the previous Saturday, covered in a blanket. They were taken in a cart to the workhouse fever hospital.[53] Illustrative of the severity of the situation is the case of a police officer who found two persons in Newhall Street, in the North End, both ill with fever. He concluded they were dying and contacted Dr Ashcroft, the district medical officer, who refused to turn out, claiming he was ill. The constable then tried to obtain a horse and trap to take the individuals to the Workhouse, but failed. He went to the Workhouse and explained the situation, only to be told that there was no places available in the fever wards. He finally obtained a car and took them to the infirmary at the Workhouse. Again, he was told there was no room. In desperation, he took the persons to the Bridewell, which at the time contained 55 people. The typhus sufferers were placed in the cells with prisoners. The latter were clearly at risk and such measures negated the efforts of the health authorities to contain the epidemic.[54]

The examples given above indicate a lack of resources to deal with the crisis. Given this fact, then the bad state of many immigrants meant they could not take advantage of the services available. The Select Vestry meeting early in March was told of a case discovered by a relieving officer:

> Amongst a certain number of individuals in a cellar in Bent Street, it was reported that four were lying down in one bed, with fever; that twenty four grown up young men and their sisters were sleeping in a filthy state in the room; and that fourteen persons were sleeping in another filthy place. Thirty six persons were found huddled together in a room elsewhere and eight had died of fever in one house.[55]

Fever and dysentery were not the only illnesses at large. In February, Irish children in Liverpool began to be affected by smallpox, very few of the children of the Irish having been vaccinated. This was followed in March by an outbreak of measles. During 1847, 381 persons died of smallpox and 378 of measles. What number of these were Irish is not recorded but the view was expressed that the children in the Irish districts were particularly affected.[56] Duncan was strongly of the opinion that many famine Irish immigrants would have lived had they stayed in Ireland instead of going to Liverpool, 'the cemetery of Ireland'.[57]

The members of the Select Vestry were far removed from the frightening reality of the squalor and dreadful scenes of suffering characteristic of so many dwellings at this time. (homes does not seem the appropriate noun). Reading the accounts of the regular meetings of the Select Vestry, one is left with a strong sense that the guardians were detached from the tragedy unfolding in the streets around them. Not so for those in the front line, the Catholic priests, relieving officers, policemen, doctors, nurses and staff of the workhouse. Press reports give some idea of the extent of the involvement of Catholic clergy in the typhus crisis. On 12 March, a man went to the stipendiary magistrates office and complained about an Irish family which had taken possession of a house in Vauxhall Road. In this house several deaths had occurred from fever, including several children. The mother refused to allow the bodies of her children to be removed. Rushton sent for Superintendent Towerson of the Vauxhall Police Station and ordered that the bodies be put into coffins but first to check if the woman's refusal was based on religious beliefs. If it was, Towerson was to get the Catholic priest to attend her.[58] In another case, a man went to Rushton's office and asked the authorities for help. He lived in a Court off Key Street. A man had died in one of the fever sheds and his friends had announced their intention of removing the body from the sheds in order to have a wake in their house in Key Street. As a consequence, the neighbours were terrified of catching fever in what was a densely packed Court. Rushton ordered the police to have the body kept in the fever sheds until arrangements for immediate burial were completed.[59] The *Liverpool Journal* of 13 March carried a report headed 'A Skibbereen in Liverpool':

> We fear that there is at this moment suffering as great and undeserved in this town as can be witnessed, even on the west coast of Ireland. Two or three cases in one court have come to our knowledge. That court is Webster's Court in Oriel Street. It was in this pest place that the Rev. Mr Nightingale caught the fever which deprived society of a most kind hearted, pious clergyman. Last week a whole family was down with fever: there was no nurse, no doctor. An infant died and the mother was only able to push the dead body from off the straw on which she herself was dying. No one came to remove the corpse until the daily call of the Rev. Mr Newsham, of St Anthony's. In house no 1, are now lying in fever thirteen cases, four on one floor, five in another, some dying, some getting better. There is *no one* in attendance on them and no medical man had seen them Sunday to Thursday. The only person who visits them is the Rev gentleman whose name has already been mentioned. The parish allows the families 8sh a week and the authorities will probably enquire why a medical man has not seen them. In another court, all the family were down with fever, but a child, and that child was burnt to death in consequence of its clothes catching fire while making for a hot drink.

The reference to the Catholic clergy from St Anthony's in Scotland Road confirms the people were Irish Catholics. At the same time as the above events were taking place, the clergy at the Roman Catholic Chapel of St Joseph's at Copperas Hill read out at one mass 130 names of parishioners for whom prayers for the sick were asked. In addition, prayers for the dead were offered for seventeen parishioners.[60] The Catholic clergy were particularly at risk because of their custom of visiting sick parishioners and their sacramental responsibilities to hear confessions and give the last rites. Early in March, Fr Nightingale caught typhus and died.[61] On 29 April Fr William Parker died; he had been one of the clergy at St Patrick's in Toxteth for about ten years.[62] He was soon followed, on 13 May, by Fr James Challinor, of St Joseph's, Grosvenor Street.[63] By 14 June, five of Liverpool's Catholic priests were dead. Fr Brown of Birkenhead wrote to a colleague in Lisbon on 14 June:

> I regret to inform you of the sickness and deaths of our Liverpool clergy. Five are dead and Mr Grayston of St Patrick's is hardly expected to last another day. Fever is making fearful ravages all over the town but especially around St Anthony's. Mr Newsham told me a few days ago that he had visited sixty eight cases... We have prayers in every congregation, to avert the scourge of famine and pestilence.[64]

St Anthony's is in Scotland Road and the area was one with very large numbers of Irish. Brown's reference to Grayston was prophetic. Fr Grayston died, Wednesday, 17 June. The previous Wednesday he had sung High Mass at St Mary's, Edmund Street, at the funeral of Fr Gilbert, also a typhus victim. The next day he complained of feeling unwell. On the Sunday before his death, Grayston had told his Irish parishioners that they must clean up their dwellings and persons unless they wished to kill all their priests. Grayston had been educated in France and Ushaw College, Durham, was thirty three when he died and like many of the Catholic clergy tending the Irish, was English.[65] At the time of Grayston's death, Fr Kelly, an Irish priest at St Patrick's, appeared to be recovering from typhus but he also died. Fr Hagger went down with the disease and died on 23 June, 40 years of age. He was also one of the clergy at St Patrick's, making three priests dead, leaving a sole priest to cope with the needs of a large Irish population.[66] On 26 June, Fr William Dale died. He was on the staff of St Mary's, Edmund Street. A Yorkshireman who had been in Liverpool for about ten years, he had been responsible for raising money and building St Mary's. The *Liverpool Mercury* reported that he had caught the fever while visiting the cellars in the North End. He took to his bed on Sunday, 20 June and died on Saturday, 26 June, 'his body covered with black spots'.[67]

Up to this point no Protestant clergy were reported dead The sole non-Catholic minister to die of typhus was the Rev. John Johns of the Liverpool Domestic Mission. He died 23 June at his home in Mill Street. He was forty seven years of age and left a wife and six young children.[68] Unlike the majority of Anglican clergy in Liverpool, Johns and his fellow workers at the Unitarian Domestic Mission were active in the slums and so were at risk from typhus. Early in July, when deaths from fever were at their highest, the *Liverpool Mercury* told its readers:

> We are glad to learn there are no new cases of fever among the Roman Catholic Clergy in this town. The Rev. O'Reilly is still improved and Mr Walker and Mr Williamson are nearly recovered. It is also satisfactory to know that the calls upon these devoted men are on the decrease in the districts of St Mary's, St Anthony's and St Nicholas. The districts of St Patrick's and St Joseph's are now in the worst condition as regards fever. The number of calls made in the first named districts average about twenty calls daily whilst in the latter they average about forty. Some idea of the wretched places into which the Roman Catholic clergy venture in their ministerial capacity may be formed when it is known that in one house alone in the district of St Patrick's there were, besides two dead bodies, twenty eight cases of fever.[69]

Soon after this report, Fathers Gillow and Whittaker died. Further evidence of the nightmarish experience is contained in a letter written by Fr Gregory Lane, on 20 July 1847. He was writing from St Mary's Presbytery in St Paul's Square, Liverpool, to Fr Benet Tidmarsh. Lane had been sent to Liverpool to help fill the gap in manpower resulting from the death of so many priests. He told Tidmarsh that he had been giving the last rites to an average of ten people per day but that on some days, this had risen to twenty. He claimed that the bodies of the typhus victims began decaying rapidly and that often their arms and legs came off. While the body of one priest was being placed in its coffin, it had 'burst'. Presumably, this was because of gases building up in the body. Lane said that the priests prepared *all* typhus victims for death. On 16 July he had been walking in a nearby street when a child told him that someone was sick in a house. He went in and found a fifteen year old girl with typhus. He assumed she was a Catholic and started to give her the last rites. However, she told him she did not understand what he was saying and it turned out she was not a Catholic. The child said her mother and father had died in the same bed two weeks previously and she also wanted to go to Heaven. Lane told her that unless she was a Catholic, there was nothing he could do. She consented to become a Catholic and Lane got her into a fever shed and recorded he had his eye on her younger brother and sister.[70] Lane's response to the child's predicament is interesting in as much as it highlights the exclusivity of Catholic claims at the times. He offered Heaven as a reward for conversion. The Protestants offered soup, and then Heaven. Writing on 27 August, Fr Brown of Birkenhead wrote to the President of the English College in Lisbon, apologising for his lack of letter writing. He explained that in addition to the Catholics of Birkenhead, he was attending the lazarettos in the Mersey, 'which contain hundreds of the worst cases of fever out of Liverpool'.[71] During the *quarter* ending 30 September, 301 died on board the lazarettos.[72] At this particular juncture in the history of the Roman Catholic church in England, it is possible to detect a sense of triumphalism among the clergy, a sense that their (Catholic) time had come. The conversion of John Henry Newman and numbers of other prominent Anglicans, many aristocratic, had bolstered confidence. The Irish immigration had vastly increased their congregations and the famine cast them into a dramatic historical event from which they emerged 'with enhanced and indeed heroic status'. Thomas Seed, a Catholic priest at St Anthony's in Scotland Road, wrote to the President of the English College in Lisbon on 16 October. By this time, the fever was lessening in severity:

> You will have heard no doubt of my present destination. Little did I expect to find on arriving at Liverpool that this priest-killing town was to be the scene of my labours. But so it is. Dr Waring, on account of the lamentable loss of so many priests in this district, has offered my services for a time to Dr Brown. So here I am, sent to the great town of Liverpool, dwelling in the midst of plenty and want, happiness and misery, healthiness and sickness, life and death. What a change for the serious farm lad, to be pitched from quiet Lisbon to the neverending commotion and hurly burly of Liverpool... I am in excellent company. The two Newshams, Thomas and Henry, lately from Ushaw, are very jovial and interesting companions. Henry who has had the good fortune to recover from a dangerous attack of the fever, is now exempt from the duty of visiting the sick... The congregation of this church amounts to the number of 26 000... Every Friday and Saturday evening from 5 till 10.0 o'clock, we sit in the confessional listening to the innocent tales of these good Liverpoolians. This town is verily a holy consecrated spot. I had no idea of the glorious fervour ... We visit the sick from ten to three o'clock. If anyone wants to have an idea of real misery, he has only to enter into the dark, filthy, cellars of the poor dying Irish. From the late deaths of Mr Gillow and of Whittaker, you will have perceived that the fever has not yet been mastered. In this district of St Anthony's, during the last two weeks, it has considerably abated. In the present state of things, we cannot promise ourselves, with any assurance, a long life. Two years seems to me a very long period to live in these perilous times. I do not, at all, feel afraid of being kidnapped by the fever. Nor do the other priests here. *We live as if we were not to die*, messy, happy and in health. How the fever rages in the north! Billington, Standon and Dugdale have in these last two weeks been carried off.[73]

This letter has overtones of a willingness to embrace martyrdom in the face of the typhus epidemic. Certainly, the groups of celibate Catholic clergy were more single minded in their pastoral duties in this dangerous situation than the majority of non Catholic clergy. However, the priests were not the only heroes. As early as March, a number of poor law officials had died as a result of fever caught in the course of carrying out their duties. On 23 March the Select Vestry was told by Archibald Campbell, the chairman, that he had written to the Poor Law Commissioners asking if parish funds could be used to give some money to the widows and children of dead officials. This was turned down, as being illegal. Campbell suggested that ratepayers should set up a fund instead. It is not clear that anything followed this suggestion and in the meantime many more officials subsequently died.[74]

Early in May the Select Vestry petitioned the Home Secretary yet again, asking for help. The petition pointed out that three relieving officers were dead, two dangerously ill; one doctor had died, another was ill; a nurse dead and another ill.[75] Soon after, doctors Steele, Gee and Grimsdale all contracted typhus while an office worker in the parish office died of the disease.[76] Two weeks later Dr John Whitely died of typhus, the third doctor to die within two weeks. He was followed by the Matron of the Night Asylum and Mr Peachey, another parish relieving officer.[77] The press published the litany of casualties among public workers. A Mr Sampson was appointed a relieving officer in June. He died of typhus two weeks later; Mr Smith Rowland, dentist, cupper and hairdresser to fever victims in the sheds, died on 26 June, having held his parish job for three weeks. His son a relieving officer, had died of typhus earlier in the year.[78]

Just how many parochial officers, workers and police died of typhus as a result of tending the Irish has not been established. In his report for 1847, Duncan noted the death of ten Catholic priests and ten doctors.[79]

VI

Though the events of 1847 in Liverpool were extensively reported by the local press, the coverage is less than one would have expected, given the calamitous nature of the fever epidemic. Far more space was given to politics, both national and local, trade and shipping and foreign news. In particular, the reporting of the parliamentary elections dominated the news in July, when typhus deaths were peaking. One reason for this is that the worst effects were felt in the working class areas, an alien world to the middle classes who made up the bulk of the readership. The members of the Select Vestry did not visit the sick and poor, the paid officers provided a barrier between them and the awfulness of the life in the poor areas. Life went on, and trade and shipping were Liverpool's lifeblood.

Figure 5.2 The Plaque placed in the Presbytery of St Anthony's Church, Scotland Road, Liverpool, commemorating the ten Roman Catholic priests who died during the afflictive year, 1847.

In Memorium

The awful visitation which it pleased Divine Providence to inflict upon Liverpool in 1847 (the most awful on record that ever befell it) will long render that year painfully memorable to its inhabitants. Pestilence, like the Destroying Angel, passed from house to house through the whole town, numbering its victims by thousands, among whom were the ten Roman Catholic priests here graphically represented to the public - a relic dear to those for whose sake, or for that of their relatives or friends, these ministers of religion sacrificed their lives. Like true champions of the Cross and valiant heroes of Christianity, they boldly went forth, in the service of the Great King to whom they had vowed allegiance, where the shafts of death fell thick around them. By their deeds they proved themselves Disciples of their Lord, who had said 'By this shall men know that ye are My Disciple, if ye love one another', they had love, and the greatest love; 'GREATER LOVE THAN THIS NO MAN HATH, THAT A MAN LAY DOWN HIS LIFE FOR HIS FRIENDS'.

Rev. William Vincent Dale, O.S.B., died June 20th, aged 48 years.
Rev. William Parker, died April 28th, aged 43 years.
Rev. Richard Grayston, died June 16th, aged 33 years.
Rev John Fielding Whitaker, died September 28th, aged 36 years.
Rev. John Austin Gilbert, O.S.B., died May 31st, aged 27 years.
Rev. Peter Nightingale, died March 2nd, aged 32 years.
Rev. James Haggar, died June 23rd, aged 29 years.
Rev. Robert Gillow, died August 22nd, aged 35 years.
Rev. James Francis Appleton, D.D., O.S.B., died May 28th, aged 40 years.
Rev. Thomas Kelly, D.D., died May 15th, aged 28 years.

They were good and faithful shepherds; 'THE GOOD SHEPHERD GIVETH HIS LIFE FOR HIS SHEEP'. They now rest from their labours, may their memory be in benediction and long preserved among all who witnessed or heard of their dedication. Spiritual consolation and temporal aid to the afflicted poor, was the business of their lives, truly acting like Good Samaritans by pouring the oil of comfort into the wounds of their stricken fellow creatures. May their example be an incentive to others in similar circumstances to 'Go and Do Likewise'. To further the cause of education among the poor Boys and Girls of their congregations, was an object dear to their whole living, and the present effect is made in the hope of assisting with benevolent intentions to those little ones whom in life they gathered under their protection, to impart to them that flame of charity which warmed their own hearts.

May Heaven's Blessing be upon the Undertaking

Restricting ourselves here to the typhus crisis, the press saw it as part of the more general unfairness of one parish, Liverpool, having to bear such a large burden. Newspaper reading provided the only way that many people in the middle class areas acquired any inkling of what was going on. Typical of such reporting was the piece which appeared in the *Liverpool Mercury* on 12 February, 1847. After drawing the attention of its readers to the dangers to the health of *all* residents, it called on government to erect large sheds in Ireland for Irish pauper fever victims. It also said all Irish embarking at Irish ports for Liverpool should be warned they would be sent back:

> We have no right to sit still and let pestilence walk in amongst us . At this moment the progress of fever in the cellars and garrets of Liverpool is most alarming. The first flush of warm weather will spread disease and death into hundreds of streets. The filthy state in which the poor people arrive and the shocking damp, dirty places in which they herd - as many as thirty in a cellar - are the most certain constituents of malignant fever; and deeply shall we suffer in a few weeks by the loss of many of our valued townsmen and townswomen, if the evil growing around us be not staid.

The paper, was wrong in assuming warm weather would spread fever. It was correct in its assertion that the town would lose many of its inhabitants. In this case 'valued' townsmen and townswomen meant members of the wealthier classes. On 19 March, the *Mercury* praised the Health of Town Committee for its actions in petitioning the Home Secretary and the Irish administration, on the subject of Irish immigration into Liverpool. The Committee had told the Home Secretary that conditions in Liverpool were so bad for the Irish that they would have been safer had they stayed at home. In its comments *The Mercury*, urged the 'public attention to self preservation'. Returning to the issue on 23 April, the *Mercury* repeated its long held view that large sheds should be erected in Ireland for Irish paupers, who should be removed from England. Referring to the 'generous' response of the inhabitants of Liverpool to the famine influx, the *Mercury* continued:

> But those inhabitants now have an imperative duty to perform and that is this, to save themselves and their families from calamities such as have never been known here and which threaten disastrous results. Unless the town is cleared of many thousands of the paupers belonging to the soil of Ireland, who are now impoverishing our parochial treasury and engendering the most frightful diseases from the dirt and destitution in which they are involved in the dark cellars and miserable garrets in which

> they are huddled together we shall indeed find Liverpool converted into, not only a Skibbereen on a large scale but a Lazar House such as England has never had within its borders since the horrible days of the great plague.

This and similar reports by *The London Times* were in turn attacked by the *Liverpool Journal* on 24 April. It accused the *Times* and *Mercury* of exaggeration. The *Journal* leader was principally concerned that the stories of the horrors in Liverpool would frighten off visitors and so adversely affect trade. 'People at a distance will imbibe a dread of the place which years may not remove, hundreds will seek their summer enjoyments in another direction'. The success of the Liverpool-Manchester railway had been followed by the growth of a big trade in day visitors from Lancashire, fascinated by Liverpool's docks and river. In a rather poor piece of investigative journalism, it reproduced statistics showing that in the period 1 January to 14 April the numbers of people treated in the Liverpool dispensaries in 1846 was 10 408 while for the same period in 1847, the total was 9765. This, concluded the *Journal* leader writer, proved that the town was in a healthy state. This is breathtakingly myopic and one can only conclude that the writer was totally cynical in his concern over profits and had never emerged from his middle class redoubt. No reference was made to the fact that thousands were being treated at home and in fever sheds. On 4 May, the *Mercury* advocated sending twenty or thirty thousands of Liverpool's Irish paupers to Westminster. It argued that the legislation in the House would be 'passed in less than a fortnight' if disease threatened Westminster on the same scale. *The Mercury* was in no doubt about the nature of the problem:

> Here we see on our piers thousands of pitiable creatures who have no choice but to get into cellars long since condemned as unfit for habitation, and into garrets already overcrowded. Disease is at work there and fastens, as if instinctively, upon their poor frames, which are predisposed to its deadly effects. When fever has marked its own, we remove the victims to temporary fever sheds for the channel of relief or death. On their first landing, we know that they pine in comparative hunger, though we relieve them, many must die because they resort for shelter to the places saturated with filth and foul air and diseased sufferers. Our police officers cannot drive them out because there are no hospitals or prisons that would hold a tithe of them. Their begging in the streets, and the disgusting exhibition they make with squalid, perishing children in their arms, cannot be suppressed, for the same reason. A prison would be a paradise for them, a luxury we cannot give them, and here the sanitary,

> and vagrant laws are at this moment, in this town, virtually bereft of all force. Parliament is now impotent.

This statement in the *Mercury* is a remarkably pithy and accurate statement of the situation in Liverpool in April. As such it can have left few of the wealthier classes ignorant of the problem facing the town. In early May, the registrar of one of Liverpool's sub-districts declared unequivocally his opinion that the famine Irish were bringing 'Irish fever' with them. Commenting on his statement, *The London Times* of 4 May declared that:

> Perhaps there is not a parallel case to Liverpool for the last two months in the history of the country... Liverpool is notoriously the most unhealthy, worst drained and most miasmic city of the Empire.

As the empire included Bombay and Calcutta the *Times* may have been guilty of exaggeration. London in the great plague was even more calamitous. However, in recent history, the claim does not look outrageous. The *Liverpool Chronicle* of 19 June told its readers that there was no reason whatsoever why the parishioners of Liverpool, or the English population, should be 'swept into their graves' to save the pockets of Irish landlords. A week later the *Liverpool Albion*, in the course of a long leader on the crisis, assured its readers there was nothing for the middle classes to worry about, at least *if they did not work for the parochial authorities*:

> Though the fever, which continues to smoulder and break forth among the multitude of Irish immigrants so perversingly thrown upon our charity, has worked melancholy results upon some of those whose duties have brought them into contact with the squalid miserables who have imported it, there is not the slightest reason for alarm or apprehension amongst those who are happily removed from its immediate influence. Though the subject is not one that will bear to be treated with the slightest approximation of levity, some of our townsmen cannot forbear laughing at the absurd fears of some of their distant friends, some of whom regard us as a city smitten with pestilence.[80]

The piece is striking for its lack of concern over what was happening in the working class districts of the town and goes on to make the claim that Liverpool was 'exceedingly healthy... Our distant friends may therefore, visit us, on business or pleasure, in transition or for a lengthened sojourn, without apprehension and they will find our citizens walking with their usual cheerfulness and alacrity, untroubled by the thought of Irish sickness'. The underlying concern was over a possible loss of visitors and trade.

Looking back over what had happened in Liverpool during 1847, Dr Duncan recorded the toll on the town. Nearly 60 000 individuals contracted typhus, 40 000 diarrhoea and dysentery. In his view, Liverpool was converted into a 'city of plague' by the immigrant Irish who 'inundated the lower districts'. In his view, 1847 had been 'calamitous'.[81]

The total deaths in Liverpool in 1847 was 17 280. Of this total, 7475 died of fever, dysentery and diarrhoea. If we assume 70 per cent of these were Irish deaths, then we arrive at an estimated 5233 deaths during 1847. This gives some kind of basis on the claims regarding Famine Irish fever deaths. Not included here are childrens' deaths from measles and scarletina. Many hundreds of Irish children died of these diseases, during the year. However, a figure of approximately 5500 deaths still justifies the label given to Liverpool by the Registrar General, 'the cemetery of Ireland'.

Notes and References

1 Chadwick Report (England) no 18. Summary of the Cases of Fever Admitted into the Fever Hospitals at Liverpool, 1834-39', p. 257. The medical services in Liverpool and other large towns were severely tested by the 1832 cholera outbreak and again, in 1836 and 1837, by fever outbreaks. During 1834, 1100 fever cases were admitted in Liverpool´s fever hospital. In 1837, the number was 2448.

2 For discussions of the state of medical thought at this time see C. Hamlin, 'Predisposing Causes and Public Health in Early Nineteenth Medical Thought', *Social History of Medicine* (1992) pp. 41-70. M. Sigworth and M. Worboys, 'The Public's View of Public Health in Mid-Victorian Britain', *Urban History,* Vol. 21, pt. 2 (October 1994), pp. 237-50. S. Gutia, 'The Importance of Social Intervention in England´s Mortality Decline: The Evidence Reviewed', *Social History of Medicine,* (1994), pp. 89-113. An illuminating study of the profession of medicine in Victorian Britain is found in R. Poster, *Diseases, Medicine and Society in England,* 1550-1860, 2nd ed. (Macmillan: 1993), ch.. 5.

3 Hamlin, op.cit. p. 58.

4 Hamlin, op.cit, Section IV. Hamlin uses the Irish typhus outbreak in 1817-19 as a case study, pp. 59-62.

5 For examinations of the nature of typhoid and typhus epidemics see, W. Luckin 'Evaluating the Sanitary Revolution: Typhus and Typhoid in London 1851-1900', in R. Woods and J. Woodward, eds. *Urban Disease and Mortality in Nineteenth Century England* (London: 1984) ch. 5. A. Hardy, 'Urban Famine or Urban Crisis? Typhus in the Victorian City', *Medical History,* 1988, 32, pp. 401-25. An excellent study of the public health problem in Victorian Britain is A. S. Wohl, *Endangered Lives: Public Health in Victorian Britain* (Cambridge: 1983), in particular see ch. 5.

6 For specific studies of 'Irish fever' see W. P. MacArthur, 'The Medical History of the Famine´, in R. Dudley Edwards and T. D. Williams, eds. *The Great Famine: Studies in Irish History, 1845-52* (Dublin: 1956) ch. 5, and L. M. Geary, 'Famine, Fever and the Bloody Flux', in C. Póirtéir, ed. *The Great Irish Famine* (Dublin: 1995).

7 MacArthur, op. cit. pp. 272-3.

8 At the time of writing (1996) there is no comprehensive biography of this remarkable man. There are two studies available to the interested reader. W. M. Fraser, *Duncan of Liverpool*, (London: 1947). This is a lightweight survey of Duncan's life. More recently, G.Kearns, P.Laxton and C.J.Campbell, 'Duncan and the Cholera Test: Public Health in Mid-Nineteenth Century Liverpool', *Transactions of the Historic Society of Lancashire and Cheshire*, volume 143 (1993) pp.85-115. This piece examines Duncan's attitude towards statistical analysis of disease and his position in the contagionist - anti-contagionist debate.
9 Liverpool Record Office (hereafter referred to as LIVRO) h.352.4.Hea, Medical Officer of Health, Report for 1847 (hereafter referred to as MOH. 1847) p. 10.
10 LIVRO. MOH. 1847, p. 6.
11 LIVRO. MOH. 1847, p. 8.
12 LIVRO. MOH. 1847, p. 18.
13 On 28 January 1847, Augustus Campbell, Chairman of the Select Committee, wrote to the Home Secretary, asking if immigration into Liverpool could be stopped, *Liverpool Mercury*, 29 January 1847, carries a copy of this letter.
14 BPP (HC) Third Report of the Select Committee on Medical Poor Relief, Appendix No 1, Liverpool Parish, p. 786.
15 Austin (1847) Appendix A, no 8, The Relief of the Irish Poor of Liverpool, dated 1 May 1847, p. 114.
16 Austin, op. cit. p. 114. Austin claimed that taking into account the temporary fever sheds at Brownlow Hill and Great Howard Street, there were, in May, 'nearly' 1000 fever patients.
17 Austin, op. cit. p. 114. Also *Liverpool Courier,* 24 May 1847, Report on the weekly meeting of the Select Vestry, held on 23 March.
18 *Liverpool Courier*, 28 April 1847, Report on the weekly meeting of the Select Vestry, held on 27 April. The issue of complaints from residents was raised at this meeting for the first time.
19 LIVRO. H352/Min/Hea/11, Minutes of the Meeting of the Health Committee of the Borough Council (referred to hereafter as Health Minutes), 15 March 1847.
20 Health Minutes, 5 April 1847. These streets contained large number of Irish.
21 Health Minutes, 19 April 1847.
22 *Liverpool Courier*, 28 April 1847, Report on the weekly meeting of the Select Vestry, held on 27 April.
23 LIVRO. Cem/Mry/4/11-13, Burial records of the parochial cemeteries of St Mary's, Cambridge Street and St Martin-in-the-Fields, Vauxhall. These have been transferred to a database and are in the process of being fully analyzed.
24 Health Minutes, 17 May 1847.
25 Health Minutes, 31 May 1847, *Liverpool Mercury*, 8 June 1847.
26 *Manchester Guardian*, 9 June 1847, *Liverpool Standard*, 15 June 1847, Report on the weekly meeting of the Select Vestry, held on 8 June.
27 *Manchester Guardian*, 19 June 1847.
28 MOH. 1847, p. 8.
29 *Liverpool Mercury*, 29 June 1847.
30 For references to the lazarettos, see *London Times*, 8 May 1847, *Liverpool Chronicle*, 15 May 1847, Report of the ratepayers meeting held 12 May, *Liverpool Mercury*, 18 May 1847, *Manchester Guardian*, 19 May, 9 and 16 June 1847, *Liverpool Standard*, 15 June 1847, Reports of the meeting of the meeting of the Select Vestry held 7 June.
31 LIVRO. 353/Sel/19/3. Workhouse Admissions and Discharges Register (names are entered alphabetically).

32 *Liverpool Mercury*, 1 June 1847.
33 For reports of this meeting see *Liverpool Times*, 13 May 1847; *Liverpool Chronicle*, 15 May 1847.
34 *Manchester Guardian*, 30 June; 3 and 7 July 1847; *Liverpool Albion*, July
35 SC (1850) Minutes of Evidence, Augustus Campbell, q. 5026, p. 369.
36 *Liverpool Albion*, 26 July 1847.
37 *Manchester Guardian*, 10 July 1847.
38 The Liverpool Workhouse Admissions and Discharges Register provides clear evidence that many Irish paupers were removed back to Ireland when pronounced cured in the workhouse fever sheds. See p.226.
39 MOH. 1847, p. 9. *Liverpool Albion*, 4 October 1847. The *Albion* also stated that seven posts of relieving officers were to be discontinued.
40 *Liverpool Albion*
41 *Liverpool Mercury* 6 November 1847.
42 *Liverpool Journal*, 6 February 1847.
43 MOH. 1847, p. 6. *Liverpool Journal*, 6 March 1847. This reports that Duncan told the town council that out of 90 patients in the workhouse hospital, 73 were Irish.
44 Health Minutes, 15 March 1847.
45 Health Minutes, 22 March 1847, Report from Inspector Fresh.
46 Health Minutes, 31 May 1847.
47 During the first week on July 1847, the Sanitary Committee emptied 56 cellars but had to stop because the inhabitants were left in the streets, most suffering from fever. *Manchester Guardian*, 7 July 1847. Rushton refused to sign any more eviction warrants.
48 *Liverpool Chronicle*, 27 March 1847, Report of the weekly meeting of the Select Vestry held on 23 March. The Vestry were told that often 1400 persons, were kept waiting in cellars below the parochial offices in Fenwick Street in conditions unsuitable for human beings. The meeting declined to do anything about this overcrowding.
49 LIVRO, Health Minutes, 22 March 1847.
50 *Liverpool Courier*, 10 March 1847, Report on weekly meeting of the Select Vestry.
51 *Liverpool Mercury*, 18 May 1847.
52 *Liverpool Courier*, 14 April 1847, Report of the weekly meeting of the Select Vestry, held on 13 April. The Head Constable told the meeting that the Vestry should provide proper transport for conveying fever victims to hospital.
53 *Liverpool Mercury*, 8 June 1847.
54 *Liverpool Times*, 11 May 1847, 'State of the Town'.
55 *Liverpool Courier*, 10 March 1847, Report of the meeting of the Select Vestry held on 9 March.
56 MOH. 1847, pp. 10-11. There is a strong correlation between under-nutrition and fatalities in measles, see D.Morley *Paediatric Priorities in the Developing World*, London, 1973. I am grateful to Bill Lukin for drawing my attention to this.
57 Health Minutes, 17 June 1847. The Registrar General described Liverpool as the 'cemetery of Ireland' in his report for the quarter ending 30 September 1847. See *Liverpool Standard*, 2 November 1847, for an analysis of the report insofar as it refers to Liverpool.
58 *Liverpool Journal*, 13 March 1847.
59 *Liverpool Mercury*, 15 June 1847.
60 *Liverpool Mercury* 19 March 1847.
61 *Liverpool Mercury*, 15 March 1847.
62 *Manchester Guardian*, 5 May 1847.

63 *Liverpool Mercury*, 18 May 1847.
64 Ushaw College, Durham. Lisbon correspondence, W.Brown to P.A.Davies, letter dated 14 June 1847.
65 *Liverpool Mercury*,18 June 1847. *Liverpool Chronicle*, 19 June 1847; *Liverpool Mercury*, 25 June 1847.
66 *Liverpool Mercury*, 25 June 1847.
67 *Liverpool Mercury*, 29 June 1847; *Manchester Guardian*, 30 June 1847.
68 *Liverpool Mercury*, 25 June 1847.
69 *Liverpool Mercury*, 6 July 1847.
70 'The Fever Year in Liverpool, 1847'. in *Downside Review*, 29 (1910) pp. 178-86. I am grateful to Maureen Walsh for drawing my attention to this letter.
71 Ushaw College, Durham. Lisbon correspondence, E. F. Brown to R. Winstanley, letter dated 25 August 1847.
72 *Liverpool Standard*, 2 November 1847, 'Registrar General's quarterly report for the quarter ending 30 September 1847, St Thomas sub-district'.
73 Ushaw College, Durham. Lisbon correspondence, T. Seed to the President, letter dated 16 October 1847.
74 *Liverpool Courier*, 24 March 1847 Report on the weekly meeting of the Select Vestry, held on 23 March.
75 *London Times*, 8 May 1847. Report on the proceedings in the House of Commons for 7 May. Sir Bernard Hall read parts of the Liverpool petition to the House.
76 *Liverpool Albion,* 2 May 1847.
77 *Liverpool Mercury*, 25 May 1847.
78 *Liverpool Mercury*, 29 June 1847.
79 MOH. 1847, p. 18.
80 *Liverpool Albion*, 28 June 1847.
81 LIVRO, MOH, 1847, p.18.

6 Glasgow, South Wales and the Irish Fever

I

Turning to other ports of entry, Glasgow has the most obvious parallels with Liverpool with respect to the typhus outbreak of 1847. The main difference was that the Scottish Poor Law provision for medical assistance to the poor was not the same as in England. Indeed, the new Scottish poor law introduced in 1845 did not impose a uniform pattern of provision on Scottish parishes and so generalisations are difficult to make. Specifically, Glasgow city did not have a workhouse with a medical ward as did Liverpool and also did not have a full-time medical officer of health. However, like English poor law authorities, Glasgow Parochial Board and the Boards of its suburbs all paid subscriptions to charitable institutions, in return for which poor people could be sent for medical treatment.[1] The situation in pre-famine Glasgow with regard to charitable institutions is shown in Table 6.1 below.

On first glance, the provision looks impressive, but placed against the size of the population living in poverty and the generally poor level of health of immigrants from Ireland and the Highlands, large numbers of the poor in Glasgow experienced severe suffering when falling ill. The normal harshness of life resulting from low incomes, intermittent employment and trade depressions was however periodically eclipsed by the devastating effect of typhus and cholera outbreaks. By 1840, the two principal institutions in Glasgow providing for the poor were the Royal Infirmary and the Towns Hospital. As Table 6.1 shows, in 1840 the Royal Infirmary had a fever hospital with 200 beds, together with a general ward of 231 beds. To obtain a bed, a pauper falling ill had to obtain papers from a church elder or district surgeon. The infirmary was managed by a committee of directors and depended on subscriptions.[2] The Towns Hospital was in effect a poor house, but it employed district surgeons to provide medical assistance to the outdoor poor. These medical officers were usually part-timers, having practices of their own.[3] Charles Baird, a Glasgow lawyer, told the Chadwick Enquiry in 1840 that: 'Much, however, as the working classes in Glasgow have suffered from the depression or fluctuations of trade, the want of employment and the high price of provisions, I conceive that their sufferings from these causes have been trifling indeed when compared to what they have annually suffered from disease, especially an epidemic'.[4]

Table 6.1 The Charities providing medical facilities at the public expense in Glasgow: 1840

	No. of Patients treated			*No. of beds*	*Cost*
	Indoor	*Outdoor*	*Total*		
Royal Infirmary	2 596	-	2 596	231}	
Royal Infirmary *Fever Hospital*	3 535	-	3 535	200}	
Royal Infirmary Dispensary	-	7 501	7 501	200}	£8 405.9s.9½d
Eye Infirmary	63	1 723	1 336	10	£263.3s.3d
Lock Hospital	369	-	369	32	£429.1s.7d
University Lying-in Hospital	136	410	546	14	£156.10s.0d
University Dispensary	-	2 708	2 708	-	£27.7s.2d
Glasgow Lying-in Hospital	104	90	194	18}	
Glasgow Dispensary	-	750	750	}	£99.0s.0d
Lunatic Asylum	11	-	11}	{	£200.4s.0
daily average			}	110{	
Lunatic Asylum Barony	22	-	22}	{	£400.0s.0d
Towns Hospital (lunatics)	43	-	43	56	£228.16s.2d
District Surgeries of city (12)	-	4 504	4 504	-	£252.0s.0d
District Surgeries Barony	-	949	949	-	£120.9s.1½d
District Surgeries Anderston	-	403	403	-	£41.0s.0d
District Surgeries Govan	-	320	320	-	£21.0d.0d
District Surgeries Gorbals	-	1 755	1 755	-	£82.0s.0d
Celtic Surgery	-	261	261	-	£48.3s.0d
Medicines for city paupers	-	-	-	-	£150.19s.3d
Total	6 879	20 926	27 805	871	£10 922.11s.4d

Source Sanitary Report (Scotland) No 9, p. 172.

The full scale of the 'Irish fever' crisis of 1847 can better be appreciated if it is examined in contrast to the number of deaths from fever in the years immediately preceding the famine, given below in Table 6.2. The numbers of deaths in the years 1837 and 1840 were the results of outbreaks of an epidemic nature, giving rise not only to an increase in the absolute number of deaths but also in the ratio of deaths to population. The data below refer to the city parish of Glasgow and the suburbs of Barony, Gorbals and Govan. Another index against which to judge the nature of the 1847 crisis is the number of burials at public expense, over the same period. The data below in Table 6.3 refers only to the city of Glasgow.

Table 6.2 The numbers of deaths from fever in the city of Glasgow and its suburbs over the period 1836-1840 (inclusive)

Year	*Deaths from fever*	*Deaths from fever as proportion of the population*
1836	841	1 in 290.1
1837	2180	1 in 116.1
1838	816	1 in 322.2
1839	539	1 in 504.6
1840	1229	1 in 229.5
Total	5605	

Source: Sanitary Report (Scotland) No. 9, Table vii, p.171

Table 6.3 The number of burials at public expense in the city of Glasgow 1836-1840 (inclusive)

Year ending 24 October	*Men*	*Women*	*Children*	*Total*
1836	120	175	363	658
1837	254	330	513	1097
1838	169	258	453	880
1839	116	182	447	745
1840	187	201	568	956
Total	846	1146	2344	4336

Source: Sanitary Report (Scotland) No 9, p.174.

Fifty four percent of all the pauper burials over these years were those of children, a pattern of child mortality occurring throughout Britain at this time. These data refer to paupers who died from all causes; we do not know the respective numbers of deaths attributed to each possible cause. However, the burials are highly correlated with the fever deaths, (r=0.85) in Table 6.2.

At the onset of the influx of Irish famine refugees towards the end of 1846, the Glasgow Parochial Board still had no hospital facilities of its own. It paid a subscription to the Royal Infirmary, in exchange it had access to beds in the fever and general wards. However, the Royal Infirmary's beds were also in demand by the Parochial Boards of Barony, Gorbals and Govan. Under normal circumstances, this hospital capacity of 200 fever beds and 231 general ward beds, was adequate. In terms of medical manpower, Glasgow Parochial Board employed seventeen district surgeons in 1846 to look after the needs of the sick poor, most of whom were treated at home or given medicine at one of the public dispensaries. The neighbouring parishes had similar arrangements. The crisis of 1847 was to precipitate an emergency on a scale that exceeded the worst years of the eighteen thirties.

The chronology of the developing typhus crisis in Glasgow reflected that of Liverpool's almost exactly. In January 1847, the *Glasgow Chronicle* expressed concern at the numbers of destitute Irish arriving in the city.[5] As elsewhere, the Irish were blamed for the typhus epidemic. On 1 March, 1847, the Glasgow Municipal Police Board were told that the majority of Irish arriving in the city were both destitute and diseased.[6] Four days later, the Glasgow Parochial Board received a report which stated that the Irish were spreading disease in the parish:

> The necessity of imposing additional assessment on ratepayers to meet the deficiency before the end of the financial year. The committee regrets to say that such an emergency has arisen, that privation, suffering and disease prevailed and still prevail to a lamentable extent in the city.[7]

Following this, reports flowed in from officials regarding the conditions in the poorest areas and subsequently these appeared in the press. By the end of March the parochial authorities in the city of Glasgow can have been in no doubt that they were facing a major health crisis. On 26 March, the Parochial Board had read to them a letter from Dr Archibald Brown, one of the district surgeons. He referred to the state of a close, number 275, High Street. After describing the lack of drains and the filth of the place, he claimed that of 105 persons who had lived in that close since June 1846, had all contracted fever.[8] At the same meeting another letter was read out, this time from Mr Willick, an assistant poor inspector. He had just visited a cellar at number 95, Bridgegate, which measured sixteen feet by ten feet. '... there four Irish families, twenty three persons, and eight had fever. None of them were more than eleven months from Ireland, a considerable portion only three months'.[9]

Clearly these were famine Irish. Willick wanted the cellar inspected, presumably with a view to removing the individuals and he also expressed concern over the lodging houses.[10] The meeting went on to adopt an increasingly popular tactic used by besieged local authorities, a petition to Parliament regarding Irish immigration. This particular petition encapsulates the views of Glasgow's middle classes regarding the nature of the crisis. After asking for an Irish Poor Law which would provide relief for the able-bodied in Ireland, the petition went on to repeat the claim that the Irish famine refugees were spreading disease among Glasgow's working classes.[11] Given the correlation between social disruption, in particular overcrowding, and the transmission mechanism for typhus, body lice, the Irish had always featured disproportionately in the fever statistics in Glasgow. For example, in 1832, 41 per cent of all fever victims admitted to the fever ward at the Royal Infirmary were Irish and in 1842 the figure was also 41 per cent. Between July 1846 and January 1847, a total of 1680 persons were taken into the Royal Infirmary fever ward and of these 879 or 52 per cent, were Irish. The *Glasgow Herald* of 22 March 1847 told its readers that 'the great majority of the cases of typhus which have occurred may be traced to the masses of diseased and famished Irish which have been thrown amongst us'. Thus at the outset of the emergency, the blame was unequivocally laid on the Irish famine refugees.

Given the organisational structure and hospital facilities available, the Parochial Board wanted to send increasing numbers of sick paupers to the Royal Infirmary. As in Liverpool, the medical strategy adopted was to take fever victims out of their homes and into hospital. However, the infirmary simply did not have the beds to cope. Before the end of March the directors of the Royal Infirmary acquired an empty cotton mill on the Dalmarnock Road with the view of converting it into a fever hospital. Immediately, local residents protested and organized an approach to Sheriff Bell for an interdict.[12] In the meantime the objectors held a meeting at Bridgeton with the objective of presenting their arguments to the Sheriff.[13] Eventually, the Royal Infirmary provided an extra 150 beds in the temporary fever hospital, financed by a £300 donation from Glasgow city parish and money from Barony parish.[14] By the beginning of May, it was clear that the number of hospital beds was massively insufficient to successfully implement a policy of isolating all fever victims in hospitals. The Towns Hospital had 643 inmates, 411 beds and 51 temporary beds. However, these were for the indoor poor and while some fever victims could be accommodated here, it provided no solution. The Parochial Board was told that 'strong measures were needed'. One district surgeon claimed he had 200 fever patients in his district, none of whom could be found a hospital bed. Sometimes he found six or seven in one house, all with fever. In some instances reported Mr Godwin, another district surgeon, there were five to eight cases in one small house, all needing hospital beds. Mr M'Lure told the Board of 17 persons in one garret, eight of whom had fever.[15] The following week the Glasgow Municipal Police Board was informed that even given the conversion of the cotton mill and the opening to a temporary fever ward at the Infirmary there would still be insufficient beds for the typhus victims. Baillie Liddell told the Board that he had reviewed returns from 15 of the 17 district surgeons belonging to the Towns Hospital. They reported that there were 526 'of the poorest classes' in these 15 districts, all with fever and needing hospital attention but for whom there were no beds. Liddell estimated that taking into account Calton, Bridgeton, Barony and Govan 'it would not be too high an estimate to say there are at present 400 cases in these districts, making a total of 1000'.[16] During May, the Glasgow Parochial Board sent 467 fever patients to hospital and on 3 June it was estimated there were nearly 500 persons being treated at home.[17] By this time the Parochial Board had grasped the nettle and acquired the old Poor Home from the Caledonian Railway Company. It was in a bad state of repair but in a remarkable effort it was converted into a parochial hospital in six weeks, opening on 29 June. It was in Great Clyde Street and provided 331 beds.[18] Despite these efforts, the majority of fever victims were treated in their dwellings. It was estimated that the total number of beds available after the parochial hospital opened was 699, including 368 at the Royal Infirmary's fever wards. Against this there were 1225 fever cases being treated at home.[19]

In reality, there was no chance of the Glasgow authorities hospitalising all fever victims and the continual arrival of famine Irish reinforced the hold of typhus in the overcrowded slums. The Glasgow Parochial Board had no hesitation in identifying the famine Irish as the source of their problems. At its Board meeting 5 March 1847, the Rate Assessment Committee had presented a report on the cost to Glasgow of the Irish influx. After expressing sympathy for the Irish, it called on the Parochial Board to petition Parliament regarding a poor law for Ireland, in the hope that:

> ... the influx of Irish paupers into this parish may be stopped, for not only are these casual Irish paupers amounting in numbers to many thousands a year, absorbing a large portion of the rate levied for the maintenance of the poor of the parish, but from their utter wretchedness, destitution and disease, are not only *spreading disease throughout the city* [my italics] but are setting a most pernicious example to the lower orders of Glasgow by accustoming them and instructing them to look for parochial aid for support instead of depending, as they hitherto have done before, on their own exertions.[20]

The Parochial Board in fact petitioned the House of Commons regarding the crisis on several occasions (see Appendix No. 6.2) In the course of spelling out its concerns over the Irish famine immigration, it went on to stress the health factor:

> ...that in addition to the extraordinary internal pressure, many thousands of diseased and starving Irish have forced themselves on this community and have become chargeable on the parish..... That those districts of the city in which the poorer classes reside have subsequently become too much overcrowded and fever is there raging to a fearful extent.... The most valuable public officers have already fallen victim to fever and the

> execution of public duties connected with this Board have become of a most hazardous character. This will go on to increase as long as multitudes of diseased and destitute Irish are permitted to enter the city.[21]

Glasgow had no more success than Liverpool in trying to stop Irish famine immigration and the petitions show the same lack of real understanding of the nature of the horrors in Ireland which propelled people out of Ireland fixed with the belief that anywhere was better than Ireland.

As in Liverpool, a vital factor in the survival strategy of the newly arrived Irish in Glasgow was the use of lodging houses. These assumed a greater importance than in the case of Liverpool and Manchester because Glasgow had fewer cellars. However, the popularity of lodging houses facilitated the spread of typhus. The worst conditioned areas of Glasgow city consisted of the Wynds and Closes on the south side of Trongate and Argyle Streets, including Saltmarket and Bridgegate, the east side of High Street and a large part of Gallowgate. On 19 April, the Superintendent of Police told the Parochial Board that in this area there were 915 lodging houses.[22] Yet despite the clearly understood correlation between lodging houses and incidence of fever, the authorities knew that a policy of emptying the lodging houses was simply not feasible. Where would those ejected live? This was the same dilemma which taxed the Liverpool authorities faced with the illegal occupation of cellars. A month later, Baillie Liddell told the Municipal Police Board that there was a need to licence lodging houses but this advice was irrelevant in term of solving the problem as it existed when he made the statement.[23]

The shortage of beds resulted in the Police Office being used as a temporary hospital ward. Mirroring the situation in other centres of Irish immigration at this time, lodging house keepers threw out any lodger suspected of having fever. For example, ten persons were ejected from lodging houses towards the end of May. Of these, four were found hospital beds but the other five were taken to the Police Office. For obvious reasons such measures were unpopular with police officers and in this particular case, officers refused to attend the men.[24] On 23 May, Brian Doyle was taken to the Central Police Office suffering from fever but he was refused admission and was sent to the Royal Infirmary where he was also refused admission. He was taken back to the Police Office, admitted and died two days later.[25] By the week ending 19 June there were 17 fever victims in the Glasgow Police Office.[26] Margaret Connor was a young Irish woman who worked in a cotton mill at Eaglesham. She became ill and expressed a desire to return to Sligo. Her employers provided a cart and she was taken with a view to boarding a steamer at Glasgow. On route she died and her body was deposited at the Gorbal's Police Station.[27] Throughout Glasgow refugees seized any opportunity to obtain shelter. In Barony parish, an Irish family of six arrived in Calton and took possession of a disused stable. The walls were totally devoid of plaster, there was no floor covering and the floor was cold and damp. All six went down with fever. 'This family had recently arrived from Ireland'.[28] The Inspector of Lodging Houses for Glasgow visited an apartment which measured 15ft x 11ft. It contained seven beds and there were eight cases of fever in one room. Nine corpses had already been removed from the same room but as soon as space in a bed was vacated, it was filled. In another apartment in the Gorbals, over a space of a few days, six corpses were removed while in another apartment in Rutherglen, there were fourteen cases of fever.[29]

Given the extra hospital accommodation available by the beginning of July, the Parochial Board determined to take extreme measures to bring the typhus outbreak under control. At its meeting on 29 July the recommendations of a crisis meeting held on 19 July were discussed and acted upon. A policy was agreed in which, following the removal of fever patients to a hospital bed, the police would arrange to have their bedding burned, the rooms cleaned and fumigated. Between July 1847 and 13 May 1848, 3127 houses were cleansed in this manner.[30] By December 1847, the number of fever deaths was falling and the immediate health crisis was over. As elsewhere in Britain, the parochial employees paid for their devotion to duty with their lives. In the case of the city of Glasgow, the following died of fever caught in the course of carrying out their jobs: Dr Thomson, surgeon and Superintendent of the Towns Hospital fever ward; Dr Ferrie and Dr Rigby, district surgeons; Dr James Short Thompson, Superintendent of the Great Clyde Street Fever Hospital; William Thomson, William Thomson, junior and Alexander Phimister, assistant poor inspectors; Mr Caldwell, Hugh M'Arthur, clerks; Peter Wishalt, van driver; Janet Leat, Jane Michan, Mary Bowman, nurses.[31] The Glasgow authorities followed the practice adopted in Liverpool of giving a financial contribution to the relatives of those officers who died as a result of their work for the parish. Mrs Phimister was given £50 while Dr Rigby's daughter was given £25.[32] In June, *The Times* reported that four Catholic priests in Glasgow had caught typhus as a result of carrying out their religious duties.[33] It was inevitable that the Catholic clergy would pay heavily for their assiduity in carrying out their sacramental responsibilities. During 1847, John Bremner (Scots), Richard Sinnot (Scots), Daniel Kenny (Irish) and William Welsh (Irish) all died of typhus caught in the course of duty.[34] A clear indication of the scale of the 1847 crisis is the number of burials in the churchyards of the city of Glasgow and its suburbs. The increase in the number of burials from 11 686 in 1846 to 18 886 in 1847 was 61 per cent, a phenomenal increase. The total number of burials in 1848 was 30 per cent less than in 1847 and in 1849, the year of the cholera outbreak, the decrease was 33 per cent. Further in 1840 there were 956 pauper burials in the city of Glasgow parish while in 1847, the number was 3298, which allowing for a population increase of approximately 17 per cent, is statistically significant. The question arises of whether or not the Irish in Glasgow suffered disproportionately compared with the indigenous population and Highlanders. Given the evidence at present available, the answer seems to be that they did. For example, between 5 June and 9 September, it was reported that upwards of 2000 cases of fever were admitted to the supplementary hospitals and of these, almost three quarters were Irish.[35] If true, then assuming 75 per cent of pauper burials were famine Irish, we arrive at an estimated 2309 deaths.

Table 6.4 The total number of burials in the city of Glasgow and its suburbs over the period 1845 to 1851 (inclusive)

Parish or Place	*Year*						
	1845	*1846*	*1847*	*1848*	*1849*	*1850*	*1851*
City of Glasgow			9 872	6 577	6 606	4 995	5 703
Gorbals			3 861	2 851	3 064	2 675	2 937
Barony			5 153	3 751	4 061	2 791	3 099
Govan			-	-	-	128	90
Total	8 259	11 686	18 886	13 179	12 731	10 589	11 829

Source: Strathclyde, *Glasgow Bills of Mortality*.

We will leave the last words to John Strang, City Chamberlain of Glasgow, as he looked back on 1847:

> During the last twelve months no city almost, in Her Majesty's dominions has been more burdened with so many wretched and starving immigrants from Ireland and from the Highlands, hundreds of families were found hurrying daily to Glasgow as a city of refuge, those families bearing with them the last rags of poverty, and exhibiting, but too frequently the last symptoms of famine fever. Thousands, in fact, while they fled from their starving homes to live, arrived here only to die and have thus not only tended to swell the figures of our city mortality but to increase to a fearful extent the amount of our parochial rate ... why should there not be some more universal poor law for the whole nation, which would prevent the helpless and famishing families of neglected districts being forced to leave their homes to seek temporary residence in the homes of the crowded city.[36]

Like the authorities in Liverpool, the members of the Parochial Boards, Police Boards and Town Councils in Glasgow and its suburbs, were bewildered by the speed and the size of the famine immigration during 1847. In addition, the typhus outbreak was on a far bigger scale than the previous cholera crises. They had no previous experience of dealing with such circumstances but more particularly, they suffered a further disadvantage compared to Liverpool. In the case of Liverpool and the South Wales ports, the authorities had had thirteen years to adjust to the new poor law. The authorities in Glasgow, by contrast, were struggling with the new Scottish poor law, which was far less centrally organized that the English and Welsh system. The Scots still didn't fully understand the mechanics of the new system while simultaneously trying to cope with a major financial and health crisis.

II

Public Health - Fever

> All paupers arriving from Ireland in any port in England or Wales should immediately be sent back by the parochial authorities at the expense of the County. The authorities neglect a paramount duty in omitting in any case to do so directly any Irish person requires relief at the expense of any parish. We in Cardiff, as well as our neighbours in Bristol and Newport, 'have no right to sit still and let pestilence walk in amongst us'. At this moment, the progress of *the fever* in the holes and cellars of Stanley Street, Whitmore Lane and elsewhere, is most alarming. The first flush of warm weather will spread the disease and death into most of our streets. The filthy state in which the poor people arrive, and the shocking condition of the places where they herd - *as many as thirty in a room* - are the most certain constituents of malignant fever.

The above headline appeared in the *Cardiff and Merthyr Guardian* of 12 March 1847 followed by the leader article. The writer went on to warn that valued citizens of Cardiff were at risk and that the cemetery of Cardiff township was already over full. Over the previous two months, it was claimed, burials at St John's churchyard had averaged 'more than one a day'. At the time this edition of the newspaper appeared, the authorities in Cardiff already knew that they were faced with a major health hazard. On 27 February, the mayor of Cardiff had told the poor law guardians that a part of Longcross barracks separate from the main buildings, could be used for the reception of Irish fever victims.[37] John and Mary Darrett were appointed to run the establishment, each at a salary of twenty shillings a week.[38] These were relatively high wages and probably included an element of danger money.

The two parishes making up the township of Cardiff at this time were St John's and St Mary's. The only cemetery was in St John's parish and the rising number of deaths was an immediate cause of concern because of the limited amount of space available. The week before the above leader article appeared, the Cardiff guardians wrote to the Poor Law Board asking for advice concerning the provision of extra burial space:

> ... all the burying ground for the dead is confined to the churchyard in St John's parish, which lies in the very heart of the town. In addition to the dead of these two parishes, the great number of deaths in the Union House situated in St John's, together with the great numbers of deaths among the Irish, who have been forced by the famine from their own country, have so filled the churchyard as to make it feared that the consequences will be fatal to the health of the town.[39]

This correspondence is of interest on a number of grounds, not least in that the reference to the famine could be taken to imply that the Cardiff guardians felt that the members of the Poor Law Board in London needed reminding that there was a crisis in Britain associated with the Irish famine. This approach to London resulted in the Cardiff guardians being given permission to use money raised from ratepayers to acquire a piece of land from the Marquis of Bute.[40] The overcrowding of the Cardiff graveyard was a process underway before the famine influx of refugees. The deaths among the Irish early in 1847 simply brought the issue to a head.

The typhus epidemic in Cardiff exhibited the same chronology as in other places, making its appearance early in spring, peaking in September but not finally disappearing until spring 1848. During this period, the assistant medical officer for the Cardiff Union visited 283 typhus victims in their own homes. Not surprisingly, the streets in which the Irish settled were worst hit, 75 cases in Stanley Street, 25 in Whitmore Lane, 14 in Little Frederick Street and 8 in Love Lane. These made up 43 per cent of all the fever cases treated at home.[41] In addition to the 283 cases of fever treated at home in Cardiff, 186 fever sufferers were admitted into the Longcross barracks temporary hospital.[42] Of this number, 61 died, a 33 per cent death rate. These figures suggest a total of 469 typhus cases during the 12 month period February 1847 to February 1848. Just how many Irish refugees died in Cardiff over this period is simply not known. If we assume a 33 per cent death rate, then 156 would have died. We do know that over the period October 1846 to September 1850, inclusive, the number of Irish paupers buried by the township of Cardiff was 493, an annual average of 123.[43] This four year period covered the 1849 cholera outbreak. It is certain that the year 1847 witnessed the largest number of deaths of Irish immigrants in Cardiff township so if we assume that twice the average died in that year, we would have an estimated 246 deaths. The statistics hide the individual tragedies and widespread suffering, most cases never to be known. In April, Mr John, a Cardiff relieving officer went down with typhus caught as a direct result of his visiting the Irish in their cellars and rooms. A substitute was appointed at a wage of two pounds a week. This was a very high rate of pay and again must reflect the element of danger money. John recovered and returned to duty.[44] On 13 May, John turned up at Cardiff town hall where the guardians were meeting. He told them that outside there was an Irish family, man, wife and a dead child. The woman was carrying the corpse of the child on her back. The couple were in a bad way and had spent the previous night in a shed, where the baby had died. John wanted to know what to do, as they were wandering the streets, carrying the corpse as they could not obtain any lodgings. The decision was to send them to Longcross barracks.[45]

The local press reporting of such tragedies exhibited the same mixture of sympathy and exasperation characteristic of similar accounts in other parts of the country. In the same edition of the *Cardiff and Merthyr Guardian* another more tragic case was also described. On 10 April, John Alley, his wife and two children were admitted into Longross temporary hospital. The family were Irish and in a very poor physical condition and obviously ill. Within a seven day period, man, wife and one child died. In reporting these deaths, the piece was headed 'The Destitute Irish' (their quotation marks). It claimed that before she died. Mrs Alley had demanded an improved hospital diet. Being dissatisfied with the food provided she asked a nurse to go to a Mrs Moss in Mary Ann Street and borrow ten shillings, telling Mrs Moss to use a blanket of the Alleys as security against the loan. A nurse went to the house and Mrs Moss confessed that the Alleys had left five pounds with her. *The Guardian* report took this as a particular example of what it alleged was an widespread Irish practice, such as claiming relief while possessing funds. Paying lip service to the tragic circumstances, the *Guardian* castigated the Irish in general:

> The following extraordinary circumstances, our account of which may be depended upon as being strictly accurate, recently occurred near this town and place the conduct of certain of the 'destitute' Irish (as they are termed) in rather an unfavourable light... There is one child now left a burden on this parish. We do not wish to make any harsh comments on these poor Irish wretches, nor uncharitably to reflect upon the training which they all

> seem to have received previous to becoming adept in deception, but we think it right to make the facts contained in the foregoing statement known to the country.[46]

The whole of this piece of reporting is remarkable in its lack of warmth or compassion at the deaths of three out of four members of one family in a strange land. Aneurin Owen, assistant poor law officer, told the Poor Law Commissioners that Cardiff was 'inundated' with Irish and that they 'introduced fever, which requires special provision'.[47] This special provision included the appointment of Dr Paine and Dr Lewis on 3 April.[48]

III

Given the much larger numbers of Irish passing through Newport, it is highly probable that the union experienced more cases of typhus, and hence more deaths than Cardiff. However, there is little hard evidence extant. Harriet Huxtable, matron at Newport's House of Refuge, claimed that during 1847, 40 per cent of the Irish who sought help were ill with infectious diseases.[49] She herself twice survived an attack of typhus contracted in the course of duty. In an effort to cope with the typhus outbreak, the Newport guardians acquired a disused Catholic schoolroom and converted it into a temporary fever hospital. The majority of Irish coming ashore at Newport went straight to the House of Refuge. Those found to be suffering from fever were sent immediately to the temporary fever ward. On 5 June 1847, there were 'fifty to sixty patients' in this hospital. Many of those who recovered in the fever ward were then sent back to the House of Refuge where they were given food and a bed for the night and then passed on to a converted police station for a period of convalescence.[50] The increased workload and the risk to the health of the union officers was recognized as early as March when the guardians wrote to the Poor Law Commissioners, asking for permission to increase the salaries of the relieving officers '...the large influx of Irish into the central district increases the work and risk from fever of the relieving officers'. The outcome was a salary increase of £15 a year.[51]

Tuthill Massy was a doctor, invited to Newport by William Brewer, coroner and himself a doctor of some repute.[52] Massy worked in Newport's temporary fever hospital between May and November 1847, inclusive, and the is the best available source of evidence concerning the typhus outbreak in Newport. He describes how the Irish poor from Skibbereen, Cork, Cloyne and Kinsale finished up in Newport applying for tickets for a nights lodging at the Newport House of Refuge, 'tottering with famine fever'.

> Morning after morning, this scene went on, and evening after evening, the grave was dug and the poor wanderer was silently interred, unknown and unregretted.

During his work at the fever hospital, 6000 Irish were treated. This figure if correct, further vindicates the argument that Newport faced the greatest problem in the region. Writing of his first day at the fever hospital, Massy records:

> The thermometer was several degrees above summer heat when I entered the barn, not worthy of the name hospital - a shocking place. The darkness terrified me as I stepped over the beds of those creatures as they lay side by side, moaning and groaning, and those who were able, calling for 'water! water! Oh the thirst'! A candle was required to examine the anxious faces, the flushed cheek and the parched tongue, of those who lay in the angles of the building. According to the report of last week, thirty had died yet the barn was still full; the places of the dead were quickly taken. Those many deaths alarmed me.[53]

He estimated that during his spell of duty at Newport, twenty four persons (sic public servants) contracted typhus from the Irish and eight of those died. The whole experience had a profound effect on Massy, witnessing as he did, many distressing cases. A woman landed from Cork, in an advanced state of pregnancy. On landing, she gave birth in the street after which, she, her husband and five children were put into one of the union wards. Within a few days, all were dead. Massy expressed the opinion that 'those seven persons would not, probably, have died or got the fever, if left unprovided for by the poor law'[54] It is almost certain that they had typhus when they arrived but Massy was repeating the views of Duncan in Liverpool, that many Irish would have lived had they stayed in Ireland. Massey tells of another occasion when he entered the fever ward:

> One morning, as I entered the hospital, I saw the priest kneeling at the side of a lovely Irish girl in the agonies of death. I sent him word that he would very likely get her fever if he continued so close to her bed. A few days later I saw him with the same disease, the head greatly engorged, fever running high, with paroxysms of delirium, requiring two men in attendance.[55]

The priest Massey referred to was almost certainly the Italian, Mr Sentini, who in fact recovered. The Catholic clergy in Wales shared the same sacramental responsibility as those in Liverpool of hearing deathbed confessions and the giving of the Last Rites. In 1847, Fr Neri and Dr Carroll were parish priests in Merthyr Tydfil. Early in June 1847, Neri was ordered to go to Liverpool to help make up the clerical losses in the port. On 19 June, Dr Carroll died in Merthyr. This left Merthyr without a priest so Neri was recalled.[56] At the other end of the Principality, Fr Mulcahy died in Bangor, Carnarvonshire, as a result of carrying out his parish duties among the Irish.[57] We do not know the total number of Irish who died of typhus and famine related diseases in South Wales and Newport but an estimate of 1000 does not seem unrealistic (see Appendix No. 6.3).

Appendices

Appendix 6.1 An example of press reporting of the Irish crisis in Newport. Taken from the *Bristol Gazette*, Thursday, 25 February 1847.

OVERWHELMING IMMIGRATION OF THE IRISH POOR TO NEWPORT - (from the *Merlin*)- The streets of our town present an alarming and lamentable appearance, being literally crowded with famished and half-naked strangers from the most distressed parts of Ireland, several ship loads of whom, amounting to many hundreds have either been induced by specious promises of work and good wages in this neighbourhood to pay their passage to Newport, or the more destitute of whom have been huddled together in the holds of coal vessels, for this country, at the expense of local committees, to lessen the number of famishing creatures at home. We have been informed, on authority to which we attach full credit, that handbills, setting forth the temptation of constant work, with half-crown a day on our railways, or as labourers about our iron works, are industriously circulated through several parts of the south of Ireland, and the bellman has been employed in many quarters to tell the Utopian tale, rounded with 'God save the Queen!' on market days, in various towns in Cork county. Hence it is, that hosts of squalid beings are induced to embark on board filthy hulks, totally unsuited for a living freight, the miseries of whom, densely stowed upon damp ballast, suffering from famine and sickness during this tempestuous season, are almost beyond human expression. Cast, as most of them have been, brutally on our shores, emaciated, and in many instances diseased, they find the hope of employment an empty vision, and thus add to the multitudes of their unfortunate country people, whom they find crying with hunger from door to door. By the books of the Refuge for the Destitute, we find that from the first of January to the 16th instant, temporary relief in lodging and food has been given to 369 men, 360 women and 402 children; whilst aid to an enormous extent has been afforded at the Union. The relieving officer has been engaged almost night and day, and Sergeant Huxtable and his wife, of the House of Refuge, have been indefatigable in their service to the poor. - This is a matter of lasting credit to our town, and we pray God that we may be enabled to keep life in these miserable strangers, until better times arrive; but it cannot be disguised, that the poor of the place complain bitterly of the increased privations thus brought upon them; and that many persons who have been subscribers to the very munificent relief fund of above £1000 - a larger sum, by the way, than the Irish landlords of half a dozen counties of Ireland have contributed, during their people's extremist need - consider that Newport has been very ungratefully treated by those committees in the sister kingdom, who have inflicted upon it this visitation. Five of the perishing beings who were removed from the hold of that floating pesthouse, the *Wanderer*, at the risk of their lives of charitable gentlemen, have since died, and it is more than probable, that the proceedings of the coroner's inquest on an adult, to be held this day, will unfold some of the horrors of the treatment experienced by persons shipped lately for Newport.

Appendix 6.2 Poor Law for Ireland: The following is a copy of the petition adopted on Friday last, at a meeting of the Parochial Board of the city parish of Glasgow, in favour of the Ministerial Poor Law for Ireland.

'UNTO THE HON. THE COMMONS OF GREAT BRITAIN AND IRELAND IN PARLIAMENT ASSEMBLED. 'The petition of the Parochial board of the city parish of Glasgow; Showeth - that your petitioners, as the representatives of the ratepayers of this populous city parish, have, in the discharge of the arduous and responsible duties imposed on them as managers of the poor's fund, experienced such difficulty and annoyance, as well as an unprecendental increase of expenditure, arising almost entirely from the extraordinary influx of impotent, infantine and diseased Irish paupers into this parish';

'That your petitioners, while deeply sympathetic with their [sic] distressed Irish fellow subjects in the calamity that has overtaken them upon the failure of the potato crop, cannot but express their surprise that so little should have been done by the wealthy classes in that country to ameliorate this distress - a distress as yet that has had to rely for its relief upon British charity and the taxation raised from British industry'.

'That, in the opinion of your petitioners, an absolute necessity exists for the introduction of a sufficient Poor Law into Ireland, whereby an adequate provision shall be made for the relief and support of the impotent, infantine, diseased and aged poor of that country, and that the fund for this purpose should be raised by an assessment upon all incomes, whether arising from real or personal property.

'That your petitioners feel persuaded, had such a law as this existed in Ireland, they would not have had to complain of the present influx of Irish paupers, who, from their wretchedness, destitution and disease, have not only absorbed and are absorbing a large proportion of the rate levied for the poor properly belonging to this parish and spreading contagion among them, but are also setting a most pernicious example to the lower classes of this city, by accustoming and instructing them to look to parochial aid for support, instead of depending as Scotsmen were wont to do, upon their own industrious exertions.

'That your petitioners have seen with alarm that her Majesty's Ministers, in the Poor Law Bill which they have introduced to your hon. house, have admitted the principle of granting outdoor relief to the ablebodied poor - a principle your petitioners hold to be opposed to sound political economy, as well as independent and sound morals among the lower orders; and, should your hon. house sanction such a principle, your petitioners do not hesitate to aver that, it will lead many to trust entirely to the poor fund for their support who, but for this enactment, would assuredly trust to their own exertions; while it will also destroy all feeling of gratitude on the part of the receiver of that aid - a feeling that ought to ever exist, and which your petitioners earnestly desire to foster and encourage, rather than destroy, and which they pray your hon. house to carefully watch over and protect, and not supersede.

'That your petitioners as the representatives of this populous parish, feel themselves especially called upon to give utterance to their opinions on this question, as they have to provide not only for the maintenance of their own destitute poor, but also, under the recent Poor Law Act for Scotland, they are compelled to provide contemporary aid for an overwhelming number of their impotent, infantine and diseased fellow subjects, having no settlement in this parish, and for the relief granted to whom they have no resources whatsoever.

'May it therefore please your hon. house to pass a measure for establishing an efficient Poor Law, by which adequate relief shall be provided for the impotent, infantine, diseased and aged poor in Ireland, and otherwise adopt such measures as shall relieve your petitioners from the intolerable and oppressive burden to which, from the causes set forth above, they are at present subjected.

'And your petitioners shall ever pray 'signed and sealed in the name of appointment of the Parochial Board of the city parish of Glasgow, at Glasgow, this 27th day of March, 1847'

Appendix 6.3 Estimates of deaths in Newport.

My estimate of deaths in Newport is based on the following assumptions. Dr Massy claimed that 6000 people passed through the fever hospital at Newport between May and November (inclusive) a rate of 857 per month. As the typhus epidemic cases increased significantly in April, then assuming the same monthly rate, over April to November, we obtain a total of 6857. Thus, assuming 70 per cent were Irish we arrive at an estimated 4800 Irish cases. Based on a death rate of 10 per cent we obtain a total of 480 Irish deaths. Add to this an estimated 246 Irish deaths in the Cardiff unions, the total becomes 726. Allowing for deaths at Merthyr and elsewhere in the region, 1000 Irish deaths seems a reasonable estimate. It we had assumed a death rate of 20 per cent, this estimate rises to 1480, say 1500 at the top side. (I am grateful to Martin Cullaford of Newport for kindly supplying me with some statistics of burials at Newport). During the whole of 1847, there was a total of 770 deaths in Newport. If one compares this with my estimate of 480 deaths, 10 per cent of fever victims, the Irish deaths at Newport would have been 62 per cent of the total, quite plausible. At the Newport dispensary, during 1847, 1285 cases of all kinds were treated, of which total, 300 were fever cases. These would be additional to the cases referred to above at the fever hospitals. During 1847 there were 539 burials at St Woolo's Church. Of these 145 had obviously Irish names, some 27 per cent. Catholics at this time were buried at the Asylum Church. (Again, thanks to Martin Cullaford).

Notes and References

1 A.Paterson, 'The Poor Law in Nineteenth Century Scotland', in D.Fraser (ed), *The New Poor Law in The Nineteenth Century,* (Macmillan: 1976) pp. 189-190. S.Blackden, 'The Board of Supervision and the Scottish Parochial Medical Service, 1845-95', *Medical History*, 1986, 30, pp. 145-172. M.W.Dupree, 'Family Care and Hospital Care: the Sick Poor in Nineteenth Century Glasgow', *Social History of Medicine*, 1993, 06, 02, pp. 195-211. C. Hamlin, 'Environmental Sensibility in Edinburgh, 1839-1840: the Fetid Irrigation Controversy'. *Journal of Urban History,* 1994, May, pp. 329.
2 Dupree, op.cit, pp. 198-99.
3 Blackden, op.cit, pp.162-63.
4 First Report (Large Towns) Local Reports, No 9, C.R.Baird, On the General and Sanitary Condition of the Working Classes and the Poor in the City of Glasgow, p. 167.
5 *Glasgow Chronicle*, 6 January 1847 '... and it is Ireland above all the rest that pours its columns of human wretchedness into all the larger towns'.
6 *Glasgow Chronicle*, 3 March 1847. Report on the Glasgow Municipal Police Board Meeting held on Monday, 1 March 1847.
7 Strathclyde. Meeting of the Glasgow Parochial Board held on the 5 March 1847, Assessment Report, pp. 74-75.
8 Strathclyde. Minutes of the Meeting of the Glasgow Parochial Board held on 26 March 1847.
9 ibid.
10 ibid.
11 ibid.
12 *Glasgow Herald*, 26 March 1847. Report on the Meeting of the Glasgow Municipal Police Board held on 22 March 1847.
13 *Glasgow Herald*, 2 April 1847. This edition contains a long account of the protest meeting.
14 Strathclyde, Minutes of the Meeting of the Glasgow Parochial Board held on 21 May 1847, p. 109.
15 Strathclyde, Minutes of the Glasgow Parochial Board held on 7 May 1847. See also report of the meeting in *Glasgow Constitutional*, 8 May 1847.
16 *Glasgow Constitutional*, 19 May 1847. Report on the Meeting of the Glasgow Municipal Police Board held on 17 May 1847.
17 Strathclyde, Minutes of the Meeting of the Glasgow Parochial Board held on 4 June 1847. Report of the Committee on Improvements, dated 3 June 1847.
18 Strathclyde. Minutes of the Meeting of the Glasgow Parochial Board held on 4 June 1847. The Improvements Board asked the Parochial Board to acquire more premises for use as a fever hospital. Minutes of the Meeting of the Glasgow Parochial Board held on 25 June 1847, p. 124. It was reported that the old fever hospital would be opened in the following week.
19 *Glasgow Constitutional*, 2 July 1847. The hospital was between Maxwell Street and Stockwell Street.
20 Strathclyde. Minutes of the Meeting of the Glasgow Parochial Board, Assessment Report, p. 74.
21 Strathclyde. Minutes of the Meeting of the Glasgow Parochial Board held on 4 June 1847. Copy of Memorial to the House of Commons, pp. 114-5.
22 *Glasgow Courier*, 20 April 1847.

23 *Glasgow Herald*, 21 May 1847. Report on the meeting of the Glasgow Municipal Police Board held on 17 May 1847.
24 *Glasgow Constitutional*, 25 May 1847.
25 *Glasgow Herald*, 28 May 1847.
26 *Glasgow Herald*, 18 June 1847.
27 *Glasgow Herald*, 7 June 1847.
28 *Glasgow Constitutional*, 5 June 1847. Report by the Chairman of Barony Medical Committee on the 'Causes and Prevention of Fever'.
29 *Glasgow Constitutional*, 19 June 1847. Statistics from the book kept by the Inspector of Lodgings in Glasgow.
30 Strathclyde. Minutes of the Meeting of the Glasgow Parochial Board held on 29 July 1847. At this meeting a report was heard of the outcome of a meeting held on 19 July at the Police Hall in Glasgow, attended by the Lord Provost and representatives of the Town Council and Parochial Boards of Glasgow, Barony and Govan. The purpose was to discuss the fever crisis.
31 Strathclyde. Minutes of the Meeting of the Glasgow Parochial Board held on 30 November 1847, p. 204-205. This meeting was given the names of officials who had died between January 1847 and 30 November. The death of Dr James Short Thompson was reported to the Board meeting held on 6 December 1847, p. 221.
32 Strathclyde. Minutes of the Meeting of the Glasgow Parochial Board held on 5 August 1847, p. 154.
33 *The Times*, 3 June 1847. In fact *The Times* report was a syndicated report from the *North British Mail*.
34 Glasgow Archdiocese Archives, Scottish Catholic Directory, 1848.
35 *Glasgow Herald*, 27 September 1847. Report of the Meeting of the Glasgow Parochial Board, 24 September 1847.
36 *Scotch Reformers Gazette*, 26 February 1848, Report on the Glasgow Mortality Rate for 1847.
37 PRO/MH12/6248/Cardiff/1847. Cardiff Guardians to Poor Law Commissioners, 19 July 1847.
38 PRO/MH12/6248/Cardiff/1847. Cardiff Guardians to Poor Law Commissioners, 2 August 1847.
39 PRO/MH12/6248/Cardiff/1847/5110B. Cardiff Guardians to Poor Law Commissioners, 7 March 1847.
40 PRO/MH12/6248/Cardiff/1847. Letter from Poor Law Commissioners to Cardiff Guardians, sanctioning the purchase of land using money from the poor rates.
41 J.Hickey, *Urban Catholics in England and Wales from 1829 to the present day*, London, 1967, p. 80. Hickey is quoting the statistics contained in the Report to the General Board of Health on the Town of Cardiff, London, 1850.
42 Hickey, op.cit, p. 81.
43 SC (1854) Appendix, No. 14. Summary of Irish Paupers Relieved in the Town of Cardiff and the Cost Thereof, From September 1846 to September 1850, Paid by The Cardiff Poor Law Unions.
44 PRO/MH12/6248/Cardiff/1847/5026B. Cardiff Guardians to Poor Law Commissioners, 12 April 1847.
45 *Cardiff and Merthyr Guardian*, 15 May 1847.
46 ibid.
47 PR0/MH12/6248/Cardiff/1847/14004B. A.Bevan to Poor Law Commissioners, 16 July 1847.
48 PRO/MH12/62481/Cardiff/1847/9017B Cardiff Guardians to Poor Law Commissioners.

49 Vagrancy (1848) p. 47-8.
50 PRO/MH12/8089/Newport/1847/12604. Report of John Lewis, Assistant to Poor Law Commissioners, on a visit to Newport Union on 5 June 1847.
51 PRO/MH12/8089/1847/6461. Newport Guardians to Poor Law Commissioners, 23 March 1847.
52 *Dublin Quarterly Journal of Medical Science*, Vol VIII, part III, 1849. Letter from Dr Massy on the recent epidemic of fever in Wales, dated 16 May 1849, pp. 438-447. I am grateful to Dr Margaret Crawford for drawing my attention to this letter.
53 Massy, op.cit, p. 439.
54 Massy, op.cit, p. 440.
55 Massy, op.cit.
56 *The Tablet*, 26 June 1847.
57 *The Tablet*, 31 July 1847.

7 Survival and Dispersal

I

For a large proportion of the Irish refugees, life in the ports of arrival was chaotic, bewildering and extremely harsh. The primary objective of many was to move on as soon as possible to those places inland where they hoped to find family, friends and work. By 1847, Liverpool was linked to its industrial hinterland by roads, canals and railways. Cardiff, Swansea and Newport were gateways to the developing industrial towns of South Wales, Merthyr Tydfil being a particular attraction for some Irish. In addition many were en route to the English industrial midlands and London and in such cases, Chepstow and Gloucester became stopping off places. The industrial and textile towns of the west of Scotland lay behind Glasgow while the route south east would take trampers to the mines, ironworks and docks of Northumberland and Durham. However, more popular ports of entry for those Irish going to the north east of England were Whitehaven and Maryport. London absorbed its own Irish arrivals. The majority of the famine Irish walked to their destinations and groups of ragged, famished, ill-looking Irish became familiar sights to travellers on the roads radiating out from the western ports.[1]

A survival strategy was essential and commonplace Specifically, it involved begging and using the poor law facilities along the chosen route, especially the vagrant sheds of workhouses. In some cases, those begging possessed money but many were penniless. Those with a few pounds were behaving rationally. Some funds would be needed on arrival at their destination, particularly if poor relief was to be avoided, and so begging allowed them to keep a small amount in reserve. Even sums such as two pounds could help a family survive for weeks while they found work. However, if any money was found when claiming relief, the claimant would incur the wrath of officials and help feed the press with stories of the 'deceitful' and 'ungrateful' Irish.

Not surprisingly, there were Irish, men and women, who abused the system but for most, the experience of the search for a new home was one of hardship and, in many cases, it was a nightmare.

Jeremiah Sullivan worked a small plot of land near Schull in County Cork.[2] Early in 1847 the family was evicted. Commenting on this event, the *Cheltenham Examiner* informed its English readers:

> He (Sullivan) had a piece of ground which he cultivated; when visited by distress and famine, with misery and despair surrounding them, their landlord, Mr Summerfield, with that peculiar species of Christian charity which forms a distinguishing characteristic of Irish landlords, turned them out of their little holding, to beg or starve, he cared not which.[3]

Sullivan owned a cow and a horse which he had sold in anticipation of being evicted, making a total of three pounds from the sales. He was married and had four small children, one of these a baby of about two months, being breastfed. The three pounds were used for lodgings and food for the family while Sullivan looked for work. When this proved fruitless, the family decided to go to England, Sullivan having an aunt in London who kept a shop. They went to Cork and negotiated a passage on a steamer to Newport at a total cost of eight shillings. This left the family penniless. By the time the Sullivans boarded the ship at Cork they were already showing the signs of malnutrition. They arrived in Newport sometime early in March 1847 and as they were literally without means of support, they started begging in the streets. A stranger gave them some bread before a police officer moved them on. They set out almost immediately to walk to London, heading north from Newport in the direction of Chepstow. Sullivan applied for relief at unions en route but the level of assistance, given their deteriorating physical condition, was inadequate for people walking long distances. Mrs Sullivan had no milk left in her breasts and the baby was being fed a mixture of water and sugar.

On 2 April, Police Constable Fowler was doing his rounds in the village of Charlton Kings, near Cheltenham, when his attention was caught by the sound of groaning coming from a ditch. On investigation, he found a crude shelter had been erected and inside were the Sullivans. Mrs Sullivan was holding the baby to her breast in an effort to keep the child warm. However, the child was already dead. The policeman realized the rest of the family were in a dying state and immediately went for Mr Feegan, a local doctor. In turn, Feegan sent for Mr Pearman, the union relieving officer. On arrival Pearman at once issued an order for the Sullivans to be taken to a nearby lodging house used by the parish as temporary accommodation for vagrants. This order was given at 9.0pm and at 9.30pm the family arrived at the house where they were refused admission because the place was full, people sleeping on the floor. Amor, the lodging house keeper went to see Mr Coombs, a guardian who ordered him to admit the Sullivans. We don't know where they slept but, despite their condition, it is almost certain they slept on the floor. There was no provision of hospital services. Coombs worried, went for Dr Brookes who came at 10.0pm and examined each member of the family. He ordered that they be given arrowroot, brandy, bread and tea. It is clear that Brookes took the situation seriously because he made further visits to the lodging house at 11.30pm and 1.30am, to monitor the condition of the family. It does appear that within the system the parish officers did all they could for the family except provide hospital beds. This meant that the family, seriously ill from exposure and malnutrition, were squeezed in among the vagrants using the house that night.

An inquest was held 5 April at Charlton Kings on the body of Anthony Sullivan, aged three months. J. Lovegrove, the area assistant coroner, presided and the verdict was 'death from starvation'. The family were still in the lodging house at the time of the inquest and their nightmare was not over. Three more Sullivan children died. Another inquest was held on 13 April at the Red Lion Inn and Lovegrove presided over the inquest held on the bodies of Dennis Sullivan, aged five years; Mary Sullivan aged ten years and Hannah Sullivan aged eleven years. It seems that another Sullivan family accompanied Jeremiah Sullivan. One of these three dead children, probably Hannah, was the daughter of Michael Sullivan. In turn he was probably the brother of Jeremiah. The verdicts were 'that the deceased had died from the effects of starvation brought on from privation previous to their arrival in Cheltenham'. It was also made clear at the inquest that the parish officers had not neglected the family. This may have been true, the deterioration in the condition of the children had gone too far for any remedial efforts to work. Equally, it may have been that living in an overcrowded lodging house, in poor health, on a parish diet, was an inadequate response to a desperate situation. Certainly the guardians were sensitive to charges of neglect but the local press exonerated the parish. We do not know what happened to Jeremiah Sullivan, his wife and their remaining child. Perhaps they eventually disappeared in the vastness of London; wherever they finished up there can be no doubt the tragedy of losing three children scarred them for life.

Alfred Austin, assistant poor law commissioner in the north west of England wrote to the Poor Law Commissioners in London 1 May 1847, telling them that '...many of those who land quit Liverpool nearly immediately upon their arrival, for the interior'. Austin claimed that the accommodation situation in Liverpool was so bad that most newly arrived Irish had little choice but to head inland.[4] The most popular route out of Liverpool was the road to Prescot, due east, eight miles from the waterfront. At Prescot, some would head north to St Helens, Wigan and Bolton. Large numbers would continue eastwards to Warrington where many turned southwards through Knutsford, Holmes Chapel, Stoke on Trent and towards Wolverhampton, Birmingham and London. Equally large numbers would keep heading east from Warrington towards Manchester, in some cases crossing the Mersey at Warrington and making for Stockport via Altrincham. From Manchester and Stockport, some would cross the Pennines to Sheffield and south Yorkshire. Charles E Mott was the district auditor of Manchester township and on the 15 May he wrote a very long letter to the *Manchester Guardian* following his visits to other unions in Lancashire. In the course of commenting on the state of the area, he dwelt on the subject of the fever outbreak, expressing the view that it was of the most 'threatening and dangerous character within living memory'. He said the universal opinion was that it was introduced and spread by the famine Irish:

> The cause of the spreading of this serious affliction is clearly marked, as to be easily traced to its source. Thus, to the northward and eastward of Manchester, the fever has at present only extended to the manufactory towns within ten or 12 miles of this town, whilst in the towns in all the great thoroughfares leading to the south its destructive effects are only too apparent. It may be traced through Warrington, to Sandbach, from Altrincham to Knutsford and Congleton, and from Stockport to Macclesfield, by the hordes of Irishmen and their families who are flocking to the south to seek work. As they beg for support at the houses near the roads by which they pass, the fever is working its deadly influence among the respectable families where they have been admitted on to the premises.

Mott was merely repeating the view of union officers he had spoken to but he was articulating a universally held opinion concerning the cause of the typhus epidemic. However, the statement provides endorsement of the view that the escape routes were well established early in 1847.[5]

The case of John Waters illustrates in a particularly poignant manner the frustration, hopelessness and bewilderment of those at the bottom of the social pile, trying to survive in an alien environment. At the second appearance of the potato blight in 1846, Waters was a 50 year old labourer who rented seven acres of land from Lord Darrens. The plot was in the parish of Barasculis in County Mayo and Waters paid a rent of five pounds ten shillings per year. At the time he had been a tenant for 18 years and during that period, he and his wife Catherine had married and raised seven children. By the end of October 1846, the family's health was beginning to deteriorate because of a lack of food. They had planted three barrels of seed potatoes and 'did not get one week's supply from them'. At the beginning of November, under no pressure from the landlord, John and Catherine Waters decided to go to England. In the words of Catherine Waters '....the want of potatoes, starvation and poverty obliged us to leave'.[6] Waters owned a horse and pig, which he sold to finance the journey to England. John and Catherine Waters and their children, Patrick aged 16, Mary and Biddy, 14 year old twins, Anthony aged seven, Annie aged three and John aged one, all walked from Mayo to Drogheda. At no time during this trek did they ask for poor relief, living off the remaining proceeds of the sale of their animals. It took them nine days to reach Drogheda where they took a steamer to Liverpool at a fare of nine shillings for the whole family. Significantly, John Waters could not speak English and his wife Catherine had never been to England in her life. They survived the chaos of Liverpool for two weeks and then joined the stream of refugees pouring inland. They planned to go to Sheffield where John Waters had a brother. This would mean walking across the Pennines in winter. They hoped to find work in the factories for the children. On their first night out from Liverpool they reached Prescot where they stayed one night in the vagrancy ward. Next day they walked to Warrington where they stayed two nights and then set out for Stockport. By this time they were all in a very weak state and the children were beginning to show signs of distress. The family survived on this section of the route by begging, the kind of sight that outraged certain elements in English society. On leaving Warrington they had only one shilling but managed to solicit another shilling as a result of begging. They had reached Stockport about 7 December.

On arrival in Stockport they headed for the Chestergate district, where many Irish lived, a place where cheap lodgings could be found. They obtained a room in a dilapidated property, run as a lodging house by an Irishman, Michael Burke. This was in Swan Court. Immediately, the Waters set out to find jobs for the children, and quickly succeeded in placing Patrick, Mary and Biddy as 'learners' in Mr Howard's factory in the adjacent Portwood district. Unfortunately, as learners, the children were not paid wages and so to survive, Catherine Waters sold her cloak and the clogs of the boys. She got a sixpence for the cloak and one shilling for the clogs. This was at a time when snow and frost were occurring. In addition, despite his lack of English, John Waters and some of the children, went out begging. At no time did they seek poor relief from the Stockport union. On 21 December John Dooley and John Hadfield arrived at Burke's lodging house. They were 'bum bailiffs' acting for John Pollitt, agent for the property owner. Burke was eleven shillings behind in his rent and the bailiffs ejected all the inhabitants of the house, including the Waters family and locked the doors. They also seized the Waters only possessions, a blanket, two sheets and a bolster. The Waters were confused, did not understand the law; the bailiffs acted illegally in seizing their bedding.

The weather was cold and frosty and in a show of compassion common among the poor, another family in the same court, the Sandfords, took the

Waters in, despite having little space themselves. There were no beds available and the Waters family sat all night round the fireplace. They stayed with the Sandford's for three nights. Catherine Waters appears to have been a woman of some strength of personality and courage. Also, she spoke English. The morning after being ejected from Burke's lodging house she found out where the rent agent Pollitt lived and went to see him, to protest about her bedding being taken. There began a process of being passed from person to person. Pollitt told her to go and see the auctioneer, who by then possessed the goods. Pollitt, either from a rush of humanity or fearing that trouble was brewing because of the illegal seizure of goods, gave her three shillings. Catherine, bereft of cloak in cold weather, tramped off to find the auctioneer who gave her a note and told her to go and see Dooley the bailiff. When she found Dooley he took the note and refused to speak with her. So she got nowhere in her efforts to reclaim her bedding. It later transpired that the bailiff, John Hadfield, had bought the goods at the auction for five shillings and twopence.

On the second and third day after moving in with the Sandfords, their condition was so bad that John Waters and four of the children applied to be admitted to the workhouse and entered the vagrancy ward. Catherine refused to apply as she feared that they might be removed to Ireland. It is significant that despite the wretchedness of their experience in England, she did not want to go back to Ireland. When John Waters and the children entered the vagrancy ward something happened which later became the subject of public debate. Because John Waters could not speak English, Bridget dealt with the Lawton, the relieving officer. He asked her where her mother was and Bridget said she did not have a mother. She probably said this because of her mother's fear of removal. The morning after John and the children entered the vagrancy ward, Catherine turned up at the workhouse and asked to see her husband and children, saying they were all going to go to Sheffield. Lawton became aggressive and accused Bridget of lying about having no mother. Whether or not she had a mother was totally irrelevant to the request of John and the children to enter the vagrancy shed. It was indicative of a common attitude to the Irish applicants for relief, a view that they were up to something which, in some vague way, was detrimental to the interests of the ratepayers. Lawton's attitude was astonishing because the whole family were obviously in a very poor physical condition and the issue of a mother was nothing to do with Lawton. Eventually, the family left the workhouse, John and Bridget each carrying one of the smaller children on their backs. It was Christmas Eve.

The Waters were put up temporarily by Biddy Plunkett and then they obtained a room in a house, 36, Swan Street, Chestergate, rented by an Irishman named Mealey, agreeing to pay one shilling a week. They shared with another Irishman, John Flanagan. By this time John Waters was visibly suffering from malnutrition and cold. On 27 December he went out begging and came back with a two pound loaf and one and halfpenny. The next day, Tuesday, 28 December he went out begging again but all the family had to eat that day was a little porridge. The room the family were using had no furniture and they had no bedding, simply lying on the flour. In the early hours of Wednesday, 29 December, Flannagan heard moans and went to the Waters' room and found John lying on the floor, almost naked, asking for water. Flanagan gave him a drink. Later he heard crying and found Catherine and the children gathered, crying, around John who was having convulsions. Flanagan held John's head while he died, at approximately 9.0am. The surgeon acting for the coroner stated there was no fat whatsoever left in his body. The *Manchester Guardian* described the scene where the Mayo man died:

> The house is in a dilapidated building, two storeys high in a damp, dark, pestilential hole, with not an article of furniture in it. In a room above, in size about four yards by three, stretched on the dirty bare floor, was the body of a man, fleshless and emaciated and naked, being only half covered with a few rags. Our reporter was told that the man, his wife and seven children slept in this room. The floor was in holes and the walls were blistered, broken and crumbling to decay. In another room, the attention of the jury was directed to another sad spectacle, though the dim twilight admitted through the dingy windows was only such that a candle was required to make the inspection. Three dirty, squalid children, stiff and stark naked, were found huddled together before the expiring members of a fire which might have been gathered up in one hand and scarcely emitted any warmth at all. In another corner, a boy was lying upon some shavings, almost without clothes and with merely the tattered remnants of an coat to cover him.

The case of John Waters has been given in some detail because it illustrates clearly the reality of the experience that was often subsumed under phrases such as, 'hordes of destitute Irish' or the statistics of numbers claiming relief. The Waters' case reminds us of the reality of the struggle to survive on the part of disorientated, sick and poverty stricken people. Coping with a relief system many of them did not understand, often faced with hostile officials, yet many were unwilling to return to Ireland. There were sympathizers in the Waters case. The coroner attacked the callous attitude of Lawton, the relieving officer, for his aggressive and irrelevant questioning of the child Bridget over her statement that she had no mother. The bailiffs were ordered to return the bedding to Catherine Waters.

However the members of the coroner's jury and the editor of the *Manchester Guardian* defended Lawton and poor law officials in general. The case generated much discussion and the *Stockport Advertiser* 15 January 1847, in publishing a leader on the general level of distress in Stockport resulting from the economic downturn, went out of it way to plea for a better treatment of the Irish refugees:

> In passing, we may be allowed to say that the guardians, at such a time, should be more than ordinarily liberal, especially towards the Irish. Their own land is the land of famine and death. They have fled to England for refuge; let us treat them kindly, and relieve their necessities as far as we can. Do not let us pack them off to their own unfortunate country, to perish, the moment they apply for relief. We feel persuaded that our own guardians will deal with the poor, at such a crisis, not in rigid principles of cold, stern justice, but with consideration and generosity.

This sounds like a rebuke to Lawton, the relieving officer in the John Waters case and it was announced that an additional reliving officer had been appointed to deal with the 'distressed Irish'.

II

The Irish heading for the west Yorkshire industrial towns usually took the St Helens road when they reached Prescot and headed for St Helens, Bolton, Rochdale and then into Yorkshire. On Thursday 5 May 1847, PC Neville was travelling from Bury in Lancashire to Heap Bridge when he found a family, man, woman and children, lying under a hedge. On stopping to investigate he saw a child lying some distance from the adults and on closer examination, established that the child was dead. The man's name was John Kearney and they had landed in Liverpool three weeks previously from Mayo. They had been walking to Leeds and over the previous few days, the dead child had been ill. The whole family were in a distressed condition and on the day before, Mr Ramsbottom, the relieving officer at Bury, had given the family three shillings. The inquest jury verdict was 'natural causes'. On the facts available in the report, this seems an odd conclusion, unless they felt the three shillings relief guaranteed it could not have been starvation.[7]

Tim Cowbrain rented six acres of land in Roscommon, about two miles from Elphin.[8] The landlord was Mr Irvine and Cowbrain paid an annual rent of £3.7s.6d. Cowbrain was originally from the parish of Kilmehgue, in Sligo. In 1846 he had sown one and half acres of potatoes and two acres of oats. The potato crop was rotten and the oats crop also failed. By the end of December, he decided to leave for England. He had two cousins working on a railroad near Huddersfield and he hoped, like many others in his position, to find work and to get the eldest children into factories. He sold his cow for five pounds, paid his rent and sometime during the first week in January 1847, joined the flood of refugees heading for England. The family consisted of Tim, his wife and six children, the youngest just over a year old.

They took a steamer from Sligo to Liverpool, the fare for all the family was 18 shillings and the journey took five days, a harrowing experience in January. They spent 10 days in Liverpool and while there, received four shillings in relief and some food for the family. They then set out to walk to Huddersfield, surviving by begging but experiencing deteriorating health, particularly the children. They arrived in Rochdale on Friday 12 February. Here one of the children, aged one and half years, died on Sunday, 14 February. Cowbrain asked Mr Abram Travis, the relieving officer for money to bury the child and was given five shillings. At this time, Cowbrain had not asked the Rochdale authorities for any relief, keeping the rest of the family alive by begging. However, by Wednesday 17 February, the condition of the members of the family was such that Cowbrain asked Travis for relief and was given two shillings and was also sent to a union doctor. The doctor told Cowbrain the children were not fit to travel and that he must claim relief in Rochdale. Cowbrain went back to Travis but Travis refused to give any more help. Cowbrain also asked for a ticket for lodgings but this was refused and so he had to pay sixpence at the lodging house. On Friday, 19 February, he went again to Travis and again, relief was refused. On that day he did not eat. On Saturday, 20 February, the family had two pounds of bread and set out to walk to Todmorden, which they reached on the same evening and stayed at Richard Holt's lodging house. On Sunday 21 February, Cowbrain had fourpence left and he bought two quarts of milk and a pound of meal.

On Monday, the family set out to walk to Halifax (it is not clear why they did not go to Huddersfield). The children were by now weak and it seems that Cowbrain took them to the union doctor who again said they were too ill to travel. They stayed in Todmorden but by the next day, Tuesday, 23 February, one of the children aged four and half years, was in a very poor state. In the evening, the family walked to the Todmorden relieving officer's house, about a mile out of the town and knocked on the door. Thomas Heyworth, the relieving officer was faced with the famished looking Cowbrain family. Cowbrain told Heyworth one of the children was dying and asked could they come in. Heyworth let them in and within five minutes the child died. The inquest was held on Thursday 25 February, and the jury verdict was 'death by starvation'. The poor law authorities at Todmorden treated the remaining members of the family well but we don't know their ultimate fate. They may well have become typhus victims themselves. On 10 April 1847, the *Halifax Guardian* reported that William Townend, the head constable of Halifax had reported on the risk of a typhus epidemic because of the state of the lodging houses.

> The attention of the magistrates was on Tuesday last called by Townend to the filthy, disgusting and dangerous state of Swallow Street, inhabited by the lowest of the Irish, who now infest every corner of the streets and lanes, and as the warm spring months advance... these resorts of the Irish may, and probably will, prove the focus from which some pestilential epidemic may arise if not timely looked to and prevented.

Note the choice of words, the Irish 'infest', such language distancing the reader from the human wretchedness under their noses. On the 24 April the paper returned to the subject, pointing out there was an increase in typhus cases in Halifax: '...which is attributed to the influx of Irish into the town. The lodging houses are most inconveniently crowded by these half starved and diseased beings'. *The Guardian* went on to describe one cellar in which an Irish family of seven lived and all had typhus. In another case quoted, a house in Chapel Fold was occupied by one family named Leonard, 20 in all, 11 of whom had fever. On 8 May, the *Halifax Guardian* claimed that the English poor in the locality of Chapel Fold were threatening the union officers because they blamed them for the 'Irish fever'.

The McAndrew family landed at Liverpool from Sligo sometime in June 1847 and made their way to Bradford, man, wife and five children. The children died in Bradford 'of hunger and measles combined'. The couple and the remaining child moved to Leeds and then to York. On arrival in York they tried to get into lodging houses but were refused entry because of a fear that they had typhus. They slept one night in the vagrant shed and then slept in a barn. On 24 June, they were found sitting in a ditch near the York fever hospital by a doctor who examined the family. Teddy McAndrew, the father, was the most distressed. The fever house was full and the family were given blankets. On Saturday 3 July, after sleeping out in the open, 36 year old Teddy McAndrew died. In the space of a few weeks, Mrs McAndrew had lost four children and her husband.[9]

Thomas Constable, of the Manor house, Otley, in Yorkshire, opened up a building on his land to be used as a shelter by Irish vagrants. This was about January 1847. Inevitably, typhus broke out and by the beginning of July, 30 inmates had died. The local population objected to the place and Constable agreed that he would not allow any new inmates and when those in were cured and moved out, he would close the place. The McQuinn family arrived in the district early in June, father, mother and four children.

For two weeks they slept under Ilkley Bridge during which time one of the boys contracted smallpox. The locals in Ilkley wanted the McQuinns moved and it was suggested that they go to Thomas Constable's vagrant shed. Thomas Rhodes, the constable, had them put in a cart at 10.0pm on Tuesday 29 June and dumped them six miles from Constable's vagrant shed. The sick boy was carried on his mother's back and they all arrived at Constable's at 4.0pm on Saturday 30 June, only to be refused permission to enter. The boy died in the afternoon. Of particular significance in this case is that at the inquest held at Otley, John McQuinn, the father, could not give evidence as he did not speak English. Mary McQuinn aged 17 years, spoke for him. The verdict was 'died by the visitation of God of a natural disease called the smallpox'. The local correspondent of the *Halifax Guardian* reported that: 'We never saw a funeral like unto this lad's pass along our street before. There were three bearers, his father at the feet, a brother on one side and his sister on the other, the mother following behind. These were the whole party, they were dressed not in mourning but in rags!' The exclamation mark in this report emphasizes that the state of the famine Irish consistently exceeded in its distress, that of the English poor.[10]

III

The west Yorkshire textile belt had attracted sizeable pre-famine Irish settlements, presenting job opportunities for immigrants. In 1847, the borough of Leeds consisted of 11 townships and of these the township of Leeds was by far the largest. Within the township of Leeds there were 8 wards. Of the 7795 Irish born persons living in Leeds borough in 1851, 92 per cent lived in the township of Leeds.[11] Of the eight wards in Leeds, the Irish were concentrated in three. The distribution of the Leeds Irish in 1851 was 27 per cent in the north ward, 25 per cent in the north east ward and 31 per cent in the east ward.[12] The Chadwick Report on Leeds had earlier revealed the usual combination of overcrowding, substandard housing, poverty, lack of water and poor sanitation.[13]

The Irish refugee crisis in Leeds unfolded along the same lines as in the other centres of Irish settlements. During March 1846, the number of Irish paupers receiving outdoor relief in Leeds was 89. In March 1847, the number had increased to 854, almost an eightfold increase. Between the 1 and 16 of April 1846, the number of Irish receiving outdoor relief was 59; the same period in 1847 saw 654 Irish recipients of outdoor relief.[14]

In Leeds township, the Irish poor were relieved at the Mendicity Office where they could also obtain temporary accommodation, or rather, a bed. By the end of February 1847, the charitable House of Recovery was filling up with typhus victims and it was reported that over half of these were

Irish. From then onwards the crisis followed a familiar pattern. Commenting on the situation at this time, the *Leeds Mercury* told its readership viz a viz the Irish:

> The condition in which they arrive in this town and become the subjects of treatment in the House of Recovery is most deplorable. Only on Thursday last a poor woman was conveyed to that establishment, having been found with no covering but a dirty rag. The clothing of the whole of these Irish inmates is more than useless. We are informed that the cast off garments of our operatives would be most respectable in comparison with them.[15]

On the 24 April, John Beckwith clerk to the poor law guardians of Leeds township, wrote to the Poor Law Commissioners, pointing out that within a very short period there had been a 'sudden access of fever cases... especially among the tramping Irish who are relieved at the Mendicity Office'. He told of the hospital 'overflowing' with fever cases and said the guardians wanted permission to provide extra hospital accommodation. This was granted.[16]

The guardians' attention was drawn to the situation in the town by a report submitted to them by Dr W.S.Taylor, surgeon of the number two medical district. In this, Taylor had called attention to the 'wretchedness, filth and disease' in certain streets in which the Irish lived, in particular Goulden's Buildings, Goulden's Square and Back York Street.[17] These were all in the north ward.[18] Taylor also told the guardians that typhus had broken out in the vagrancy ward at the Mendicity Office and that the House of Recovery could not cope with the outbreak. Taylor's report seems to have jolted the authorities into action. On the 26 April the borough magistrates met to discuss the crisis. They were told by the chairman of the poor law guardians that in the quarter ending 25 March 1846, 278 Irish had been given outdoor relief. For the quarter ending 25 March 1847, the number was 1896, 'many of them labouring under fever'.[19] On the 1 May, Beckwith again wrote to the Poor Law Commissioners on behalf of the guardians, pointing out that there had been a considerable increase in applications for outdoor relief in districts number one and three, 'many being Irish poor'. The guardians requested the go ahead to appoint an additional relieving officer.[20] On the following day, 2 May, the guardians hired a plot of land in the appropriately named Accommodation Road, in Richmond Hill. On this a wooden shed was to be erected, to be used as a temporary fever hospital. Later, on the 28 June, further hospital beds were provided by using Victoria mill in Cleveland Street.[21] Simultaneously with the announcement of the acquisition of land in Accommodation Road, the Mendicity officer announced that in future all vagrants wanting beds would have to bath using newly provided bathing facilities.[22] The police were active in the campaign to control the typhus outbreak. On the 4 June, a police report gave some statistics regarding the spread of fever. In the East ward there had been an increased number of cases. In Lower Cross Street in two cellars, there were no beds and seven fever victims. In two other houses in the same street there were two houses, six beds and 14 persons ill with fever. At no 13 Brussels Street, there were no beds and seven fever victims.[23] By this time, the Nuisance Committee of the Town Council had decided to initiate a policy of cleansing the rooms of the poor. The *Leeds Mercury* reported that the cleansing of rooms was proceeding, in effect whitewashing walls, and informed its readers:

> We understand the great difficulty that has to be contended against arises from the number of Irish families who came to take possession of cottage houses - in some cases cellar dwellings. Owing to their filthy habits and the large numbers of individuals who are crowded together, these houses are in a short time rendered wholly unfit to live in and become the nurseries of disease.[24]

The problem was similar to that in Liverpool, Glasgow and Manchester. As long as thousands of destitute Irish poured ashore, there would be extreme pressure on even the most abominable accommodation available. By the time people had walked from Liverpool to Leeds, they would be even more desperate for a place to sleep. The authorities could not eject them for the simple reason they might have died in the streets. A Leeds police return of 18 June told of the fact that in the Rose and Crown yard in Union Street, there were seven houses, three of which had no beds. In these houses 28 persons were ill. In Brussels Street, in three houses (only two having beds) 20 persons were ill. The fever hospital was full. The number of burials in the churchyard at Leeds Parish Church for the half year ended 30 June 1847 was more than 900, an increase of over 200 on the corresponding period in 1846.[25]

The epidemic in Leeds peaked in July and the *Leeds Mercury* of 7 August 1847 announced that 'the extent of typhus fever has very much diminished in Leeds during the last fortnight'. However, those in contact with the poor had been exposed to great danger and, as in Liverpool, the Catholic priests paid heavily for their devotion to duty. Early in May, the Reverend George Wilson became the first Catholic priest to die in the typhus epidemic. The senior Catholic priest in Leeds at the time was Henry Walmsley, Dean of the District of York. He also visited Catholics in the House of Recovery and in their rooms. On the 27 May, at 3.0pm, Walmsley died of typhus.[26] The following day, the Rev Mr Metcalfe, a Catholic priest sent to replace Wilson, also died of typhus.[27] The Rev Joseph Curr was sent to Leeds to replace Walmsley as head of the Catholics in Leeds; by the 26 June he had contracted typhus. He died within a week, aged 55 years.[28] Another Catholic priest, the 33 year old James Coppinger, arrived in Leeds from Hull, again to replace losses. Within four weeks he was dead of Irish fever.[29] Over a period of nine weeks, five Catholics priest died as a result of carrying out their sacramental duties.

Unlike Liverpool, the Anglican clergy of Leeds were involved in administering to the sick Irish, presumably Protestants. At the end of May, the Rev Edward Jackson of Leeds parish church, contracted typhus 'from visiting one of the poor members of his church'. Fortunately, he recovered. William Stanley Monck was a 26 year old curate at Leeds parish church, the youngest son of Colonel Monck, of Cowley Park in Berkshire. He had been ordained at Ripon in March 1847. For several weeks the Anglican clergy from the parish church had been visiting sick poor, Irish and English, in some of the worst streets:

> In one cellar not more than twelve feet square, the clergy found nineteen wretches with only a few shavings under them; and upon inquiry as to what sustenance they had received, the reply was 'only occasionally a bucket of water reached down to quench their thirst'. The cleansing of these dreadful places was immediately undertaken, and fresh straw and blankets supplied. To effect this, the clergymen had themselves to assist in order to induce others to lend their help, and Mr Monck undressed some of the sufferers and aided in the removal of filth from the dwellings.[30]

There is something particularly moving in the thought of the young Anglican priest, transferred from a landed estate in Berkshire, to a filthy cellar in Leeds, handling dirty, smelly bodies in surroundings beyond his family's comprehension. He died of typhus on 11 July, four months after being ordained. Other members of the middle classes who died were Francis Sharpe, district surgeon, contracting typhus in the course of his duty. Sharpe was 40 years of age.[31]

IV

Compared with Liverpool, Manchester had the additional problem of even larger numbers of unemployed workers, victims of the economic downturn. At the beginning of 1846, business in Manchester was booming; by December it was clear that the economy was not healthy and by April 1847, there was a slump.[32] In November 1847, of 91 cotton mills in Manchester, only 38 were working full time, 34 were on part time production and 19 were closed. All other sectors of the textile industry suffered similarly, for example, of 20 dye works, 15 were working part time.[33] It was against this background of a depressed textile industry that the Irish famine refugee problem erupted in Manchester.

Table 7.1: Payments of outdoor relief in the township of Manchester in each of the financial years 1846/7 and 1847/8, each year ending 25 March.

Year	*Quarter*	*Manchester settled poor*		*English Casual poor*		*Irish poor*		*Total*	
		Nos	*Cost*	*Nos*	*Cost*	*Nos*	*Cost*	*Nos*	*Cost*
1846/7	1	23 816	3534	1 463	260	6 856	805	32 135	4 599
	2	22 978	3474	1 413	259	5 558	625	29 949	4 358
	3	22 042	3407	6237	772	7 636	911	35 915	5 090
	4	25 737	4023	13 550	1672	17 174	2 310	56 461	8 005
1847/8	1	33 882	5360	24 093	3142	32 914	4 886	90 889	13 388
	2	36 517	5399	27 886	4068	35 726	5 915	100 129	15 382
	3	37 686	5282	27 581	3861	30 042	4 602	95 309	13 745
	4	39 937	5917	28 097	3932	36 373	5 641	104 407	15 490

Source: MCL, M3/3/6B, *Statistics of Poor Relief in Manchester township.*

For the quarter ending 31 December 1846, the number of Manchester settled poor receiving outdoor relief was 22 042. In the quarter ending 25 March 1847, this category cases had risen to 25 737, an increase of 17 per cent. Over the same period, the number of Irish receiving relief had increased by 125 per cent. Similarly, over the same period, the numbers of English non settled poor increased by 117 per cent. For the quarter ending 30 June 1847, the total number of Manchester settled recipients on outdoor relief had increased by 54 per cent compared with the last quarter of 1846 while the Irish cases, numbering 32 914, were 310 per cent up on the quarter ending 31 December 1846. In the case of English non settled, the corresponding increase was 286 per cent. This indicates that the newly arrived English were badly hit by the closure of mills and factories.[34]

On the 31 December 1846, the level of distress among the working population was such that a meeting was held, called by concerned members of the middle classes. The Mayor, Elkanah Armytage chaired the proceedings at Manchester's town hall. The purpose of the gathering was to decide whether or not to open up a soup kitchen, financed by voluntary contributions. Three relieving officers claimed there was no need for such action but the Dean of Manchester and Dr Howard argued in favour.

George Pierce, the relieving officer for the St George's district told the meeting of great distress among the Irish in the district. John Harrop, clerk to the guardians of Manchester township claimed that over 'the last few weeks', between three and four hundred Irish families had arrived in Manchester and were claiming relief, about 1500 individuals. Dr Howard, surgeon to one of the dispensaries, told the meeting that there was great distress among the English but that there was a widespread reluctance to claim poor relief. This opinion must be viewed against the fact that increased numbers of Manchester's settled poor did claim relief.

The final outcome of the meeting was the opening up of a subscription list to finance a soup kitchen.[35] This was clearly desirable as the increasing number of press reports of destitution showed unequivocally that there was a crisis. On the 16 January the *Manchester Courier* described the developing situation in Manchester township:

> The stream of Irish mendicants which has for some weeks poured into our town, appears to increase and the wretched families to be met with at every street corner are painfully numerous. It is harrowing to the feelings to mark the suffering children, the almost infants who, without shoes or stockings, and with nothing but rags to cover them in this inclement weather, crowd after their parents, really and truly, we believe, because their parents have no place to shelter them until they go out and beg the means of procuring the scantiest and coarsest food. The number who find their way to the main offices [sic parish] increases in a fearful ratio, considerably more than in proportion than the English.

There is no doubt that poor relief and charitable soup kept large numbers of Irish alive. On 25 March 1847, the soup kitchen dispensed 1300 gallons of soup and 2000 loaves. The following day, the figures were 1000 gallons and 2000 loaves.[36] A correspondent of the *Manchester Guardian* gives us some idea of the scenes at the distribution of soup. An Irish woman and her children turned up without having first obtained a ticket:

> The woman herself was emaciated but the appearance of the children, with their sunken eyes and their wasted faces (more, as we were told by an eye-witness, like monkeys than of human beings) with their little knees bare of clothing and as bare of flesh (the bones nearly protruding through the skin) told of how greatly they must have suffered from the lack of food. They had no tickets but were supplied with bread and soup at the kitchen and ate voraciously. It appears they only arrived at Liverpool from Ireland on Thursday and the woman had been induced to come over in consequence of having a married sister living in Manchester.

It transpired her sister, who lived in Little Ireland, was herself dependent on the soup kitchen for her own survival.[37] In May the *Manchester Guardian* claimed that the system of distributing soup and bread was being abused and that the system itself was badly organized. It also commented on a falling level of interest in the kitchen activities by those organising it. Despite these criticisms a decision had been made to open a second soup kitchen in Ancoats. Between 1 and 10 of May, an extra 2000 people had lost their jobs because of factory shutdowns.[38]

The authorities in Manchester had watched events at Liverpool with alarm and by March 1847, the signs of a typhus epidemic appeared. The township of Manchester had the usual array of charitable institutions which provided medical aid to the poor, including a lying-in hospital, an eye hospital, the Royal Infirmary, various dispensaries and the House of Recovery. The latter treated fever victims. In addition, the Manchester workhouse at Strangeways had a medical ward. Before the famine influx, the Irish were already identified as major consumers of medical services. Edmund Lyon, physician to the Royal Infirmary, told the Cornwallis enquiry that the Irish in Manchester were more liable to epidemic diseases than the indigenous population because of their poor diet and grossly overcrowded living conditions.[39] James Phillip Kay also informed the same enquiry that among the people treated by staff of the Ardwick and Ancoats dispensary, the Irish were disproportionately represented.[40] John Robertson, surgeon to the lying-in hospital, claimed that at least 50 per cent of all births assisted by the charity were Irish.[41]

The records of the House of Recovery give some idea of the scale of the fever problem in Manchester before the 1847 outbreak. In Table 7.2 below the data for 1847 has been added.

During the 1837-8 outbreak in Manchester, the increase in the number of typhus sufferers was too great for the House of Recovery and a temporary fever hospital was opened in Balloon Street. This remained opened for six months and treated 182 patients.[42] In 1840, Dr Howard, physician to the Ardwick and Ancoats dispensary, claimed that during 1839, the various medical charities in Manchester treated 40 858 patients. He estimated that only 2432 of this total or six per cent, were fever patients. Assuming this includes those who died in the House of Recovery, it is a smaller number than one would expect in such urban conditions.

The fever outbreak of 1837-38 convinced Howard that effective treatment required the isolation of fever sufferers from the rest of the population. He arrived at this conclusion, like many other doctors, without the knowledge that body lice spread typhus.[43] The 142 deaths in the House of Recovery in 1847 was only previously exceeded in 1838 and 1839.

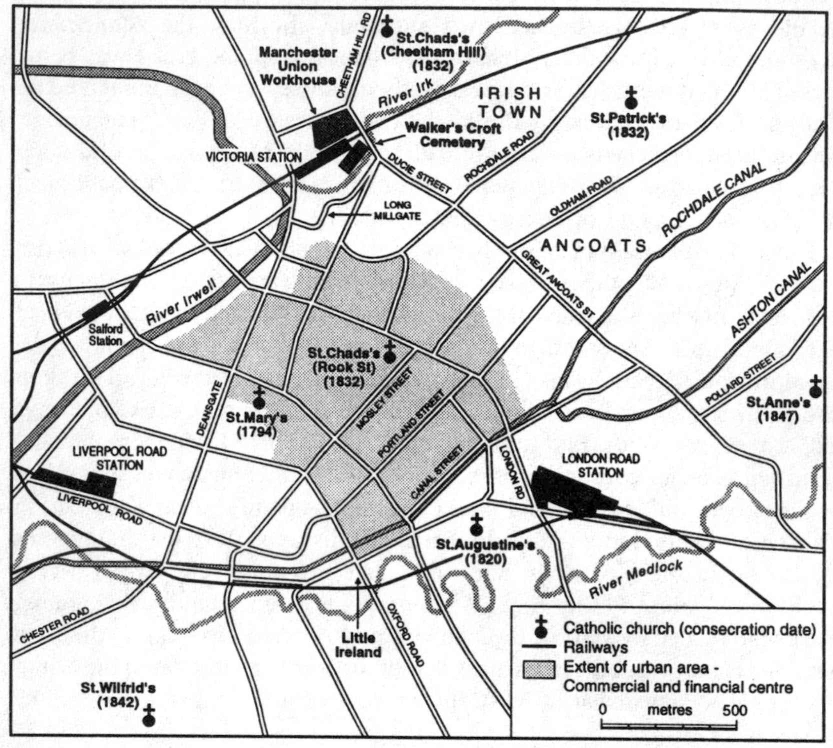

Figure 7.1 Manchester Township 1847

The organisational structure of medical provision for the poor in Manchester was one in which the union was divided into seven districts and within each district at least one doctor was employed by the poor law guardians. At the onset of the Irish famine influx, the districts were defined as Newton, Deansgate, Ancoats, Market Street, London Road, St George's and Cheetham.[44] As in other towns, there was a confusing allocation of responsibilities for the health of citizens. For example, at the beginning of 1847, Manchester Borough had responsibility for sanitary matters while the Board of Guardians had to provide medical services for the poor. In addition there were various medical charities. Apart from charitable medical provision, Manchester's principal workhouse at Strangeways had a medical ward to treat sick indoor paupers. A second workhouse was in Canal Street.[45] By the beginning of 1847, at the time when the economic depression was already putting extreme pressure on the union, the famine refugees began to arrive in numbers.

Table 7.2 The numbers of persons treated in the Manchester House of Recovery Fever hospital over the period 1832-44 and 1847.

Year ending 31 May	*Number admitted*	*Number who died*	*Deceased as a % of admissions*
1832	774	88	11.4
1833	287	30	10.4
1834	404	36	8.9
1835	400	56	14.0
1836	592	99	16.7
1837	800	120	15.0
1838	1402	240	17.1
1839	1103	200	18.1
1840	848	131	15.4
1841	733	116	15.8
1842	752	126	16.8
1843	737	85	11.5
1844	603	72	11.9
1847	955	142	14.7

Source: MCL. For 1832-44 inclusive, 'Report of the Board of Health in Manchester', 1 June 1844, p.4. For 1847, 'Report of the Board of Health in Manchester', 1 June 1847, p.5.

The logistics facing the poor law guardians were similar to those in Liverpool and Glasgow. First, the sick poor had to be identified and this meant visiting the homes of the poor. Second, given the prevalent medical view that fever victims should be isolated, when persons were diagnosed as being in need of treatment they had to be conveyed to hospital. Once there, then nurses and doctors were needed to give them treatment. Under normal circumstances, the charitable institutions such as the House of Recovery would have had adequate accommodation but the increased incidences of 'Irish fever' meant that by the end of March 1847 the town was facing an extraordinary situation. The capacity of the House of Recovery was about 100 at the most. The reaction of the guardians was to reorganize the medical districts, replacing the existing ones with five districts, namely Deansgate, London Road, Ancoats, St Georges and Market Street, together with two rural districts, Newton and Prestwich. A district relieving officer was responsible for visiting every applicant for relief. In addition, the officer would note anyone in need of medical assistance and inform the district medical officer. If a sick person was in need of hospital treatment and was too weak to walk, a cart would be sent to convey the person to the sick ward. In practice this arrangement often broke down. Those not in need of hospital treatment would be given a note to obtain medicine at one of the district dispensaries. Unfortunately, no central body of archives have survived regarding the incidence of typhus and other diseases associated with social disruption in Manchester. Fortunately, the *Manchester Guardian* carried detailed reports of the weekly meetings of the Manchester guardians of the poor. Though not consistent in the details reported, they do enable a fairly clear picture of the crisis to be traced through the medium of weekly fever reports.

By the end of March the guardians realised that the rapidly rising number of fever cases would, if they continued, be beyond the capacity of the House of Recovery to provide for. An approach was made to the owner of an empty mill on Long Millgate, to rent the building and convert it into a fever hospital. At their meeting held on 8 April, the guardians were told that the Bank of Manchester had agreed to the mill being rented at a cost of £200 per annum. With remarkable speed, the hospital opened for patients on 10 April.[46] Basically, floors were whitewashed and beds put in the rooms. In addition other emergency measures were taken. An auxiliary workhouse was in Tib Street, it had formerly been a military barracks and before that a mill. The guardians decided to convert this into another fever hospital, a move which prompted immediate protests but these were brushed aside.[47] The mill in Long Millgate was eight storeys high and the six upper floors were appropriated as wards for women and each ward had forty five beds. A master was appointed, a matron and 35 nurses.[48] These decisive measures were vindicated when the House of Recovery statistics are examined, the number of patients being much lower than was the case for each of the years 1838 and 1839. For the year ended 31 May 1847, the House had treated 955 patients, an increase of 58 per cent over the previous year. The number of deaths was 142, an increase of 97 per cent (see Table 7.2 above).[49] By the end of June, Millgate hospital had 300 beds but this was still insufficient and the guardians decided to convert the auxiliary workhouse in Minshull Street into a fever hospital with 180 beds. This latter opened in the last week of June and within one week had 180 patients. Despite these draconian measures, the shortage of hospital beds persisted. The central strategy was to transfer all fever patients into a hospital. This was shown to be failing when, in June, several cases of fever occurred in the Canal Street workhouse and there were no available hospital beds. At their meeting 1 July, the guardians decided to transfer all the indoor paupers out of the Canal Street workhouse onto outdoor relief or into the other workhouses, and convert Canal Street into a fever hospital. The owner of the building reluctantly agreed, subject to a firm commitment on the part of the guardians to compensate him for any loss of tenants in nearby property and any other loss which might follow as a consequence.[50] The situation on Saturday 3 July, 1847 was that Long Millgate hospital had 388 patients, Tib Street workhouse 110 and Canal Street workhouse 65.[51] A problem for the union officers was that instead of sick persons being taken by friends or relatives to Long Millgate they were dumped at the workhouses so increasing the danger to healthy inmates. Despite the expanded hospital provisions, some typhus victims had to be treated at home. For example, during the week ending 26 June 1847, 484 persons with typhus and other fevers were visited at home. Of this total, 138 or 29 per cent were in the St Georges district. By contrast, only five cases were in the rural districts of Newton and Prestwich.[52] The provision of hospital beds was a necessary but not sufficient condition for controlling the epidemic. Nurses and doctors were needed and the speed with which the crisis developed meant that little time was available for training. John Walsh, assistant surgeon at Long Millgate, in his report for the quarter on the running of Millgate hospital, stated: '...our staff of attendants, too, were not at times very efficient. Many of the nurses were not by any means prepared for their duties. We had to drill them ourselves, and when tolerably well instructed, it too often happened that they became patients themselves'.

One of these nurses, Catherine Burns, went into a delirious state and while unattended got onto a window ledge on the 5th floor, jumped into the River Irk and drowned. Eventually, fifty one of the staff at Long Millgate contracted fever. Of these six died.[53] To back up the hospital facilities, a second pronged attack was needed on the sanitary conditions in which the majority of fever victims lived.

On 8 May, eight police officers were seconded from the borough police force as sanitary inspectors, to be assisted by three labourers and a clerk. Their terms of reference were to inspect cellars and lodging houses and if deemed necessary, order the cleaning of accommodation and the whitewashing of walls. This action followed a decision by the town council to use its powers under existing legislation. The *Manchester Guardian* estimated that each officer would have to visit 150 dwelling per week.[54] The reports of these sanitary inspectors provided the local press with much evidence regarding the progress of the typhus epidemic in Manchester. By 22 May, the union had appointed eight more relieving officers and three assistant relieving officers, backed by three extra clerks. It was hoped this additional manpower would enable each family on its books to be visited weekly. The problem was that typhus, measles and diarrhoea could strike at any time. By now the Sanitary Inspectors had visited 184 streets and 496 lodging houses, of which 136 were whitewashed by the tenants and 88 by the Sanitary Police, as the inspectors became known. They found 534 conveniences in a filthy state and in the course of their visits they also found 204 persons ill, of which number 121 had typhus.[55] The situation was that, by June 1847, both the guardians and the town council had acted promptly with a whole range of measures concerning accommodation and manpower to deal with a major health crisis. This is all the more impressive when it is remembered that the trade depression had hit the textile industry particularly hard and many thousands of English were experiencing great hardship. However it is central to this study to claim that the Irish suffered disproportionately. The records of hospital cases does not distinguish the nationality of patients and so we have no direct evidence in support of this claim. However, much secondary evidence points to the fact that, as in Liverpool, Glasgow and South Wales, a high incidence of Irish patients occurred in Manchester.

In his report for the year 1846, the Registrar General comments with regard to the last quarter: '...the sad condition of these poor Irish immigrants have, no doubt, contributed to deteriorate the health of Liverpool, Glasgow and Bristol, ports through which they enter, as well as to raise the mortality of Manchester and other inland towns'.[56]

The Registrar of St George's district in Manchester, also referring to the last quarter of 1846, noted the large number of deaths in his district, 406 and recording that typhus and measles accounted for most:

> The population of the district is to a great extent composed of the lower order of Irish who live and lodge together in great numbers in the same home. In one part of the district called 'Angel Meadow' it is not uncommon to find 20 or 30 persons living in one house when there is not accommodation for one third of that number if health is to be in the least considered. During the last two or three months, large numbers of the poor from Ireland have crowded themselves in the district, droves of them rambling about the street seeking lodgings, and no doubt being exposed to the severe and inclement weather. Many of the poor creatures

have died from cold producing fever and other diseases. Owing to the great increase in mortality, during the last few weeks, I instituted enquiries as to the length of time the deceased had been in England and found in many cases they had been only a few weeks. The poverty and destitution of the district at the present time is very great. The homes are badly ventilated and the unhealthy odour arising from so many persons huddled together in a confined apartment must have an injurious affect. It cannot be surprising that while such a state of things exists, mortality should be so great.[57]

The Registrar, with access to the official statistics of registered deaths must be regarded as authoritative. Local medical statistics highlight the vulnerability of the population of St George's. During the week ending 10 July 1847, the district surgeons visited 577 fever cases. Of this total, 211 or 36 per cent were in St George's. However, other areas experienced high levels of sickness. Writing 21 July from his home in Medlock Street, Joseph Murphy, surgeon, told the guardians that from 1 April up to date, 987 persons had been treated by the doctors in the London Road district. Of these some 378, 38 per cent were fever cases and of these, 286 or 76 per cent were in Little Ireland.[58] It was as late as 18 November when the guardians were told by Dr Noble that the fever was 'now spread among the lower population' and was 'no longer confined to the Irish'. This remark can reasonably be interpreted to mean that before this a minority of victims were English. However, despite the increase in English patients, of the 266 patients in Long Millgate at this time, 47 per cent were Irish. On 9 September, Dr Noble told the guardians that the epidemic was subsiding and a week later they were told it was hoped to close the Minshull Street hospital.[59] During the whole of the calendar year 1847, 3946 patients were treated at the Long Millgate hospital and of these 592 died, a death rate of 15 per cent (see Appendix No 7.3)

To the deaths in Long Millgate must be added the deaths in the House of Recovery. Irritatingly, the reports of the House are based on a year ending 31 May and so a direct comparison with Long Millgate is not possible. During the year ended 31 May 1848 the number of fever patients treated was 1049 and of these, 136 or 13 per cent died.[60] If we assume an average monthly death rate of eleven, then for the seven months June to December 1847, 77 deaths occurred. Added to those in Long Millgate we have a total of 669. We do not know the numbers who died in the workhouse wards at Tib Street, Canal Street, Strangeways and Minshull Street. However, these will not add up to many as a policy of transferring to Long Millgate when beds were available, was vigorously pursed. The Registrar General's report for 1847 records 1444 deaths from fever in Manchester township. (see

Appendix 7.1). If we deduct the estimate of 669 dead in the hospitals, this leaves a net total of 775 deaths, most of which have occurred at home. If we assume that 70 per cent of all fever deaths were Irish, then we obtain an estimated 1011 Irish deaths in the epidemic. The Manchester union had been using a place called Walkers Croft in Strangeways as a pauper burial ground but by the beginning of December 1847 it was becoming 'unhealthy and unsanitary' and the guardians decided to enter into a contract with Harpurhey Cemetery Company for a pauper plot.[61]

The pattern of the disease in Manchester, in respect of its chronology, followed that of Liverpool, in that it peaked in July/August in terms of numbers of hospital patients. For example, at the end of the week ending 29 May 1847, the number of patients in Long Millgate was 211. At the week ending 3 July the number was 388. (see Appendix No 7.4). In the case of sick cases visited at home, these also peaked in July, with 4170 visits of which number 2733 or 66 per cent, were described as typhus. Of all 4170 visits, 38 per cent were in the St George's district and 19 per cent in Ancoats, a total of 57 per cent of all visits being in districts with large Irish populations. (see Appendix No 7.1).

Turning from the statistics of the epidemic, we can obtain some idea of the horror of the experience. The efforts of the sanitary inspectors revealed that there were 150 lodging houses all 'in an extremely filthy state' and chiefly occupied by the Irish. As well as visiting the lodging houses, the Inspectors surveyed cellars and cottages. Many of the latter were sublet and grossly overcrowded and it was estimated that 70 per cent were in a filthy state confirming the pre-famine reports of Kay and Adshead. On 12 May 1847, the *Manchester Guardian* carried a report on the work of the Sanitary 'police':

> We have heard of one house in which there are about forty Irish paupers, seven of them sick, and a child lying on a table, having measles. In the whole house there were only three filthy beds and a little furniture most wretched in kind and dirty in condition. In another house, thirteen beds were found in three rooms; one room nine feet square, had fourteen occupants and into this house forty lodgers were received at night... To this house there was neither convenience nor ash-pit.. In a cellar containing only one bed, were found two families, in all, eleven individuals, one man, his wife and five children having to lie on the cellar floor without any covering but a few filthy rags. Here too, as might be expected, two sick persons were found. In another cellar, a woman and four children were found all sick and in a state of extreme destitution: the husband had been removed to the fever ward.

There is no reason to doubt the accuracy of the *Guardian*'s reporting, it was consistent with many other accounts of events. During the weekend Saturday and Sunday, 8 and 9 May, nature intervened to increase the misery of the Irish. Heavy rain fell throughout the Saturday and on Sunday morning. This caused the River Medlock to rise and on Saturday evening, despite floodgates being opened, it continued to rise, overflowing its banks at the bend of the river near Oxford Road in Central Manchester. The consequent floods ran all over the wretched collection of streets known as 'Little Ireland' (see Appendix 7.4). The police evacuated the Irish families at 5.30am on the Sunday morning so averting any loss of life. However, the water from the River Medlock was filthy and dangerous and had soaked whatever bits of furniture the inhabitants of Little Ireland possessed. The police immediately ordered the *owners* of the houses to clean them up.

Commenting on the event, the *Manchester Guardian* told its middle class readership:

> After years hence, and we trust Little Ireland, which in years past has been the scene of many an Irish riot and faction fight; which in 1821 was one of the worst centres of the Asiatic cholera and which has long been, and still is, a seat of squalor, nucleus of fevers and other foul diseases, will have passed away for ever, its hollows filled up with its wretched abodes levelled with the ground.[62]

Within two weeks, the misery of Little Ireland's population was exacerbated when the owners of the property in Aughton Street ejected the tenants. The properties in this street had been sold to the South Junction and Altrincham Railway Company *before* the typhus outbreak and notices had already been served on the tenants to quit. The ground was needed for what is today Oxford Road Railway Station, but despite the awful housing, the tenants refused to go. However, the order to clean up the flooded houses probably decided the landlords to get rid of the Irish and their property. On 20 May the inhabitants of Aughton Street were ejected, four labourers, their wives, five widows, a woman whose husband was in Ireland and 34 children. The relieving officer gave them some assistance; while some stood over their pathetic belongings, the rest went begging.

Simultaneously, in the surrounding streets of Little Ireland, the scenes of the worst distress in Manchester were found. Emery Street consisted of 18 houses and was only 15 feet wide. In one house, on the same day, two people had typhus and a third was found dead. No neighbours would go in to help the sick as they were afraid of catching the fever. In another house a man and two of his children had fever while in yet another, six persons were found in conditions of extreme destitution. One house in Winckley

Street had four occupants with fever; in James Leigh Street two were in a destitute state and in four more houses in Little Ireland, twenty four persons were destitute. Also in James Leigh Street two children, living in a cellar, had small pox and in each of six other cellars in the vicinity, there was a child with smallpox. Bent Street had eighteen houses; a woman in the street took in an Irish woman named Mary Carroll on Tuesday 19 May. Mary died early on the following morning. She had no relations in Manchester and the woman who took her in was also ill, with six children, all in a poor way. There was no money to bury Mary Carroll and so she had a pauper burial.[63]

Dr Noble, the Manchester union medical officer, had told the clerk to the union on 3 June that the fever was spreading and expressed doubts about the capacity of the authorities to provide sufficient hospital beds. One of the many problems was that people being discharged from fever wards were returning to the same overcrowded rooms and contracting fever again. Two people living in a cellar under No 5, Back Nicholas Street contracted typhus, went into a fever ward, recovered and went back to the same cellar. They were later re-admitted to the fever wards.[64] By the week ending 29 May 1847, the Long Millgate Fever Hospital had, since opening on 10 April admitted 554 patients and of these only 63 had died. The argument that the transient Irish propagated the spread of fever received some support when Dr Noble exonerated the resident Irish of Manchester from blame for the typhus outbreak. He accused migrant Irish, most of whom had moved up from Liverpool and who crowded into the lodging houses and other low price accommodation.[65] The local press echoed this condemnatory explanation of how typhus came to Manchester. *The Manchester Guardian* proclaimed: '...from enquiries we made yesterday, we regret to learn that the fever, which has been brought hither by Irish immigrants and which is found to exist amongst them wherever they are huddled together in lodging houses, so far from being on the decline, appears to be increasing'.[66]

As the summer progressed, Little Ireland continued to present the worst scenes of destitution and suffering in Manchester. On Tuesday 29 June, no fewer that ten people, four males and six females, all Irish, were found lying in the open in Wakefield Street, in a poor physical condition. They had been thrown out of the lodging houses because of the fear of typhus. One of these, Anne Gaffney, was the daughter of the lodging house keeper, at no 1, James Leigh Street. She had obtained a certificate from a visiting surgeon several days previously, specifying that she had fever. Her father took the certificate to the authorities, hoping to have her removed to a fever ward. No one came so he put her in the street, hoping the Sanitary Inspectors would find her and take her to hospital. Several others of the people in this group had certificates but no one had come to take them to hospital. The Inspector who found them immediately procured a cart and they were all taken to the Manchester Workhouse fever ward.[67] One problem facing the police at this time was that cart owners were becoming increasingly reluctant to carry fever victims out of a fear of contagion. The next day, Wednesday 30 June, William Spetch went to the A Division police station at the Town Hall and stated that a lodging house keeper, Thomas Smith, of 28 Spinning Field, had put him in the street because he had contracted fever. A policeman escorted him back to Smith's and paid for another night's lodgings and promised a surgeon would visit Smith the next day. We don't know what happened. At 9.0am the next morning, two young women, aged 16 and 20 years of age were discovered lying in Wakefield Street, Little Ireland, by a Sanitary Inspector. Both were very ill and had been turned out of a lodging house. They were physically unable to move and apparently had no relatives or friends. Again, a cart was hired and they were taken to a fever ward.[68] On 12 July, a five year old child was found lying in the street in Little Ireland apparently with no one to look after him. Both his parents had been taken to fever wards. He was taken to the workhouse.[69]

Distressing as these cases were, it is not clear that the Manchester parochial authorities can be accused of deliberate neglect or unconcern. As elsewhere, the organisational problems were considerable and the scale of the outbreak initially overwhelmed the poor law guardians and police. There are many examples of this. An Irish woman who had been in Manchester over twenty years, had been deserted by her husband, leaving her with four children. The eldest, aged 17 years, had been out of work five months and by 24 June, had had fever of some kind for five weeks. On the same day a surgeon advised that he be taken to a fever ward. The family had been surviving on a parish allowance of four shillings a week and by 24 June had no food in the cellar, no bedding and had not changed their clothes for weeks. On a subsequent visit they told the Sanitary Inspector they had not eaten since the previous day.[70]

In a cellar in James Leigh Street, Michael Smith, an Irishman, his wife and three children, aged 2, 8 and ten years were all found sick with fever. They were so ill they couldn't assist each other. They had had only two and sixpence parochial relief, possibly because they were frightened of applying for more in case they were removed, having been in Manchester only three years.[71] In another instance, four children were found in a house, aged 11, 7, 3 years and a baby of eleven months. They were looking after themselves as both parents were in a fever ward. A Sanitary Inspector visited a cellar in Tame Street and found an Irish woman living with her four sisters. They also had lodgers, a man his wife and six children. All 13 slept on the flagged floor of the cellar on shavings and rags. Eight had fever.[72]

An official view of this particular period in Manchester's social history is that of the Registrar for the Market Street district in his report for the quarter ending 30 June 1847. Commenting on the 711 deaths in the quarter, 12 per cent up on 1846, he wrote: 'this is perhaps attributable to the extraordinary number of Irish persons; men, women and children, naked, hungry and diseased, who have inundated this country, especially the various districts of South Lancashire'.[73]

As in all other areas of Irish settlement, the efforts of the authorities to control typhus continued to be hampered by people who had been pronounced cured and then returning to their former homes and again contracting the disease because of bodily contact. The Manchester poor law guardians were informed of such a case, the gist of the complaint was that property owners were often taking no steps to clean homes when the occupants were in hospital.

> An Irish family lived in a cellar at 51a Gas Street. Patrick Egan, his wife Catherine and their children Thomas, John, Patrick, Bridget and Mary shared the cellar with another Irish family of eight. Bridget and Mary Egan died of typhus in the cellar and the rest of the family were sent to the fever ward. When pronounced cured, the Egans returned to the 'filth and dirt' of the cellar which had been neither cleaned nor whitewashed while they were in the fever ward. Of the other family who shared the cellar with the Egans, three were sent to the fever ward on 19 July. In 53a, another family lived in the cellar and all were sent to the fever ward where the father died. The Catholic priest paid for this cellar to be whitewashed. These two cellars had provided cases for relief to the guardians incessantly for nearly 12 months, arising from sickness.[74]

This report in September 1847 suggests that the sanitary inspectors were not able or willing to deal with all cases of dirty cellars.

Inevitably, there were deaths among those whose duty took them into close proximity with the paupers. Reference has already been made to the six deaths at Long Millgate by July. Dr Noble, surgeon, survived typhus; Mr Davenport, the master of the Long Millgate hospital went down with typhus, as did the deputy matron.[75] Roberts, a relieving officer died of typhus caught escorting Irish paupers to Liverpool for removal.[76] Early on in the crisis, Fr Walker, a Catholic priest died, as a result of his duties in Little Ireland.[77] On 2 February 1848, Fr Edward Unsworth, priest at St Patrick's in Manchester died. He was 26 years of age and contracted typhus giving the last rites to dying Catholics. He had been ordained in Rome only 18 months previously.[78]

Looking back at the events in Manchester during 1847 it seems fair to suggest that the authorities acted with reasonable speed to an unexpected crisis. The provision of hospital space, and medical manpower undoubtedly kept the death rate from typhus down to levels well below what they could have been. By comparison with Liverpool and Glasgow, Manchester escaped fairly lightly but the experience shook the middle classes who had feared for their own lives.

Given the large number of Irish in Manchester township in 1847, it is notable that most of the comments on the suffering of the Irish refer to Little Ireland. This was the smallest of the three Irish settlements. The lack of comment on the conditions in the other areas could be taken to mean that the Irish in these did not suffer disproportionately. More likely, it reflected the fact that the cases in Little Ireland were the most desperate. News from the other Irish settlements was competing with other events for newspaper attention at a time of crisis. Reflection on the year inevitably lead to blame being placed on the Irish. Looking back over 1847, the Health Committee of the House of Refuge wrote in their report for the year 1847: '...this disease, imported from Ireland, and popularly known as the 'famine fever' became prevalent in Manchester late in 1846'.[79]

In conclusion, the views of the Manchester Board of Guardians concerning the cause and nature of the emergency of 1847 are best appreciated by reading the memorial they sent to the Home Secretary in February 1848. It states unequivocally that the crisis had its roots in the arrival of the famine refugees.[80] In preparing their memorial, the guardians were almost certainly reflecting the views of those in the front line of the battle against typhus. Their own medical officer, Dr Noble, in his report of 30 October on the fever hospital in Long Millgate, claimed that until August 1847, 90 per cent of patients were Catholics.[81]

V

Distance from the west coast ports was no guarantee of immunity from the arrival of Irish famine refugees and the consequent financial, health and social problems. Relatively large numbers of Irish arrived at the ports of Whitehaven and Maryport, some of the settling in the mining and iron ore villages of Cumberland, particularly Cleator Moor. Large numbers made their way across the hostile landscape which runs parallel with Hadrian's Wall, making their way to Newcastle, Sunderland, Durham City and the mining villages of County Durham. Events in the north east soon followed the by now familiar pattern of rising claims for outdoor relief, rising numbers of fever victims and distressing scenes of wretchedness. As early as 2 January 1847, the *Newcastle Journal*, in the course of commenting on events in Ireland, claimed that large numbers of Irish were arriving in Newcastle, adding that there was no work for them. In March, it was reported that the 'town of Sunderland is overrun with Irishmen who are in a most miserable condition.[82] Such claims were soon bolstered with the publication of statistics of spending on poor relief. During the quarter ended 25 March 1847, 6061 vagrants had been relieved at the Morpeth workhouse and of these, 51 per cent were Irish.[83] In May, the *Newcastle Journal* carried a piece headed 'Fearful increase in Pauperism', in which it was reported:

> The influx of Irish into the town over the last three months, all of whom become chargeable to their different parishes in which they locate themselves immediately on their arrival, has so far increased the expenditure of the union during the last quarter, that the guardians reckon it is nearly double the amount it has usually been.[84]

The thought of the poor rate doubling was enough to upset the most sympathetic and sanguine of ratepayers but any such worries there may have been turned out to be unfounded. The total expenditure on poor relief by the Newcastle union in the year ending 25 March 1848 was only 13 per cent up on the previous year.[85] This compares with the 74 per cent in Liverpool and 88 per cent in Manchester over the same period.

On the eve of the 1847 crisis, the situation in Newcastle regarding fever victims was one in which a charitable institution, 'the Institute for the Cure and Prevention of Contagious Diseases' took patients from both Newcastle and Gateshead. In December 1846, the Newcastle guardians were criticized for having no provision for vagrant fever victims outside of the workhouse wards. Vagrants put into these wards were responsible for spreading disease. It was recommended that *all* paupers with contagious diseases be sent to the House of Recovery (Institution) and all fit vagrants be sent to the workhouse as an alternative to outdoor relief.[86] Though the typhus epidemic appeared in the region it seems to have been on a much smaller scale than in Lancashire, South Wales and Glasgow. The number of patients treated in the House of Recovery in December 1846 was five. In April 1847 the number had risen to 24 and in June it was 61. At this juncture, the Roman Catholic clergy in Newcastle entered the debate about the fever epidemic in a dramatic way. William Riddell, Catholic bishop in Newcastle, and James Standon and Joseph Cullen, priests, produced a report based on their first hand knowledge of the conditions in the slums. This is reproduced here, almost in its entirety, it being one of the few eye witness accounts of the Irish in Newcastle at the time. It is dated 3 June 1847:

> The great influx of Irish during the last few months has caused all the lodging houses to be overflowing. In rooms of very small dimensions and very imperfect ventilation, sixteen or twenty persons sleep at night. In these rooms, fever has of late been greatly on the increase, and we beg to lay before you a few instances which we have observed in Anchor Entry, Sandgate, which is extremely narrow, with a dirty stream running down it. We found in a room 12 feet by eight feet and but seven feet high, with a single window against a dead wall at four feet distance, twelve persons lying ill of fever, they were huddled four of five together upon straw and covered with a single rug or blanket, four other persons sleep in the same room at night. In Maningham's Entry, Sandgate, in a wretched garret, fifteen feet by ten feet (the average height not six feet) with a window but eighteen inches square, lay a poor woman called Bridget Carroll, with her four children, all ill of fever, in a most abandoned state, for being unable to keep themselves, their neighbours, for fear of contagion, had refused them any aid. In Dock Entry, a family of the name of Naughton, consisting of eight children, has suffered severely, everyone being either at present affected or but just recovering from fever. In White Boar Entry, Sandgate, the rooms are very small; in one inhabited by Patrick Conley, about eight feet square and seven feet high, with a very small window, five people sleep and two of these are in the last state of fever. In another, inhabited by Mary Coulson, thirteen feet by twelve feet, and eight feet high, fourteen people sleep every night, and nine of them have already had the fever. In Downs Entry we have found five cases of fiver, four others having only just recovered, the whole nine inhabiting only one house. In Soap Entry, behind the Rose and Crown public house kept by Mr Lattery, lives Patrick Henry with a family of eight children, six of whom are suffering from fever. These facts, however striking, are not to be compared to what has occurred in Cobourg Stairs; we have observed during the last three weeks, thirty six cases of fever in but six rooms.

Riddell and his co-investigators urged the Guardians to provide more accommodation for fever victims.[87] The report seems to have jerked the authorities into action. The magistrates of Newcastle met on the 5 June and passed a resolution urging the Board of Guardians to provide proper accommodation for fever victims.[88] On the 8 June the guardians met to discuss the same issue.[89] The outcome was the provision of two fever sheds at the workhouse.

The committee of the House of Recovery met on the 6 July 1847 and the secretary reported that during the past month the admissions had been so numerous as to make any additional numbers of beds absolutely necessary.

A room used for mangling washing was appropriated as a fever ward and 18 beds installed.[90] The number of patients under treatment peaked September at 95.[91] On the 2 May 1848, Dr White, the physician who had been in charge of the House of Recovery over the past year, suggested to the committee: 'The propriety of rewarding the servants of the institution for their unprecedented exertions during the late fearful visitation of fever, the extraordinary number of 710 patients having been treated'.[92]

Dr White's report does not indicate how many died of typhus. In addition to the House of Recovery, another charitable institution, the Newcastle Dispensary, also provided medical facilities for persons with letters of recommendation. Over the year ending 31 August 1847, the Dispensary treated 10 470 people. Of these 349 were typhus cases of which number 56 died, a death rate of 16 per cent. In its annual report it was explained:

> Continued [sic relapsing fever] typhus has been more than usually prevalent, owing in a great measure to the enormous influx of wandering Irish who have continued to pour into the town during the greater part of the year. Numbers of them labouring under fever on their arrival and it is surprising that the disease has not spread more extensively than it has hitherto done, among the inhabitants, when the crowded state of the lodging houses and tenements in the lower part of the town is considered.

The most affected locality in Newcastle was the Sandgate district.[93] During the next 12 months, ending 31 August 1848, 9830 persons were treated, of these 469 were cases of fever and 25 died, a death rate of only 5 per cent.[94] Again we have the constantly repeated identification of the famine refugees as the principal perpetrators of contagion. Under normal circumstances, the poor law guardians in Gateshead sent their fever patients to the House of Recovery in Newcastle. However, as we have seen, Newcastle had problems of its own and in September the Gateshead guardians were told that they could not longer send fever patients to Newcastle. They searched for suitable, empty accommodation in the Gateshead union but failed to find anything. Instead, they negotiated the lease of a building at Eighton Bank, 20 yards over the union border in the Chester-le-Street union, to be used as a temporary fever hospital. This was unusual, one union wanting to erect a fever hospital in another union and so the Gateshead guardians had to ask permission of the Poor Law Commissioners. The guardians, in an effort to cajole the Commissioners, stressed the short term nature of the project: '...that it is likely to be quite of a temporary nature will induce you to sanction their proceedings; at present fever cases seem to be spreading rapidly in the various lodging houses where the Irish poor principally report and also in some degree among our resident labouring poor'.[95]

Permission was given and a lease was taken out until the following 28 February. Immediately, the churchwardens of the parish of Gamesley objected to the setting up of a fever hospital.[96] Their reactions were a manifestation of the strains appearing in the relationships between the authorities in different unions, as a result of the growing cost of Irish vagrants in terms of relief and medical expenses as well as a fear among the populations near the fever sheds. In some instances, poor law authorities took legal action against those whom they felt were abusing the system. For example, in September 1847, Patrick Doyle was taken before the magistrates in Newcastle by the master of the workhouse vagrant ward. It seems he pushed Daniel O'Connell 22 miles from the parish of West Chevington to St Nicholas parish in Newcastle. O'Connell had typhus. It was suggested at the court hearing that parishes outside were sending their fever victims to Newcastle, to save the expense of providing treatment. Charging Doyle was meant to send out a warning to others who might consider taking fever victims into Newcastle.[97]

The Catholic clergy in Newcastle and the surrounding areas paid heavily for their devotion to duty. Fr O'Connell died in June 1847, to be followed by Fr James Stephen, at Newcastle on 11 October.[98] On the 4 November, Bishop William Riddell, died of typhus caught on his visits to the Irish poor of Sandgate. He was the third son of Ralph Riddell, the family being one of the Catholic landed families of Northumberland. Bishop Riddell was 42 at the time of his death. At his requiem mass in Newcastle, celebrated by Nicholas Wiseman, leader of England's Catholics, it was claimed that 23 Catholic priests had died of typhus so far.[99] Other priests in the region to die were James Standon, 11 October 1847 and William Fletcher, 22 February 1848.[100] Despite these deaths of priests, the total number of Irish deaths from typhus appears to have been much smaller than was the case in Liverpool, Newport and Glasgow, when allowing for different sized populations.

Appendices

Appendix 7.1 The number of deaths from fever in the various districts of the township of Manchester, 1838, 1845 and 1847.

	Deaths all causes			*Deaths from fever*			*Fever deaths as %*		
Districts	*1838*	*1845*	*1847*	*1838*	*1845*	*1847*	*1838*	*1845*	*1847*
Ancoats	1341	1253	2085	61	26	207	4.5	2.1	9.9
St Georges	1075	912	1509	59	10	136	5.5	1.1	9.0
London Rd	1197	950	1253	231	46	331	19.2	4.8	25.6
Market St	1291	1257	2379	75	16	618	5.8	1.3	26.0
Deansgate	1127	910	1467	74	19	149	6.6	2.1	10.2
Total	6031	5282	8693	500	117	1441	9.1	2.2	16.5

Source: Manchester Guardian, 15 April 1848. Report of the meeting of the Poor Law Guardians held 13 April 1848: Report submitted by Dr Noble.

Appendix 7.2 The number of patients admitted to the Newcastle Dispensary between 1 September 1846 and 31 August 1848, inclusive.

1 September 1846 to 31 August 1847		*1 September 1847 to 31 August 1848*	
Outcome		*Outcome*	
cured	10 001	cured	9330
died	178	died	163
relieved	41	relieved	29
irregular treatment	18	irregular treatment	16
incurable	1	incurable	1
sent to fever house	8	sent to infirmary	8
remaining in house	223	sent to fever house	58
		remaining in house	225
Total admissions	10 470	*Total admissions*	9830

Notes: (i) over the year ending 31 August 1847, of the total admissions, 349 were typhus cases and of these, 56 died, a 16 per cent mortality rate. (ii) over the year ending 31 August 1848, of the total admissions, 469 were typhus cases and also continual fever. Of these 469 cases, 25 died, a 5 per cent death rate.

Appendix 7.3 The number of admissions and deaths, during each week at the Tib Street, Minshull Street and Long Millgate fever hospitals, Manchester, from the 10 April 1847 to the 8 April 1848.

Wk/ ending	Admissions	Deaths	Wk/ending	Admissions	Deaths
1847					
April 17	66	3	Oct 23	98	8
April 24	75	9	Oct 30	115	13
May 1	89	6	Nov 6	86	5
May 8	61	12	Nov 13	104	11
May 15	84	16	Nov 20	76	13
May 22	75	6	Nov 27	97	13
May 29	105	10	Dec 4	87	10
June 5	125	15	Dec 11	64	15
June 12	141	15	Dec 18	38	7
June 19	172	16	Dec 25	52	7
June 26	281	23	**1848**		
July 3	185	18	Jan 1	41	7
July 10	221	27	Jan 8	51	3
July 17	268	38	Jan 15	45	8
July 24	232	25	Jan 22	52	9
July 31	264	29	Jan 29	34	1
Aug 7	224	24	Feb 5	60	4
Aug 14	222	23	Feb 12	31	6
Aug 21	203	23	Feb 19	40	5
Aug 28	184	25	Feb 26	30	0
Sept 4	160	16	Mar 4	36	6
Sept 11	183	21	Mar 11	21	6
Sept 18	133	15	Mar 18	32	5
Sept 25	163	26	Mar 25	18	2
Oct 2	88	13	April 1	34	4
Oct 9	106	12	April 8	12	7
Oct 16	104	17			
			Total	5567	658

Note: The Minshull Street hospital ward opened on 26 June 1847 and closed 9 October 1847. The Tib Street fever ward opened 10 July 1847 and closed 11 September. The Long Millgate hospital opened 10 April 1847 and was still open at the time of this report.
Source: Manchester Guardian, 15 April 1848, Report of the weekly meeting of the Manchester Guardians held 13 April 1848.

Appendix 7.4 The streets constituting 'Little Ireland' in Manchester in May 1847, and their condition following the floods of Saturday night, 8 May 1847.

Name of street	*Length in yards*	*Width in feet*	*Number of owners*	*Number of houses*	*Remarks*
James Leigh	40	23	2	12	Flooded.
Cayley	40	8	2	13	Flooded, bad conditions.
Mary	40	17	2	18	Not drained.
John	40	13	2	18	Flagged, but not drained.
Bent	40	16	2	18	Flagged, but not drained.
Emery	40	15	1	16	Flagged, not drained, water deep in cellar.
Winkley	40	13	3	15	Stone paved, not drained, foul water.
Great Marlborough	196	47	6	16	Passages to cellars full or mud.
Wakefield	196	36	7	27	Not paved or drained.
Anvil	71	17	6	29	Worst street, not paved or drained.
Forge	71	17	5	18	Mud paved, but very bad conditions.
Frank	71	17	2	8	Mud paved, but very bad conditions.
William	-	17	1	4	Mud paved, but very bad conditions.
Johnson's Buildings	-	13	1	12	Mud paved, but very bad conditions.
Bakehouse	-	12	1	1	Mud paved, but very bad conditions.
Aughton	-	13	1	6	Mud paved, but very bad conditions.
Totals			44	241	Houses flooded, cellars and ground floor.

Source: Manchester Guardian, 12 May 1847.

Notes and References

1 The propensity of the Irish to walk long distances was noted by many commentators before the famine crisis. See BPP (HC) 1844 (318) 1, Report of the Select Committee on Railways, Appendix no 4. Evidence of Charles Mott of Manchester. See also correspondence in the *Liverpool Mercury*, 1 January 1847.

2 See *Cheltenham Examiner*, 7 April 1847; *Sunderland Herald*, 16 April 1847; *Bristol Gazette*, 27 April 1847; *Cheltenham Examiner*, 28 April 1847.

3 *Cheltenham Examiner*, 7 April 1847.

4 Austin (1847), Relief of the Irish Poor in Liverpool, p. 112.

5 BPP (HC) 1850 (1142) XXVII, 2nd Report of the Poor Law Board. Letter from J.Roscoe, Clerk to the Altrincham Union to Poor Law Commissioners, dated 20 October 1849. Roscoe wrote 'In consequence of this place being situated on the great road from Liverpool to the south, we have always been much infested with vagrant poor, particularly the Irish'. See *Manchester Guardian*, 22 May 1847, Report on the meeting of the Manchester guardians held on 20 May 1847.

6 *Manchester Guardian*, 2 January 1847; *Manchester Guardian*, 6 January 1847; *Bradford and Wakefield Observer*, 7 January 1847; *Stockport Advertiser*, 8 January 1847.

7 *Manchester Guardian*, 12 May 1847. The same edition had an account of an unemployed English labourer dying of starvation at Todmorden.

8 The account of the death of the baby Cowbrain has been based on the reports of the inquest. See, *Halifax Guardian*, 27 February 1847; *Manchester Courier*, 3 March 1847; The *Sheffield Iris*, 11 March 1847.

9 *Halifax Guardian*, 10 July 1847. Mrs McAndrew gave birth in Bradford.

10 ibid.

11 T.Dillon, 'The Irish in Leeds', 1851-61, *Publication of the Thoresby Society, Miscellany*, volume 16, part 1, No. 119, pp. 1-28. This is as yet the only study of the Irish in Leeds. The data quoted is on p. 2.

12 Dillon, op.cit. Table No. 6, p. 9.

13 Chadwick Report (England) 1840. Robert Baker, 'On the State and Condition of the Town of Leeds in the West Riding of the County of York'. For information on the Irish in Leeds, see pp. 362-371.

14 SC (1847) Minutes of Evidence, J Beckwith, Clerk to the Guardians of Leeds Township, q. 4041.

15 *Leeds Mercury*, 27 February 1847.

16 PRO/MH12/15228/ Leeds Township/1847/9286B. John Beckwith to Poor Law Commissioners, 24 April 1847. On the 26 April the Poor Law Commissioners gave permission for the expenditure.

17 *Leeds Mercury*, 24 April 1847.

18 Dillon, op.cit, pp.7-14.

19 *Leeds Mercury*, 1 May 1847.

20 PRO/MH12/15228/ Leeds Township/1847/9824B. John Beckwith to the Poor Law Commissioners, dated 1 May 1847. A John Sanderson was appointed to the job.

21 PRO/MH12/15228/ Leeds Township/1847/10950B, also J.Mayhall, *Annals and History of Leeds, York and the Surrounding District*, Leeds, 1860, volume I, part 3, p. 543. In fact, the Board of Guardians announced at their meeting held on 2 June that on land in Accommodation Road, they were going to erect fever sheds near to an existing convalescent ward. See, *Leeds Mercury*, 5 June 1847.

22 *Leeds Mercury*, 5 June 1847, 'The Fever'.
23 *Leeds Mercury*, 5 June 1847.
24 *Leeds Mercury*, 19 June 1847. The policy of whitewashing walls was similar to the action taken in Glasgow, Liverpool and Manchester. A group of private citizens suggested to the Guardians that they would set up a bath house with disinfecting liquids if the guardians would take on the continuing permanent charges that would accrue. The guardians agreed, see PRO/MH12/15228/ Leeds Township/1847/12162B.
25 J.Mayhall, op.cit. p. 543.
26 *Leeds Mercury*, 29 May 1847.
27 ibid.
28 *Leeds Mercury*, 26 June and 3 July 1847.
29 *Leeds Mercury*, 3 and 10 July 1847; *The Tablet*, 10 July 1847.
30 *Leeds Mercury*, 10 and 17 July 1847.
31 *Leeds Mercury*, 17 July 1847. Also J.Mayhall, op.cit. p. 543-4. 1847-48 (996) XXV.
32 BPP 1847-8 (996) XXV. Ninth Annual Report of the Registrar General of Births, Deaths and Marriages in England, pp. x-xi.
33 H.M.Booth, 'Unemployment and Poor Relief in Manchester, 1845-50', *Social History*, volume 15, No. 2, May 1990, Table No 1, p.219. This article examines the expenditure on poor relief and economic activity in Manchester over what is in effect the Irish famine crisis.
34 MCL, Archives M3/3/6B. Manchester Board of Guardians, Accounts of Monies disbursed each week by the Churchwardens, 1830-48.
35 *Manchester Guardian*, 6 January 1847, 'Meeting to establish a soup kitchen'.
36 *Manchester Guardian*, 27 March 1847, 'The soup kitchen'.
37 ibid.
38 *Manchester Guardian*, 15 May 1847, 'Distress in Manchester'.
39 Irish Poor (1836) p.54.
40 Irish Poor (1836) p. 56.
41 Irish Poor (1836) p.56.
42 Chadwick Report, England (1842) Manchester pp. 304-5.
43 Chadwick Report, England (1842) Manchester, p.295.
44 *Manchester Guardian*, 15 April 1847. When the guardians began to publish fever reports in April 1847, the medical districts were listed.
45 The Strangeways workhouse was the largest and it was sited between Bridge Street and Victoria Station. On the otherside of the station was the pauper churchyard, known as Walkers Croft.
46 *Manchester Guardian*, 10 April 1847. Meeting of the Board of Guardians, 8 April.
47 *Manchester Guardian*, 24 April 1847. Meeting of the Board of Guardians held on 22 April. A letter of complaint re Tib Street was read, also a memorial complaining of the use of Tib Street as a fever hospital ward.
48 *Manchester Guardian*, 3 July 1847, 'Long Millgate Fever Hospital'.
49 MCL, Archives. Report of the Board of Health in Manchester, 1 June 1847.
50 *Manchester Guardian*, 10 July 1847, Meeting of the Board of Guardians, 3 July 1847.
51 ibid.
52 *Manchester Guardian*, 3 July 1847. Meeting of the Board of Guardians held 1 July. Fever Returns.
53 *Manchester Guardian*, 17 July 1847. Meeting of the Board of Guardians held 15 July 1847. The details concerning Long Millgate were contained in a report from Dr John Walsh.
54 *Manchester Guardian*, 22 May 1847, 'State of the Town as to Disease and Distress'.

55 ibid.
56 BPP (HC) 1847-48 (996) XXV. Ninth Annual Report of the Registrar General of Births, Deaths and Marriages in England, p. xxvii.
57 ibid, p.xxvii
58 *Manchester Guardian*, 24 July 1847. Meeting of the Board of Guardians held on 22 July. Report of Joseph Murphy, 21 July 1847.
59 The Tib Street fever ward was closed 11 September and the Minshull Street ward 9 October 1847.
60 *Manchester Guardian*, 15 April 1848. Meeting of the Guardians held on 13 April. The report of this meeting contains a complete breakdown of the number of patients treated at Long Millgate from its opening in April 1847 to 8 April 1848. The numbers for the House of Recovery are taken from annual reports for the years ending 1 June 1847 and 1 June 1848. MCL Archives. The Reports of the Board of Health in Manchester, vols L11 and L111.
61 *Manchester Guardian*, 13 April 1848. Meeting of the Guardians held on 13 April. The report includes the Registrar General's statistics of deaths in each of the five medical districts. Dr Noble, the Union's medical officer, claimed that in the first four months of Long Millgate's opening, 90 per cent of admissions were Catholic. See *Manchester Guardian*, 6 November 1847. Meeting of the Guardians held 4 November 1847.
62 *Manchester Guardian*, 12 May 1847, 'Floods in Little Ireland'.
63 *Manchester Guardian*, 22 May 1847, 'State of the Town as to Disease and Distress'. This report covers these events in 'Little Ireland'.
64 *Manchester Guardian*, 5 June 1847. Meeting of the Board of Guardians, 3 June 1847.
65 ibid.
66 *Manchester Guardian*, 26 June 1847. 'Famine Fever - State of Health'.
67 *Manchester Guardian*, 3 July 1847, 'Famine Fever - Destitution'.
68 ibid.
69 *Manchester Guardian*, 24 July 1847, 'Famine Fever'.
70 *Manchester Guardian*, 30 June 1847, 'The Famine Fever - Destitution'.
71 ibid.
72 ibid.
73 *Manchester Guardian*, 4 August 1847, 'Quarterly Returns of Public Health and Mortality'.
74 *Manchester Guardian*, 5 June 1847. Meeting of the Board of Guardians held on 3 June 1847. The death of Dr Walker, surgeon to the workhouse.
75 *Manchester Guardian*, 26 June 1847, 'The Health of Union Officers'. Also *Manchester Guardian*, 3 July 1847.
76 *Manchester Guardian*, 25 September 1847. Meeting of the Board of Guardians held 23 September 1847.
77 So far, I cannot establish exactly how many priests died in Manchester.
78 *Manchester Guardian*, 5 February 1847, 'Death of another Catholic Priest'.
79 MCL, Archives. The Report of the Board of Health in Manchester, year ending 1 June 1848, p. 3.
80 *Manchester Guardian*, Saturday 12 February 1848. Report to the weekly meeting of the Manchester Board of Guardians.
81 It is important to remember that large number of English factory workers were suffering at the time. For a moving and detailed account of the destitution among the hatters of Denton, nr Manchester, see *Manchester Guardian*, 16 January 1847, 'Severe Distress in Denton'.

82 *Newcastle Journal*, 27 March 1847.
83 Many Irish stopped at Morpeth en route for Scotland.
84 *Newcastle Journal*, 1 May 1847.
85 BPP (HC) 1849, XXV, First Report of the Poor Law Board for the year ending 25 March 1847, Appendix B, no 2, p.38.
86 TWA, Archives. NG/359/1/6. Minutes of the meeting of the Newcastle Board of Guardians held 4 December 1846, p.282.
87 TWA, Archives. NG/359/1/6. Minutes of an Extraordinary meeting of the Newcastle Board of Guardians held 8 June 1847. Copy of a report 'Fever in Newcastle, especially in Sandgate', signed by Bishop Riddell and Frs J. Standon and J.Culley, p.411. The same report was presented to a meeting of the magistrates on 12 June 1847. See *Newcastle Journal*, 19 June 1847.
88 TWA, Archives. NG/359/1/6. Minutes of an Extraordinary meeting of the Newcastle Board of Guardians held 8 June 1847. Copy of the resolution of the meeting of magistrates held 5 June, p.410.
89 ibid.
90 TWA, Archives. HO/NG/1. Minutes of the monthly meeting of the committee of the Institution for the Cure and Prevention of Contagious Diseases in Newcastle and Gateshead (House of Recovery) held 6 July 1847.
91 TWA, Archives/HO/NG/1. Minutes of the monthly meetings of the House of Recovery. The statistics have been compiled from information given at the various monthly committee meetings held throughout 1847 upto 2 May 1848.
92 TWA, Archives. HO/NG/1. Minutes of the monthly meeting of the committee of the House of Recovery held 2 May 1848. Dr White stated that over the 'late fearful visitation', 710 patients had been treated.
93 TWA, Archives. Accounts of the Newcastle Dispensary for the Seventeenth year ending Michaelmas 1847. Of the 10 470 patients treated only 178, 56 of these by typhus.
94 TWA, Archives. Accounts of the Newcastle Dispensary for the Seventy first year, ending Michaelmas 1848.
95 PRO/MH12/3069/Gateshead/1847. William Rowntree, clerk to the Gateshead Union to Poor Law Commissioners, 4 September 1847. Rowntree told the Commissioners that the provision for vagrants in Gateshead was being expanded.
PRO/MH12/3069/Gateshead/1847. Rowntree told the commissioners that the guardians were taking a room over the union boundary.
96 TWA, Archives. T37/1/3. Minutes of the meeting of the Gateshead Board of Guardians held 28 September 1847, p.138. Minutes of meeting held 12 October 1847, p.142, records that the Poor Law Guardians of Chester-le-Street objected to the siting of a fever ward at Eighton Bank.
97 *Newcastle Journal*, 2 October 1847.
98 *Newcastle Journal*, 13 June 1847.
99 *The Tablet*, 6 November 1847. For an account of his Requiem Mass see *Newcastle Journal*, 13 November 1847 and *The Tablet*, 20 November 1847.
100 *The Tablet*, 23 October 1847 reported death of Standon. The death of Fletcher was recorded in *The Tablet*, 26 February 1848 and *Manchester Guardian*, 8 March 1848.

8 Removal

I

Faced with the arrival of large numbers of destitute Irish famine refugees, individual poor law unions had a limited number of options open to them in terms of protecting local ratepayers from the consequences of Irish poverty. As has been described in earlier chapters, English, Welsh and Scottish poor law unions had a responsibility not to allow paupers to die, in effect, to provide them with relief and medical treatment. When these primary responsibilities had been met, what then? British poor law unions had no legal obligation to provide *long term* assistance to any newly arrived Irish. The last line of defence for beleaguered unions was the body of legislation subsumed under the heading 'Laws of settlement and Removal'. Throughout this study, there have been frequent references to the fact that many famine refugees stopped claiming relief because of the threat of being removed back to Ireland. The point has also been made that the *threat* of removal was successful in that expenditure on Irish poor relief in Liverpool, Glasgow and Newport fell dramatically in 1848. The question remains, given that some Irish refugees did claim relief, how frequently was the threat of removal translated into action? In other words, how many Irish were removed during the famine crisis and under what conditions did this occur? To appreciate how the system operated it is necessary to understand the laws of settlement and removal as well as the administrative structure within which they were applied. These basic administrative and financial features of poor relief in Britain were described in chapter four (see p. 89). By the beginning of the nineteenth century, the basic unit of administration for the provision of poor relief was the parish. The Poor Law Amendment Act of 1834 amalgamated parishes into larger administrative units known as 'poor law unions'. These unions became the focus of poor relief in England and Wales, with a Board of Poor Law Commissioners in London exercising strong central control. In some instances, for example, Liverpool, the parish was so big that the parish *was* the union.

The validity of a person's claim to poor relief depended on whether or not he or she had acquired the status of being 'settled' within the parish where the claim was made. Settlement status could be achieved in a variety of ways but the principal means of doing so was that of inheriting settlement from one's father. Illegitimate children took the settlement of the parish of birth on reaching 16 years of age. If a pauper's inherited settlement could not established, the magistrates would settle for the parish of birth. In situations where a claimant for poor relief could not prove settlement in the parish within which poor relief was being claimed, he or she could be forcibly removed back to the parish of their settlement. However, resort to forcible removal was not always undertaken. It was often difficult to establish *where* someone could be removed to, sometimes involving lengthy and expensive litigation, while in many instances, humanitarian considerations prevailed over the concern for ratepayers. In some cases in which a claimant's parish of settlement was established, that parish would compensate the parish of residence for relief paid.[1]

One consequence of this system was that in inhibited the geographical mobility of English labour and from the seventeenth century onwards, itinerant Irish workers were an increasingly important source of agricultural labour in England. The Irish did not have settlement in English parishes, which meant they could be forcibly removed back to Ireland if they were forced by circumstances to claim poor relief. English pragmatism, recognizing the value of Irish labour, gave rise to legislation (17. Geo.II Cap.5) which enabled any destitute Irish to apply voluntarily to be 'passed' back to Ireland. If the application was granted by the justices, the fare was paid by the parish. Thus there were two legally distinct situations that gave rise to a traffic in Irish paupers back to Ireland at local expense. First, there were those Irish who applied for poor relief while in England and were forcibly *removed* back to Ireland under the laws of Settlement and Removal. Second, there were those Irish, wanting to return to Ireland, who asked the magistrates to be *passed* back to Ireland, which meant their fares were paid. The essential difference in the removal, as opposed to the passing, of an Irish man or woman back to Ireland, was one of voluntary versus forcible removal.[2] A clear statement of the operation of the pass system was given by Edward Rushton in evidence to the Select Committee on Removals. He was explaining the difficulties facing the Liverpool authorities in the developing famine crisis during December 1846 and January 1847.

> When you remove with a pass, that is a voluntary business on the part of the distressed Irish; he applies for a pass to the magistrates and you then remove him under the regulations of the Secretary of State. You cannot pass without a certain form. He swears that he had no settlement in England and then two justices give instructions to pass him but he is passed under regulations approved by the Secretary of State, one of which is he shall not be passed in inclement seasons, except under cover; there are not enough craft in the port of Liverpool. Suppose I ordered 10 000 people to be passed between decks on steamers in the month of December and January?

The problem was widespread. In 1833, the assistant overseer of St Giles parish in London stated that one district within the parish was almost entirely Irish. Each year large numbers of Irish harvesters made their way to the parish, which had a large stock of cheap housing. Each year St Giles issued 800 passes and of these 88 per cent were Irish.[3] John Wall, Vestry clerk to the parish of St Luke's, Middlesex, claimed that Irish harvesters from 50 miles away came to the parish to obtain a pass to Ireland. They did not apply to the magistrates in the country areas because 'they will not send them ...they know the London police magistrates will pass them without difficulty'.[4]

Rushton's reference to the impossibility of finding cover on board steamships because of the large number of paupers involved is interesting because it highlights the fact that the pass system was a burden on the town. Itinerant Irish workers from all over the country made their way to Liverpool and then asked the Liverpool magistrates to be passed back to Ireland. In effect, the system gave many Irish workers a free trip home at the expense of the Liverpool ratepayers, who consistently alleged that many Irish harvesters hid their earnings before declaring themselves destitute and asking to be passed.

The body of law regarding settlement and removal dates from the Act of Settlement and Removal, passed in 1662 (13 and 14 Charles II, Cap. 12). The extent to which the law was invoked varied depending on local conditions and individual cases but in most cases before the influx of famine Irish, it had been used sparingly because of the widespread use of Irish labour. For example, it was given in evidence to the Select Committee on Removal that between 1835 and 1846 inclusive, only 764 removal orders were taken out in Liverpool, resulting in 477 families, Irish, English and Scots, being removed.[5] Under the Poor Removal Act of 1845 (8 and 9 Vic.Cap. 117), any persons applying for poor relief and not having settlement could be summoned to appear before the magistrates, who could order their removal by signing a warrant. However, if a pauper chose not to answer the summons, no removal could take place. The conditions prevailing in Liverpool from 1846 onwards were such that it was impossible to seek out the people concerned and physically serve a summons; the Irish moved lodgings frequently and the police simply had not got the manpower to search for them. Even if the applicants for relief had been served summonses, having been proved not to have settlement, Liverpool parish, it was claimed, did not have the resources to ship back the large numbers of paupers in this category. Rushton had no doubt the system would not work because of the scale of the problem in Liverpool:

> ...the Irish are quick enough to see what you wish to do, they would never come. It is perfectly futile to attempt it, supposing it was practicable for other reasons... Suppose the summonses availed, how is he to be removed to the place or port from where he came in Ireland, or nearest to the place he resided; we should have 40 000 to remove; where are the officers to take charge of them? [6]

The Poor Law Commissioners were extremely concerned at Rushton's reluctance to implement the law, and after consulting their law officers, told him he was wrong. Rushton's view of the problem seems to have been based on the view that under the law, the parish ordering the removal of the pauper to Ireland would have to send a parish officer with him. This in fact was not the case. Under the 1845 statute (8 and 9 Vic. Cap. 117), the English ratepayers were only liable for the expense of conveying the pauper to one of the English ports mentioned in the Act. The responsibility of the parish ended when the person was handed over to the master of the steamship, so Rushton's view concerning the expense of providing parish officers to escort paupers to Ireland was erroneous. In the case of port authorities, there was little cost involved in escorting people from the magistrate's office to the docks. The major practical difficulty early in 1847 was that of physically serving a summons, a legal necessity. In addition, the removal of Irish paupers had been made more difficult with the passing, in August 1846, of the Five Years Residence Act (9 and 10 Vic. Cap. 66), which introduced the new concept of *irremovability*. Under this Act it became illegal to remove paupers who had lived continuously in a parish for five years, so introducing a new category of Irish pauper, the 'irremovable Irish'. In addition, the Act provided that widows could not be removed within 12 months of their husband's death nor could persons applying for temporary relief on account of sickness. The provisions of this Act did not apply to a large part of Liverpool's Irish population which numbered well over 50 000 at the time the Act was passed. In Manchester, the situation was different, large numbers of Irish had been long term residents. In most towns with large Irish populations the manpower needed to check out claims of five years residency was enormous and prohibitive.

The simple fact was that, by the beginning of the nineteenth century, the laws of Settlement and Removal were virtually inoperable in the large towns of the Midlands and north of England, and, as already noted, in the special case of Liverpool, in the first six months of 1847, the number of Irish coming ashore simply overwhelmed the authorities. The result of this inflow was a sustained political campaign, spearheaded by the authorities in Liverpool and Glasgow and supported by *The Times*, aimed at bringing about a change in the law. Basically, the demand was based on two propositions. First, the Irish should be given a legal right to poor relief in Ireland. Second, the removal of Irish paupers from England should be made easier, in particular, the need was not to have to serve a summons. In June 1847, the campaign paid off with the passing of the Poor Relief (Ireland) Bill and the Poor Removal Act (10 and 11 Vic. Cap. 33). Under the provisions of this latter Act a relieving officer simply had to prove that a pauper was in receipt of relief and then take the person before two magistrates. On establishing that the pauper had been born in Ireland, did not have settlement and had received relief that day, a removal order could be made out. In effect, the problems associated with serving a summons had been removed. The passing of this Act was greeted with jubilation in the Liverpool press and the *Manchester Guardian* of 8 July 1847 reported that:

> Arrangements on terms favourable to the parish have been made with the agents of the various Irish steamers for the conveyance of Irish paupers to the ports of Dublin, Dundalk, Belfast, Newry, Drogheda and Sligo and a negotiation is pending for renting commodious warehousing near the Clarence dock, to which all Irish poor now or hereafter chargeable to the town, will be removed, preparatory to their prompt removal to their respective unions in Ireland.

In the case of poor law unions in ports, the mechanics of the system involved a parish officer taking a pauper to the docks after the magistrates had signed an order and handing him over to the master of the vessel, to whom a duplicate copy of the order was given. The relieving officer purchased the steamer tickets from the company office for the port nearest to pauper's parish or, often any other port of the pauper's choice. The unfortunate person was given some bread and a small sum of money, usually a shilling. On the master taking on board the pauper and signing the receipt, the parish had fulfilled its legal responsibility. The master had a legal obligation (17 Geo. II Cap. 5) to carry the pauper on board. On putting the person ashore in Ireland the master had discharged his responsibility and the pauper was left to his own devices. This abandoning of Irish paupers at Irish ports caused great resentment in Ireland during 1847.

The immediate result of the simplifying of the removal procedure was an increase in the number of removals to Ireland and the greatest proportion of all such removals was from towns in northern England, particularly Liverpool. Authorities were particularly concerned that 'casual' Irish claimants for relief should not obtain 'irremovable' status.[7]

II

Turning to the issue of how many Irish were removed in 1847, the facts concerning the volume of traffic involved in removals and passes are to be found in the evidence given to various Select Committees' official investigations. In practice, it is not always possible to distinguish between removals and passes because many officials used the terms interchangeably in their verbal and written evidence. From the point of view of the steamship companies the distinction was academic, for both removals and passes provided them with revenue. Table 8.1 below shows the number removed from Liverpool and Manchester over the whole period of the famine crisis. The figures for Manchester are included because, together with Salford, the number of Irish in the locality was the biggest in England, outside of Liverpool and London.

Table 8.1 Numbers of Irish paupers removed from Liverpool and Manchester over the period 1846 to 1853 inclusive.

Year	*Liverpool*	*Manchester*	*Total*
1846	5 313	286	5 599
1847	15 008	553	15 561
1848	7 607	1902	9 509
1849	9 409	617	10 026
1850	7 627	275	7 902
1851	7 808	400	8 208
1852	5 506	337	5 843
1853	4 503	362	4 865
Total	62 781	4732	67 513

Source: SC (1854) Minutes of Evidence, J.Harrop, Table C, p.445 (Manchester data). SC (1854) Appendix No. 8, p.595 (Liverpool data).

A significant feature of these figures is the much larger number of removals from Liverpool compared with Manchester. In 1851, the Irish-born population of the township of Manchester was 37 958 while that of Liverpool was twice as many but, over the eight-year period, the number of removals from Liverpool was 13 times the number removed from Manchester. How is this to be explained? This difference did not reflect a harsher attitude on the part of the Liverpool officials but rather the economic facts of life. The Manchester poor law guardians had to face a higher cost of removal because the pauper had to be transported to Liverpool, by rail, accompanied by a relieving officer. This factor alone put Manchester, and all other inland towns, at a disadvantage.

The following breakdown of the costs of removal from Manchester indicates the relative importance of the rail fare from Manchester to Liverpool, a major item of expenditure, whereas in Liverpool, the authorities did not incur any rail charges. By contrast, the average cost of removing an Irish pauper from Liverpool to Dublin in 1847 was usually four shillings and only six shillings in 1854. It would be cheaper for the Manchester authorities to pay the casual Irish pauper relief for a number of weeks and try to get him to move on; such incentives applied to all towns that were not near the ports of departure. The other, more important, explanation of Manchester's lower level of removals is that the overwhelming majority of the Irish in Manchester in 1847 were protected by the Five Year Residency Act, in effect were 'irremovable Irish' The 15 008 removals from Liverpool in 1847 represented a peak, never to be achieved again, although the number of removals remained relatively high in subsequent years.

Table 8.2 Average cost of removal of one person to Ireland from the township of Manchester, 1854.

Item	*Cost*
Pass	2s. 9d
Rail	2s. 7½d
Vessel	3s. 0d
Relief	1s. 6d
Bus	6d
Refreshments	6d
Total	10s. 10½d

Source: SC (1854) Minutes of Evidence, Appendix 5, Table F.

The reason for the fall-off in removals after 1847 was that the number of Irish seeking relief fell as the Irish, newly arrived, tried to avoid removal proceedings. The majority of Irish did not want to return to Ireland and preferred to resort to begging rather than risk removal. However, of those who were removed, there were many who *wanted* to return home and the parochial authorities in Liverpool claimed about two-thirds of all removals were voluntary, (for example, passed) in contrast to the West Derby union, next to Liverpool, where it was claimed that not more than ten per cent of their (much smaller number) of removals were voluntary. The extent to which the traffic in paupers removed to Ireland was localized is illustrated by the fact that, in the year ended 25 March 1853, the *total* number of removal *orders* made out with respect to the Irish, in the *whole of England and Wales*, was 4823. Of this number, 3840 of them were in Lancashire and, of this total, 3549 were made out in Liverpool.[8] It should be pointed out that the Manchester authorities produced a return showing the number of Irish passed voluntarily to Ireland over the period 1846 to 1853 and this totalled 3006. However, this does not change the fact of the overwhelming preponderance of Liverpool removals over the total from those in Manchester (see Appendix No. 8.1)

In 1846 the Liverpool authorities had laid down a scale of fares to be paid for the transporting of Irish paupers removed back to Ireland and these were approved by the Secretary of State on 25 April 1846. The fares quoted below were the maximum amounts to be paid.

Table 8.3 Fares to be paid for paupers removed to Ireland, as deck passengers, from Liverpool, 1846.

Irish port of destination	*Above 10 years of age*	*10 years of below*
Cork	13s. 0d	6s. 6d
Waterford	10s. 6d	5s. 0d
Derry	7s. 0d	3s. 6d
Wexford	7s. 0d	3s. 6d
Dublin	4s. 6d.	4s. 6d
Belfast	4s. 6d.	4s. 6d
Dundalk	4s. 6d.	2s. 3d

Source: SC (1854) Minutes of Evidence, Appendix No. 10, pp. 606-7.

Some critics of the steamship companies repeatedly argued that one reason why the companies brought over paupers free of charge was that such actions provided them with a return traffic paid for by poor law unions. This claim was never substantiated, but it could not be denied that there were obvious advantages to be exploited by the companies. Even bringing paupers over at one shilling a head was profitable if a significant number were removed back to Ireland at the expense of poor law unions.

On 17 November 1847, the Select Vestry discussed the allegation that Irish steamers were bringing paupers over at one shilling per head and taking them back at four shillings. The meeting agreed to approach the companies on this and, on doing so, the City of Dublin Company denied that it charged four shillings per head for paupers going to Dublin; they claimed the charge was two shillings and sixpence and offered to take them back at one shilling. However, nothing more was heard of this offer.[9] The majority of removals were to Dublin and, over much of the period, the fare from Liverpool was four shillings. Naturally, the conditions under which the paupers travelled back to Ireland as deck passengers were no better than those experienced on the journey over to England. However, local authorities had a responsibility for the conditions under which paupers were removed but in practice were slow to exercise their duty in this respect.

In 1846, the Liverpool magistrates had written provisions into the regulations concerning removals which aimed at giving some protection to the paupers on the crossing to Ireland: 'that all such persons shall be conveyed on the decks of vessels or in the steerage, according to the season of the year, or on the deck part of the way and in the steerage the remainder, as the Justices who order their removal may direct'. The provision was inoperable. As has been noted, there was little steerage accommodation on the cross-channel steamers so that it would have been impossible to remove the number involved if steerage accommodation had been insisted on.

III

It needs to be recognized that individual ports had their own specific problems. In the case of Cardiff, a system was adopted of giving the famine refugees relief and then to warn them that they would be sent back to Ireland. In fact, no action was taken on the first application for poor relief. If however, a person returned again, then removal proceedings were triggered off. Also, if a person applied for relief and was absolutely destitute, appearing as though he or she might become a permanent charge on the union, then they were removed. During 1847, the Cardiff union removed 201 Irish for whom warrants had been obtained. Cardiff had no direct steamer connection with Ireland and so paupers were often put on board coal vessels sailing to Ireland. The masters of these vessels, in many cases, put the Irish back ashore further down the channel, having pocketed the fare. To avoid this, the Cardiff authorities started to send the paupers for removal direct to Bristol, to be put on the regular steamer to Cork.[10]

Liverpool had quite different problems. Because of the port's connection with all Irish ports, large numbers of Irish from other towns made their way to Liverpool in order to obtain a free trip home. As a report of a sub-committee of Liverpool recorded, 'Liverpool, in short, is made the pass house of all England'. The same report claimed that many Irish committed crimes in order to be hauled before the magistrate and removed. It was further claimed that knowledge of this system was widespread throughout Ireland and that significant numbers of Irish came from Ireland to Liverpool for all kinds of purposes, including seeing their friends off to America. One example was cited in which an Irish woman came from Dublin to Liverpool at the cheap steamer rate and then got herself removed to Cork, where her husband was. This was much cheaper for her than paying the fare from Dublin to Cork.[11] One mechanism which the Liverpool authorities used was the fact that in 1847, over 6750 Irish were admitted to the workhouse, many of them suffering from typhus. (these were in addition to those in the auxiliary fever sheds in Chadwick Street). Of these Irish admissions, 1124 died in the workhouse. The Irish in general were reluctant to enter the workhouse because it was widely known that once admitted, there was a high probability of being removed if a person did not have five years residency. During 1847, 997 Irish were removed from the workhouse to Ireland, men, women and children. The awfulness of the Irish experience in 1847 is easily illustrated. For example, on 8 April 1847, James Welsh, aged 48 years, his wife Catherine, aged 38, were admitted to the Liverpool workhouse, together with their five children. These were Mary, aged 15 years, Thomas 12 years, Catherine nine years, Bridget two years, and Winifred aged five weeks. James Welsh died on 12 April, followed by his daughters Winifred on 22 April and Mary on the 14 May. In turn Thomas died 16 May. In a space of 12 weeks, Catherine Welsh lost her husband, her only son and two daughters. On 15 July she was removed to Ireland, with her two remaining daughters, Bridget and Catherine.[12] On 30 April, 1847, Bridget McGiveran aged 45 years was admitted into the fever ward at the workhouse and her four children were put into a general ward, probably because they were not displaying signs of typhus. It is probable that her husband was already dead. The children were Michael, aged 15 years, Bridget 11 years, John aged nine years, and Patrick aged seven years. Patrick died on 3 May and Bridget his mother on 26 May. The remaining three children were removed to Ireland on 12 July.[13] It is not known whether anyone accompanied them or what they did on arrival in Ireland.

Table 8.4: The number of Irish removals from selected Poor Law Unions in Britain over the years 1849-54 inclusive.

	Year ending 25 March					
Unions	*1849*	*1850*	*1851*	*1852*	*1853*	*1854*
Liverpool (Parish)	6964	9095	8327	7125	5043	4545
Bristol (incorporated)	93	111	68	29	54	78
Newport (union)	-	15	24	49	66	34
Cardiff (union)	134	96	9	47	42	42
Swansea	16	23	2	6	4	8
London (Met. Districts)	2163	2197	897	1223	1252	1693

Note: Among the Metropolitan districts, St Martins in the Fields parish, City of London and Whitchapel unions were the principal places involved in removals.
Source: BPP (HC) 1854 (488) LV 325, A Return on the Number of Paupers Removed to Ireland in the year ending 25 March 1849, 1850, 1851, 1852, 1853, 1854, from the parishes within the Metropolitan Districts of the Registrar General and from Liverpool, Bristol, Newport (Monmouthshire), Cardiff and Swansea.

How did they make their way back to their own parish in Ireland? On 4 June Bridget Moran aged nine years, her sister Catherine aged six and brother Thomas aged two, were all admitted into the fever ward at the workhouse. Once more, the absence of parents suggests that they had already died of typhus. On 10 July, all three children were sent to Ireland, at their own request.[14] Again, it is not clear how these children made their way to their home parish or whether or not they had a family in the parish. All of these examples, and many other cases, illustrate the determination of the Liverpool parochial authorities to try and contain the Irish famine refugee problem. The relative scale of the removals from various English and Welsh centres of Irish settlement is given above. (Table No. 8.4)

Where in Ireland did the British poor law unions send those Irish they removed? We simply have no data concerning ports of destinations regarding the 1847 and 1848 removals. With reference to the end of the famine crisis, the only port for which such data exists is Liverpool.

Table 8.5: The numbers of Irish removed from Liverpool to various Irish ports over the calendar years 1849-1854, inclusive.

Port of destination	*Year of removal*						*Total*
	1849	*1850*	*1851*	*1852*	*1853*	*1854*	
Dublin	6749	5335	5809	4110	3225	1343	26 571
Drogheda	999	274	286	219	234	78	2 090
Newry	454	264	214	121	129	26	1 208
Belfast	399	523	404	360	286	173	2 145
Dundalk	324	193	198	106	135	58	1 014
Sligo	109	158	176	116	77	32	668
Cork	126	369	314	188	170	64	1 231
Waterford	128	392	243	165	165	88	1 181
Londonderry	77	81	72	51	73	10	364
Wexford	37	37	21	49	28	10	182
Portrush	2	-	1	5	1	-	9
Youghal	5	-	-	-	-	-	5
Limerick	-	-	-	-	2	3	5
Totals	9409	7626	7738	5490	4525	1885	36 674
Costs in pounds	2519	1488	1951	1456	1130	443	8987

Source: BPP (HC) 1854 (488) LV. 325. A Return of the Number of Irish Poor Removed from the Parish of Liverpool, Distinguishing The Ports to which such Paupers were Removed, with a statement of the cost of such Removals upto 24 June 1854.

Not surprisingly, the greatest number of removals were to those ports which provided the greatest number of arrivals, Dublin and Drogheda accounting for the overwhelming majority of removals.

IV

An examination of poor law correspondence at the Public Record Office and press reporting of maladministration by poor law authorities, reveals a great deal of confusion regarding what, precisely, the law required with regard to removals, particularly the Irish. Unlike removal of English, the removal of the Irish involved sea passages. Often local magistrates added rules to be applied locally. County magistrates sometimes added their own rules, further complicating the job of relieving officers and guardians. It is certain that throughout the famine crisis, there was much misunderstanding of the law regarding removals. For example, Rushton's view that the law required paupers to be escorted on the voyage to Ireland by parochial officers was widely held. In most cases, poor law guardians made ad hoc arrangements for such chaperoning of people being removed. In addition, there was a great deal of confusion regarding the issue of whether paupers could be removed on deck in bad weather. Most of these issues were never resolved during the period under review. Even Captain Denham's report in 1849 did not clear up the ambiguities.

There are many well documented cases of Irish, men, women and children, who after long periods of residence in England, were removed illegally. For example, Mary Ann King had lived in Manchester for 18 years. In August she travelled to Liverpool to collect a letter from her brother in America and while there became ill with fever. She was admitted into the fever hospital. After a month she was released, taken in front of magistrates and admitted that, to the best of her knowledge, she was born in Raharney, West Meath. She was marched off with 40 other people, totally confused about what was happening until some other women in the group told her they were being removed to Ireland. Mary King had left a child in Manchester and, on reaching the Clarence dock, refused to board the steamer. She was given 2 lbs of bread and threepence and the police put her on board saying 'you are forced to go to Ireland, and you have a parish there as well as in England'. She was landed in Dublin and made her way to Raharney.[15] Patrick Kelly, aged 16 years, was from the parish of Kilbride, in Roscommon. He arrived in Prescot in 1845 and found work as a farm labourer in the district. About September 1847 he contracted typhus and was taken into the fever ward at Prescot workhouse. When he recovered he was immediately removed to Dublin where he had a relapse and was again taken into the fever ward. When he recovered, he was removed to Liverpool and made his way back to Prescot. This removal was illegal.[16] Sarah and James Murray and their three children lived in Prescot. Towards the end of 1847, James Murray killed a man and was sent to prison for two years after being found guilty on a manslaughter charge. In September 1848,

Sarah Murray and the children moved to the neighbouring parish of Eccleston, within the same union. By moving parish she lost her irremovable status and the Prescot guardians wanted to remove her and the children to Ireland. Unsure of their ground, they asked the Poor Law Commissioners whether they could proceed with this removal and were told it was illegal.[17]

Another example of the hazards under which the system operated is illustrated by the case of James and Margaret Kelly. With their three children, they were being removed from Salford to Ireland. The relieving officer accompanying them from Salford to the Liverpool docks got drunk, spent all the money he had been given, lost the removal warrants which guaranteed the Kelly's passage to Dublin and disappeared. The Kellys went aboard the steamer but the master would not accept them as passengers and so, destitute, they went begging in the streets of Liverpool, where they were arrested and brought before Rushton. At the magistrates's hearing it emerged that Kelly had been in England 18 years and so was not eligible for removal. The Salford authorities had acted illegally.[18] The case of Michael Duignan illustrates all of the difficulties facing pauper and authorities in 1847.[19] The Duignan family came from the parish of Mohill in County Leitrim. Just before Christmas 1846 they landed in Liverpool absolutely destitute, man, wife and their children, Patrick 14 years, Michael 12 years, Catherine four years and Mary under 12 months. They made their way to Rochdale where Mrs Duignan had a brother, John Keegan. John Keegan was a labourer and lived with his wife Mary at a house in Park Lane, Rochdale. On arrival at Rochdale, the Duignans stayed with the Keegans for several nights, being provided with food by the Keegans and some neighbours. As early as 6 March 1847, the Rochdale guardians wrote to the Poor Law Commissioners referring to the 'large influx of Irish paupers'. By May, typhus was prevalent and the guardians wrote again to the Poor Law Commissioners concerning 'numerous cases of Irish fever' and stating that R.W.Barber, one of the union's doctors had died on 30 April as a result of carrying out his duties. The letter also pointed out that the local 'citizens' were alarmed. To cope with the increased numbers of typhus cases, a building was rented at Spotisland.[20] On 26 May, Austin, the assistant Poor Law Commissioner for the region visited Rochdale union and condemned the workhouses as inadequate.[21] In response to these criticisms and the growing crisis, on 19 June, John Metcalfe was appointed as master of the fever ward and soon after Dr Thomas Collingwood was appointed temporary medical officer of the fever ward. Collingwood was to figure significantly in the fortunes of the Duignan family.

By this time the Duignans had left the Keegans' house and were drifting in and out of temporary accommodation in Dawson Square and Spring Lane, both districts with a relatively large Irish presence. On the first of July 1847, Michael Duignan applied to the relieving officer for medical assistance and on the following day was taken to the workhouse by his mother. From here Michael was put into a fever ward. On 23 July he was discharged as cured. In the meantime both his parents went down with typhus and died in the fever ward. This left Patrick at home in Dawson Square, looking after his two sisters, but on 27 July he was also sent to the fever ward suffering from typhus. At parish expense, Catherine and Mary were put in the care of Mary Elson in a house in Stock Road, Rochdale. Here Mary, aged one year, died. On the 2 August, Patrick was discharged, his being a mild case of fever according to Dr Collingwood.

Among both acquaintances and officials who knew the Duignans there was a general opinion that Michael Duignan was badly deformed around the legs and feet and that he could only walk by holding a strong stick in front of himself, using both hands, and dragging himself along. Whatever the actual diagnosis of Michael's disability, he was not capable of looking after himself. It also appears that Patrick was also lame but less severely. In addition to his problems of walking, Michael suffered from epileptic fits. The situation by 2 August 1847 was that both Duignan parents were dead as was Mary, the baby, leaving a badly disabled Michael and a lame Patrick living in a room in Dawson Square. Catherine was boarded with a family. Their relatives, the Keegans seem not to have bothered with them after their initial help. Michael and Patrick lived off poor relief and begging. From this point onwards, the Duignan children were sucked into the administrative procedure involved in removal, with tragic consequences.

The Rochdale guardians met each Friday at the Flying Horse Inn to transact union business. Those attending would include guardians, relieving officers, union doctors and others concerned with the poor law administration. The procedure regarding removals was that the relieving officers would ask the guardians to make out removal orders for specified persons. When a removal order was so made out, the person named for removal had to be brought before a magistrate and a warrant signed for the removal. These were legal requirements. Also any paupers removed had to be accompanied to the steamer by a union officer and then placed on board and a receipt obtained from the master of the vessel. There remained a great deal of uncertainty as to whether or not a parochial officer had to accompany paupers on the voyage to their port of destination. Rushton in Liverpool thought so but others disagreed.

On 9 August 1847, John Whitehead, a relieving officer, was attending a meeting of the guardians at the Flying Horse when he was approached by two Irish women, Bridget Gallagher and Mary Goharty. Both *asked* to be removed to Ireland. This was not as strange a request as it might at first seem. They probably wanted a free trip home. On 12 August, Mr Bower, an apprentice to one of the union doctors, was asked to go and visit Michael Duignan at a house in Dawson Square. Bower found the boy lying on the floor and immediately had him removed to the fever shed, probably suffering from relapsing fever. On 13 August, the Rochdale Board of Guardians signed removal orders for Patrick, Michael, Catherine and Mary Duignan together with orders for Bridget Gallagher, Mary Goharty and a child. The administrative system was lacking in that Mary Duignan was dead and Michael was in the fever shed. On 26 August, Michael Duignan was sufficiently recovered as to be moved into the convalescence ward. Given the existence of the guardians' removal order, John Whitehead, the relieving officer asked Dr Collingwood whether Michael Duignan was fit to be removed. Collingwood had little experience of removals and even less of the conditions on the steamships for deck passengers. Whitehead knew that someone would have to look after the Duignan children during the voyage and decided to ask Bridget Gallagher and Mary Goharty to undertake that task. Before asking the women to act as chaperones to the Duignan children, he checked with Fr Dowling, a local Catholic priest, that they were responsible persons. Dowling appears to have endorsed the arrangement. Whitehead still needed two more procedures to be completed before the removals could take place. He needed a certificate from Dr Collingwood to the effect that Michael Duignan was fit enough to be removed. Second, the Duignans needed to be brought before the magistrates who, after questioning them, could complete the warrants for their removal.

On 30 August, Dr Collingwood signed a certificate to the effect that Michael was fit to be removed. It was to become a matter of some heated argument as to whether Michael Duignan was it fact fit to travel as a deck passenger to Ireland. On obtaining such a certificate, Whitehead took Patrick and Catherine before the magistrates in order to obtain a removal warrant. The difficulty in this case was that the children were orphans, normally their parents would have been questioned. In fact, Patrick, aged 14, was not even spoken to while Catherine was only four years of age. Michael never appeared before the magistrates. Had he done so, they may well have not signed the warrant given his sickly condition. All this meant that it was extremely doubtful that the removals were legal.

Early on the morning of Wednesday, 1 September, after breakfast, a cart came to the convalescent ward and collected Michael Duignan. Already in the cart were Patrick Duignan and other persons picked up earlier. Catherine Duignan was not among those being removed despite her name being on the original list. Patrick later claimed it was raining and by the time the cart reached Rochdale station, they were wet. In all 11 Irish paupers were being removed that morning. Abraham Travis, one of the

Rochdale union's officers was told on the Monday morning of that week that he was to escort 11 paupers to Liverpool to be removed to Ireland. The first time he saw the paupers was when the cart arrived at the station. Travis claimed that the Duignan boys were covered with a rug and though it was raining they weren't getting wet. The train left at 9.35am for Manchester, stopping at three stations, Blue Pits, Middleton and Miles Platting. The paupers travelled in a third class compartment. At Manchester, they had to change trains and Patrick Duignan carried Michael on his back. They arrived at Liverpool Lime Street at 12 noon. From there the paupers were carried in a cart to the Clarence dock, stopping only at the offices of the City of Dublin Steam Packet Company. Here Travis bought 11 tickets at five shillings each.

On arrival at the steamship dock, the 11 paupers were taken on board the *Duchess of Kent* which was preparing to sail for Dublin. This in itself is noteworthy. Under the law, paupers had to be removed to the port of arrival nearest to the home parish. In practice, paupers were given a choice. In this instance, *before the tickets were bought*, Travis should have asked the persons being removed whether or not they wished to go to Dublin. The Duignans came from Mohill in Co Leitrim, Bridget Gallagher and her child came from O'Draugh, Co Leitrim. A man named McNulty was from Roxford, Co Mayo, Mary Bradley and her three children, Anthony, James and Thomas belonged to Swinscot, in Co Mayo. In fact, Travis only asked them whether they were willing to go to Dublin when he was giving the tickets out. They all said yes. When on board, Michael Duignan was put on the floor at the side of a box, under the paddle housing, a relatively sheltered spot. However, in most instances as the decks filled up with passengers, the stronger people forced the weaker away from the best spots and occupied them.

When the paupers were on board, Travis found Captain Jones, who signed for the 11 passengers, thus becoming responsible for them on the voyage. Jones did not bother to visit them and so had no idea of their condition. Also, no one among the crew was given any responsibility for the paupers during the voyage. Before going ashore, Travis gave the group some bread and butter and some money to help them when they arrived in Dublin. Patrick Duignan received one shilling and Michael Duignan one shilling and sixpence. There was no legal necessity to pay them anything and to that extent the Rochdale authorities were being generous. When the vessel sailed at 2.30pm, there were estimated 550 deck passengers aboard. This produced dreadful crowding, with hardly room for anyone to sit down. The journey should have taken 13 to 14 hours; in fact it took 23 hours. The weather was in Captain Jones's own words, 'very rough', the decks were awash before the vessel left the Mersey. In the desperate overcrowding,

Michael Duignan was helpless, he could not stand up and people eventually were sitting on him. The women supposed to be looking after him failed to do so. A cabin passenger stated subsequently that there was hardly room for the deck passengers to stand and that, 'the deck, yesterday, when we arrived was as much covered with blood as it a bullock had been killed there'. By eight o'clock, Michael Duignan was dead. During the night another man died. When the *Duchess of Kent* arrived at Dublin, the authorities were notified and a coroner's inquest was quickly organized. Surgeons Wright and Hatchell examined the body and on 3 September issued their report. After detailing the condition of the body they concluded:

> The vital powers being so much exhausted by recent disease, that his constitution was unequal to bear the sudden revulsion and caused death. He seems to be about twelve years old, a passenger aboard the *Duchess of Kent*, on the night of 1st September instant. In this case, death was produced by the exposure of his delicate frame to the cold of a tempestuous night.

A third doctor concurred with these findings and Dr Wright unequivocally accused the Rochdale guardians of inhuman treatment of Michael Duignan. In their deposition to the coroner's inquest, several passengers testified to the poor physical condition of the Rochdale paupers when they boarded the steamer. Benjamin Crabbe, a Dublin stationer, was a cabin passenger on the voyage. He swore that 'I saw the deceased man on deck, he was very weak and in bad health... he appeared to be in a dying state when he came on board'. Robert English, a gentleman, also a cabin passenger, testified of the Rochdale paupers that 'they were all in a very bad, weakly and exhausted state. I saw amongst them a boy much emaciated and sickly'. The verdict of the Dublin coroner's jury was that:

> We find that Michael Duignan was removed on a cart at seven o'clock on the morning of Wednesday last, from the fever hospital in the town of Rochdale, in England, to the railway station there; and thence transmitted by railway, a distance of 47 miles, to Liverpool, and then put on board the steamer on the same day, as a deck passenger, in a weak and very exhausted state; a state quite unfit to undertake a voyage across the channel; and we find that his death was caused by the exposure of his weak and diseased frame to the cold of a tempestuous night on the deck of a steamer. We cannot too strongly condemn this treatment of the said Michael Duignan by the parish authorities of Rochdale, and attribute his death to their inhuman conduct in sending him in such a state of weakness to Ireland.

This tough uncompromising verdict captured widespread press interest. W.H.Somerville wrote from Dublin Castle to Sir George Grey at the Home Office, drawing his attention to the inquest.[22] He in turn had had his attention drawn to the event by the Lord Mayor of Dublin.[23] Sir George Grey, the Home Secretary, noticed the furore in the press and on 6 September ordered the Poor Law Commissioners to set up an inquiry into the whole affair.[24] The following day, Edwin Chadwick wrote to Albert Austin in Manchester and ordered him to set up an inquiry into the Duignan affair. Austin wrote to Dublin for the depositions of witnesses at the inquest and on Monday, 13 September, the inquiry opened at the board room of the Wardlesworth workhouse in Rochdale. [25]

The picture which emerged reflects the problems of day to day administration of the poor law at a time of crisis. The arrival of relatively large numbers of Irish paupers took the Rochdale authorities by surprise. Their workhouse accommodation was deficient in terms of space and the outbreak of typhus scared the townspeople, particularly as two English nurses and a doctor died. The guardians met the usual opposition to the purchase of property for use as a fever ward. On 12 May or thereabouts, a buildings was acquired and from that date until 25 September, 128 patients were admitted, of which number 112 were Irish, including the Duignans. From the outset of the inquiry, the Rochdale guardians vigorously defended their treatment of the Duignans and rejected absolutely the Dublin inquest verdict that Michael Duignan should not have been sent as a deck passenger as he was in a bad physical condition. They argued that the Irish medical evidence regarding the state of the corpse was flawed. In their opinion, Michael had been trampled to death because of the gross overcrowding of the steamer. Why, they demanded, had the Dublin inquest jury never referred to the fact that 550 deck passengers were carried by the *Duchess of Kent*?

The inquiry revealed a trail of administrative sloppiness. Dr Collingwood, who signed the certificate saying that Michael Duignan was fit to be removed had never seen the conditions suffered by deck passengers on board the Irish steamers. Despite the evidence of middle class cabin passengers that the Rochdale paupers looked in a bad way, Collingwood stuck to his view that Michael Duignan was fit, saying that Michael did not complain when told he was being sent back to Ireland. The boy was 12 years of age, he had just lost his parents and his baby sister, he was unable to walk and he had epileptic fits. Under the law, those being removed should have been brought before the magistrates. Only Patrick Duignan appeared before the magistrates. He was 14 years of age and recovering from typhus. He was never questioned or indeed, never spoken to. It is probable that had Michael been presented to the magistrates they would not have signed the warrant. The reasons given to explain these administrative failures were that the Guardian's office was busy at the time the Duignans' case came before them and that as the parents were dead, they did not think it necessary to see all the children.

Patrick Duignan claimed that Michael was so weak he could not sit upright in the cart taking them to the Rochdale railway station. He also claimed that they were not covered and they were soaked by the rain. Abraham Travis, one of the union officers, who accompanied the paupers to Liverpool admitted that it was raining when the cart arrived at the station but that Michael and Patrick were covered with a counterpane. On arrival at the Clarence dock in Liverpool, a 12 year old boy, unable to stand because of his disability, was placed sitting on the deck, wearing outsize clothes given to him by the workhouse. Neither the captain or the crew paid any attention to him. Nor it seems, did the women, Gallagher and Goharty, who were charged with his care.

Captain Jones of the *Duchess of Kent* took no responsibility for allowing so many passengers on board. The authorities did not prosecute him. The journey started in wet, rough weather, with gross overcrowding of deck passengers. It seems certain that he was sat upon in the jostling for space and was dead by 8.0pm, five and a half hours after sailing. Before arriving in Dublin, an adult male also died. A dispassionate reading of the whole of the evidence concerning Michael Duignan's experience, from being declared fit by Collingwood, to his death, would lead most people to conclude that the whole system was responsible for Michael Duignan's death. There seems little doubt he was ill, that he suffered from being trampled upon but as a cripple, he would have been unable to take evasive action. One witness, Mary Hobson of Dawson Square in Rochdale, knew Michael before he became ill with typhus. She told the inquiry:

> When he lived in Dawson Square, Michael walked with a stick, not so well. He was lame and I never saw him walk without a stick. In the case of danger I do not think he would be able to get away. When he walked, he walked slowly and I considered him a cripple. Patrick was also lame, he had a foot turned in. When Michael walked, he put his stick before him and seem to drag his feet. I remember a fire in the house at Dawson Square where the Duignans lived. Michael was on the first floor and he was got out at the window. He hung by his hands from the window, with his feet from the ground and was lifted down by two women. He would not have saved himself... I think the boy tried to get out of the window because of his not being able to get down the stairs alone.

Other witnesses testified to his incapacity, yet he was left on the deck of an overcrowded steamer. In fact, the Rochdale authorities used the fact of his disability to defend themselves. He did not die because of being in a poor physical condition as a result of typhus, he was, they argued, trampled because of the overcrowding. Why, they demanded, did not the coroner's jury in Dublin, mention the overcrowding on the *Duchess of Kent*? Because they were anti-English. On the 6 October, Austin sent his report on the inquiry to the Poor Law Commissioners. Astonishingly, he concluded that Michael Duignan had been treated 'reasonably' by the Rochdale guardians and that he 'probably' died of suffocation. He also expressed the opinion that had Michael Duignan appeared before the magistrates, the fact that he was 'lame' may have been noticed and thus might have caused them not to sign a warrant for removal. Again, he admitted there was some confusion regarding the law governing the conditions under which paupers were to be removed on steamers. In particular, the Justices of the Peace in Lancashire had one set of regulations while the Rochdale guardians had another set. Travis, the officer who took the paupers to Liverpool seemed not to have read the regulations. Overall, the case of Michael Duignan highlights the experience of many Irish paupers who were removed during 1847. As we have noted, the conditions on the steamers became so bad as to require a special investigation by Captain Denham.

From June 1847 onwards, the threat of removal provided many poor law guardians with a weapon that did reduce the volume of claims for relief on the part of the Irish who did not have the status of irremovability. However, as a deterrent to would-be claimants it was not entirely successful because of the difficulty of disproving a claim to five years residence. However, it *did* discourage many and to that extent it was a limited success, as the statistics of expenditure on relief demonstrate. However, it did not stop Irish paupers coming to Britain at any time during the famine. It did not succeed because there was simply no way of stopping those who were removed, returning to Britain, as many did. The numbers removed cannot be taken as an index of the success of the poor law union's determination to use the law to remove Irish paupers because the system was used by those wanting a free trip home. The total number of removals from England and Wales during the famine, when compared to arrivals, was relatively small. After allowing for voluntary removals, the number of famine refugees removed was even smaller. For those who were forcibly removed it was a bitter experience.

Appendices

Appendix 8.1 The number of removal orders for Irish born persons made out in the year ending 25 March 1853, with respect to England

Place	*Number of persons*
Liverpool	3549
London (Middlesex part)	420
Manchester and Preston	217
Newcastle on Tyne	24
Bradford, Leeds and Sheffield	124
Camberwell and Lambeth (Surrey)	31
Pontypool (Monmouthshire)	31
East Stonehouse (Devon)	27
Stockport and Wirral (Cheshire)	51
Total	4474

Note: the number of orders is not identical to the number of individuals as one order may cover several individuals.

Source: SC (1854) Minutes of Evidence, Appendix No 17, p. 667.

Appendix 8.2 The number of persons born in Ireland and removed from Scotland to Ireland in each of the years 1846-1853, inclusive, distinguishing between compulsory and voluntary removals.

Counties	*1846*		*1847*		*1848*		*1849*	
	Orders	*Voluntary*	*Orders*	*Voluntary*	*Orders*	*Voluntary*	*Orders*	*Voluntary*
Lanarkshire	32	3063	100	8 047	227	7 866	445	5614
Renfrewshire	10	262	16	1 124	81	685	32	373
Rest	247	373	259	1 181	374	1 458	457	607
Total	289	3698	375	10 352	682	10 009	934	6594

Counties	*1850*		*1851*		*1852*		*1853*	
	Orders	*Voluntary*	*Orders*	*Voluntary*	*Orders*	*Voluntary*	*Orders*	*Voluntary*
Lanarkshire	450	3550	299	3508	199	1495	44	793
Renfrewshire	25	133	17	140	51	169	42	117
Rest	485	416	460	271	459	302	276	288
Total	960	3999	776	3919	709	1966	362	1198

Source: SC (1854) Minutes of Evidence, Appendix No 6.

Notes and References

1 M.E.Rose, 'Settlement, Removal and the New Poor Law', in D.Fraser (ed) *The New Poor Law in the Nineteenth Century,*(Macmillan: 1976), pp. 25-44. D.Ashworth, 'Settlement and Removal in Urban Areas: Bradford, 1834-71', in M.E.Rose, *The Poor and the City: the English Poor Law in its Urban Context, 1834-1914*, pp. 58-91 (Leicester University Press: 1985).
2 G.W.Place, 'The Reparation of Irish Vagrants from Cheshire, 1750-1815', *Journal of Chester Archaeological Society*, Volume 68, 1985, pp. 125-141. Also G.W.Place, 'The Labouring Passengers', *Chetham Society*, Volume XXXIX, 1994, pp. 172-191.
3 Vagrancy (1848) Minutes of Evidence, John Easter, Assistant Overseer, St Giles Parish, q. 164, q.193, q.226.
4 Vagrancy (1848), Minutes of Evidence, James Wall, Vestry Clerk of the Parish of St Luke's, Middlesex.
5 SC (1847) Minutes of Evidence, E.Rushton, q.4336, p. 54.
6 ibid, q.4379.
7 SC (1854) Minutes of Evidence, George Grey, Assistant Overseer of the parish of All Saints, Newcastle on Tyne, qq. 436-457, pp. 31-32. Grey's evidence provides clear example of the removal procedures used by a parish with a large Irish population.
8 SC (1854) Minutes of Evidence, Appendix No 17, p. 666. See also p. 667 for an analysis of the numbers of removals in Britain up to 1853.
9 *Liverpool Mercury*, 1 December 1847. Meeting of the Select Vestry.
10 SC (1854) Minutes of Evidence, E.David, qq.695-6505
11 PRO/MH12/5968/Liverpool/42433/51. Copy of a report of a sub-committee of the workhouse appointed on 12 June 1851. Also the charge famine Irish are claiming five years residency.
12 LIVRO. 353/Sel/19/3. Liverpool Workhouse Admissions and Discharges Register, 4 November, 25 March 1848. Entry nos. 301-307.
13 LIVRO. 353/Sel/19/B. Liverpool Workhouse Admissions and Discharges Register. Entry nos. 936-940.
14 LIVRO. 353/Sel/19/3. Liverpool Workhouse Admissions and Discharges Register. Entry nos. 2219-2221.
15 SC (1854) Appendix No. 15, Case No. 91.
16 PRO/MH12/6095/Prescot/1847-49. Copy of an affidavit regarding Kelly's removal from Dublin to Liverpool.
17 PRO/MH12/6095/Prescot/1847-49. Prescot Guardians to Poor Law Commissioners, letter dated 5 December 1848.
18 *Liverpool Mercury*, 26 December 1847.
19 Poor Law Inquiry held at Rochdale by the Manchester Guardians. See *Manchester Guardian*, 25 and 29 September and 20 October 1847. See also SC (1854). Evidence of A.Power, qq.414-8.
20 PRO/MH12/6176/Rochdale/1846-7. (known hereafter as PRO Rochdale). Rochdale Guardians to Poor Law Commissioners, 19 May 1847.
21 PRO Rochdale. Poor Law Commissioners to Rochdale Guardians, 21 June 1847.
22 PRO Rochdale. Somerville to Sir Denis le Merchant, 6 September 1847.
23 PRO Rochdale. Denis le Merchant, Home Office to Poor Law Commissioners, 6 September 1847.
24 PRO Rochdale. Albert Austin to Rochdale Poor Law Guardians, 8 September 1847.
25 *Manchester Guardian*, 25 September 1847. Carries a full account.

9 The Cost of the Famine Immigration

I

Clearly, the term 'cost' can have various connotations. Importantly, with regard to the famine immigration, there was the cost to the recipient towns of social disruption, deteriorating housing conditions and, in many instances in the north of England, bad inter-communal relations. Such social costs are difficult, though not impossible, to assess. A relatively easy cost to measure is the financial cost of providing relief and medical aid. The issue to be addressed in this chapter is that of the *financial* cost of the famine immigration to those British towns receiving the refugees. In particular, how large was that cost? What was the incidence of the taxation or, in other words, who paid? Did the cost have a deleterious effect on business? However, before attempting such analysis, the perceptions regarding such matters on the part of contemporary observers and administrators will first be established in order to see if their fears matched the reality. This is important because the resentment over perceived financial burdens influenced attitudes towards the Irish refugees. Then in section III we examine the *levels* of expenditure on the relief of the Irish in particular towns and the cost of the famine Irish in particular. The expenditure, as a rate per pound is then estimated in section IV. We conclude with an assessement of the effects of this tax burden.

II

Given the scale and nature of the immigration described in chapter four, it is not surprising that many individuals and poor law officials were alarmed. A particular source of adverse comment was the belief that the Irish famine refugees were imposing an 'intolerable' financial burden on ratepayers. Such concerns surfaced in 1846 from October onwards when the rate of arrivals from Ireland at British ports began to significantly increase. The press, provincial and national, played a central role in disseminating information regarding the immigration and in generating fears over the social and financial consequences of the influx of refugees. The financial cost of the crisis was not simply the value of direct relief handed out in terms of food, clothing and money. It also included the increased administrative costs resulting from the need to have extra relieving officers, overseers and gravediggers; the employment of extra doctors and nurses to deal with the typhus victims, the provision of extra hospital accommodation, the cost of medicines, coffins and removals. Thus the extra expenditure was either a variable cost such as labour, materials and cash relief payments or a fixed cost such as interest on loans taken out to finance capital projects and items such as insurance premiums for buildings cover. In all cases, the funding of such expenditure had to come principally from the poor rates.

At the beginning of 1847, though the press adopted various ideological stances when commenting on the Irish crisis and displayed disparate nuances in identifying culpability with regard to the economic problems of Ireland, there was general agreement on one point. There was a consensus that the Irish famine was a *national* calamity and that *central* taxation ought to finance the provision of poor relief for the famine Irish in Britain, it should not be the responsibility of ratepayers in those towns in which the Irish immigrants congregated. Combined with this conviction was the opinion, equally strongly expressed, that outdoor relief should be available in Ireland and, in the absence of national financing of poor relief, Irish landlords should pay for Irish poverty in Ireland. Not surprisingly, such views were passionately expressed in Liverpool, the worse affected town. The *Liverpool Mercury* of 15 January 1847, commenting on the desperate condition of many of the Irish coming ashore at the port, mirrored a widely held opinion among its mainly middle-class readership:

> ... the numbers of starving Irish, men, women and children - daily landed on our quays is appalling, and the parish of Liverpool has at present the painful and most costly task to encounter, of keeping them alive - if possible. Never was the simple truth so plainly discernible as at this moment, that the pauperism of a nation ought to be provided for by national means. The barbarism of local taxation for such provision - one of the results of the wisdom of our ancestors - stands forth now in all its deformity. Liverpool is at this moment bearing a burden which belongs neither to itself or the county; nor even to England but to the United Kingdom and that burden will bring bitter distress upon hundreds of struggling tradesmen and small householders...

This piece is of interest in that it articulated a general acceptance that the famine Irish immigrants could not be allowed to die. At the same time, it imparts a widespread sense of grievance that particular towns were bearing the main burden of alleviating the poverty of another part of the United Kingdom. The *Mercury* was a Liberal paper, often locked in conflict with its Tory rivals. However, on this occasion, there was a common conviction that Liverpool was bearing the brunt of the famine influx. The Tory

Liverpool Courier of the 27 January carried a column headed 'Pauperism Invasion'. The *Courier* claimed that more than anywhere else, Liverpool was best placed to form a judgement on the famine influx. 'This influx of Irish poor has had several consequences of much importance over and above the *principal one*, which is the exaggeration of the poor rates'.

Such views were not confined to Liverpool. The *London Times*, throughout the whole of the famine crisis took a lead in attacking the Irish landlords. On the same day the *Liverpool Mercury* carried the above report, the *Times* drew the attention of its readers to events in Glasgow:

> ... the state of things which the administration of the new Scotch Poor Law in that city have at the moment to meet, is as remarkable as it is embarrassing and painful. Glasgow is to become, so to speak, a very focus of difficulties. On the stage of municipality, a national drama develops itself. As closely connected with Ireland as with Scotland, a city which has long borne an ill name for pauperism on the one hand, and economy on the other, is now the hard refuge of literally myriads flying from the blighted soil. Day after day, steamers arrive laden with the most absolute destitution, casting itself on the mercy of strangers.

The Times reported that the Glasgow Parochial Board was considering approaching Sir George Grey, the Home Secretary, for central government help in relieving the Irish poor. As it was to do many times in the succeeding months, *The Times* argued that if there was an adequate poor law in Ireland, Glasgow (and by implication other towns) would not have to bear such a heavy burden. *The Glasgow Chronicle*, in a leader article, on 6 January 1847 had warned its readers that if the Irish immigration were to continue unchecked, it would 'ultimately corrode the vitals of society and render property almost valueless in all the hives of industry'.[1] In May, the *Newcastle Journal* carried a piece headed *Fearful Increase in Pauperism* and informed its readers that over the last three months there had been a considerable immigration of poor Irish into the Newcastle Union, 'all of whom become chargeable to the different parishes'. It was claimed the poor relief expenditure had doubled during the last financial quarter (ending 25 March 1847)[2] The *Halifax Guardian* took a particularly jaundiced view of the Irish in the area. In February it commented on the large number of Irish in the district, claiming that they were imposing a considerable cost on the ratepayers and that they were 'ungrateful'.[3] Three weeks later it returned to the attack, describing the large number of Irish beggars in Huddersfield and labelling them 'lazy'.[4] The *Times* turned its attention to Newport in Monmouthshire. After describing the scale of the problem facing the poor law authority, the paper stated that the 'Board of Guardians are almost paralysed at the onerous duties which now devolve upon them, and are earnestly deliberating what measures should be adopted for the protection of ratepayers...'[5] On 25 February 1847, the *Bristol Gazette* carried a report concerning the famine Irish influx into Newport. It alleged that the indigenous poor ' complain bitterly of the increased privation brought upon them'. The implication of the report was that the relief expenditure on the Irish in Newport meant less for its own poor. Weeks later, the paper warned its readers, with reference to the Irish crisis: 'This is no question of party, sect or class. All feel the pressure - all are interested. Through every pore is felt the exhausting drains of Irish distress and except the property of Ireland is made to bear its share of Irish burdens, England will be dragged down to the level of Irish pauperism'.[6]

Thomas Baines writing in the *Manchester Guardian* 20 January 1847 warned its readers that the Liverpool authorities had saved thousands from dying of starvation. However, this fact would, he claimed, be transmitted to Ireland and that the rate of immigration at the time of his writing was 'only the first flood'. Throughout the whole of the famine crisis, a continual stream of articles on the cost of Irish immigration into Britain was placed before the newspaper reading public. Even the amendment to the Irish Poor Law in June 1847 did nothing to stem editorial concern over the issue.

It is not possible to quantify the effect the press reporting had in shaping public attitudes towards the immigrant Irish, in particular, the creation of the opinion that the immigrants were an unreasonable financial burden on the British ratepayer. It is highly probable that it *was* influential. Was it accurate in its portrayal of the problem? The views of those intimately involved in dealing with the crisis provides an alternative means of checking the media claims of crisis. In January 1847, the Mayor of Stockport called a meeting of ratepayers of the borough 'in consequence of the great distress thrown upon the Stockport District by the large importation of Irish poor people...' Reporting on this meeting to the Poor Law Commissioners in London, the clerk to the Stockport poor law union told them that 'it was not advisable to hold out any inducement for other families to come into this already overburdened district'; he claimed this was in order to protect the ratepayers.[7] This can be interpreted to mean that the relief to be offered to the newly arrived Irish should be kept to a minimum. Later in 1847, the poor law guardians in Ashton-under-Lyne expressed a similar concern that the provision of poor relief should not attract more famine Irish. Again, alarm over the possible consequences for ratepayers was the primary worry. The fear expressed was not simply about the numbers of Irish arriving in the town but also reflected the belief that, given the same number of destitute English on the one hand, and Irish on the other, a greater proportion of Irish would apply for relief. Enoch Turner, an Assistant overseer, and

Joseph Tipping, Relieving Officer, both of the Ashton Union, told the Poor Law Commissioners, that with respect to the provision of poor relief:

> .... the effect on the Irish greatly exceeds that of the English, for as soon as you relieve an Irish family in any district, the fact becomes notorious; numerous applications are immediately made by their neighbours and there is no possibility of checking it without offering the workhouse and promptly removing them in the event of their accepting it.. We could refer to families who, immediately on their arrival in this town from Ireland, some members of them were taken ill, which sickness was protracted by different members of their family for several months and in one instance, seven medical orders were given at a cost of two pounds nine shillings and relief to the amount of £8.

It is not clear whether these officials feared the Irish were imposing on the guardians or whether they were simply protesting about the cost of Irish sickness in Ashton.[8] The same union had complained to the Commissioners in London that it could not provide a fever ward in the workhouse as there was no room. They were told to consider building a new workhouse 'in view of the inadequate provision'.[9] This was rather a silly proposal for dealing with an immediate and temporary crisis. Similarly, in the north east, the Gateshead guardians of the poor told the Commissioners that 'owing to the influx of Irish poor' they had inadequate accommodation for vagrants. This was despite the fact they had built two extra rooms to cope with the crisis.[10] Three weeks later, William Rowntree, clerk to the Gateshead Guardians, wrote to the Commissioners again. He said that Gateshead had been sending fever patients to the Newcastle fever hospital but that Newcastle was refusing to take any more. The only building now available to Gateshead for renting as a fever shed was over the union border, in Chester-le-Street. The situation was desperate '... at present fever cases seem to be spreading rapidly in the various lodging houses where the poor Irish principally resort...' Permission was granted and the shed was leased for a year, thereby increasing the costs of the union.[11]

Two doctors attending the Irish poor in Newport wrote to the Newport Guardians in April 1847, asking for salary increases because of the bigger workload. The guardians sought the permission of the Poor Law Commissioners, who agreed that the money could be spent.[12] On 4 November 1847, Charles Tyrer, relieving officer at the Prescot Union, on the outskirts of Liverpool, asked for a pay rise as a result of the large increase in his workload consequent on Irish immigration.[13] These examples of the cost of Irish famine immigration contained in the correspondence of the Poor Law Commissioners could be expanded. However, the point made here is this, the views of officials involved in the provision of poor relief confirms the validity of the sense of crisis reported in the press. There are other sources. Edward Rushton was the stipendiary magistrate of Liverpool throughout the whole of the famine crisis. On 22 April 1847, he gave evidence to the Select Committee on Settlement and Poor Removal. He told the Committee that in the financial year ending 25 March 1847, the rates in the parish had been two shillings one penny. Because of the Irish influx he claimed a three shilling rate was contemplated for the current financial year but he did not think that would be enough.[14]

The public's perception of financial crisis arising from the famine immigration was particularly widespread in 1847. *Equally, concern was not confined to the year 1847.* Despite claims to the contrary, the famine was not over in that year and as we have noted, *throughout* 1847-53, a high level of Irish pauper immigration into Britain continued. At a meeting of the Select Vestry in Liverpool on 4 January 1848 a call was again made for central government financing of the cost of relieving the Irish poor in Liverpool.[15] Such requests were pointless but they reflected the frustration arising from the town's position as the main port of entry. Three weeks later the *Liverpool Journal* carried a leader article headed 'The Irish are Coming'.

> Last year the people of Liverpool lived in the shadow of death. The streets swarmed with misery, and pestilence sat down in horror in our populous places. The unhappy poor of Ireland, flying from famine at home, or exported on economic speculation, came here as the nearest port and soon after their arrival breathed a tainted atmosphere, each inhalation a death to nature. Hunger, neglect and filth, which like a parasite, exhausts even the life of poverty, had prepared them for the reception of fatal disease; and devoid of resources, they shrink into the fetid depositories of typhus. The returns of the Registrar contain the sequel. The authorities did their duty humanely and liberally, but the visitation was nevertheless, awful and appalling... but the symptoms are showing themselves that the evil is returning.

The *Journal* went on to state that the Irish preferred English gaols to their chances in Ireland. Significantly, it argued that starvation was still the reality in Ireland and that the 'desire now is any land but Ireland'.[16] In July 1848, at the time of rising national concern over Chartism and the Irish Confederates, the *Times* launched a ferocious attack on the financial burden imposed on Britain by Ireland. The piece carried the statement that 'every hardworking man in this country carries a whole Irish family on his shoulders'.[17] In November 1848 the Select Vestry in Liverpool was still complaining to the Poor Law Commissioners of the cost to Liverpool of Irish paupers, in particular the cost of removing them to Ireland.[18] (see Appendices Nos 9.1 and 9.2).

III

There is little doubt that by the end of 1847, there was a deeply ingrained belief that the famine Irish had imposed an intolerable burden on local ratepayers. Were such fears justified? Any attempt to answer such a question first runs into the problem of the availability of primary evidence and its reliability. Crucially, not all poor law unions distinguished between expenditure on the Irish and non-Irish. In those unions where the distinction was made, not all of the records have survived. Of those unions for which records exist, some provide data on both indoor *and* outdoor expenditure on the Irish, while others simply record outdoor expenditure. In such cases, the total cost of relief for the Irish poor in the unions cannot be calculated. A major problem is the failure to distinguish between money spent on newly arrived Irish and that spent on those Irish who were permanent residents of a town. A cardinal rule in the discipline of statistics is that data should refer to clearly defined phenomena. Unfortunately, in those instances of unions providing information on Irish poor relief to various government bodies, select committees and the Poor Law Commissioners, this rule has not been observed. For example, in the case of statistics referring to expenditure on *outdoor* relief for the Irish poor in English Unions, many refer to money spent solely on the provision of bread, soup and cash payments while in other cases, they may also include the provision of clothing, medicine and the cost of doctors and nurses. Similarly, with respect to data on expenditure on *indoor* relief, they may allude simply to maintenance of Irish poor in the Workhouse or they may have included elements of fixed costs and capital charges. A particularly irritating feature of the available data is that in some instances they refer to a financial year ending Lady Day, 25 March, and in other cases, they refer to a calendar year. In the case of Glasgow and other Scottish parochial boards, the financial year ended in May of each year. Illustrative of the difficulties facing the researcher trying produce comparable data is the case of the Manchester poor law guardians. Long before the famine, they adopted the policy of treating those Irish paupers who had been in Manchester a long time, on a par with the English who had settlement rights. This means that with regard to expenditure on outdoor poor relief for such long stay Irish in the township, it is not clear if such spending is recorded under the heading 'Manchester cases' or 'Irish'.[19] Finally, and most important, when analysing the available data on famine Irish poor relief expenditure in Britain, it is absolutely essential to include in the analysis, an assessment of the effects of specific legislative measures which directly affected the Irish in the context of the poor law. It follows from this latter point, that though it is necessary to make allowance for the state of the labour markets and macro-economic forces when examining fluctuations in poor relief, expenditure on *Irish* relief may not reflect the demand for labour nor the amount of destitution. Keeping all these factors in mind, it *is* possible to make some meaningful assessment of the financial consequences of the famine immigration.

The starting point for any analysis of the financial burden of Irish pauperism within a poor law union must be the system of raising poor rates. It is important to note that the English and Welsh systems differed significantly from that operating in Scotland. Dealing first with England and Wales, during the period under discussion, the value of property in each parish within a union was assessed, usually each year, in order to establish the tax base on which the poor rate would be levied. This means, for example, that the significance of the *absolute* level of expenditure on the Irish poor in two different unions must, for purposes of comparison, take into account the rateable value of property in each. In principle, in the case of two unions possessing the same rateable value of property assessed for the poor rate, a given rate in the pound would bring in the same amount of money. In practice, this was not the case. There were two main reasons for this.

First, in some unions, many ratepayers were excused the payment of rates on the grounds of poverty. In general, such persons rented property at the bottom end of the housing market, usually below £12 a year. To the extent that this happened, a given sum of money would have to be raised from those *not* excused payment, thereby increasing the amount paid in rates by that particular section of the ratepayers. This point is illustrated by the situations in Liverpool, Manchester and Stockport during the famine crisis. In 1847 there was 38 199 tenements assessed in Manchester township for the poor rate, 449 being excused payment on the grounds of poverty. In 1848, 43 090 tenements were assessed for the poor rate in Liverpool, of these, 20 805 were excused payments on poverty grounds. (see Appendix 9.4) In Stockport the situation in 1841 was 1134 tenements excused payment, out of a total of 7464 (see Appendix No 9.3). A second reason why a given rate in the pound levied on two identical gross rateable values of property would yield differing revenues, was the inefficiency of some guardians of the poor in organising the collection of rates.

The two towns for which there are fairly complete datasets regarding poor relief expenditure on the Irish over the whole famine period, are Liverpool and Manchester. The categories of expenditure to be examined first are expenditure on Irish outdoor relief, indoor relief and the cost of removals. The table below illustrates the amount spent by each of the two unions on *outdoor* relief over the whole period of the famine crisis. This category of expenditure is the most likely to provide an index of the provision of relief for the newly arrived immigrants.

Table 9.1 A comparison of the expenditure on outdoor relief for the Irish poor in Liverpool parish and Manchester township: 1844-54

Year ending 25 March	*Liverpool* £	*Manchester* £
1844/45	498	2 863
1845/46	648	2 427
1846/47	9 648	4 651
1847/48	20 750	21 044
1848/49	8 337	15 191
1849/50	8 066	10 331
1850/51	6 835	9 250
1851/52	6 731	10 754
1852/53	5 970	7 185
1853/54	6 595	7 495

Sources: SC (1847) Appendix No 8, p. 592. For Manchester, Weekly Reports of the meetings of the Manchester poor law guardians, published weekly in the *Manchester Guardian*.

The most striking feature of these data is that during the financial year 1845/46, for example, at the onset of the famine, though both towns spent relatively little on Irish outdoor relief, Manchester spent nearly four times as much as Liverpool. The next financial year, 1846/47, shows a big increase in this category of spending by both unions. There then follows a peaking of spending during the financial year ending 25 March 1848, succeeded by a falling off but the subsequent outdoor relief settling *at a much higher level than was the case in the pre-famine period*. How is this pattern to be explained? In particular, can we assume that it reflects accurately the financial consequences of the famine immigration?

Turning first to Liverpool, if we use the financial year 1845/46 as the base line for comparison, outdoor relief expenditure over the next year rose from £648 to £9648, an increase of some fifteen times over. Similarly, the next financial year, 1847/48, witnessed an expenditure of £20750, nearly thirty-two times higher than that of 1845/46. This financial year encompassed the height of the influx of famine refugees but the increased expenditure cannot be all attributed to this fact. This pattern reflects three forces at work, namely the effect of the changes in the law regarding removal, the local demand for labour and the famine influx. First we consider the effects of the Five Year Residency Act of 1846. As we noted earlier, this act (9 and 10 Vic.Cap. 66) granted the status of irremovability to anyone who could prove five years continuous residency in a parish. A direct consequence of this was that many Irish who were long term residents could, and did, claim poor relief without risking the threat of removal to Ireland. Previously such a threat had acted as a deterrent to many potential Irish claimants, causing them not claim relief. The significance of this is that some of the expenditure on outdoor relief for Irish immigrants from the financial year 1846/47 onwards, reflects relief for those acquiring the status of irremovability ie. *non-famine Irish*. In the case of Liverpool, the stipendiary magistrate told the Select Committee on Removal that as a direct result of the Five Year Residency Act, 2491 Irish born persons had immediately become a charge on the Liverpool ratepayers, together with 956 English. The cost of these extra Irish claims was estimated to be £7037 per year. Such costs would clearly increase with the passing of time as more destitute Irish would have obtained the necessary five years residence in the parish. Rushton gave his evidence 22 April 1847, just after the end of the financial year.[20] It is plausible to argue, therefore, that of the total of £9648 spent on outdoor relief for the Irish during the year ending 25 March 1847, £7037 was spent on Irish long stay residents, leaving a *maximum* of £2611 spent on the famine Irish in that year. Similarly over the financial year 1847/48, using a conservative estimate of £7037 spent on irremovable Irish, a maximum of £13713 would have been spent on the famine refugees (£20750 - £7037). This was still a considerable increase in outdoor relief expenditure on the Irish poor but much less than £20750, the figure which centred in the heated debate about the financial impact of the famine on Liverpool. At first sight, the fall in spending on outdoor relief for the Irish over the financial year 1848/49 is surprising. After all, refugees were still arriving in large numbers. If we deduct the same £7037 from the total of £8337, it leaves only a maximum of only £1300 spent on Irish immigrants. Though this was still twice the amount spend in the year 1845/46, it does not seem to reflect the crisis described in chapter four. There are two possible explanations for this dramatic fall in outdoor expenditure on the Irish.

One is that the demand for unskilled labour picked up so that fewer of the newly arrived Irish needed to claim relief. This is implausible because such an improvement in the labour market would also have affected the English; Table 9.2 below shows the expenditure by the Liverpool Select Vestry on both English and Irish. During the financial year ending March 1846, £18796 was spent on the English poor, rising to £19 576 over the next year. This was a rise of 4.1 per cent compared to the 1500 per cent rise in expenditure on the Irish over the same period. It is noteworthy that over the financial year 1847/48, there was only a relatively small increase in expenditure on the English compared with the increased expenditure of £20 750 on the Irish during Black '47.

Table 9.2 Total expenditure on outdoor poor relief in Liverpool for the financial years 1844-5 to 1853-4 inclusive.

Financial year	*Non Irish outdoor relief (£)*	*Irish outdoor relief (£)*	*Total outdoor relief (£)*	*Irish as a % of total*
1844/45	19 578	498	20 076	2.4
1845/46	18 796	648	19 444	3.3
1846/47	19 576	9 648	29 224	33.0
1847/48	21 340	20 750	42 090	49.0
1848/49	24 451	8 337	32 788	25.4
1849/50	26 608	8 066	34 674	23.3
1850/51	25 653	6 835	32 488	21.0
1851/52	26 121	6 731	32 852	20.5
1852/53	21 473	5 970	27 443	21.7
1853/54	22 217	6 595	28 812	22.8

Note: indoor relief includes the cost of children.
Source: SC (1854) Appendix No 8, p. 592.

Significantly, this spending on non-Irish poor *increases* during the year ending 25 March 1849 simultaneously with a dramatic falling off in expenditure on the Irish. This implies that the demand for labour was *not* increasing and so a buoyant labour market was not responsible for the fall in outdoor relief for the Irish. It *is* possible that employers at the docks were substituting Irish for English labour, indeed there is anecdotal evidence that this was occurring but not on a scale that would explain the large decline in spending on Irish outdoor relief.[21] This brings us to the second, more likely explanation, the Poor Law Removal Act (10 and 11 Vic. Cap. 33). This became law 21 June 1847, making the removal of the Irish much easier and as a direct consequence, there followed in a dramatic fall in Irish applications for relief. The Irish who had not achieved the status of irremovability under the Five Year Act risked removal if they applied for relief. From 1848/49 onwards, the data measuring expenditure on outdoor relief for the Irish refer principally to spending on those Irish born persons who were long stay residents, people who had contributed their labour to the port and town over many years. This lower level of expenditure therefore does not mean the famine crisis was over, it simply reflects the reduced level of applications for relief following the real threat of removal (see p.221).

Turning to the case of Manchester, the analysis of data on *outdoor* relief for the Irish involves similar considerations. The recorded expenditure on the Irish in the township of Manchester refers to both removable and irremovable Irish. In broad terms, the pattern of change shown in Table 9.3 below, is similar to that of Liverpool. At the onset of the famine crisis, that is the period covered by the financial year ending March 1847, spending in Manchester township on the Irish poor rose from £2427 to £4650, an increase of 92 per cent. The effects of the 1847 Irish immigration are enmeshed in the spending of £21 044 during the next financial year, a rise of over 800 per cent on the year 1845/46. As in the case of Liverpool, a large part of this increase reflects both the famine immigration *and* the consequence of the Five Year Residency Act of 1846. It is surprising to see that Manchester's expenditure on Irish outdoor relief exceeds that of Liverpool. One reason was the fact that it was cheaper to remove the Irish from Liverpool than from Manchester, so that Manchester guardians paid outdoor relief rather than incur the cost of the removal of casual claimants.

Table 9.3 Total annual expenditure on outdoor relief in the township of Manchester over the financial years 1845/46 to 1853/54

Year ending 25 March	*English settled*	*English non-settled*	*Irish all categories*	*Total expenditure*	*Irish as % of total expenditure*
1845/46	12 373	4 126	2 427	18 926	13
1846/47	12 219	5 091	4 650	21 960	21
1847/48	21 171	15 084	21 044	57 299	37
1848/49	17 600	10 469	15 191	43 260	35
1849/50	13 769	5 939	10 331	30 039	34
1850/51	12 029	5 003	9 250	26 282	35
1851/52	11 853	5 410	10 754	28 017	38
1852/53	8 766	4 344	7 185	20 295	35
1853/54	7 843	4 526	7 495	19 864	38

Source: SC (1854) Minutes of Evidence, John Harrop, clerk to the Board of Guardians of the township of Manchester, qq. 6208-6219, Table A, p. 442.

More importantly the charge on Manchester township arising from *irremovable* Irish was greater than in the case of Liverpool. There is strong evidence to support this claim. We are fortunate that John Harrop, clerk to the Manchester Guardians produced a detailed report on the consequences of the Five Year Act for Manchester. The relevant statistics are given in Table 9.4 below. The evidence is clear, the Five Year Residency Act imposed a considerable increase in costs on Manchester's ratepayers. During the quarter ended September 1846, 427 removable Irish families cost Manchester township £48 per week. The corresponding period during 1851 saw an increase to 1478 irremovable families, a rise of 346 per cent, with associated costs of £180 per week. This represented a net increase of £132 or 275 per cent., equivalent to £6864 a year. The significance of these data is that of the total annual expenditure of £9250 on outdoor relief for the Irish poor in Manchester during the financial year 1850/51, something like 75 per cent was on Irish who had the status of irremovability.

Table 9.4 The average weekly number of families in receipt of outdoor relief in the township of Manchester and the associated costs, 1846 and 1851.

Quarter ended	*Number*	*Cost*		
September 1846		£	s	d
English families having settlement in Manchester	1775	226	1	10
English families not having settlement in Manchester but removable	688	85	3	8
Irish families removable	427	48	0	11
Total	2890	359	6	5
September 1851				
English families having settlement in Manchester	1833	219	12	4
English families not having settlement in Manchester but irremovable	791	99	5	9
Irish families irremovable	1478	179	16	4
Total	4102	498	14	5

Source: Report presented to the Manchester Poor Law Guardians 24 October 1851 by J Harrop, clerk to the Union. Published in the *Manchester Guardian*, 25 October 1851

This argument further is supported by a return to the House of Commons concerning expenditure on the Irish poor in various poor law unions, for the calendar year ending 31 December 1848. In the case of Manchester township, £20 505 was recorded as having been spent on the Irish poor in terms of relief and of this sum, £20 306 was spent on relief for the Irish who had irremovable status.[22]

The implication is that 99 per cent of Manchester township's expenditure on Irish relief during 1848 was on those who were long term contributors to the local labour force. It also follows that very little was spent on 'casual' relief for recently arrived Irish. Clearly the policy of threatening removal was successful and so the published data regarding the expenditure on outdoor relief for the Irish in Manchester, as in the case of Liverpool, is not a true index of Irish destitution. There is anecdotal evidence to support this view. At the meeting of the Manchester Guardians of the Poor, at which Harrop's report was presented, C H Richards told members that:

> As a point somewhat of credit to the Irish, it should be remembered that they came here because they found labour connected with our manufactory operations and that we kept them because they were useful. When they grow old, after having given the benefit of their life of labour to the community, they ought not to be pursued [sic removal]. This was the first district in which Irish labour was demanded to any considerable extent and those who were among the first of the immigrants have become old. When a period of depression came, numbers of persons were thrown upon the guardians for relief who afterwards were never got rid of; I have no doubt that an examination would show that a great number of our regular Irish paupers first became so during 1847.

These views of Richards are of interest on a number of counts. He was the Senior Vice Chairman of the Manchester Board of Guardians and had been a guardian since 1840. He was also a magistrate and as a paper manufacturer, was an employer of local labour. There is an unequivocal acknowledgement of the contribution of the Irish to the economy of Manchester and also a recognition of a moral obligation to support such long stay Irish residents when they fell on hard times. Also important was his view that the numbers of long stay Irish being thrown on the rates were high during the economic depression of 1847. At the same meeting, J Hodgson claimed that a major cause of the increase in outdoor relief for the Irish was the number of *new* immigrants claiming five years residence. Hodgson did not produce any evidence of this and Alderman Walker, Chairman, said that as a magistrate he had come across few such cases.[23] There is no doubt the cost of the relief for the famine refugees would have been higher but for the fact that the Manchester guardians took a tough line with regard to threatening removal. In the context of analysing the financial implications of Irish famine immigration into Manchester, it is certain that the threat of removal kept down expenditure on outdoor relief for the Irish. As in the case of Liverpool, outdoor relief spent on the Manchester Irish as a proportion of total outdoor spending, was permanently higher after the famine. Over the eight years 1846/47 to 1853/54, it averaged 35 per cent, compared with the 16 per cent in 1845/46. The data in Table 9.3 display a contrast with the Liverpool situation in that the expenditure on the Irish is highly correlated with the expenditure on the English. More particularly, it follows the conditions in the local labour market more closely than was the case of expenditure on the Irish in Liverpool, reflecting the high proportion of settled Irish in Manchester.

In Scotland the main destination of Irish immigration during the famine years were, as already noted, Glasgow and its immediately surrounding areas. What the data reveal is that the pattern of expenditure in Glasgow parish follows that observed for both Liverpool and Manchester in important respects. In the calendar year 1847, spending on the Irish poor was £20812, expenditure followed in 1848 by expenditure falling to £3950. It differs from the Lancashire experience, however, in that the numbers claiming relief did not fall in proportion to the decline in the absolute amount of spending. This means that 1848 saw a dramatic reduction in *spending per head*.

Table 9.5 below illustrates the absolute levels of expenditure on the Irish poor in key Scottish towns and parishes for the years 1847 and 1848.

Table 9.5 **The number of Irish poor receiving relief out of the poor rates and the cost of such relief: Scotland at Glasgow, Paisley and Edinburgh, calendar years 1847 and 1848.**

	1847			*1848*	*Change*	*Change*
Place	*Nos*	*Cost (£)*	*Nos*	*Cost*	*Nos*	*Cost*
City of Glasgow						
Glasgow *parish*	17 864	20 812	14 880	3 950	-2 984	-16 862
Barony *parish*	13 952	9 092	2 709	1 107	-11 243	-7 985
Gorbals *parish*	nd	nd	133	126	nd	nd
Govan parish annexation	nd	nd	500	295	nd	nd
Borough of Paisley						
Paisley *parish*	nd	nd	297	202	nd	nd
Abbey	nd	nd	419	220	nd	nd
City of Edinburgh						
Edinburgh *parish*	nd	nd	3904	6816	nd	nd
St Cuthberts *parish*	nd	nd	834	276	nd	nd
Canongate *parish*	nd	nd	165	78	nd	nd
Total	31 816	29 904	23 841	13 070	-	-

Source: Irish Poor (1847) and Irish Poor (1848).

In the case of Glasgow parish during 1848 a reduction in expenditure of £16862 was accompanied by a fall in the numbers of Irish claiming relief of only 2984. In 1847, the neighbouring parish of Barony spent £9092 on Irish paupers, this category of spending falling to £1107 in 1848. As Glasgow parish and Barony parish constituted the greater part of Glasgow city, then the city spent a minimum of £29 904 on Irish paupers during 1847. In 1848, this aggregate fell to £5057. In terms of spending per head, during 1847, Glasgow parish spent on average, £1. 3s. 4d, per annum. In 1848, this figure fell to 5s.4d. per head, per year. This low level of outdoor relief demonstrates that the majority of claimants were casual, not long term residents. It is interesting to note that during 1848, Edinburgh parish spent an average of £1.15s. per head in contrast to Glasgow's 5s.4d. In all probability, these paupers were long stay Irish.[24]

Turning to South Wales and the south-west of England, compared to Liverpool and Manchester, data concerning the costs of relief are hard to come by. Referring to Cardiff, table number 9.6 below shows the number of Irish relieved and the cost of such relief over the period October 1846 to 25 March 1854, inclusive.

Table 9.6: The number of Irish paupers relieved in Cardiff township over the period 30 September 1846 to 25 March 1854, and the associated costs

Period	*Number*	*Cost*	*Cost per head*
Half year ending 25 March 1847	1804	302	3s.4d
Year ending 25 March 1848	2971	948	6s.5d
Year ending 25 March 1849	2219	717	6s.6d
Year ending 25 March 1850	3152	812	5s.2d
Year ending 25 March 1851	1338	495	7s.5d
Year ending 25 March 1852	1474	527	7s.2d
Year ending 25 March 1853	1934	694	7s.2d
Year ending 25 March 1854	2016	815	8s.1d

Notes: For the four years ending 25 March 1854, Evan David stated that the total amount paid to Irish paupers was £2531 and a total of 8074 individuals received relief.

Sources: For the period ending 25 March 1850, SC (1854) Minutes of Evidence, Appendix No 14, Summary of Irish Paupers Relieved in the Town of Cardiff and the cost Thereof, from September 1846 to September 1850, paid by the Cardiff Poor Law Union. For the four years ending 25 March 1854, the same Select Committee, Minutes of Evidence, Evan David, Chairman of the Cardiff Union, qq. 6465-6494 and 6560.

The six months ending 25 March 1847 covered the period which witnessed the onset of the crisis associated with the influx of famine refugees. The year ending 25 March, 1848 covered the greater part of Black '47. If we assume that the total cost of Irish pauper relief for the year ending 25 March 1847 was £604 (twice the six month total), then the expenditure of £948 in the following year represented an increase of 57 per cent. The fall in expenditure to £717 in the year ending 25 March 1849, reflects both the tougher policy on removals and the lower numbers of arrivals from Ireland. What is clear is that the secular trend of expenditure by Cardiff on Irish paupers was permanently higher after 1846. This in turn, almost certainly reflects the effects of the Five Year Residency Act giving more Irish the right to poor relief as their residency reached five years.

This view is supported by the cost per head of relief in the years following 1846. Low levels of expenditure per head on outdoor relief reflect claims by transients often spending only one or two nights in the vagrant shed. Even more so than Cardiff, Newport was a port of entry, most arrivals wanting to move inland into Wales and England. This means that most claims for relief on the part of Irish arrivals in 1847 were on the part of people using Newport as a temporary stopping off place. As a consequence, cost per head was initially low and then increased as the famine crisis receded. Unfortunately, no data exist for 1847.

Table 9.7 The number of Irish applications for poor relief at the Newport union and the cost of such relief, 1848-1853 inclusive.

Year	*Numbers of applications*	*Cost*	*Cost per head to nearest penny*
1848	12 661	£184.15s.7d	4
1849	11 007	£467.7s.5¼d	10
1850	7 713	£410.10s.10½d	13
1851	4 992	£324.4s.9d	16
1852	6 698	£317.12s.10d	11
1853	3 299	£319.2s.9d	23

Source: For 1849-53, SC (1854) Minutes of Evidence, J. Salter, q. 6778, p.496. For 1848, BPP (HC) 1849. Returns of the Irish Poor Relieved out of the Poor Rates during the year ended 31 December 1848, in the parishes comprised in the Borough of Newport.

The area described in parliamentary papers as London consisted of 33 unions and parishes. In turn, these can be subsumed under the cities of London and Westminster and the London boroughs. For ease of presentation this latter classification is adopted in Table 9.8.

Table 9.8 The number of poor Irish relieved in London and the cost of such relief in each of the calendar years 1847 and 1848.

Place	*1847*		*1848*	
	Number	*Cost (£)*	*Number*	*Cost (£)*
City of London	5 640	3 193	4 685	3 446
Borough of Marylebone	17 598	5 294	7 303	1 409
City of Westminster	18 292	989	10 640	1 220
Borough of Southwark	5 708	2 060	6 797	1 927
Borough of Lambeth	2 052	1 010	2 561	1 857
Borough of Tower Hamlets	22 808	8 274	10 778	3 299
Borough of Finsbury	8 421	5 803	8 920	6 852
Total	80 519	26 623	51 684	20 010

Source: Irish Poor (1847) and Irish Poor (1848)

It is not clear whether these data refer to individuals receiving relief or the number of instances. Either way, the borough of Tower Hamlets incurred the greatest absolute cost of relieving Irish poverty in 1847, followed closely by the boroughs of Finsbury and Marylebone. However, the total cost of Irish outdoor relief to the city of London would be higher than the £3193 recorded because one union in the city of London did not send a return in 1847 whereas in 1848 the Irish cost the same union £1949. The breakdown of the totals is given in Appendix No. 9.12. In terms of absolute levels of expenditure by the individual parishes during 1847, the parish of St Giles in the Fields and St George's, Bloomsbury topped the list with spending of £4509 followed next by the parish of St Marylebone with a total outdoor relief expenditure of £3437. In the year 1848, St Giles in the Fields and St Georges, again spent more in absolute terms than any other parish or union for which data exists, some £3694. St Mary-le-bone did not return any statistics and in 1848 the next highest spender on Irish outdoor relief was the parish of Holborn, with £2594. These data must be regarded as the *minimum* spent on the Irish in the London area. We do not know the medical expenditure in these two years, the additional labour costs nor the indoor relief expenditure. Also we do not have any information on the numbers of the Irish who had acquired the five year residency status.

IV

The *levels* of expenditure in various unions revealed above leaves unresolved the issue of whether or not this expenditure on Irish paupers imposed a burden on ratepayers in Britain. It is obvious that had there been no expenditure on Irish poor relief in Britain, then ratepayers would not have lost personal purchasing power. However, as there is overwhelming written evidence that the Irish were considered to have made a considerable contribution to economic growth in the regions where they had a presence, then to the extent that they were 'five year residents' by 1847, they were in no different category than English, Welsh and Scots paupers. We have noted that many famine Irish did not claim relief in 1847 because of a fear of removal. Despite this, many famine Irish did claim relief and this was a cost to be attributed to the famine, together with other associated costs such as medicine, nurses, doctors, relieving officers and so on. Unfortunately, the available data often do not make clear what they refer to. However, some reasonable estimates can be made of the burden of Irish poor relief attributed to the famine. Liverpool and Glasgow are the only two places for which reasonably good evidence exists regarding the total cost of the famine Irish in 1847. By total, I mean all the costs associated with the immigration in that year, medicine, burials, etc.

We shall deal first with Liverpool. The estimated costs of the Irish poor relief are given below for Liverpool. The figure of £33 159 is the estimated cost of the famine Irish to the Liverpool ratepayers.

Table 9.9 The estimated cost of the relief for the Famine Irish in Liverpool during the year 1847.

Type of expenditure	*Costs per £*
Outdoor relief for the Irish, year ending 25 March 1848	13 713
Indoor relief for the Irish, year ending 25 March 1848	3 167
Irish children in the industrial schools (orphans)	715
Wages of crews on lazarettos [1]	525
Pauper burials (graveyards, coffins, clergymen's fees, etc.) [2]	1 332
Fever sheds [3]	7 375
Medical officers' salaries [4]	2 263
Removals to Ireland (15 000 at five shillings per head)[5]	4 068
Medical relief for paupers	1 240
Total	34 398
Less government grant	1 239
Net total expenditure	33 159

Note: see Appendix No. 9.5 for the basis of these estimated costs.

The rateable value of property on which this sum was levied was £1109798. However, after allowing for ratepayers excused on the grounds of poverty, the tax base fell to £929 645. As a result, the rate per pound attributed to the famine crisis in 1847 was 8½ pence per pound (the cost of all poor Irish in Liverpool over the same period was £35 258 or 9¼ pence in the pound). The statistical results given above are robust. By this is meant that if the total amount of expenditure attributable to the Irish refugees differs from my estimate, within reason, the results will not change in any significant way. If the actual expenditure was ten per cent higher than £33 159, we have £36475. This would result in a rate of 9 pence per pound or one half penny more. Conversely, if the actual expenditure had been £ 29 843 or ten per cent less, the rate would have been 7¾ pence per pound. The point being made is that my estimate would have to be seriously out to change the conclusion concerning the burden of the famine Irish on ratepayers. The wealthiest rate payers contributed 84 per cent of the poor rates.

In the case of the parish of Glasgow the on-costs of the famine Irish over the period January-November 1847 amounted to £21 306. Extrapolated over 12 months, this gives a total expenditure of £23 243. These costs were attributed specifically to the famine crisis. In addition during 1847, the parish of Glasgow paid out £20 812 in relief to Irish paupers, but not all of these would have been famine Irish. If we assume 70 per cent were famine refugees we have an estimated £14 568 paid out in relief. Added to the on-costs based on Table 9.10, this gives a total of £37 811. However, this includes £8000 spent on a new workhouse and it is debatable whether this can be attributed to the famine refugees. Deducting this, the total would fall to £29 811. The rateable value of property in the parish of Glasgow in 1847 was £615 452 and using the figure of £29 811, we obtain a rate of 11½ pence per pound, being 35 per cent greater than the estimated rate for Liverpool (see Appendices Nos 9.6, 9.7 and 9.8).

Table 9.10 The cost to the parish of Glasgow of destitute famine Irish in January-November, 1847 (inclusive).

Expenditure	*Cost in pounds (£)*
Infirmary	3 713
Grant to the infirmary	300
Temporary relief	6 000
Internments	565
Wine, rice, etc.	577
Clothing	170
Transmission of paupers	761
Inspection of steamboats	500
Cost of erecting new Poor house	8 000
Extra officials' salaries	350
Extra pay to district surgeons	170
Medicine	200
Total	21 306

Source: Strathclyde, Meeting of Glasgow Parochial Board, held 30 November 1847, p. 204.

With regard to Manchester township, the estimated costs of the famine resulting from the 1847 crisis are given in Table 9.10. Given a total of rateable value of property of £759 862 in the township of Manchester, the above expenditure of £17 661 works out at a rate of 5½ pence per pound. For a ten pound householder this was a rates bill of four shillings and 7 pence per annum. Unlike Liverpool, few ratepayers were excused payments on the grounds of poverty.

Table 9.11 The estimated cost of the famine Irish to the township of Manchester during the calendar year 1847.

Item	*Cost (£)*
Outdoor relief	7 002
Removals	999
Fever sheds and medical expenses	8 580
Pauper burials	270
Extra relieving officers, and clerks	810
Total	17 661

Note: for basis of calculations see Appendix 9.10

The only other place for which reasonable data exists regarding the cost of the famine crisis is Cardiff.

Table 9.12 The estimated costs to the Cardiff Union of the famine refugees during the year ending 25 March 1848.

Item of expenditure	*Cost (£)*
Cost of Irish paupers, for the year ending 25 March	947
Cost of medical expenses attributed to Irish fever	160
Cost of Irish pauper burials	102
Removals of paupers to Ireland	138
Total	1347

Source: For the basis of these costs see Appendix 9.14

In 1847, the rateable value of property in Cardiff assessed to the poor rate was £145 799. The estimated expenditure of £1347 on the famine Irish would have needed a rate of 2¼ pence in the pound. In the case of London unions and parishes, there are no easily available data regarding the on-costs associated with the influx of famine refugees. Of the 33 poor law areas, the highest rates resulting solely from outdoor relief for the Irish, were in the parishes of St George in the East and St Georges, Bloomsbury (see Appendices Nos 9.12 and 9.13). A summary of all these costings is given below.

Table 9.13 The rate per pound reflecting the total cost of Irish famine refugees in selected unions and parishes, during the year 1847.

Union or Parish	*Rate per pound in pence*
Liverpool	8½
Glasgow	11½
Manchester	5½
Cardiff	2¼
London	
St George in the East	4¼
St Georges, Bloomsbury	4½

Glasgow emerges as the most highly rated of the unions which became centres of Irish settlement. One reason for this was that Glasgow's tax base was much smaller than Liverpool's.

For other towns, there is simply an absence of detailed costs incurred by the unions as a direct result of the 1847 famine influx.

V

Finally, we come to the issue of whether or not the press campaign against the alleged burden of taxation on local ratepayers resulting from the famine immigration, was justified. Was the cost of the famine refugees a crippling burden in that it forced businesses into bankruptcy and individuals on to the parish? During 1847, in all urban areas, some firms did go out of business under the joint effect of the business slump and increased rates. Similarly, some people on low incomes must have had their consumption expenditure severely curtailed as a result of the rate increases. These effects would not have been evenly distributed. As we have observed, in some towns large numbers of ratepayers were excused payments of poor rates on the grounds of poverty. The two contrasting towns in this respect were Manchester and Liverpool. However, the *total* increase in the poor rate during 1847 also reflected the large increase in the numbers of English, Welsh and Scots claiming poor relief. Despite this, it cannot be denied that the Irish famine refugees did exert pressure on ratepayers in what was a disastrous year for the economy. There were also knock on effects into the future. For example, many of the cholera patients in the 1849 outbreak were among the newly arrived destitute Irish. In Cardiff, this cost the union more than ten times the expenditure on famine fever.

Given the range and quality of data available, the tentative conclusion must be that with respect to the wealthier or business ratepayers it was not a disaster. This is not to deny that certain towns, particularly Liverpool and Glasgow, incurred severe and long lasting social consequences as a result of the famine immigration. However, here we are considering specifically, the burden of local taxation. With regard to most host communities it has not been possible to identify the rates burden arising from the famine refugees as opposed to the cost of the long term resident Irish. In the case of Liverpool, however, a plausible estimate has been made and the evidence does not support the press claims that the local taxpayers incurred a crushing financial burden. In 1847, nearly 25000 ratepayers in Liverpool were excused payments of rates on the grounds of poverty. This means that though there was widespread poverty in the town, the working classes in general, did not finance the payment of poor relief for the Irish during the famine crisis. The threat of removal reduced the volume of Irish claims after 1847 and so expenditure on the Irish poor in Liverpool fell dramatically. It is true that expenditure on the Irish in general remained higher after 1847 than was the case before, but this was spending on the resident Irish who were long term contributors to Liverpool's labour force. This increased volume of expenditure on the long term Irish was mirrored in a permanent increase in expenditure on poor relief for the non-Irish in Liverpool, that is,

English and Welsh. A further factor to be taken into account is that those wealthier members of Liverpool society who did pay rates were, in many cases, employers of unskilled labour and so benefitted from the downward pressure on wages exerted by the reserve army of unemployed Irish. The prosperity of the port of Liverpool was not affected by the Irish famine influx; indeed, the massive reserve army of unemployed labourers benefited employers.

Manchester's Irish appear to have been principally long stay Irish and the *pattern* of poor relief expenditure appears to have been the same. The year 1847 saw a large increase in poor relief expenditure on the Irish, followed by a dramatic falling off in 1848 and subsequent years. This reflected the effects of the trade cycle and the fact of a majority of the Irish having five years residency. As in the case of Liverpool, the threat of removal kept down the claims from the newly arrived Irish immigrants. More was spent on the Irish in Manchester than in Liverpool, reflecting the fact of a more permanent Irish population in Manchester. The experience of Glasgow is more related to that of Manchester than Liverpool, but it has not been possible to separate spending on the long term residents from that on the famine refugees. Though spending in total fell in 1848 compared with 1847, the numbers claiming relief remained high. The evidence of the London unions does not support the argument that Irish pauperism was crushing the business communities. Again, in both Manchester and Glasgow, the rates paid do not seem to have been 'crippling' or 'disastrous'. Also, the employers of labour benefitted from the presence of a large permanent labour force. Similarly, the same pattern of expenditure arising from the same considerations occurred in south Wales, Bristol and Newport. None of this should be taken to mean that there were no social costs to British towns resulting from the famine crisis. On the contrary, the major areas of settlement incurred severe and long lasting costs in terms of overcrowding, health and, in some areas, public order. In most cases, much of these social costs were intimately linked with the poverty of the immigrants and, in turn, this partly reflected the effects of deterring claims for relief by the threat of removal. In judging the reactions of ratepayers nationwide to the 1847 crisis it is important to keep in mind the severity of the economic downturn. There was widespread distress and many businesses were folding. Looking back on the year, the Barony Parochial Board recorded that:

> ... the increase in pauperism during those nine months is without parallel in any year preceding since the passing of the Poor Law Amendment Act (sic August 1845)... the great increase in pauperism is not so much wondered at - first the failure of the potato crop and the consequent dearth and high prices of provisions, next the fever pestilence which

followed thereon and lastly, the unprecedented depression in trade, have all concurred in causing the increase... the Committee without mentioning names, may state that many very wealthy merchants from whom hundreds of pounds of an assessment on their incomes were anticipated, paid nothing, having lost the whole of their means and that distress pervaded all classes...

Given the perception of economic disaster, the increased rates bills resulting from famine Irish immigration rubbed up raw feelings already inflamed by the trade depression and a high level of unemployment.

In the case of Liverpool, a rate increase of 11½ pence because of Irish famine destitution meant that for a working class householder paying £10 a year rent, these extra rates amounted to nine shillings seven pence. This was roughly the equivalent to half a week's wage for a labourer. Ratepayers would not be aware of how much the Irish famine refugees were costing them personally but the press outcry over the expense of poor relief would, in all towns, have created the perception of the Irish in particular as a cause of their troubles. Had the Irish famine crisis not occurred, the non Irish poor in Britain would not have received more in poor relief but there was a feeling among sections of the working class that the Irish were diverting funds which would have been available to relieve their distress. This belief damaged inter-communal relations in Britain's areas of Irish settlement.

Appendices

Appendix 9.1 **Expenditure on the Irish poor in Liverpool, indoor and outdoor relief, and Irish children in the Industrial School, 1844-54**

Year ending 25 March	*Outdoor* £	*Workhouse* £	*Industrial Sch* £	*Total*
1844/45	498	2642	-	3 140
1845/46	648	2221	47	2 916
1846/47	9 648	2487	479	12 614
1847/48	20 750	4223	953	25 926
1848/49	8 337	3727	610	12 674
1849/50	8 066	5450	533	14 049
1850/51	6 835	5102	591	12 258
1851/52	6 731	6172	576	13 479
1852/53	5 970	5639	642	12 251
1853/54	6 595	6843	994	14 432

Source: SC (1854) Minutes of Evidence, Appendix 8, p. 592.

Appendix 9.2 Numbers and costs of Irish paupers removed from the parish of Liverpool, 25 June 1846 to 25 December 1847.

Quarter ending	*Numbers*	*Cost (£)*
25 June 1846	998	£106 16s 6d
25 September 1846	1136	£128 2s 9d
25 December 1846	2201	£234 7s 0d
25 March 1847	2271	£242 6s 9d
25 June 1847	3809	£526 7s 3d
25 September 1847	4323	£820 4s 6d
25 December 1847	4274	£862 19s 3d

Total Expense of Removing Irish for the Quarter ending 25 December 1846

Fares on steamers	£862 19s 3d
Maintenance at Vulcan Street	£57 0s 0d
Magistrates' Fees (clerks)	£276 2s 0d
Rent at Vulcan Street	£75 0s 0d
Maintenance on board ship	£252 0s 9d
Parish officers' wages	£94 18s 0d
Total cost:	£1618 0s 0d

Source: *Liverpool Mercury* 7 January 1848; Meeting of the Select Vestry, 4 January 1848.

Appendix 9.3 An account of the different classes of tenements valued to the poor rates in the township of Stockport

Tenements rateable value	*Numbers in the rate in November 1841*	*Description of dwelling & by whom chiefly occupied*
£2 and under	975	Cellars and backhouses, occupied by
over £2 and under £4	2 307	operatives and labourers, including the Irish.
over £4 and under £8	2 898	The better paid classes of operatives, including mechanics, artisans, etc.
over £8 and under £12	476	Overlookers, book-keepers and other persons holding positions of trust.
over £12 and under £20	303	Small shopkeepers and persons of small independent means.
over £20 and under £40	235	Larger shopkeepers, publicans and the higher
over £40 and under £60	62	classes of private residences.
£60 and over	44	
Mills	40	
Land	124	
	7 464	

Note: 1632 dwelling houses empty at the time. 3000 defaulted in paying rates; 1950 defaulters summoned, of whom 1134 were excused on the grounds of poverty.
Sources: BPP (HC) 1842 , Vol XXXV, p. 6, 'Report of the Commissioners for Inquiry into the State of the Population of Stockport.

Appendix 9.4 The number of tenements assessed for the poor rate and the number of each category excused payment of the poor rate on the grounds of poverty of the tenant, Manchester and Salford townships, Borough of Liverpool, Toxteth Park.

Rateable Value	*Manchester township*		*Salford township*		*Liverpool borough*		*Toxteth Park*	
	No of tenants	*Number excused*	*No of tenants*	*Number excused*	*No of tenants*	*Number excused*	*No of tenants*	*Number excused*
under £4	2 326	35	1 012		27	25	299	287
£4 and under £5	3 990	24	1 643		142	118	95	93
£5 and under £6	6 302	56	2 196		679	606	374	333
£6 and under £8	6 983	56	3 068		7 137	6 984	2 307	2 285
£8 and under £10	4 504	62	1 699		8 957	8 752	1 750	1 738
£10 and under £12	2 990	82	877		4 241	3 978	1 500	1424
£12 and under £15	2 648	91	568		5 032	136	1 345	1 066
£15 and under £20	1 647	24	711		4 374	134	1 440	787
£20 and over	6 809	19	1 071		12 501	72	2 545	504
Total	38 199	449	12 845		43 090	20 805	11 655	8 517
Date of Rate	27 June 1847		12 September 1848		29 May 1848		30 July 1847	
Amount of such a rate	£145 675 13s 11½d				£160 257 15s		£17 007 12s 9d	
Numbers such assessed at such a rate	38 499		12 688		43 090		11 646	
Total no. of dwelling houses in assessment of such a rate	30 283		12 151		37 435		11 295	

Source: BPP (HC) 1849 (630) XLVII, 'A Return from the Several Parishes and Townships in the Counties of Lancashire, Suffolk, Hampshire and Gloucestershire, respectively, of the number of tenements asessed to the rate for the Relief of the Poor'.

Appendix 9.5 Estimating the cost of the famine Irish refugees on the parish of Liverpool and identifying on which category of ratepayer on which the taxation burden fell, 1847.

It is first necessary to undertake three calculations:-

1. Measure the total cost of providing for the famine refugees during the year 1847.
2. Identify the amount of rated property that actually paid the poor rate.
3. Identify which category of ratepayer incurred the tax.

The cost of the famine Irish during 1847

The main categories of cost were indoor relief, outdoor relief, removals, nurses, doctors, burials, renting of extra hospital space and administrative costs of the police. Unfortunately, the financial year ending 25 March 1848 covers only threequarters of the famine crisis, and so there is a problem in allocating costs which fell in the period January-March 1847. I have taken the financial year as the basis of my calculations. With respect to allocating costs to the Famine Irish, I have had to make certain assumptions. The principal ones are (i) of the total expenditure of £20 750 in Irish outdoor relief over the year ending 25 March 1848 (Table 9.1) I have deducted £7037 as a (minimum) cost of outdoor relief for long term Irish relief, this gives a balance of £13 713. (ii) In respect of the expenditure of £4223 on Irish in the workhouse over the same period, I have here assumed 75 per cent of this, £3167, was on the Famine Irish. This is a conservative estimate but even if it was 100 per cent it would not make much difference to the rate per pound. (iii) In the same financial year, £953 was spent on Irish children and orphans in the Industrial School, again I have assumed 75 per cent was on the Famine Irish, this yields a figure of £715.

The incidence of taxation

Using the data in Table 9.4, we can establish that 22 785 tenements paid the poor rate ie 20 805 were excused payment on the grounds of poverty. The gross rateable value of property in the Borough of Liverpool was £1109 798, using again the Table in Appendix 9.4 as a frequency distribution we can estimate the total rateable value of property excused payment of rate, this comes to £184 045. In calculating this, I have assumed the average rateable value of property in the category of £20 or over, to be £63. These calculations mean that the estimated total rateable value on which the poor rate was levied was £929 645.

The amount of property that actually paid poor rate during 1847

Again using appendix no 9.4 we can calculate the amount of rateable property in each category. For example, for tenements rated £5 and under £6, 73 incurred rates, so that 73 x £5.50 = £401.50 rateable value on average. Repeating this exercise, we arrive at the total of £929 645 rateable value of property on which the occupiers were *not* excused payment. Of this total, £923 323 fell on property rated at £12 or over the type owned at the lower end by the 'respectable working class' (£12-£15) while £783 027, or 84 per cent, was paid by the occupiers of houses rated at £20 or over. I have assumed an average of £63 rateable value for this class. Homes rated at £20 or over were those occupied by the business and middle classes.

Notes[1] The lazarettos were supplied by the government. The Select Vestry reported on 5 July that the government had sent a bill for £700. I have attributed 75 per cent of this to the Famine Irish. See *Liverpool Mail*, 9 July 1848. [2] During 1847, 7219 paupers were buried by the parish

in the two pauper graveyards, St Mary's, Cambridge Street, and St Martin's in the Fields, Vauxhall. Of these, 5237 were Catholics. I have assumed all were either fever victims or died of famine related diseases, and also assumed all were Irish. Those Catholics who were English will balance out the unknown numbers of Irish who were Protestants. The age distribution of the dead suggests old age was hardly a factor in these burials. I have costed a funeral at 5 shillings per head; this was the average cost of burying a Catholic at St Anthony's over the same period. [3] The fever sheds and related expenses cost £8677, but a government grant was received reducing the net cost. I have assumed 85 per cent of patients were Irish.
[4] Data given at a meeting of the Select Vestry held on 14 May 1850. See *Liverpool Mail*, 18 May 1850. Again I have attributed 75 per cent of the total to the Irish. See also *Liverpool Chronicle*, 20 April 1850. [5] SC (1854) Minutes of Evidence. A. Campbell, q. 5026, p. 369. A Table gives the number of Irish removals.

Appendix 9.6 Receipts and expenditures relating to the relief of the poor in England and Wales.

Financial year ending 25 March	*Receipts from Rates*	*Receipts from aid*	*Total Receipts*	*Expenditure for the relief of the poor*	*Average price of wheat by imperial qtr*	
	£	£	£	£	*sh.*	*d*
1839/40	6014 605	227 966	6242 571	4576 965	68	6
1840/41	6351 828	226 904	6578 732	4760 929	65	3
1841/42	6552 890	201 514	6754 404	4911 498	64	0
1842/43	7085 595	219 066	7304 661	5208 027	54	4
1843/44	6847 205	219 592	7066 797	4976 093	51	5
1844/45	6791 006	218 508	7009 514	5039 703	49	2
1845/46	6800 623	187 043	6987 666	4954 204	53	3
1846/47	6964 825	152 527	7117 352	5298 787	59	0
1847/48	7817 430	1586 64	7976 094	6180 764	64	6
1848/49	7674 146	199 751	7873 897	5292 963	49	1
1849/50	7270 493	230 002	7500 495	5393 022	42	7
1850/51	6778 914	181 408	6960 322	4962 704	39	11
1851/52	6552 298	318 070	6870 368	4897 685	39	4
1852/53	6522 298	282 971	6805 269	4939 064	42	0
1853/54	6973 220	278 061	7251 281	5282 853	61	7
1854/55	7864 149	310 805	8174 954	5890 041	70	0
1855/56	8201 348	295 110	8496 458	6004 244	75	4
1856/57	8139 003	301 981	8440 984	5898 756	65	3
1857/58	8188 880	303 240	8492 120	5878 542	53	10

Source: BPP Poor Law Board 11th Annual Report.

Appendix 9.7 A return of the size of populations, annual value of property and rate of assessment, together with expenditure on poor relief in selected parishes of Scotland for the year 1847.

Parish	*Population 1841*	*Annual value of property* £	*Amount of assessment* £	*Rate per pound*	*Expenditure* *Management* £	*Litigation* £	*Actual relief* £	*Total relieved*	*% of total*
Barony	106 075	415 948	15 920	9d	1 062	162	15 271	19 351	18.2
Glasgow	120 183	615 452	41 091	1s.4d	11 178	69	29 844	16 474	13.7
Glassford	1 736	6 700	221	7d	20	10	181	45	
Gorbals	[1]10 200	-	1 138 }		209	446	1 004	1 262	
Govan			}	11d					
i Gorbals district 38 075}	45 885	[2]154 619	5 908 }		575	23	5 250	8 080	12.3
ii Govan district 7 810}									
Edinburgh	56 330	[3]657 664	39 696	1s.2½d	1 753	470	19 123	4 558	17.6

Notes: [1]included in Govan; [2]includes Gorbals; [3] includes Cannongate and St Cuthberts
Source: BPP (HC) 1850 (5) L.265, 'Return of Population, Value of Property and Rate of Assessment. Amount spent on Management, Litigation and Relief: Number of Paupers Relieved in Scotland 1847-48'.

Appendix 9.8 A return of the size of populations, annual value of property and rate of assessment, together with expenditure on poor relief in selected parishes of Scotland for the year 1848.

Parish		Population 1841	Annual value of property £	Amount of assessment £		Rate per pound	Expenditure: Management £	Expenditure: Litigation £	Expenditure: Actual relief £	Total relieved	% of total
Barony		106 075	415 948	30 420		1s.6d	1769	299	26 250	33 496	31.5
Glasgow		120 183	615 452	58 441		1s.10¾d	5470	58	61 881	59 465	49.0
Glassford		1 736	6 700	310		11d	36	-	185	73	4.2
Gorbals		[1]10 200	-	2 027	}		552	22	1 457	895	8.7
Govan					}	1s.2¾					
i Gorbals district	38 075}	45 885	[2]154 619	7 499	}		720	38	7 597	3 925	8.5
ii Govan district	7 810}										
Edinburgh		56 330	[3]657 664	51 844		1s.7d	1872	294	24 834	8 480	15.0

Notes: [1]included in Govan; [2]includes Gorbals; [3] Includes Cannongate and St Cuthberts

Source: BPP (HC) 1850 [5] L.265, 'Return of Population, Value of Property and Rate of Assessment. Amount spent on Management, Litigation and Relief: Number of Paupers Relieved in Scotland 1847-48'.

Appendix 9.9 The expenditure on Irish poor relief in the principal areas of Irish settlement in Scotland: 1847 and 1848

Parish	1847 expenditure				1848 expenditure			
	Irish £	*Total £*	*Irish as %*	*Irish as rate per pound*	*Irish £*	*Total £*	*Irish as %*	*Irish as rate per pound*
Glasgow	20 832	29 844	70	8.12	3950	61 881	6.4	1.5
Barony	9 092	15 271	60	5.25	1107	26 250	4.2	0.63
Gorbals	nd	1 004	-	-	126	1 457	8.6	0.2
Govan	nd	5 250	-	-	295	7 597	3.9	0.46
Paisley	nd	-	-	-	202	-	-	-
Abbey	nd	-	-	-	220	-	-	-
Edinburgh } St Cuthberts } Canongate }	nd	19 123	-	-	7176	24 834	-	2.62

Sources: Irish Poor (1847) and Irish Poor (1848)) The data for total poor relief in Scotland BPP (HC) 1850 (5) L.265, Return of the Population, Value of Property and Rates of Assessment, Amounts spent on Management, Litigation and Relief of the Poor in Scotland, 1847-48.

Appendix 9.10 The estimated rates burden of the famine Irish in Manchester township for the year 1847.

Outdoor poor relief for the Irish

1. The total spent on Irish applicants was £28,007. If we assume that 25 per cent of this was on newly arrived Irish then we obtain a figure of £7,002. This assumption is not unreasonable given the fact that many famine Irish stopped applying for relief because of a threat of removal. In 1848, over 90 per cent of all expenditure on the Irish was on 'settled Irish'.

Pauper burials

2. During 1847, a total of 1492 deaths occurred from fever (report of Dr Noble, Long Millgate Hospital, *Manchester Guardian* 15 April 1848). If we assume 75 per cent of all these deaths were newly arrived Irish or the friends with whom they lodged, then we have 1119 deaths. I have assumed a cost of five shillings per burial.

Removals

The number of removals was given by J. Harrop, Clerk to the Manchester Union to the Select Committee on Poor Removal, 1854, qq. 6231-6232. The average cost of removing 1902 Irish from Manchester to Ireland was ten shillings and sixpence, Appendix no. 5, Table F.

Medical costs

The medical costs of the epidemic, including fever sheds, given by *Manchester Guardian,* 12 May 1849. It is not clear if this total covers the cost of doctors, nurses and medicine.

Rateable value of property

The rateable value of property in 1847 in the union of Manchester was £885,785. However within the union, the overwhelming majority of Irish were in the township of Manchester which had property valued at £759 862 or 86 per cent of the union. I have used this as a tax basis.

Appendix 9.11 The number of Irish poor relieved during the year ending 31 December 1847

Place	*Numbers*	*Expenditure*[1] *(£)*
Borough of Liverpool[2]	47 194	20 750
City of Glasgow Parish	17 864	20 832
Barony *Parish*	13 952	9 092
City of London	5 640	3 193
Borough of Marylebone	17 598	5 294
City of Westminster	18 292	1 134
Borough of Southwork	6 008	2 060
Borough of Lambeth	2 052	1 010
Tower Hamlets	22 868	7 773
Finsbury	8 421	5 802

[1] Expenditure rounded off to nearest pound.
[2]. Liverpool number estimated by the Liverpool authorities

Source: Irish Poor (1847)

Appendix 9.12 The numbers of Irish receiving outdoor poor relief in the parishes and unions of London during the calendar years of 1847 and 1848 and the cost of such relief

Union or parish	*1847*		*1848*	
	Number	*Cost (£)*	*Number*	*Cost (£)*
City of London				
City of London unions	nd	nd	2151	1949
East London union	2 768	1561	2534	1497
West London union	2 872	1632	nd	nd
Borough of Marylebone				
St Mary-le-Bone parish	7 864	3437	nd	nd
St Pancras parish	9 660	1813	6072	1341
Paddington parish	74	44	1231	68
City of Westminster				
Strand union	1 118	492	1129	445
St Margaret & St John parish	nd	nd	nd	nd
St George, Hanover Sq. parish	4 000	150	3500	130
St James', Westminster parish	1 600	337	1131	396
St Martin in the Fields parish	11 574	145	4880	249
Borough of Southwark				
Rotherhithe parish	272	162	283	126
Bermondsey parish	571	144	1175	213
St Olave's parish	2 536	317	3727	900
St Saviour's parish	1 183	960	553	560
St George the Marthyr parish	1 146	277	1029	128
Borough of Lambeth				
St Mary, Newington parish	231	276	537	425
Camberwell parish	326	216	1273	640
Lambeth parish	1 495	518	1231	792
Borough of Tower Hamlets				
Bethnal Green parish	53	105	28	18
St George in the East parish	5 941	2454	nd	nd
Hackney union	52	3	55	26
Poplar union	879	666	5230	1719
Stepney union	7 783	2529	nd	nd
Shoreditch parish	1 847	858	1987	44
Whitechapel union	6 253	1659	3478	1493
Borough of Finsbury				
St Giles in the Fields & St George, Bloomsbury	4 974	4509	2578	3694
St Mary, Islington	682	126	2114	564
Clerkenwell parish	nd	nd	nd	nd
Holborn parish	2 765	1168	4520	2594

Source: Irish Poor (1847) and Irish Poor (1848)

Appendix 9.13 The expenditure on poor relief for the Irish in the Poor Law Union and Parishes of London calendar years 1847 and 1848

Name of parish/union	*Rateable value of property in 1847 (£)*	*Poor relief expenditure on the Irish 1847*			*Poor relief expenditure on the Irish 1848*			*Expressed as rate of pence per pound 1847*	*Expressed as rate of pence per pound 1848*
		£	*s*	*d*	*£*	*s*	*d*		
Bethnal Green (P)	95 549	104	16	8	18	8	7	0.26	0.05
Chelsea (P)	123 200			-			-	-	-
Hackney (U)	160 981	3	4	0	25	11	6	0.004	0.04
Holborn (U)	182 860	1167	19	6	2593	18	7	1.53	3.40
Kensington (P)	148 368			nd			nd	-	-
City of London (U)	613 883			nd	1948	12	5	-	¾
East London (U)	140 139	1561	2	10	1497	4	6	2.67	2.56
West London (U)	108 089	1632	7	7			nd	3.62	-
Paddington (U)	209 076	43	13	2	68	8	9	0.05	0.08
Poplar (U)	160 657	666	1	4	1719	0	0	1.00	2.57
St George in the East (P)	141301	2453	16	3			nd	4.17	-
St Martin in the Fields (P)	239 996	144	13	6	249	7	3¼	0.14	2.0
Stepney (U)	212 603	2528	12	1			nd	2.85	-
Strand (U)	211 521	492	1	9	444	11	4	0.55	0.5
Whitechapel (U)	197 524	1658	11	11	1492	12	5	2.01	1.81
Bermondsey (P)	88 492	144	1	9	212	12	6	0.39	0.58
Camberwell (P)	153 278	216	2	4	639	14	1	0.34	1.0
Lambeth (P)	449 142	518	6	6	791	18	0	0.28	0.42
Rotherhithe (P)	49 806	161	13	3	126	7	0	0.78	0.61
St George the Martyr (P)	119 963	277	0	3	127	17	0	0.55	0.26
St Olave (U)	84 076	517	0	4	900	7	0	1.48	0.27
St Saviors (U)	84 372	960	3	10	560	12	0	2.73	1.59

Appendix 9.13 continued

Name of parish/union	*Rateable value of property in 1847 (£)*	*Poor relief expenditure on the Irish 1847*			*Poor relief expenditure on the Irish 1848*			*Expressed as rate of pence per pound 1847*	*Expressed as rate of pence per pound 1848*
		£	*s*	*d*	*£*	*s*	*d*		
St George, Hanover Sq (P)	604 176	150	0	0	130	0	0	0.06	0.05
St Giles in the Field & St George, Bloomsbury (P)	236 970	4508	10	6	3694	0	0	4.57	3.74
St James, Clerkenwell (P)	176 338			nd			nd	-	-
St James, Westminster (P)	240 648	337	0	7	395	18	3	0.34	0.39
St Leonards, Shoreditch (P)	169 133	358	3	8	43	19	5	0.51	0.06
St Lukes, Middlesex (P)	136 676			nd	105	14	5	-	0.19
St Margaret & St John Westminster (P)	168 440			nd			nd	-	-
St Mary's, Islington (P)	212 283	126	7	8	561	10	2½	0.14	0.63
St Marylebone (P)	816 480	3437	0	6			nd	1.01	-
St Pancras (P)	582 000	1813	4	0	1340	11	7	0.75	0.55
St Mary, Newington (P)	161 802	275	10	7	425	3	8	0.41	0.63

Source: Irish Poor (1847) and Irish Poor (1848),'Rateable values: BPP (HC) 1851 Vol. 'A Return showing the Rateable Value of the Property Assessed To the Relief of the Poor in the Several Parishes of the Metropolis'.

Appendix 9 14: The number of Irish paupers relieved in the township of Cardiff and the cost of such relief, together with other related costs associated with the famine influx.

		Number	*Cost*
Half year ending	25 March 1847	1 804	£302.1s.0½d
Year ending	25 March 1848	2 971	£947.9s.0¼d
Year ending	25 March 1849	2 219	£716.11s.2¾d
Year ending	25 March 1850	3 152	£811.12s.6½d
Half year ending	30 September 1850	1 308	£265.19s.2½d
Total		11 454	£3043.13s.0½d
Other Expenses incurred over same period			
Funerals of Irish paupers		493	£448.0s.8d
Midwifery cases		183	£130.0s.0d
Removals to Ireland *over last 3 years*		326	£223.17s.5d
Expenses paid to Cardiff Union *on account of Irish famine fever*		-	£160.3s.4d
Expenses paid to Cardiff Union on account of Cholera in 1849 mainly Irish cases		-	£1670.3s.0d
Total			£2632.4s.5d
Grand total cost over the four years			£5675.17s.5½d

Note: The number of pauper burials averaged 123 per year over this period. However, many of these would have occurred in the 1849 Cholera outbreak so I have averaged these, 112 per annum.

Source: SC (1854) Appendix 14.

Appendix 9.15 The comparative number of Irish relieved in several unions in the March quarter of 1846 and 1847

Lancashire	*1846*	*1847*	*Yorkshire West Riding*	*1846*	*1847*
Ashton under Lyne	173	997	Leeds	756	3120
Blackburn	12	65	Pateley Bridge	0	20
Bolton	209	1815	Rotherham	265	611
Burnley	194	892	Selby	40	230
Bury	60	271	Sheffield	178	859
Chorlton	290	762	Skipton	0	899
Clitheroe	76	309	Thorne	5	194
The Fylde	39	309	Wakefield	73	463
Garstang	109	500			
Haslingden	18	229	*Yorkshire (East Riding)*		
Lancaster	46	70	Beverley	259	570
Leigh	25	153	Howden	11	56
Manchester	3103	12 256	Patrington	2	3
Ormskirk	16	2 211	Sculcoates	13	167
Rochdale	37	648			
			Derbyshire		
Salford	231	1 072			
Warrington	28	310	Chapel-en-le-Frith	27	393
Wigan	460	1 657	Glossop	88	405
			Hayfield	21	446
Yorkshire (West Riding)					
			Cheshire		
Bradford	567	1 428			
Dewsbury	58	592	Congleton	690	1617
Doncaster	145	505	Macclesfield	47	90
Halifax	194	2 066	Northwich	123	384
Huddersfield	136	544	Stockport	84	1270
Keighley	1	247			

Source: Austin (1847), Appendix A, p.188.

Notes and References

1 *Newcastle Journal*, 2 Jan 1847.
2 *Newcastle Journal*, 1 May 1847.
3 *Halifax Guardian*, 20 February 1847.
4 *Halifax Guardian*, 13 May 1847.
5 *London Times*, 16 February 1847.
6 *Bristol Gazette and Public Advertiser*, 18 March 1847.
7 PRO/MH12/Stockport Union /805B/1847. Letter from Henry Coppock, clerk to the Stockport Union, to Poor Law Commissioners, dated 11 January 1847. ...'very great destitution does exist in some districts and especially amongst that class of inhabitant who are of Irish origin..' The Poor Law Commissioners wrote to the Stockport Guardians 20 January, agreeing to the appointment of an extra relieving officer. '... in

consequence of the great destitution which exists in the Stockport district owing to the influx of Irish paupers..' See MH12/Stockport Union/1141/805B/1847. Letter dated 20 January 1847.

8 PRO/MH12/Ashton-under-Lyne Union/5415/23418/1847. Letter from E.Turner and J.Tipping to Poor Law Commissioners, dated 15 December 1847.

9 PRO/MH12/Ashton under Lyne Union/5415/1847.
Letter from Poor Law Commissioners to the Ashton Guardians, 17 February 1847.

10 PRO/MH12/Gateshead Union/3069/1847. Letter from William Rowntree, clerk to the Union, to Poor Law Commissioners, dated 4 September 1847.

11 PRO/MH12/Gateshead Union/3069/1847 Letter from William Rowntree to Poor Law Commissioners, 26 September 1847.

12 PRO/MH12/Newport Union/8089/1847. Letter from William Brown and James Hawkings, Medical Officers, to Newport Guardians, dated 3 April 1847.

13 PRO/MH12/Prescot Union/6095/1847-49. Letter from John Heyes to Poor Law Commissioners, dated 11 November 1847.

14 SC (1847) Minutes of Evidence. E. Rushton, q.4328-4332, p.54.

15 *Liverpool Mercury*, 7 January 1848. Report on the meeting of the Select Vestry held 4 January 1848.

16 *Liverpool Journal*, 29 January 1848.

17 *The Times*, 26 July 1848.

18 *Liverpool Times*, 30 November 1848. Report on the meeting of the Select Vestry held 28 November 1848.

19 Irish Poor (1836) Evidence of Mr Rose, Visiting Overseer of Manchester Township, p.54.

20 (S.C. 1847) Minutes of Evidence, E.Rushton, q. 4339-4355.

21 During 1848 there were a number of disputes between dock porters and the stevedore companies and it was variously claimed that untrained Irish were being taken on.

22 Irish Poor (1849)

23 *Manchester Guardian* 25 October 1851, Report on the meeting of the Manchester township Poor Law Guardians.

24 Strathclyde. Minutes of the Parochial Board of Barony, held on 12 September 1848.

10 Postscript

How is one to assess the events of 1847 described above? What can be asserted without fear of contradiction is that they were an integral part of the Famine tragedy. The suffering endured by so many on their journey to Britain, and the horrific nature of the experience of the battle for survival in Britain, mirrored the anguish of the catastrophe in Ireland. Captain Denham's report on the conditions in which the Famine Irish were carried to Britain revealed a picture of lethal overcrowding of vessels and an apparent unconcern on the part of the shipping companies. No matter how low the fares charged, it was all profit. What options were open to the steamship companies? They could have employed staff to ensure the number embarking on a vessel was limited. At worse, such a control would have increased the time refugees spent on the quaysides in Ireland by 24 hours. Alternatively, the local authorities in the ports of departure could have supplied the necessary crowd control. They did not. Why not? Probably because the decision-makers did not witness the scenes on the dockside while the seamen simply struggled to cope. More culpable were the ships' masters, they had the authority to limit numbers boarding. As the Duignan case illustrated it appears that deck passengers did not command their attention. The shipping companies argued in defence that their vessels were not in the passenger business and that they helped people escape from Ireland. However, it is clear they *did* compete for passengers and so had a responsibility for their safety, a responsibility frequently neglected.

The questions asked of the poor relief operation in Ireland can also be posed concerning the response of the poor law authorities in Britain. To be more specific, did the authorities in British towns act responsibly with respect to the Famine refugee crisis? The reports of Chadwick and others revealed the enormous problems of poor housing, sanitation and water supplies which rapid urban growth had created by 1840. Throughout Britain, town and borough councils were struggling to bring about improvements in the urban environment. The Famine refugee problem erupted at a time when this process had hardly touched the squalid slums of Britain. Also, the year 1847 witnessed a major trade depression, resulting in a significant increase in destitution among the British working classes. The combined effect of heavy local unemployment and the immigration of Famine refugees strained many poor law unions faced with the fact that large numbers of low income ratepayers could not pay the poor rate. The prospect of British ratepayers facing increased rate bills occurred at the same time that Irish relief committees throughout Britain were holding meetings to raise funds for the relief of distress in Ireland and the Highlands. In effect, many concerned persons were sending money to Ireland in January and February who, a little later, were paying increased rates, partly for the support of Irish paupers in Britain. The strains were not simply financial. The sheer volume of destitution tested almost to breaking point the organisation of poor relief.

The poor law guardians had a legal obligation to prevent deaths from starvation and disease among the Famine refugees who in fact had no legal claim to long term relief. The people making up the membership of the guardians were principly the petty bourgeoisie, shopkeepers, publicans, farmers, solicitors and so on. Their mental horizons were local rather than national or international. In particular, they were generally obsessed with the idea that the relief system was being abused by the 'undeserving poor'. They were also conscious of the fact that they had to stand for re-election each year by the ratepayers. By the time of the Famine crisis, there is evidence that the reformed poor law system was increasingly under strain due to the growing mobility of labour within Britain. The sudden arrival of tens of thousands of pauperised, destitute and diseased Irish from November 1846 onwards was an unprecedented experience. One of the fears felt by guardians, particularly in the ports of arrival, arose from the fact that no one knew how long pauper immigration would go on. In 1997, *we* know that in the case of Liverpool, it fell dramatically in 1854. However the poor law guardians of 1847 could not have foreseen this. The fears among the guardians of the poor in Liverpool and Glasgow of becoming permanent providers of Irish poor relief were not unreasonable.

How do we judge their response to the crisis? There are three factors which can be easily be identified for some towns, the amount spent on the Irish poor, the number of deaths from starvation and the number of deaths from famine related diseases. It has been established in this study that during 1847, all the poor law unions receiving Irish famine refugees increased their spending in proportion to the increased numbers seeking relief. Though there was much confusion, incompetence and irresponsibility among individual officials, there is no evidence whatsoever of any collective attitude that the Irish refugees did not deserve help. There were few villains and many heroes and heroines. Individual relief officers in some instances, treated the Irish badly but the official view was that they had to be helped and this was financed by rate increases. The criticisms evoked by this situation were mainly aimed at the central government and Irish landlords. Turning to the claim of the contemporary press that the financing of relief for Irish pauper immigrants in Britain was crippling business, this charge cannot be sustained. In the case of those businessmen who could not pay their rates, it is not demonstrable that this would not have been the case had

Irish famine immigration not occurred. The economic downturn was severe and pushed many companies into bankruptcy. The total expenditure on the poor of all types in England and Wales during the financial year ending 25 March 1848, was £6180 760. Taking into consideration the estimated costs of the Famine Irish crisis analysed in the previous chapter, and adding on extra for those English and Welsh towns with smaller Irish populations, a gross amount of £155 000 is not an unreasonable figure for the total expenditure on the Famine Irish. This was just over 2 per cent of all expenditure on the poor. Of course, as we have seen, this burden was not evenly spread out. However, there is no evidence of any kind to support the argument that, for example, the economic wellbeing of Liverpool, Glasgow or Manchester, was adversely affected by their expenditure during the crisis. On the contrary, all of these places benefitted from a large pool of unemployed unskilled labour.

Given the evidence that British poor law authorities responded to the crisis with increased expenditure, how effective was this? Given the desperate physical condition of many of the refugees, there can be no doubt that many would have died of starvation on arrival in Britain had it not been for the provision of outdoor relief. Despite the horrific instances of death from starvation described in this book, the absolute number was small compared to the number of famine refugees entering Britain during 1847. In Liverpool it is probable that the *maximum* number of such deaths was 22. This does not change the fact that the level of relief offered was only such as to support a minimal level of existence. This was a deliberate policy aimed at discouraging welfare dependency. The point has been made, you do not have to die to have suffered. However, there is little evidence to sustain the argument that the Famine Irish refugees received less relief per head that the casual English, Scots and Welsh paupers.

The number of deaths from starvation is perhaps the wrong criterion to use in judging the response of the poor law authorities to the refugee crisis. Most people in famines die of famine related diseases. We have seen that in Liverpool, Manchester, Newport and Glasgow, the authorities acted swiftly to commandeer buildings for conversion into temporary fever hospitals. Equally rapidly, they recruited extra doctors and nurses and also implemented policies aimed at cleaning the cellars and rooms of typhus victims. Many of the refugees already had the seeds of typhus within them when they arrived and in the case of the ports of arrival, the stream of immigrants made it extremely difficult for the authorities to gain the upperhand. There is ample evidence that many parochial workers, doctors, nurses and clergymen, particularly Catholic priests, behaved heroically and paid a heavy price. It is probable that 30 priests died during 1847 and a much greater number of medical staff and parochial workers. The majority of all these victims were English. Such losses were unprecedented and in the worse affected centres of Irish settlement, the response of the authorities to the typhus epidemic undoubtedly averted a much greater crisis. I estimate the total number of Irish deaths from typhus and other famine related diseases to have been in the order of 10-15 000, with a large proportion of these in Liverpool and Glasgow. Given the transmission mechanism of typhus, the overcrowded cellars and lodging houses played a central role in spreading the disease.

The authorities *could* have emptied these abodes of typhus sufferers by acquiring more empty buildings, and this would have reduced the number of deaths. Such a policy would also have to have been applied to British victims, but the provision of hospital facilities on such a scale was beyond the experience of guardians of the poor at the time, the question remaining of where could the people have lived on discharge from hospital? In addition, there was the worry that by providing lavish facilities for medical poor relief, Liverpool, Glasgow and Newport would be solving Ireland's problem, something they believed was the responsibility of the Irish landlords. The guardians can be accused, with the benefit of hindsight, of a lack of imagination but to the people on the ground, there was the fear of incurring an unending burden of Irish poverty, financed by a regressive tax which hit hardest the poorest ratepayers. The central government was clearly culpable in terms of not recognizing that Liverpool, Glasgow and other places were dealing with a national crisis on the basis of funding provided by local ratepayers. More hospital ships would have relieved the pressure on temporary hospitals. The actions of the poor law unions in Britain in pressing for a change in the Irish poor law, aimed at giving the Irish poor in Ireland the right to outdoor relief, was primarily aimed at Irish landlords rather than a desire not to fulfill their own responsibilities to the Irish refugees in Britain.

The decision of the central government, in the late summer of 1847, to throw the whole burden of poor relief in Ireland onto the Irish ratepayers reflected the absolute refusal to help the poor law unions in Britain struggling with the provision of relief and aid to Irish refugees. Ironically, the same poor law guardians in Britain, pressing for Irish ratepayers to bear the burden of famine relief, were simultaneously pressing for central government in Britain to relieve them of the cost. Their basic argument was that the famine disaster was a national problem and local taxation should not bear the responsibility of solving a national disaster. The decision of many poor law unions in Britain in the summer of 1847 to use the laws of removal as a threat to famine refugees claiming poor relief, did succeed in deterring many claimants, so increasing the destitution of many Irish in Britain. This was a harsh policy and can be criticised as penny pinching and it failed in its objective. It did not stop pauper immigration but did force many Irish into even more desperate poverty.

Overall a tentative conclusion regarding the response of local British poor law authorities during the 1847 Famine refugee crisis is that they fulfilled their responsibilities regarding the welfare of the Irish Famine refugees. They were not generous but they were not generous to the British poor. The apparent indifference of the middle classes to the squalor and suffering under their noses was not confined to the Irish. It is no part of this study to analyse the reason for this social apartheid but it existed and was based on class not ethnicity. A definitive judgement on the actions of the British poor law authorities at this time must await more detailed studies, the cases of John Waters and Michael Duignan suggest caution before making a final assessment.

Bibliography

Books on Ireland and the Irish in Britain

Boyce, D. George, *Nationalism in Ireland* (3rd ed. Routledge: 1995).

Boyce, D. George and O'Day, A., *The Making of Modern Irish History: Revisionism and the Revisionist Controversy* (Routledge: 1996).

Crawford, N., *Famine: The Irish Experience 900-1900* (John Donald: 1989).

Daly, M.E., *The Famine in Ireland* (Dungalgan Press: 1986).

Davis, G., *The Irish in Britain, 1815-1914* (Gill and Macmillan: 1991).

Devine, T.M., (ed) *Irish Immigrants and Scottish Society in the Nineteenth and Twentieth Centuries* (John Donald: 1991).

Edwards, R.D. and Williams, T.D., *The Great Famine: Studies in Irish History 1845-52* (Brown and Nolan: 1956 new edition, Lilliput: 1994).

Fielding, S., *Class and Ethnicity: Irish Catholics in England, 1880-1939* (Open UP: 1993).

Finnegan, F., *Poverty and Prejudice: Irish Immigrants in York, 1860-1875* (York UP: 1982).

Fitzpatrick, D., *Irish Emigration, 1801-1921* (Economic and Social History of Ireland: 1984).

Fitzpatrick, D., *Oceans of Consolation: Personal Accounts of Migration to Australia* (Cork UP: 1994).

Foster, R.F., *Modern Ireland, 1600-1972* (Allen: 1988).

Gallagher, T., *Glasgow, the Uneasy Peace: Religious Tensions in Modern Scotland, 1819-1914* (Manchester UP: 1987).

Gray, P., *The Irish Famine* (Thames and Hudson: 1995).

Killen, J., *The Famine Decade: Contemporary Accounts, 1841-51* (Blackstock: 1995).

Kinealy, C., *This Great Calamity: the Irish Famine, 1841-52* (Gill and Macmillan: 1994).

Lees, L.H., *Exiles of Erin: Irish Migrants in Victorian London* (Manchester UP: 1979).

Lowe, W.J., *The Irish in Mid-Victorian Lancashire* (Peter Lang: 1989).

Lyons, F.S., *Ireland since the Famine* (Weidenfeld and Nicolson: 1971).

Miller, K.A., *Emigrants and Exiles: Ireland and the Irish Exodus to North America* (Oxford UP: 1985).

Mokyr, J., *Why Ireland Starved: A Quantitive and Analytical History of the Irish Economy, 1800-45* (1st ed. London: 1980 revised ed. 1985).

Neal, F., *Sectarian Violence: the Liverpool Experience, 1819-1914* (Manchester UP: 1988).

O'Day, A., (ed) *A Survey of the Irish In England, 1872* (reprint, Hambledon Press: 1990).

O'Grada, Cormac, *The Great Irish Famine* (Macmillan: 1989).

O'Grada, Cormac, *Ireland before and after the Famine: Exploration in Economic History, 1800-1925* (Manchester UP: 1988 2nd ed. 1993).

O'Grada, Cormac, *Ireland: A New Economic History* (Clarendon: 1994).

O'Sullivan, P., *The Irish World Wide: History, Heritage and Identity* (Leicester UP: 1992-1996) Series: Volume 1: *Patterns of Migration* (1992), Volume 2: *The Irish in the New Communities* (1992), Volume 3: *The Creative Migrant* (1994), Volume 4: *Irish Women and Irish Migration* (1995), Volume 5: *Religion and Identity* (1996), Volume 6: *The Meaning of the Famine* (1996).

O'Tuathaigh, Geroid, *Ireland before the Famine, 1798-1848* (Gill and Macmillan: 1990).

Portéir, C., *The Great Irish Famine* (Mercier Press and RTE: 1995).

Swift, R. and Gilley, S., (eds) *The Irish in the Victorian City* (Croom Helm: 1985).

Swift, R. and Gilley, S., (eds) *The Irish in Britain, 1815-1939* (Pinter: 1989).

Vaughan, W.E., (ed) *A New History of Ireland*, Volume 5, *Ireland under the Union, 1, 1801-70* (Clarendon Press: 1989).

Books on Britain

Adshead, J., *Distress in Manchester: Evidence of the State of the Labouring Classes in 1840-42* (London: 1842).

Burnett, J., *A Social History of Housing* (Methuen: 1980).

Cage, R.A., *The Working Class in Glasgow 1750-1914* (Croom Helm: 1987).

Corlett, C., *The Iron Ship* (2nd ed., Moonraker Press: 1990).

Crouzet, F., *The Victorian Economy* (Methuen: 1982).

Dennis, R., *English Industrial Cities of the Nineteenth Century* (Cambridge UP: 1984).

Faucher, L., *Manchester in 1844: Its Present Conditions and Future Prospects* (London: 1844, reprint F.Cass: 1969).

Finch, J., *Statistics of the Vauxhall Ward of Liverpool* (Liverpool: 1842).

Floud, R. and McCloskey, D., (eds) *The Economic History of Britain since 1700,* Volume 1, 1700-1860 (Cambridge UP: 1981).

Fraser, D., (ed) *The New Poor Law in the Nineteenth Century* (Macmillan: 1976).

Fraser, D., (ed) *Power and Authority in the Victorian City* (Blackwell: 1979).

Fraser, W., *Duncan of Liverpool* (London: 1947).

Garrard, J., *Leadership and Power in Victorian Industrial Towns, 1830-80* (Manchester UP: 1983).

Hickey, J., *Urban Catholics: Urban Catholics in England and Wales from 1829 to the Present Day* (London: 1967).

Hume, A., *Missions at Home* (London: 1850).

Jackson, G., Freidman, M.J. and Aldcroft, D.K., *Transport in Victorian Britain* (Manchester UP: 1988).

Jenkins, P., *A History of Modern Wales, 1536-1990* (Longman: 1990).

Jones, G.E., *Modern Wales: A concise History, c.1485-1979* (Cambridge: 1984).

Jones, G. Stedman, *Outcast London: A Study of Relationships between the Classes in Victorian Society* (Oxford UP: 1971).

Kay, James Phillip, *The Moral and Physical Condition of the Working Classes Employed in the Cotton Manufacture in Manchester* (London: 1832).

Kennedy, J., *The History of Steam Navigation* (Liverpool: 1903).

Kidd, A., *Manchester* (Keele UP: 1993).

Mayhall, J., *Annals and History of Leeds, York and Surrounding Districts* (Leeds: 1860).

O'Brien, P.K. and Quinault, R., (eds) *The Industrial Revolution and British Society* (Cambridge UP: 1993).

Parkinson, Richard, *On the Present Condition of the Labouring Poor in Manchester, with Hints for Improving It* (London: 1841).

Pickstone, J.V., *Medicine and Industrial Society: A history of hospital development in Manchester and its region, 1752-1946* (Manchester UP: 1985).

Porter, R., *Diseases, Medicine and Society in England, 1550-1860* (2nd ed. Macmillan: 1993).

Reid, R., *The Land of Lost Content: the Luddite Revolution of 1812* (Penguin: 1986).

Rose, M., (ed) *The Poor and City: The English Poor Law in its Urban Context, 1834-1914* (Leicester UP: 1985).

Redford, A., *Labour Migration in England, 1800-1850* (Manchester: 1926).

Smith, F. B., *The People's Health* (Weidenfeld and Nicolson: 1990).

Treble, J.H., *Urban Poverty in Britain, 1830-1914* (Methuen: 1983).

Ville, S., (ed) *Shipbuilding in the United Kingdom in the Nineteenth Century: a regional approach* (International Maritime Economy History Association: 1993).

Wood, P., *Poverty and the Workhouse in Victorian Britain* (Alan Sutton: 1991).

Wohl, A.S., *Endangered Lives: Public Health and Victorian Britain* (Methuen: 1983).

White, B.D., *A History of the Corporation of Liverpool, 1835-1914* (Liverpool UP: 1951).

Articles and Chapters in Books

Busteed, M.A and Hodgson, R., 'Irish Migration and Settlement in Early Nineteenth Century Manchester, with special reference to Angel Meadow in 1851', *Irish Geography,* 27, 1994, pp. 1-13.

Busteed, M.A and Hodgson, R., 'Coping with Urbanisation: The Irish in Early Manchester' in Neavy, S.J., Symes, M.S. and Brown, F.C., (eds) *Proceedings of the 13th Conference of the International Association for People Environment Studies* (Chapman: 1994).

Busteed, M.A., and Hodgson, R., 'Myth and Reality of Irish Migrants in Mid-Nineteenth Century Manchester: a preliminary study' in O'Sullivan, P., (ed) *The Irish World Wide*, Volume 2, (Leicester UP: 1992) pp.26-51.

Blackden, S., 'The Board of Supervision and the Scottish Parochial Medical Services, 1845-95', *Medical History*, 1986, 30, pp. 145-72.

Cairncross, A., 'Trends in Internal Migration', *Transactions of the Manchester Statistical Society*, 1938-39, Group meeting, pp. 21-25.

Childers, J.W., 'Observation and Representation: Mr Chadwick Writes the Poor', *Albion*, Spring, 1994, pp. 405-32.

Dillon, T., 'The Irish in Leeds, 1851-61', *Publications of the Thoresby Society,* Miscellany, Volume 16, pt. 1, No.119, pp. 1-28.

Dupree, M.W., 'Family Care and Hospital Care: the sick in the nineteenth century', *Social History of Medicine*, 1993, 06, 02, pp. 195-211.

Fitzpatrick, D., 'Irish Emigration, 1801-70', in Vaughan, W.E., (ed) *New History of Ireland,* Volume 5, *Ireland under the Union, 1801-70* (Oxford UP: 1989) chapter 28.

Fitzpatrick, D., 'A Peculiar Tramping People: The Irish in Britain, 1801-70', in Vaughan, W.E., (ed) *New History of Ireland* (Oxford UP: 1989) chapter 29.

Geary, L.M., 'Famine, Fever and the Bloody Flux', in Portéir (ed) *The Great Irish Famine* (Dublin: 1995) pp. 74-85.

Grey, P., 'Idealogy and the Famine', in Poitiér (ed) *The Great Famine* (Dublin: 1995).

Gutia, S., 'The Importance of Social Intervention in England's Mortality Rate: the evidence reviewed', *Society History of Ireland*, 1994, pp. 89-113.

Hamlin, E., 'Predisposing causes and Public Health in early Nineteenth Century Medical Thought', *Social History of Medicine*, 1992, pp. 41-70.

Hamlin, E., 'Environmental Sensibility in Edinburgh, 1839-1840: The Fetid Irrigation Controversy', *Journal of Urban History*, 1994, May, pp. 329-331.

Harcourt, F., 'Charles Wye Williams and Irish Steam Shipping', *Journal of Transport History* (3rd series) Volume 13, No. 2, September 1992, pp. 141-62.

Hardy, A., 'Urban Famine or Urban Crisis? Typhus in the Victorian City', *Medical History*, 1988, 32, pp. 401-25.

Irvine, H.S., 'Some Aspects of Passenger Transport Between England and Ireland, 1820-1850', *Journal of Transport History*, Volume IV, 1954-60, pp. 225-41.

Luckin, W., 'Evaluating the Sanitary Revolution: Typhus and Typhoid in London, 1851-1900' in Woods, R. and Woodward, J., (eds) *Urban Disease and Mortality in Nineteenth Century England* (London: 1984) chapter 5.

McArthur, W.P., 'The Medical History of the Famine' in Dudley Edwards, R. and Williams, T.D., (eds) *The Great Famine: Studies in Irish History, 1845-52* (Dublin: 1956) chapter 5.

Neal, F., 'Liverpool, Irish Steamship Companies and the Famine Irish', in *Immigrants and Minorites*, Volume 5, No. 1 (March, 1986) pp. 28-61.

O'Sullivan, P. and Lucking, T., 'The Famine Worldwide: the Irish Famine and the development of Famine Policy and Famine Theory', in O'Sullivan, P., (ed) *The Irish Worldwide*, Volume 6, *The Meaning of the Famine* (Leicester UP: 1996) chapter 9.

Patterson, A., 'The Poor Law in Nineteenth Century Scotland', in Fraser, D., *The New Poor Law in the Nineteenth Century* (Methuen: 1976) pp. 171-93.

Place, G.W., 'The Reparation of Irish Vagrants from Cheshire, 1750-1815', *The Journal of the Chester Archaeological Society*, Volume 68, 1985, pp. 125-141.

Place, G.W., 'The Labouring Passengers', *Chetham Society*, Volume xxxix, 1994, pp. 172-91.

Scally, R., 'Liverpool Ships and Irish Emigrants in the Age of Sail', *Journal of Social History*, Volume 17, No. 1, (Fall, 1983) pp. 5-30.

Sigworth, M. and Worbeys, M., 'The Public View of Public Health in Mid Victorian Britain', *Urban History*, Volume 21, pt 2, (October, 1994) pp. 237-50.

Williams, F.J., 'The Irish in the East Cheshire Silk Industry 1851-61', *Transactions of the Historic Society of Lancashire and Cheshire*, Volume 136 (1986) pp. 99-126.

Williamson, J.G., 'The Impact of the Irish on British Labour Markets during the Industrial Revolution', *Journal of Economic History*, XIV, No.3, (September, 1986) pp. 639-721.

Index

* Note: Because of the frequency which certain place names appear in the text, and are individually the subject of chapters, they have not been indexed. These include Cardiff, Glasgow, London, Liverpool, Manchester (and Salford) and Newport.